LEGION of SUPER-HEROES

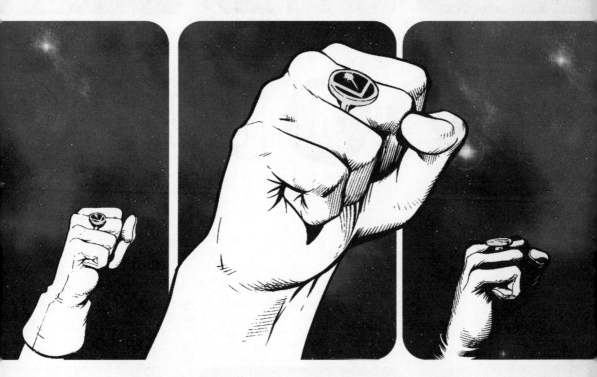

DEATH OF A DREAM

   LEGION *of*

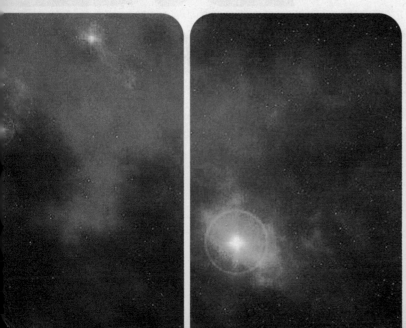

SUPER-HEROES

DEATH OF A DREAM

MARK WAID
WRITER

BARRY KITSON
PENCILLER

INTERLUDE WRITTEN BY **Stuart Moore**

Kevin Sharpe   **Georges Jeanty**   **Ken Lashley**
ADDITIONAL PENCILS

Art Thibert   **Mick Gray**   **Drew Geraci**
Prentis Rollins   **Paul Neary**
INKERS

Sno-Cone
COLORISTS

Nick J. Napolitano   **Travis Lanham**
Phil Balsman   **Jared K. Fletcher**
LETTERERS

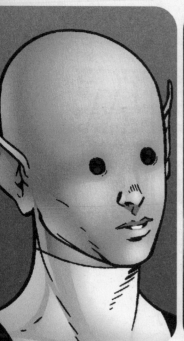

LEGION OF SUPER-HEROES: DEATH OF A DREAM
Published by DC Comics.
Cover, introduction and compilation
copyright © 2006 DC Comics. All Rights
Reserved.Originally published in single magazine
form in LEGION OF SUPER-HEROES 7-13
Copyright © 2005, 2006 DC Comics
All Rights Reserved. All characters, their
distinctive likenesses and related elements
featured in this publication are trademarks
of DC Comics. The stories, characters and
incidents featured in this publication are
entirely fictional. DC Comics does not read
or accept unsolicited submissions of ideas,
stories or artwork.

DC Comics, 1700 Broadway, New York, NY 10019
A Warner Bros. Entertainment Company
Printed in Canada. First Printing.
ISBN: 1-4012-0971-8
ISBN 13: 978-1-4012-0971-1
Cover art by Barry Kitson with Chris Blythe.
Publication design by Peter Hamboussi.

TEENAGE REVOLUTION

By the 31st century, the known universe has enjoyed a near-millennium of utopian peace. Everyday existence is shiny, optimistic and bright.

Secure, stable and orderly.

And deadly dull.

In defiance, a teenage revolution has swept the universe. The members of the LEGION OF SUPER-HEROES, inspired by the legendary crimefighters of the 21st century, have adopted colorful costumes and code names. They fight for freedom, to make their voice heard, and spur society out of its numbing complacency. With a core group of about 20 individuals and approximately 75,000 members spread out across the galaxy, they are constantly harassed by the United Planets' peacekeeping force, the Science Police, but they can handle it.

Dream Girl, the Legion's precognitive, has witnessed the image of a man who is masterminding the downfall of the United Planets. He is Praetor Lemnos, a shadowy manipulator who can be seen, detected, and even remembered only when he wants to be, which is rarely. Even with his face clear in Dream Girl's mind, the Legionnaires have no idea who it is they're trying to stop.

On a planet at the galaxy's edge, Lemnos has gathered a super-powered strike force and used them to destroy Orando, the U.P.'s wealthiest planet, creating economic havoc and shattering the life of Orando's Princess Projectra. Even more brazenly, he has appeared privately to Brainiac 5 and announced that his next attack will be on Brainy's home world of Colu.

Unfortunately, thanks to Lemnos's power, Brainy has no way of remembering this....

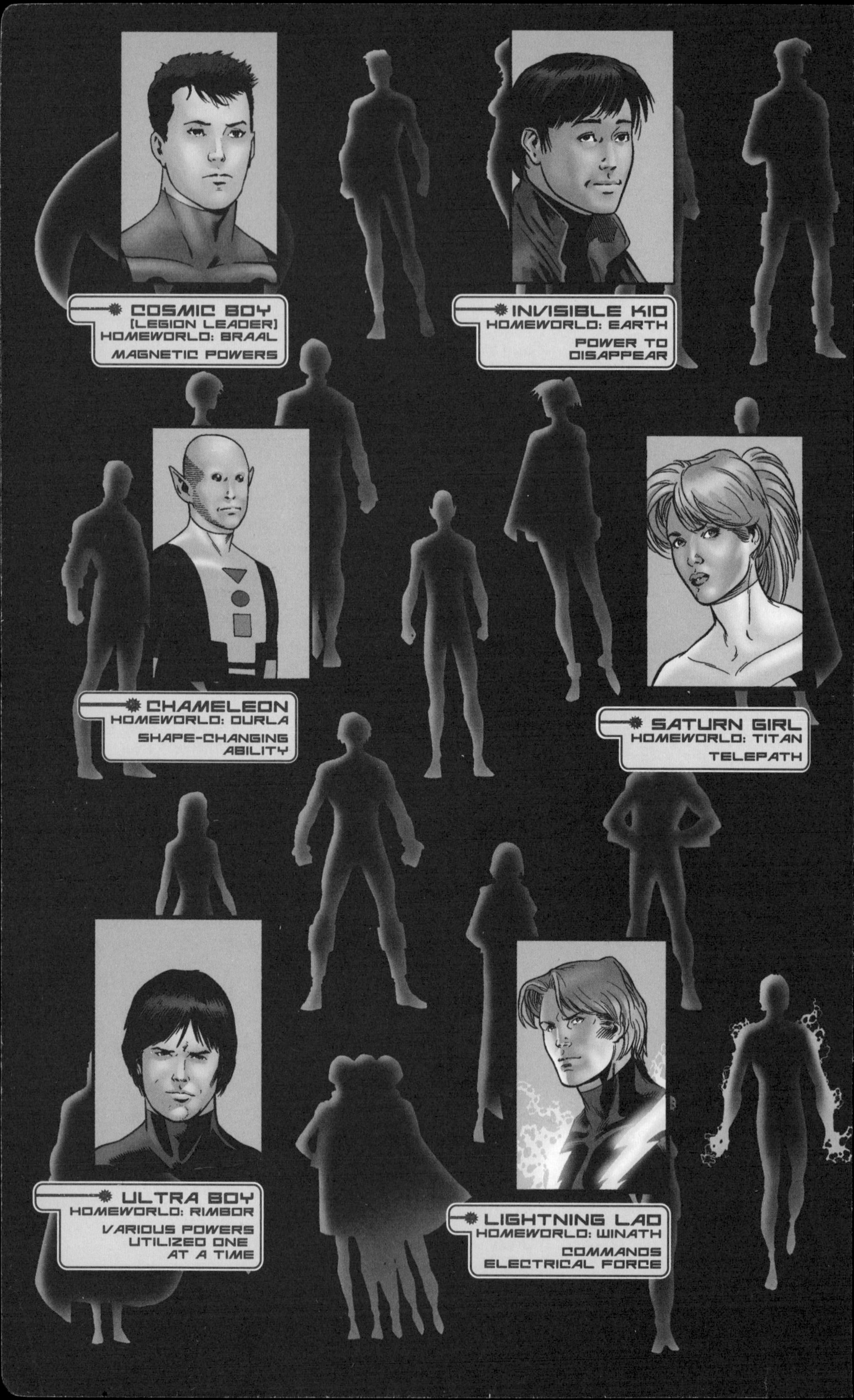
COSMIC BOY
[LEGION LEADER]
HOMEWORLD: BRAAL
MAGNETIC POWERS
INVISIBLE KID
HOMEWORLD: EARTH
POWER TO DISAPPEAR
CHAMELEON
HOMEWORLD: DURLA
SHAPE-CHANGING ABILITY
SATURN GIRL
HOMEWORLD: TITAN
TELEPATH
ULTRA BOY
HOMEWORLD: RIMBOR
VARIOUS POWERS UTILIZED ONE AT A TIME
LIGHTNING LAD
HOMEWORLD: WINATH
COMMANDS ELECTRICAL FORCE

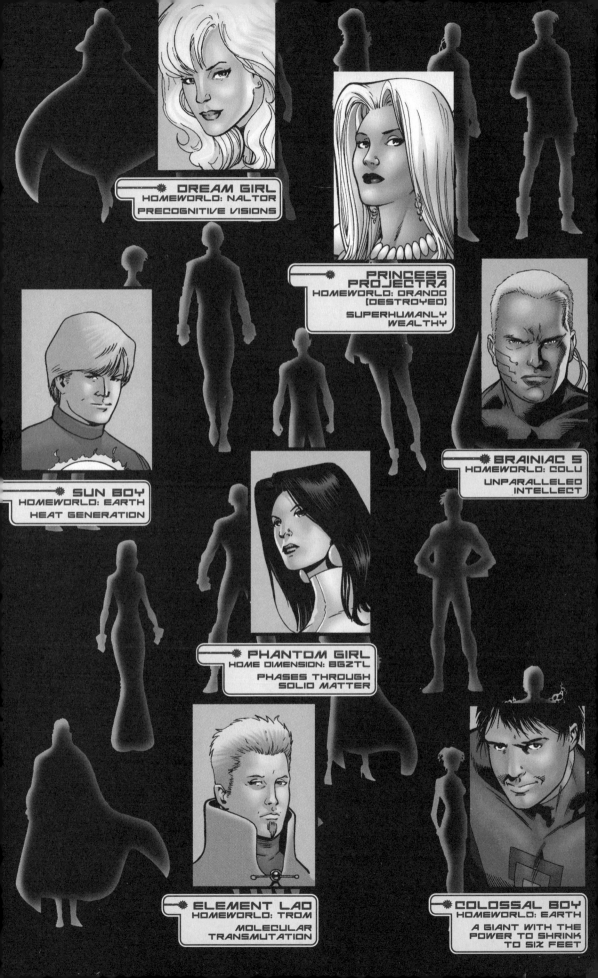

DREAM GIRL
HOMEWORLD: NALTOR
PRECOGNITIVE VISIONS

PRINCESS PROJECTRA
HOMEWORLD: ORANDO
(DESTROYED)
SUPERHUMANLY WEALTHY

SUN BOY
HOMEWORLD: EARTH
HEAT GENERATION

BRAINIAC 5
HOMEWORLD: COLU
UNPARALLELED INTELLECT

PHANTOM GIRL
HOME DIMENSION: BGZTL
PHASES THROUGH SOLID MATTER

ELEMENT LAD
HOMEWORLD: TROM
MOLECULAR TRANSMUTATION

COLOSSAL BOY
HOMEWORLD: EARTH
A GIANT WITH THE POWER TO SHRINK TO SIX FEET

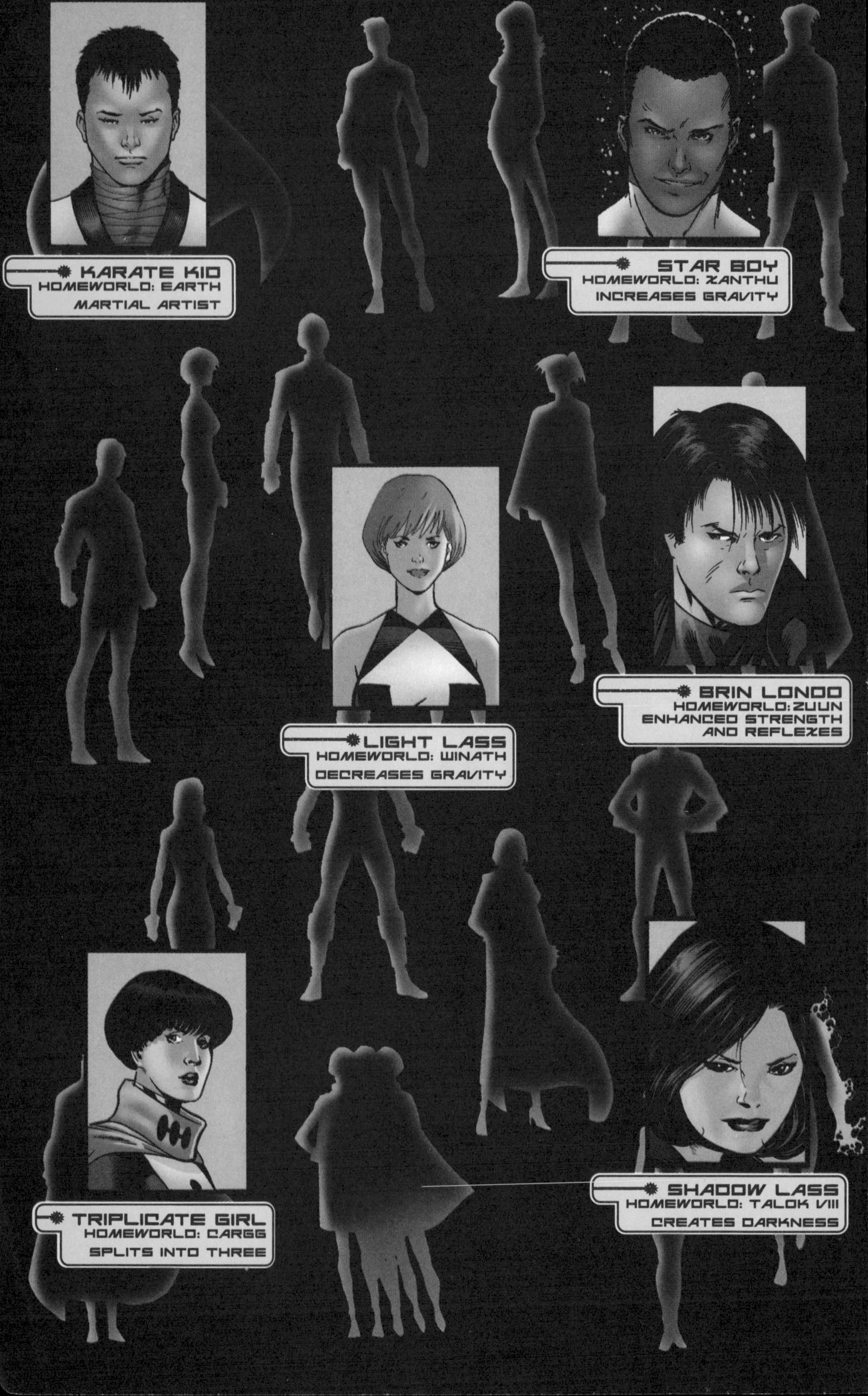
KARATE KID
HOMEWORLD: EARTH
MARTIAL ARTIST
STAR BOY
HOMEWORLD: XANTHU
INCREASES GRAVITY
BRIN LONDO
HOMEWORLD: ZUUN
ENHANCED STRENGTH
AND REFLEXES
LIGHT LASS
HOMEWORLD: WINATH
DECREASES GRAVITY
SHADOW LASS
HOMEWORLD: TALOK VIII
CREATES DARKNESS
TRIPLICATE GIRL
HOMEWORLD: CARGG
SPLITS INTO THREE

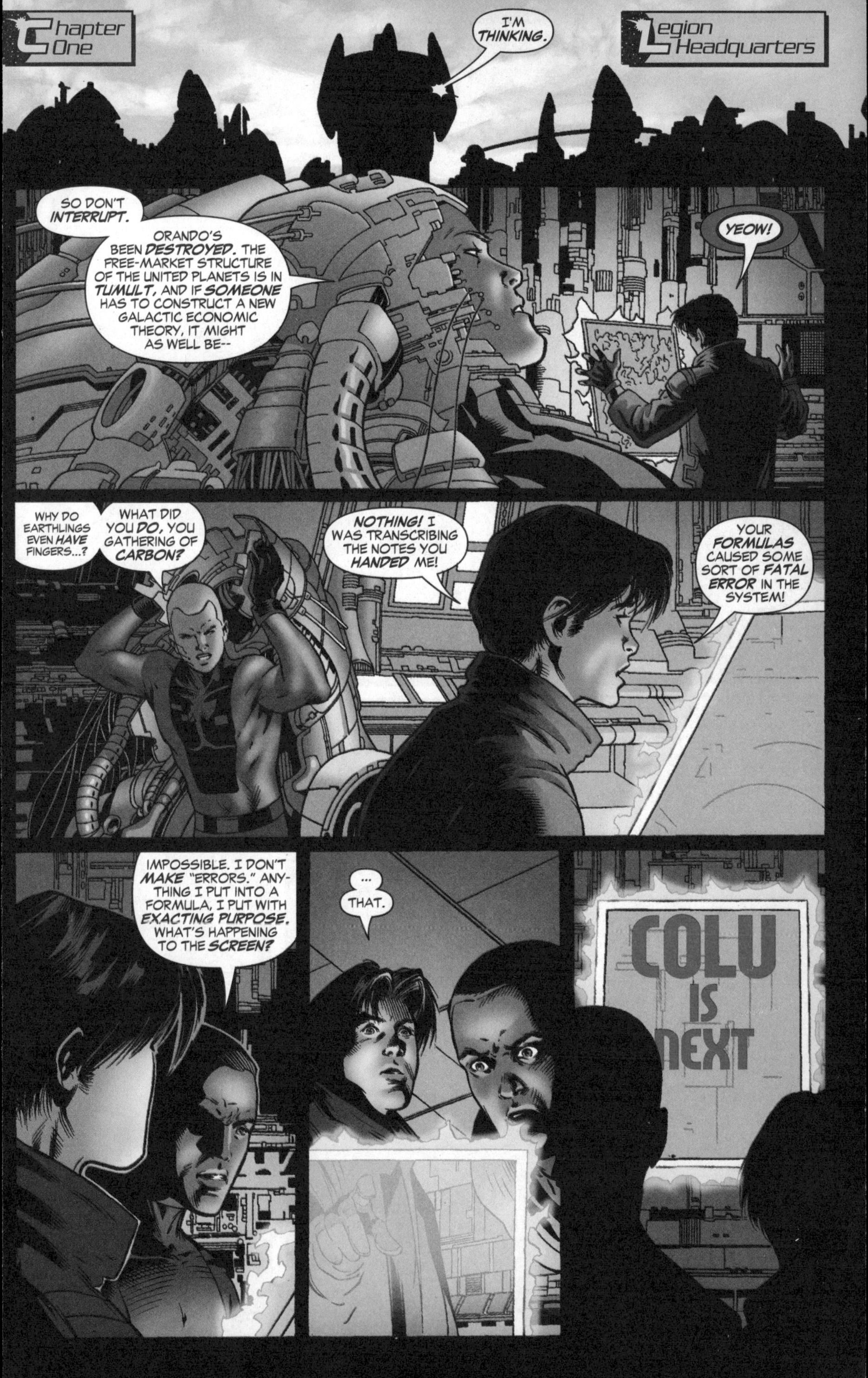
Chapter One
I'M THINKING.
Legion Headquarters
SO DON'T INTERRUPT.
ORANDO'S BEEN DESTROYED. THE FREE-MARKET STRUCTURE OF THE UNITED PLANETS IS IN TUMULT, AND IF SOMEONE HAS TO CONSTRUCT A NEW GALACTIC ECONOMIC THEORY, IT MIGHT AS WELL BE--
YEOW!
WHY DO EARTHLINGS EVEN HAVE FINGERS...?
WHAT DID YOU DO, YOU GATHERING OF CARBON?
NOTHING! I WAS TRANSCRIBING THE NOTES YOU HANDED ME!
YOUR FORMULAS CAUSED SOME SORT OF FATAL ERROR IN THE SYSTEM!
IMPOSSIBLE. I DON'T MAKE "ERRORS." ANYTHING I PUT INTO A FORMULA, I PUT WITH EXACTING PURPOSE. WHAT'S HAPPENING TO THE SCREEN?
... THAT.
COLU IS NEXT

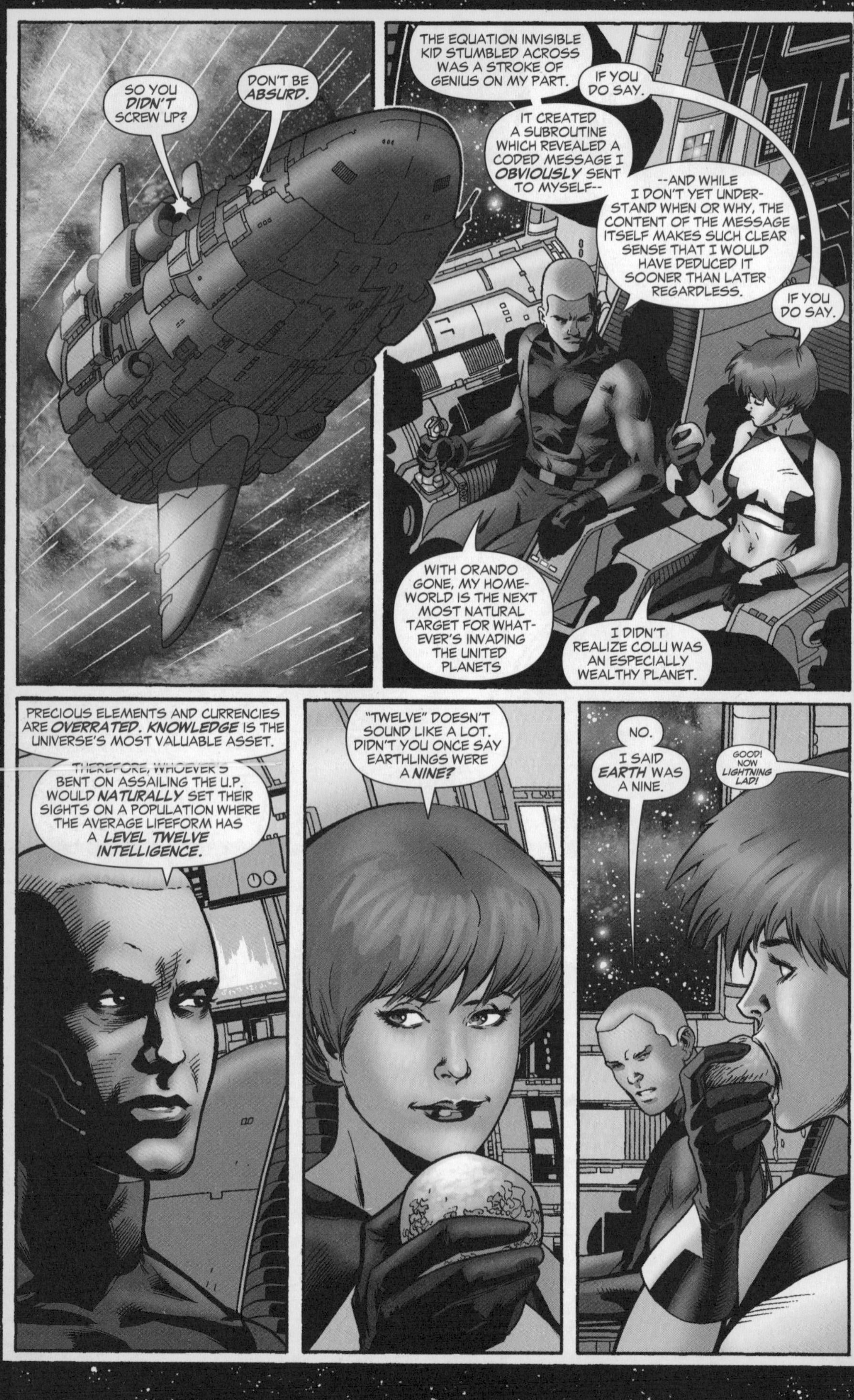
SO YOU *DIDN'T* SCREW UP?
DON'T BE *ABSURD.*
THE EQUATION INVISIBLE KID STUMBLED ACROSS WAS A STROKE OF GENIUS ON MY PART.
IF YOU DO SAY.
IT CREATED A SUBROUTINE WHICH REVEALED A CODED MESSAGE I *OBVIOUSLY* SENT TO MYSELF--
--AND WHILE I DON'T YET UNDERSTAND WHEN OR WHY, THE CONTENT OF THE MESSAGE ITSELF MAKES SUCH CLEAR SENSE THAT I WOULD HAVE DEDUCED IT SOONER THAN LATER REGARDLESS.
IF YOU DO SAY.
WITH ORANDO GONE, MY HOMEWORLD IS THE NEXT MOST NATURAL TARGET FOR WHATEVER'S INVADING THE UNITED PLANETS
I DIDN'T REALIZE COLU WAS AN ESPECIALLY WEALTHY PLANET.
PRECIOUS ELEMENTS AND CURRENCIES ARE *OVERRATED. KNOWLEDGE* IS THE UNIVERSE'S MOST VALUABLE ASSET.
THEREFORE, WHOEVER'S BENT ON ASSAILING THE U.P. WOULD *NATURALLY* SET THEIR SIGHTS ON A POPULATION WHERE THE AVERAGE LIFEFORM HAS A *LEVEL TWELVE INTELLIGENCE.*
"TWELVE" DOESN'T SOUND LIKE A LOT. DIDN'T YOU ONCE SAY EARTHLINGS WERE A *NINE?*
NO.
I SAID *EARTH* WAS A NINE.
GOOD! NOW *LIGHTNING LAD!*

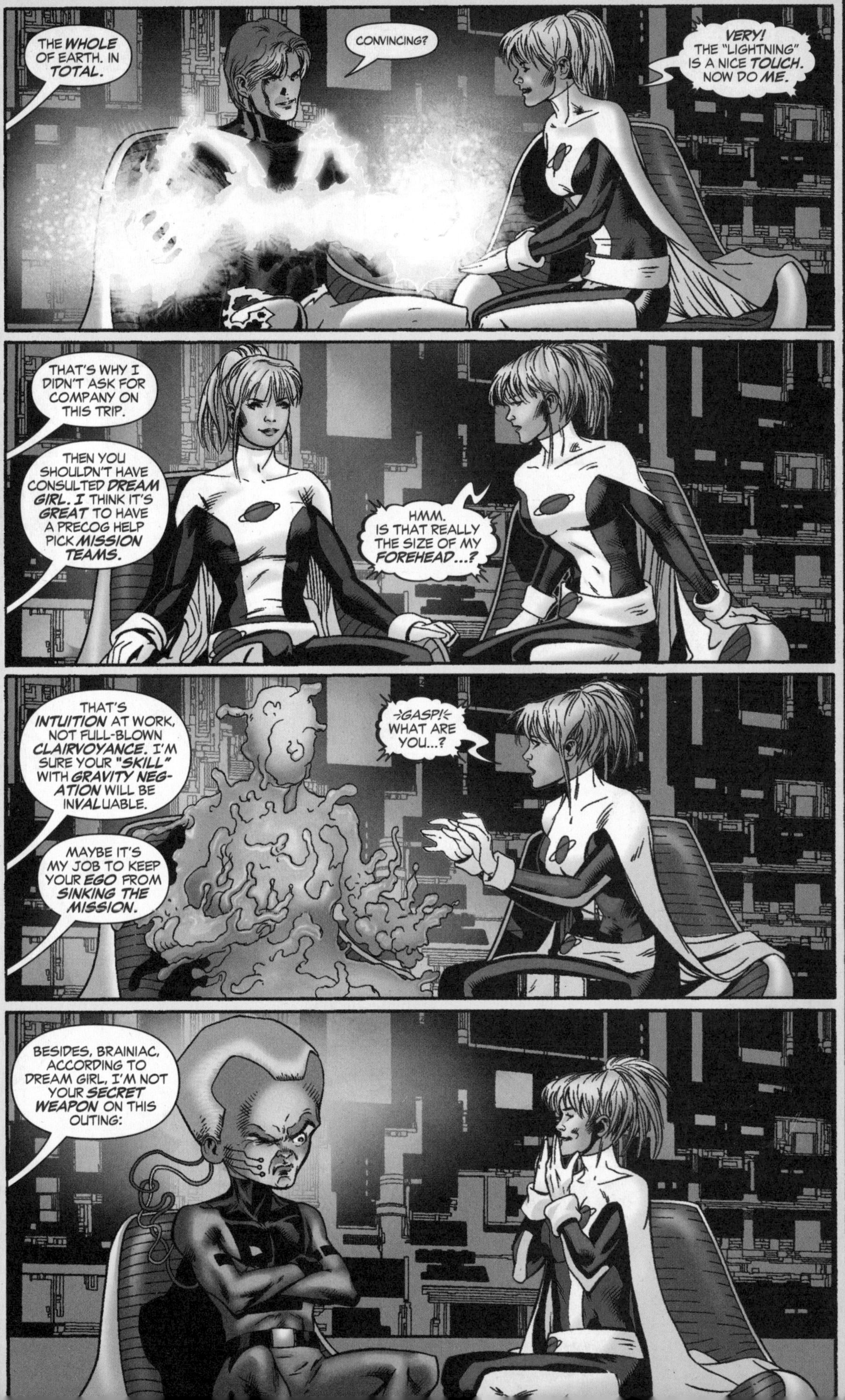

THE WHOLE OF EARTH. IN TOTAL.
CONVINCING?
VERY! THE "LIGHTNING" IS A NICE TOUCH. NOW DO ME.
THAT'S WHY I DIDN'T ASK FOR COMPANY ON THIS TRIP.
THEN YOU SHOULDN'T HAVE CONSULTED DREAM GIRL. I THINK IT'S GREAT TO HAVE A PRECOG HELP PICK MISSION TEAMS.
HMM. IS THAT REALLY THE SIZE OF MY FOREHEAD...?
THAT'S INTUITION AT WORK, NOT FULL-BLOWN CLAIRVOYANCE. I'M SURE YOUR "SKILL" WITH GRAVITY NEGATION WILL BE INVALUABLE.
MAYBE IT'S MY JOB TO KEEP YOUR EGO FROM SINKING THE MISSION.
GASP! WHAT ARE YOU...?
BESIDES, BRAINIAC, ACCORDING TO DREAM GIRL, I'M NOT YOUR SECRET WEAPON ON THIS OUTING:

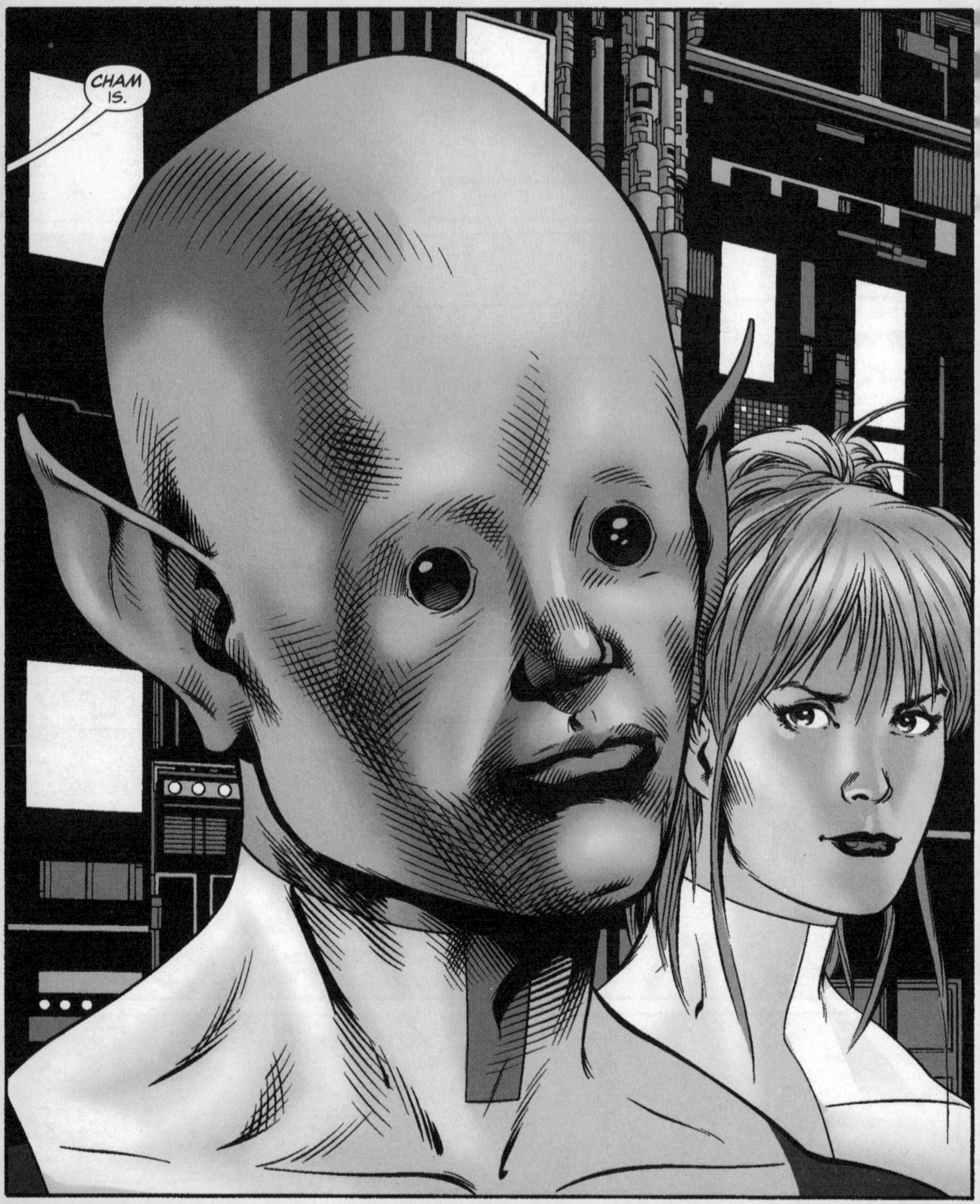
CHAM IS.

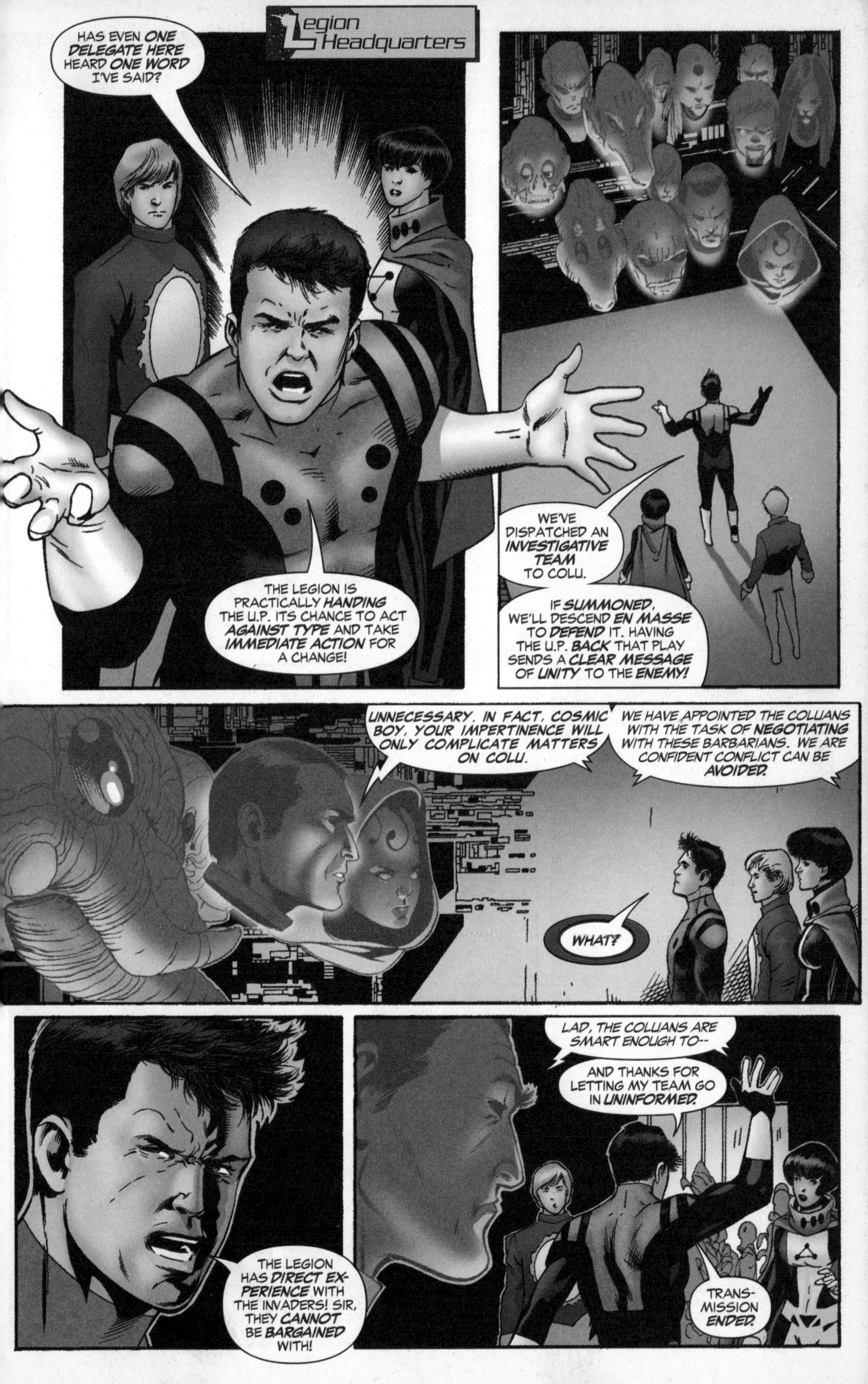
Legion Headquarters
HAS EVEN ONE DELEGATE HERE HEARD ONE WORD I'VE SAID?
THE LEGION IS PRACTICALLY HANDING THE U.P. ITS CHANCE TO ACT AGAINST TYPE AND TAKE IMMEDIATE ACTION FOR A CHANGE!
WE'VE DISPATCHED AN INVESTIGATIVE TEAM TO COLU.
IF SUMMONED, WE'LL DESCEND EN MASSE TO DEFEND IT. HAVING THE U.P. BACK THAT PLAY SENDS A CLEAR MESSAGE OF UNITY TO THE ENEMY!
UNNECESSARY. IN FACT, COSMIC BOY, YOUR IMPERTINENCE WILL ONLY COMPLICATE MATTERS ON COLU.
WE HAVE APPOINTED THE COLUANS WITH THE TASK OF NEGOTIATING WITH THESE BARBARIANS. WE ARE CONFIDENT CONFLICT CAN BE AVOIDED.
WHAT?
THE LEGION HAS DIRECT EXPERIENCE WITH THE INVADERS! SIR, THEY CANNOT BE BARGAINED WITH!
LAD, THE COLUANS ARE SMART ENOUGH TO--
AND THANKS FOR LETTING MY TEAM GO IN UNINFORMED.
TRANSMISSION ENDED.

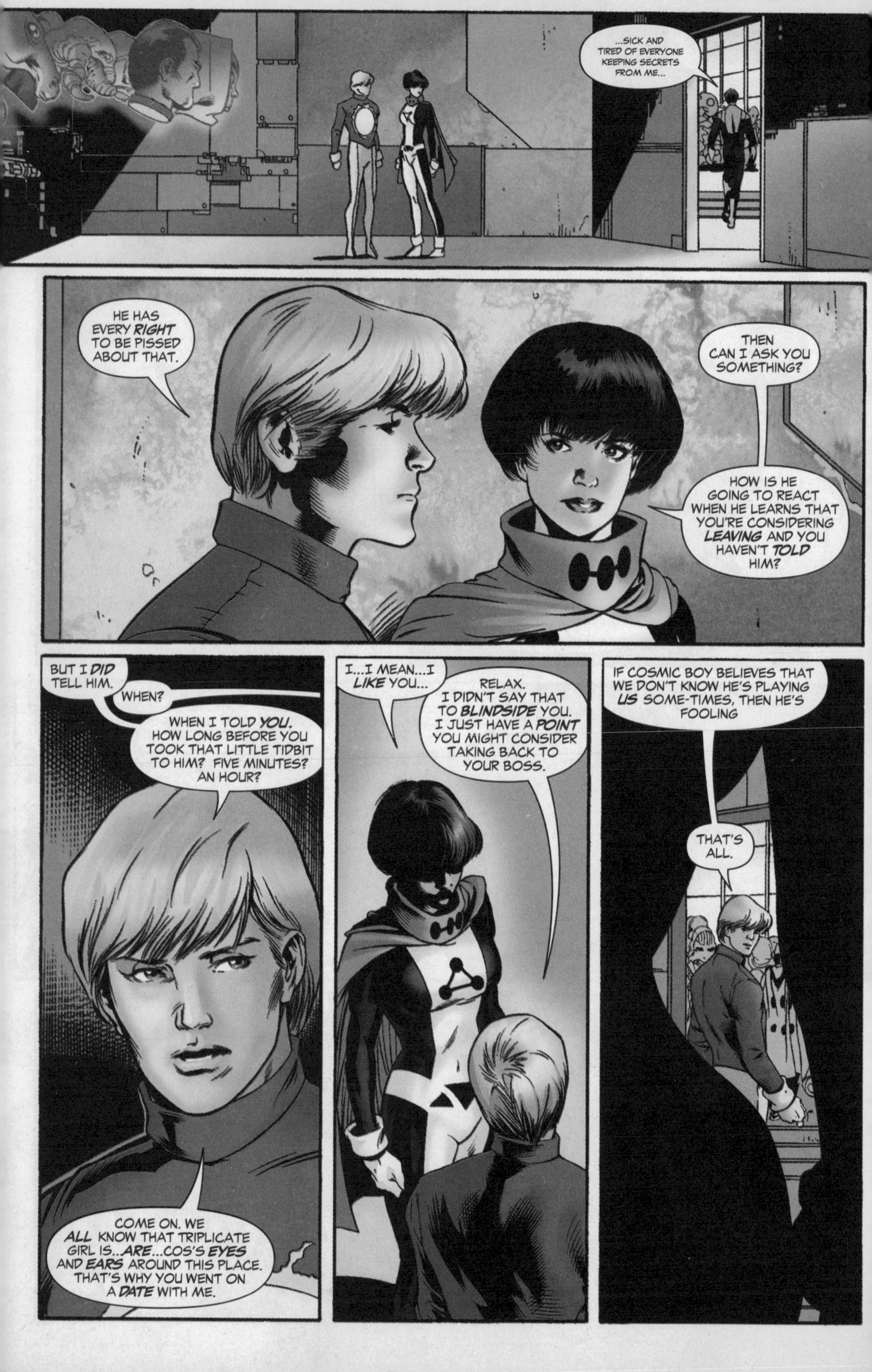

...SICK AND TIRED OF EVERYONE KEEPING SECRETS FROM ME...
HE HAS EVERY RIGHT TO BE PISSED ABOUT THAT.
THEN CAN I ASK YOU SOMETHING?
HOW IS HE GOING TO REACT WHEN HE LEARNS THAT YOU'RE CONSIDERING LEAVING AND YOU HAVEN'T TOLD HIM?
BUT I DID TELL HIM.
WHEN?
WHEN I TOLD YOU. HOW LONG BEFORE YOU TOOK THAT LITTLE TIDBIT TO HIM? FIVE MINUTES? AN HOUR?
COME ON. WE ALL KNOW THAT TRIPLICATE GIRL IS...ARE...COS'S EYES AND EARS AROUND THIS PLACE. THAT'S WHY YOU WENT ON A DATE WITH ME.
I...I MEAN...I LIKE YOU...
RELAX. I DIDN'T SAY THAT TO BLINDSIDE YOU. I JUST HAVE A POINT YOU MIGHT CONSIDER TAKING BACK TO YOUR BOSS.
IF COSMIC BOY BELIEVES THAT WE DON'T KNOW HE'S PLAYING US SOME-TIMES, THEN HE'S FOOLING
THAT'S ALL.

CHAM?

OOOH!

WHAT IS THAT? WHAT *IS* IT?

THIS? YOU'VE NEVER SEEN A *KONAPPLE* BEFORE?

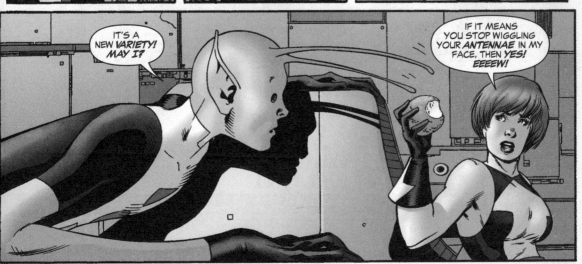

IT'S A NEW *VARIETY!* MAY I?

IF IT MEANS YOU STOP WIGGLING YOUR *ANTENNAE* IN MY FACE, THEN *YES!* EEEEW!

SORRY. DURLAN *INSTINCT.* WHENEVER WE ENCOUNTER AN UNFAMILIAR *ORGANIC,* WE AUTOMATICALLY *SCAN* IT.

IT'S *INVOLUNTARY.*

SO IS *THIS* GESTURE.

MMMM. PULPY.

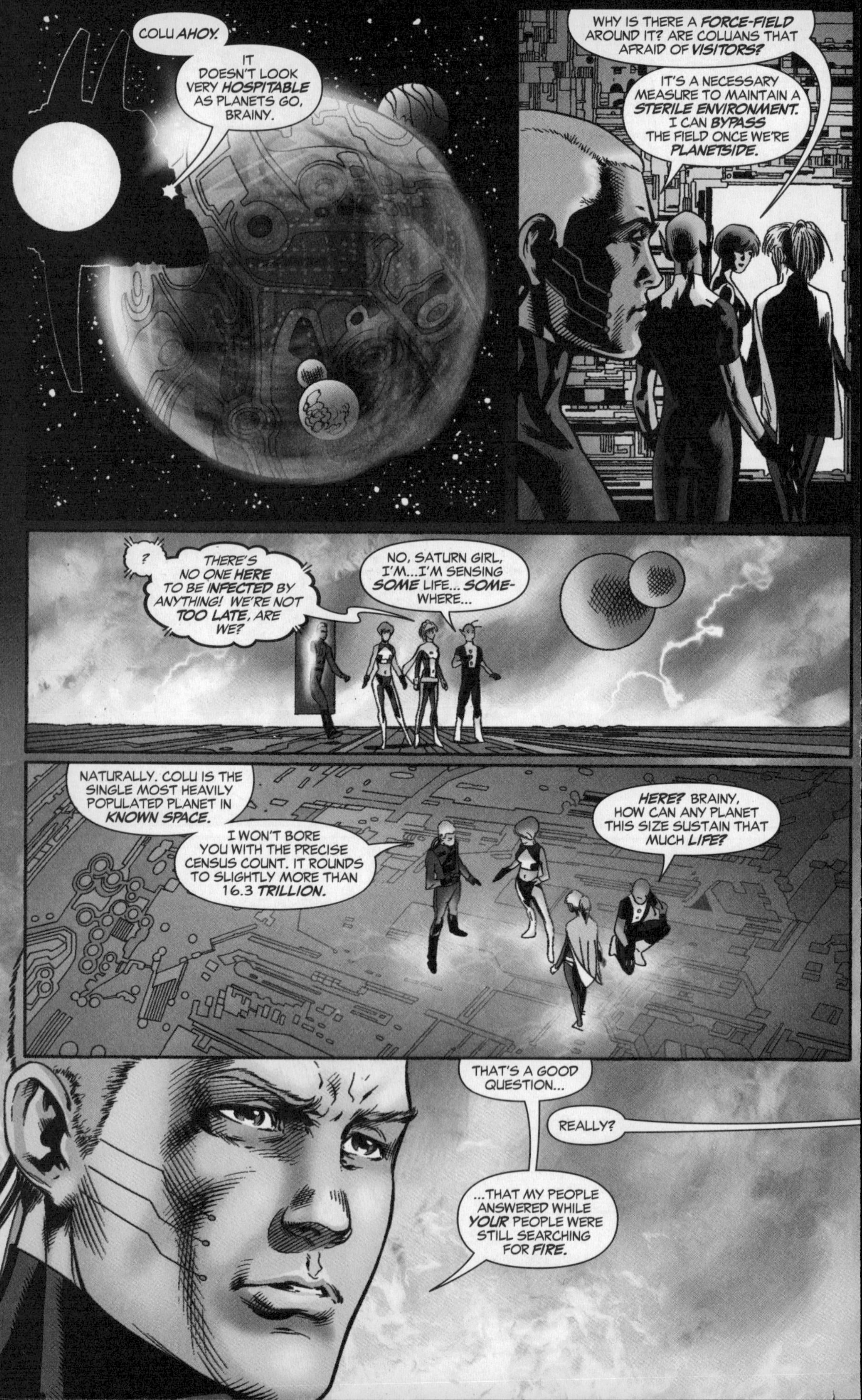
COLU AHOY.
IT DOESN'T LOOK VERY HOSPITABLE AS PLANETS GO, BRAINY.
WHY IS THERE A FORCE-FIELD AROUND IT? ARE COLUANS THAT AFRAID OF VISITORS?
IT'S A NECESSARY MEASURE TO MAINTAIN A STERILE ENVIRONMENT. I CAN BYPASS THE FIELD ONCE WE'RE PLANETSIDE.
?
THERE'S NO ONE HERE TO BE INFECTED BY ANYTHING! WE'RE NOT TOO LATE, ARE WE?
NO, SATURN GIRL, I'M...I'M SENSING SOME LIFE... SOME-WHERE...
NATURALLY. COLU IS THE SINGLE MOST HEAVILY POPULATED PLANET IN KNOWN SPACE.
I WON'T BORE YOU WITH THE PRECISE CENSUS COUNT. IT ROUNDS TO SLIGHTLY MORE THAN 16.3 TRILLION.
HERE? BRAINY, HOW CAN ANY PLANET THIS SIZE SUSTAIN THAT MUCH LIFE?
THAT'S A GOOD QUESTION...
REALLY?
...THAT MY PEOPLE ANSWERED WHILE YOUR PEOPLE WERE STILL SEARCHING FOR FIRE.

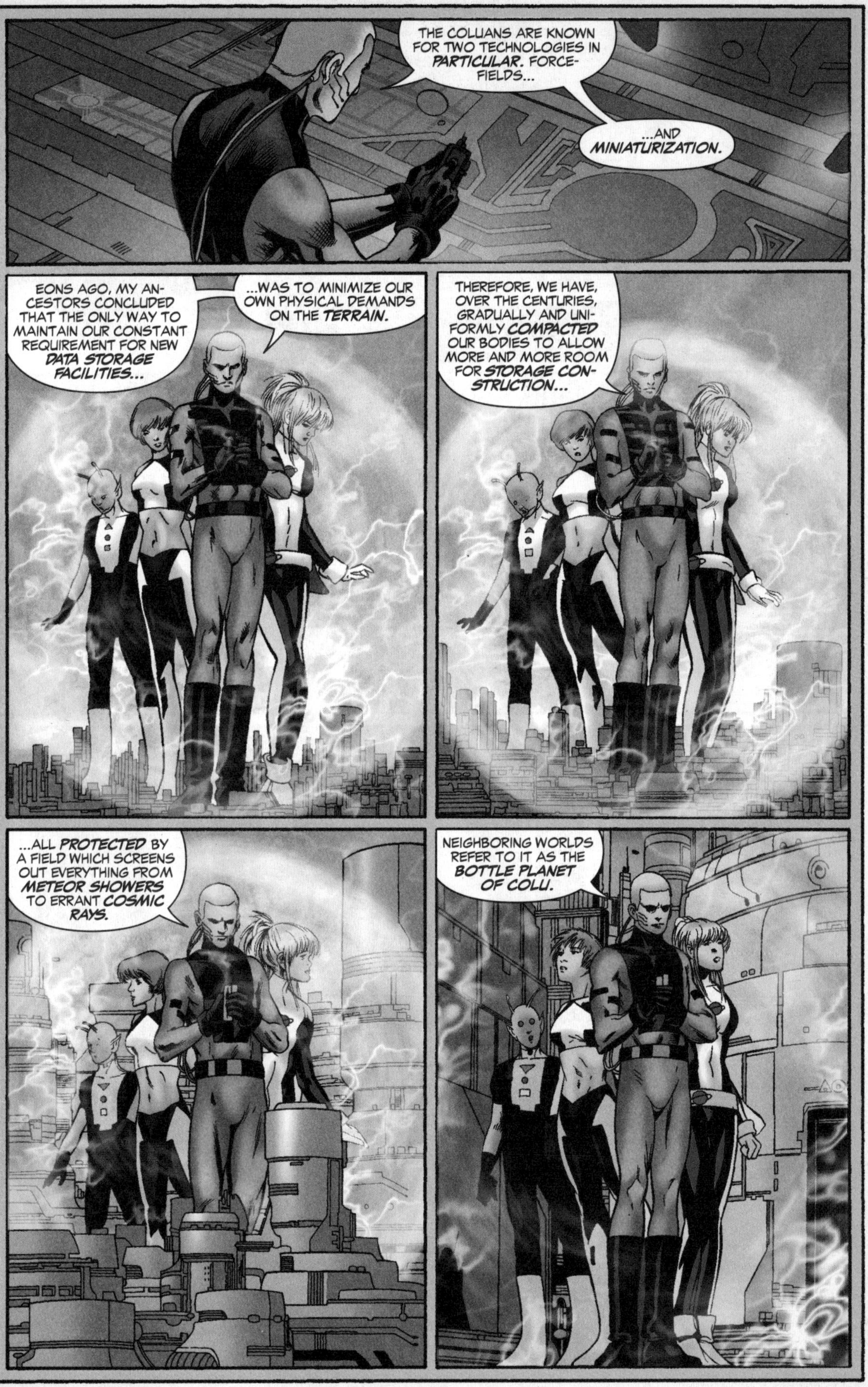
THE COLUANS ARE KNOWN FOR TWO TECHNOLOGIES IN PARTICULAR. FORCE-FIELDS...
...AND MINIATURIZATION.
EONS AGO, MY ANCESTORS CONCLUDED THAT THE ONLY WAY TO MAINTAIN OUR CONSTANT REQUIREMENT FOR NEW DATA STORAGE FACILITIES...
...WAS TO MINIMIZE OUR OWN PHYSICAL DEMANDS ON THE TERRAIN.
THEREFORE, WE HAVE, OVER THE CENTURIES, GRADUALLY AND UNIFORMLY COMPACTED OUR BODIES TO ALLOW MORE AND MORE ROOM FOR STORAGE CONSTRUCTION...
...ALL PROTECTED BY A FIELD WHICH SCREENS OUT EVERYTHING FROM METEOR SHOWERS TO ERRANT COSMIC RAYS.
NEIGHBORING WORLDS REFER TO IT AS THE BOTTLE PLANET OF COLU.

UP AHEAD IS THE *CORTEX,* OUR *CENTRAL ROUTER.*

THAT WILL BE OUR *FIRST STOP.*

I'M RECEIVING SOME VERY ODD MENTAL ACTIVITY INSIDE, BRAINY. BE AWARE.

NONSENSE. WHAT YOU'RE SENSING IS YOUR INABILITY TO COMPREHEND *COLUAN THOUGHT.* FOR YOU, IT MUST BE NOT UNLIKE STARING DIRECTLY AT THE *SUN.*

THIS IS WHERE COLU'S *GREATEST MINDS* CONVENE TO PONDER THE MYSTERIES OF *SCIENCE* AND--

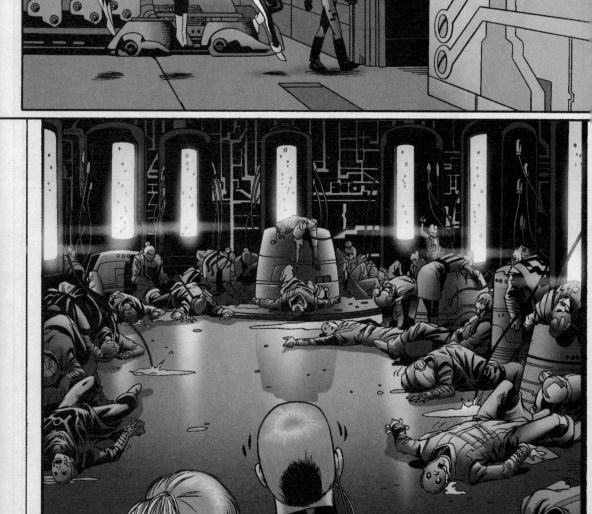

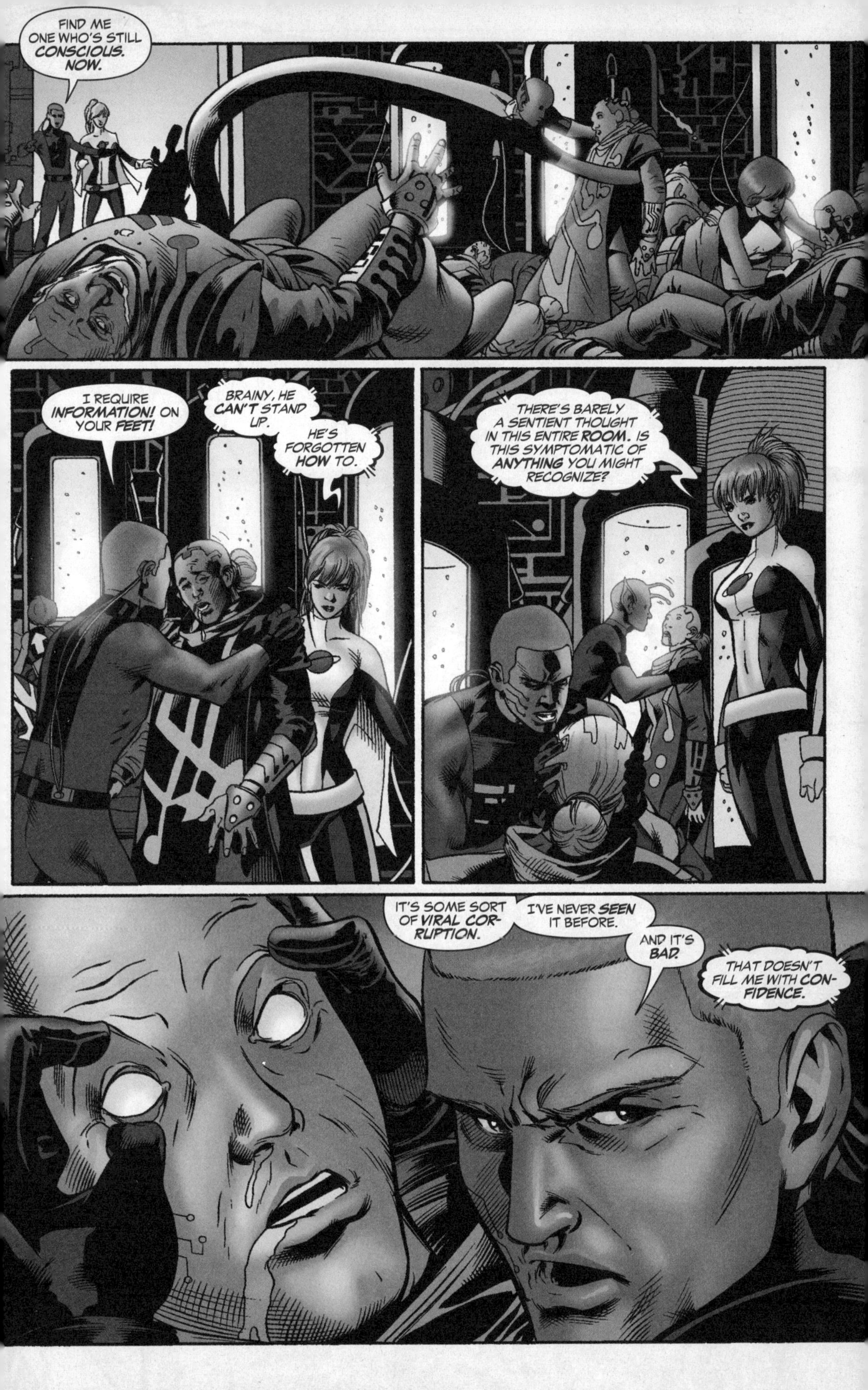
FIND ME ONE WHO'S STILL CONSCIOUS. NOW.
I REQUIRE INFORMATION! ON YOUR FEET!
BRAINY, HE CAN'T STAND UP.
HE'S FORGOTTEN HOW TO.
THERE'S BARELY A SENTIENT THOUGHT IN THIS ENTIRE ROOM. IS THIS SYMPTOMATIC OF ANYTHING YOU MIGHT RECOGNIZE?
IT'S SOME SORT OF VIRAL CORRUPTION.
I'VE NEVER SEEN IT BEFORE.
AND IT'S BAD.
THAT DOESN'T FILL ME WITH CONFIDENCE.

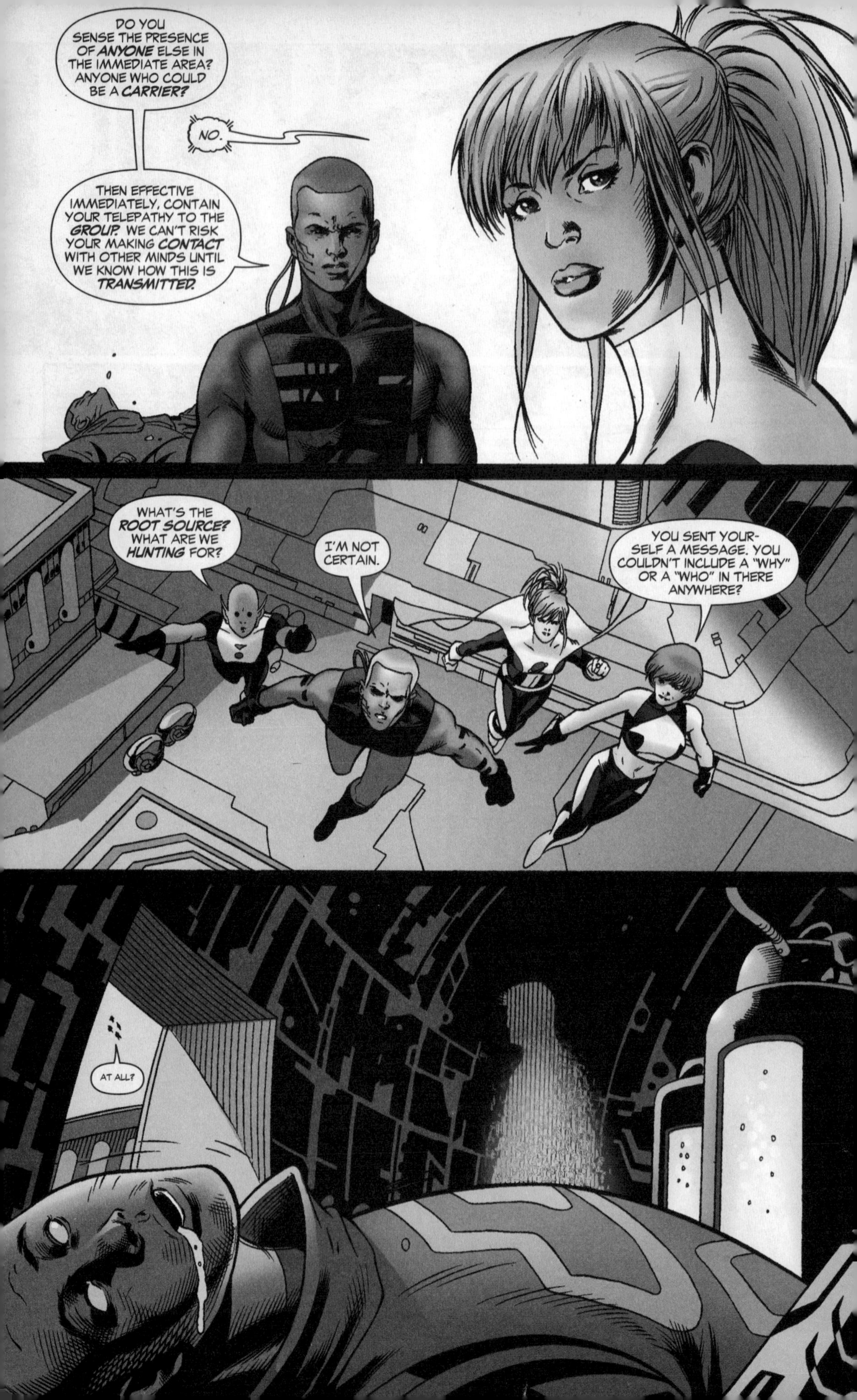

DO YOU SENSE THE PRESENCE OF ANYONE ELSE IN THE IMMEDIATE AREA? ANYONE WHO COULD BE A CARRIER?
NO.
THEN EFFECTIVE IMMEDIATELY, CONTAIN YOUR TELEPATHY TO THE GROUP. WE CAN'T RISK YOUR MAKING CONTACT WITH OTHER MINDS UNTIL WE KNOW HOW THIS IS TRANSMITTED.
WHAT'S THE ROOT SOURCE? WHAT ARE WE HUNTING FOR?
I'M NOT CERTAIN.
YOU SENT YOURSELF A MESSAGE. YOU COULDN'T INCLUDE A "WHY" OR A "WHO" IN THERE ANYWHERE?
AT ALL?

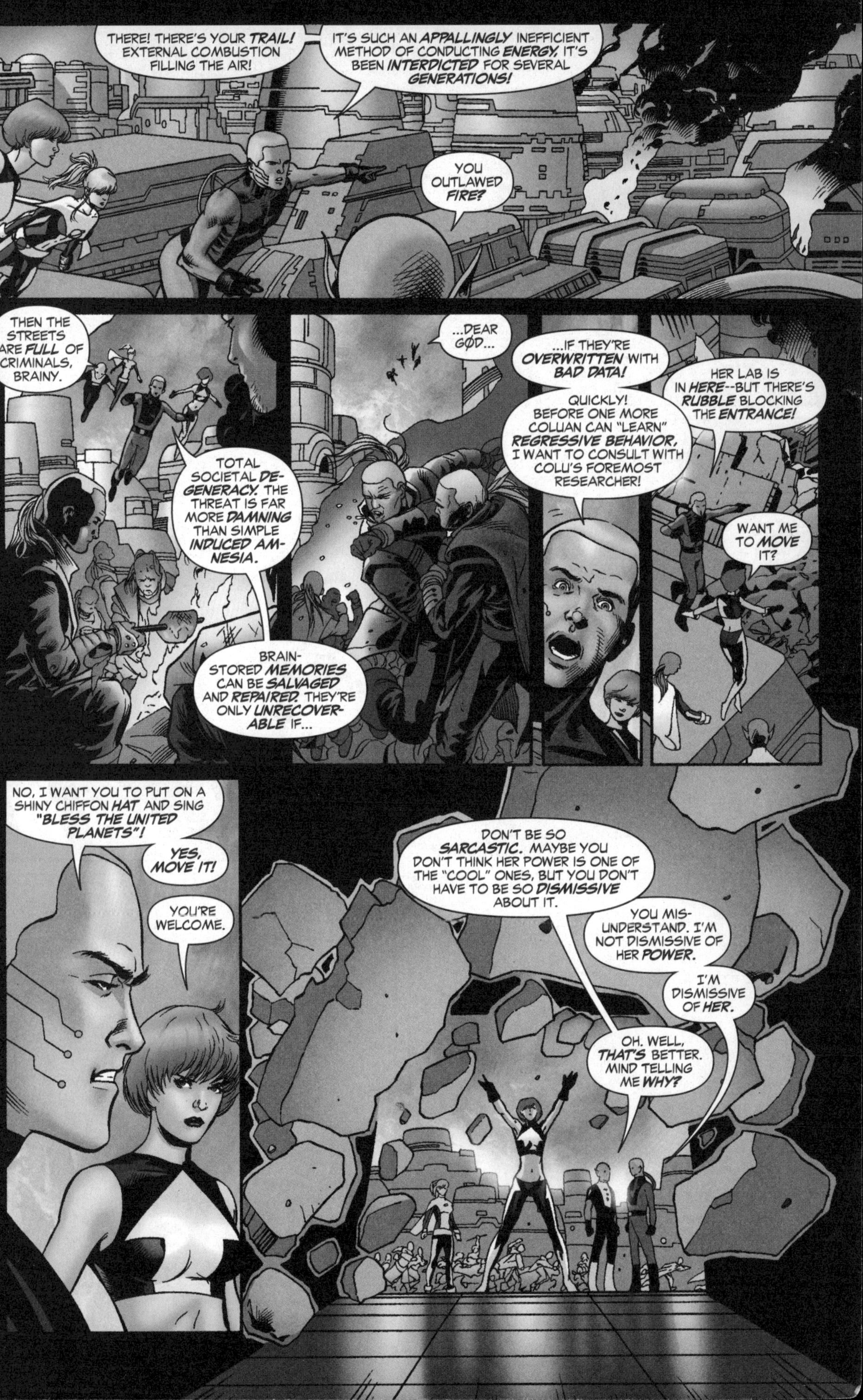
THERE! THERE'S YOUR TRAIL! EXTERNAL COMBUSTION FILLING THE AIR!
IT'S SUCH AN APPALLINGLY INEFFICIENT METHOD OF CONDUCTING ENERGY, IT'S BEEN INTERDICTED FOR SEVERAL GENERATIONS!
YOU OUTLAWED FIRE?
THEN THE STREETS ARE FULL OF CRIMINALS, BRAINY.
TOTAL SOCIETAL DEGENERACY. THE THREAT IS FAR MORE DAMNING THAN SIMPLE INDUCED AMNESIA.
BRAIN-STORED MEMORIES CAN BE SALVAGED AND REPAIRED. THEY'RE ONLY UNRECOVERABLE IF...
...DEAR GØD...
...IF THEY'RE OVERWRITTEN WITH BAD DATA!
QUICKLY! BEFORE ONE MORE COLUAN CAN "LEARN" REGRESSIVE BEHAVIOR, I WANT TO CONSULT WITH COLU'S FOREMOST RESEARCHER!
HER LAB IS IN HERE--BUT THERE'S RUBBLE BLOCKING THE ENTRANCE!
WANT ME TO MOVE IT?
NO, I WANT YOU TO PUT ON A SHINY CHIFFON HAT AND SING "BLESS THE UNITED PLANETS"!
YES, MOVE IT!
YOU'RE WELCOME.
DON'T BE SO SARCASTIC. MAYBE YOU DON'T THINK HER POWER IS ONE OF THE "COOL" ONES, BUT YOU DON'T HAVE TO BE SO DISMISSIVE ABOUT IT.
YOU MISUNDERSTAND. I'M NOT DISMISSIVE OF HER POWER.
I'M DISMISSIVE OF HER.
OH. WELL, THAT'S BETTER. MIND TELLING ME WHY?

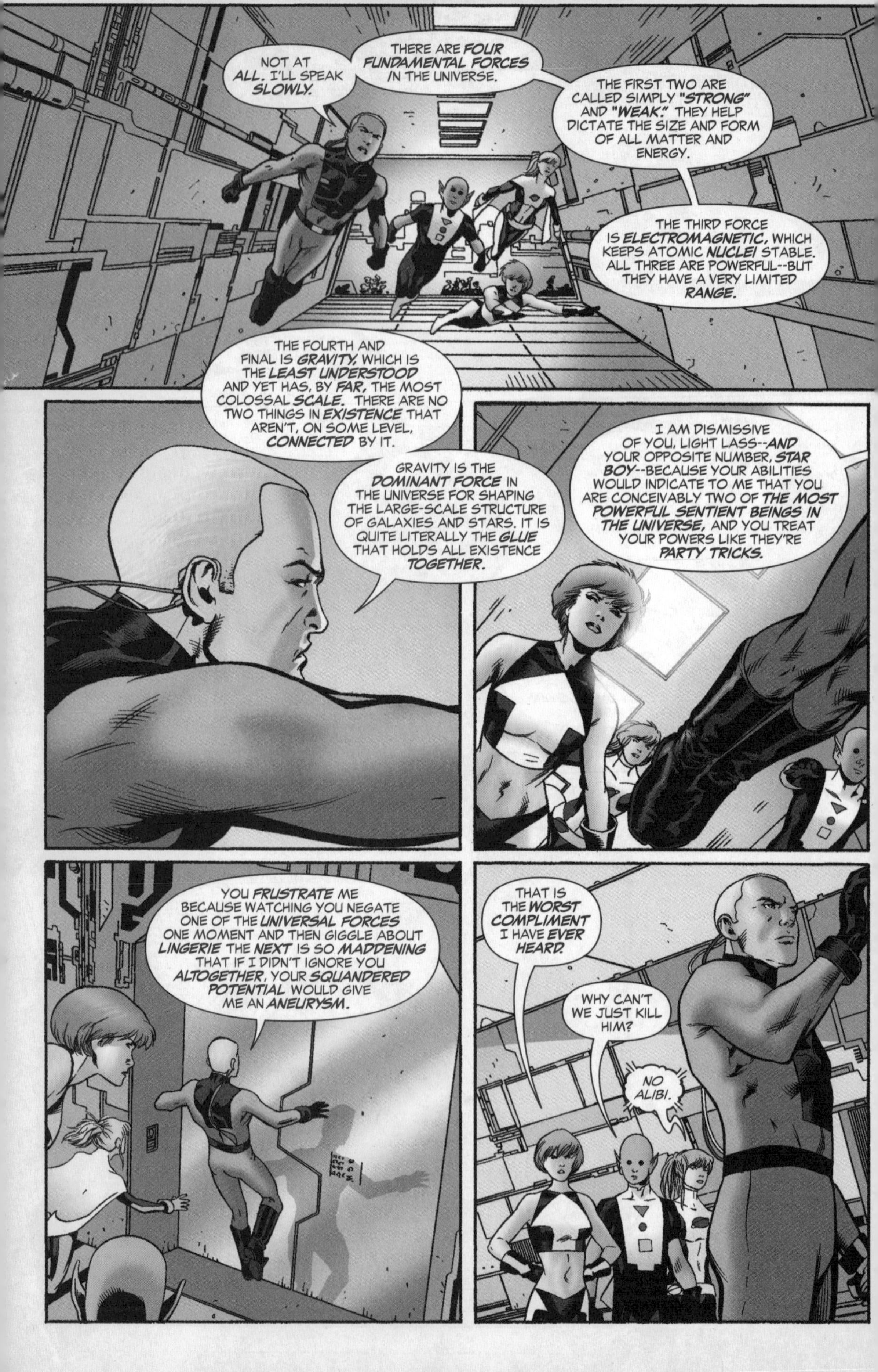

NOT AT ALL. I'LL SPEAK SLOWLY.
THERE ARE FOUR FUNDAMENTAL FORCES IN THE UNIVERSE.
THE FIRST TWO ARE CALLED SIMPLY "STRONG" AND "WEAK." THEY HELP DICTATE THE SIZE AND FORM OF ALL MATTER AND ENERGY.
THE THIRD FORCE IS ELECTROMAGNETIC, WHICH KEEPS ATOMIC NUCLEI STABLE. ALL THREE ARE POWERFUL--BUT THEY HAVE A VERY LIMITED RANGE.
THE FOURTH AND FINAL IS GRAVITY, WHICH IS THE LEAST UNDERSTOOD AND YET HAS, BY FAR, THE MOST COLOSSAL SCALE. THERE ARE NO TWO THINGS IN EXISTENCE THAT AREN'T, ON SOME LEVEL, CONNECTED BY IT.
GRAVITY IS THE DOMINANT FORCE IN THE UNIVERSE FOR SHAPING THE LARGE-SCALE STRUCTURE OF GALAXIES AND STARS. IT IS QUITE LITERALLY THE GLUE THAT HOLDS ALL EXISTENCE TOGETHER.
I AM DISMISSIVE OF YOU, LIGHT LASS--AND YOUR OPPOSITE NUMBER, STAR BOY--BECAUSE YOUR ABILITIES WOULD INDICATE TO ME THAT YOU ARE CONCEIVABLY TWO OF THE MOST POWERFUL SENTIENT BEINGS IN THE UNIVERSE, AND YOU TREAT YOUR POWERS LIKE THEY'RE PARTY TRICKS.
YOU FRUSTRATE ME BECAUSE WATCHING YOU NEGATE ONE OF THE UNIVERSAL FORCES ONE MOMENT AND THEN GIGGLE ABOUT LINGERIE THE NEXT IS SO MADDENING THAT IF I DIDN'T IGNORE YOU ALTOGETHER, YOUR SQUANDERED POTENTIAL WOULD GIVE ME AN ANEURYSM.
THAT IS THE WORST COMPLIMENT I HAVE EVER HEARD.
WHY CAN'T WE JUST KILL HIM?
NO ALIBI.

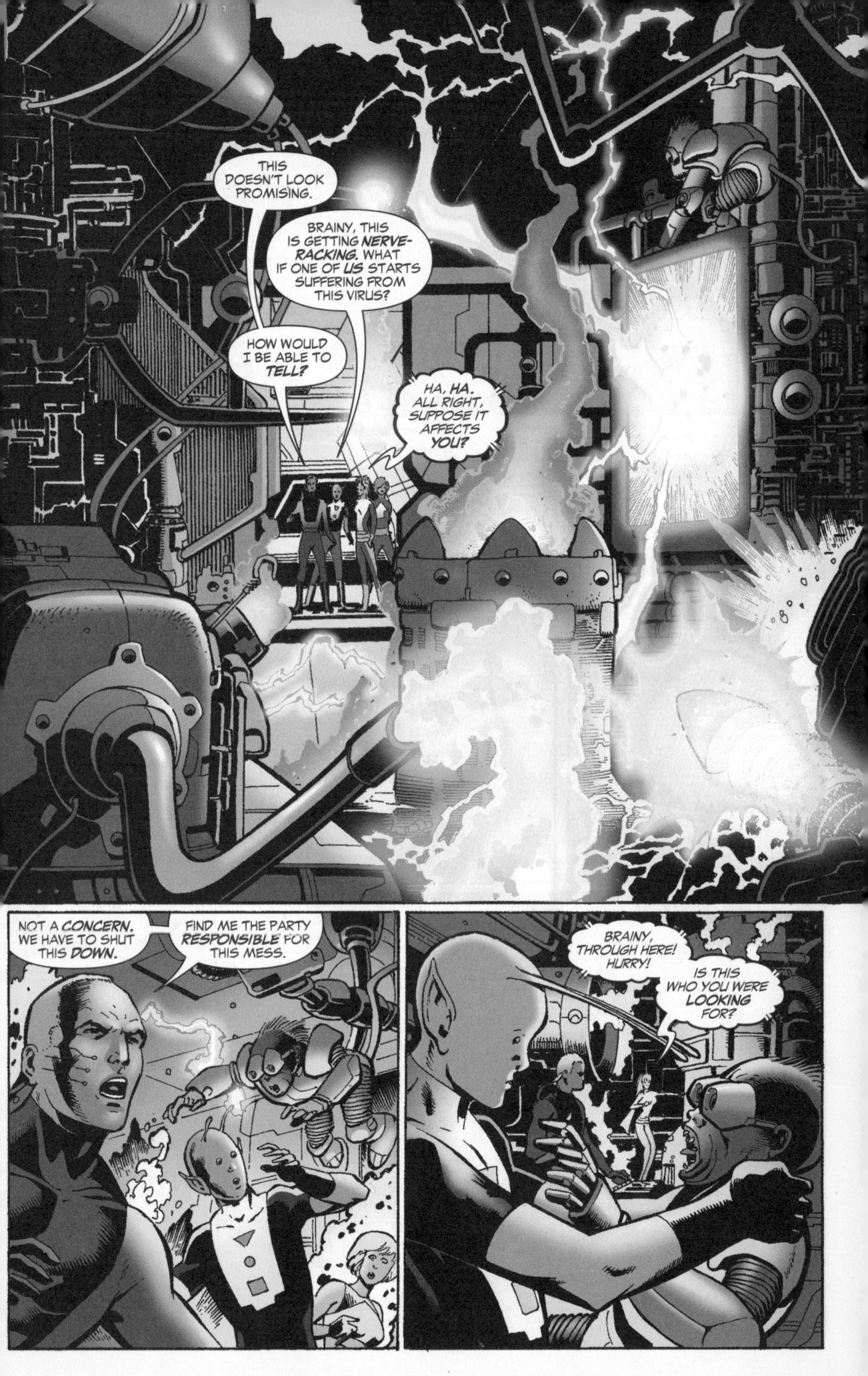
THIS DOESN'T LOOK PROMISING.
BRAINY, THIS IS GETTING NERVE-RACKING. WHAT IF ONE OF US STARTS SUFFERING FROM THIS VIRUS?
HOW WOULD I BE ABLE TO TELL?
HA, HA. ALL RIGHT, SUPPOSE IT AFFECTS YOU?
NOT A CONCERN. WE HAVE TO SHUT THIS DOWN.
FIND ME THE PARTY RESPONSIBLE FOR THIS MESS.
BRAINY, THROUGH HERE! HURRY!
IS THIS WHO YOU WERE LOOKING FOR?

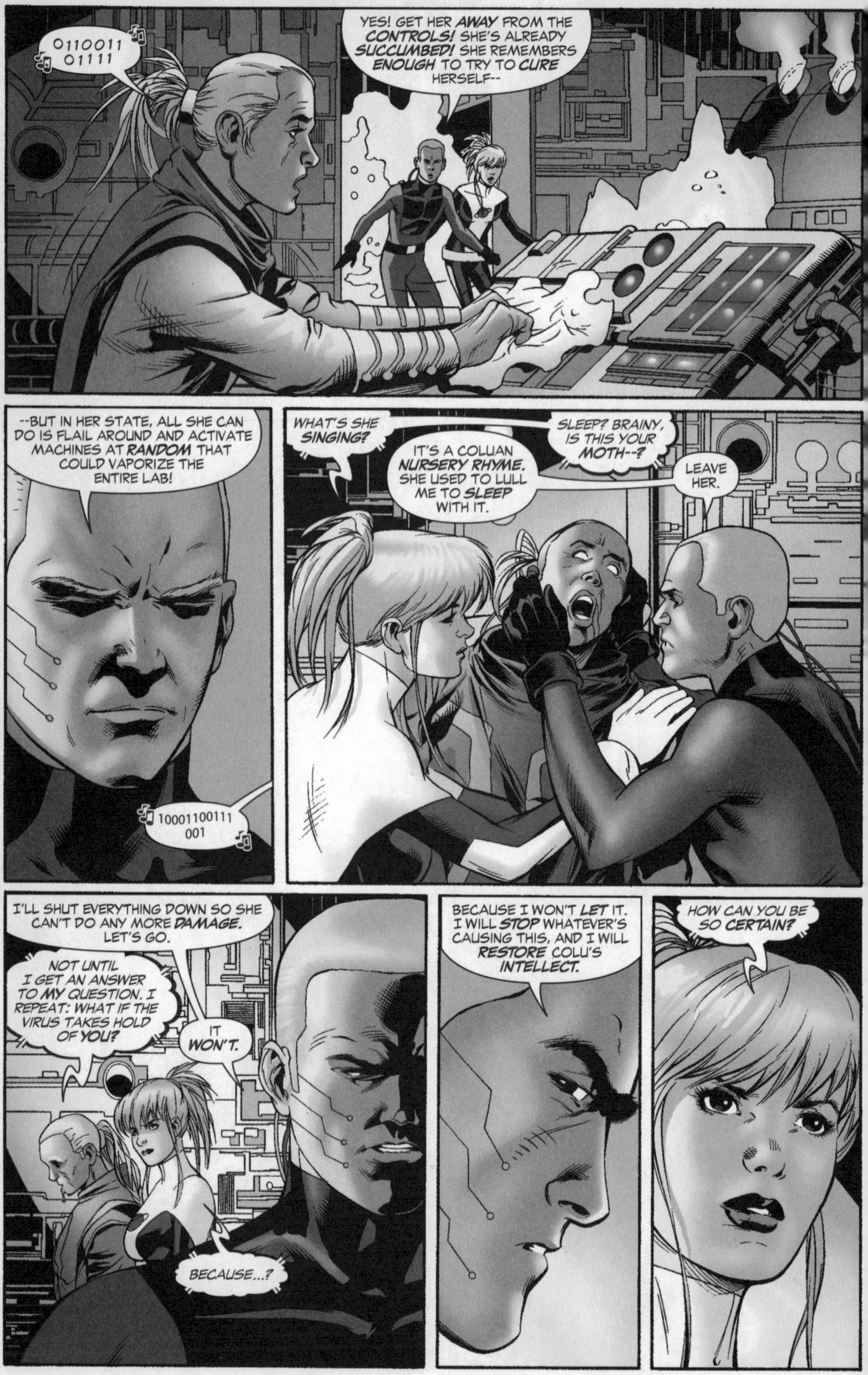
0110011 01111
YES! GET HER AWAY FROM THE CONTROLS! SHE'S ALREADY SUCCUMBED! SHE REMEMBERS ENOUGH TO TRY TO CURE HERSELF--
--BUT IN HER STATE, ALL SHE CAN DO IS FLAIL AROUND AND ACTIVATE MACHINES AT RANDOM THAT COULD VAPORIZE THE ENTIRE LAB!
1001100111 001
WHAT'S SHE SINGING?
IT'S A COLUAN NURSERY RHYME. SHE USED TO LULL ME TO SLEEP WITH IT.
SLEEP? BRAINY, IS THIS YOUR MOTH--?
LEAVE HER.
I'LL SHUT EVERYTHING DOWN SO SHE CAN'T DO ANY MORE DAMAGE. LET'S GO.
NOT UNTIL I GET AN ANSWER TO MY QUESTION. I REPEAT: WHAT IF THE VIRUS TAKES HOLD OF YOU?
IT WON'T.
BECAUSE...?
BECAUSE I WON'T LET IT. I WILL STOP WHATEVER'S CAUSING THIS, AND I WILL RESTORE COLU'S INTELLECT.
HOW CAN YOU BE SO CERTAIN?

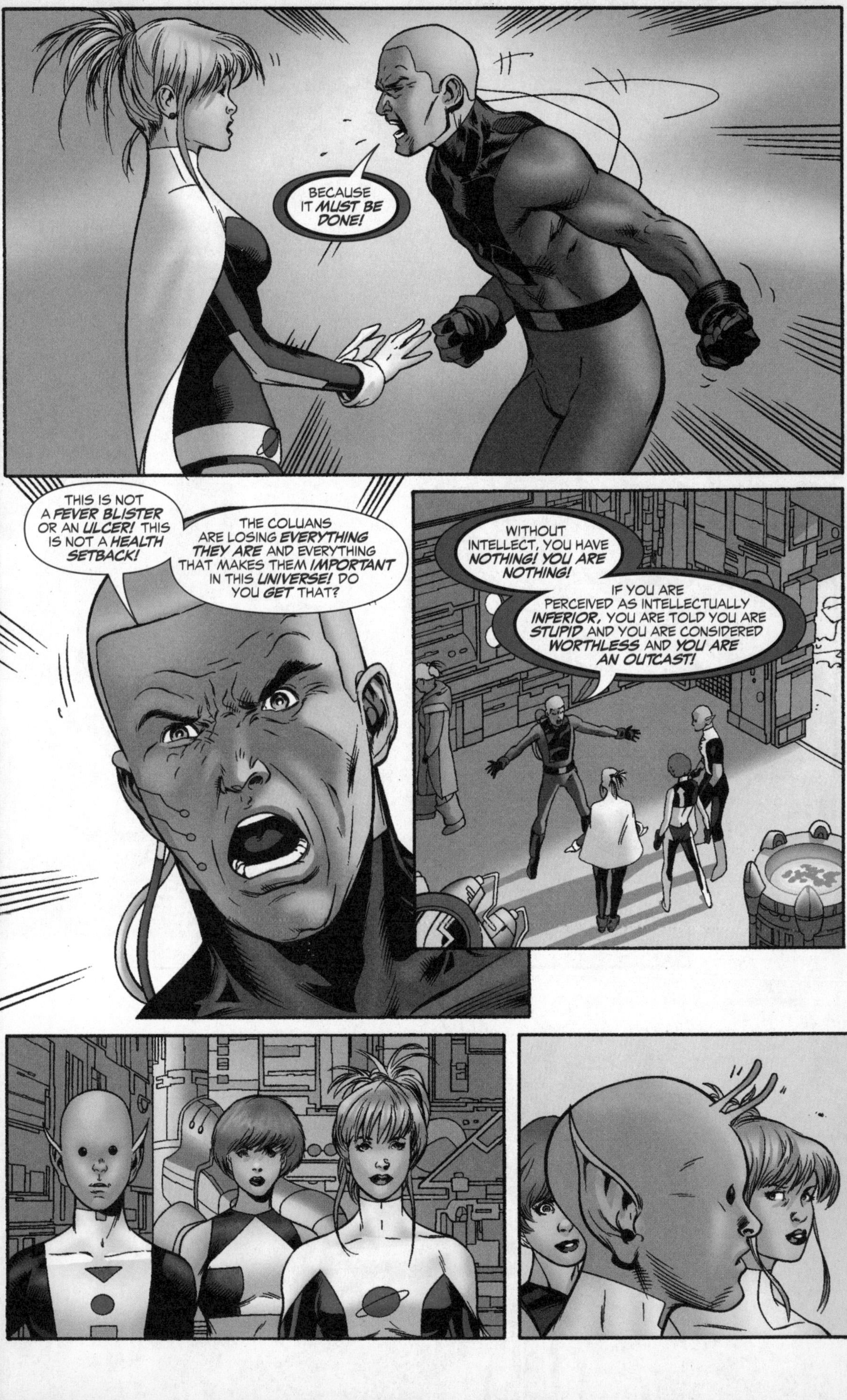
BECAUSE IT MUST BE DONE!
THIS IS NOT A FEVER BLISTER OR AN ULCER! THIS IS NOT A HEALTH SETBACK!
THE COLUANS ARE LOSING EVERYTHING THEY ARE AND EVERYTHING THAT MAKES THEM IMPORTANT IN THIS UNIVERSE! DO YOU GET THAT?
WITHOUT INTELLECT, YOU HAVE NOTHING! YOU ARE NOTHING!
IF YOU ARE PERCEIVED AS INTELLECTUALLY INFERIOR, YOU ARE TOLD YOU ARE STUPID AND YOU ARE CONSIDERED WORTHLESS AND YOU ARE AN OUTCAST!

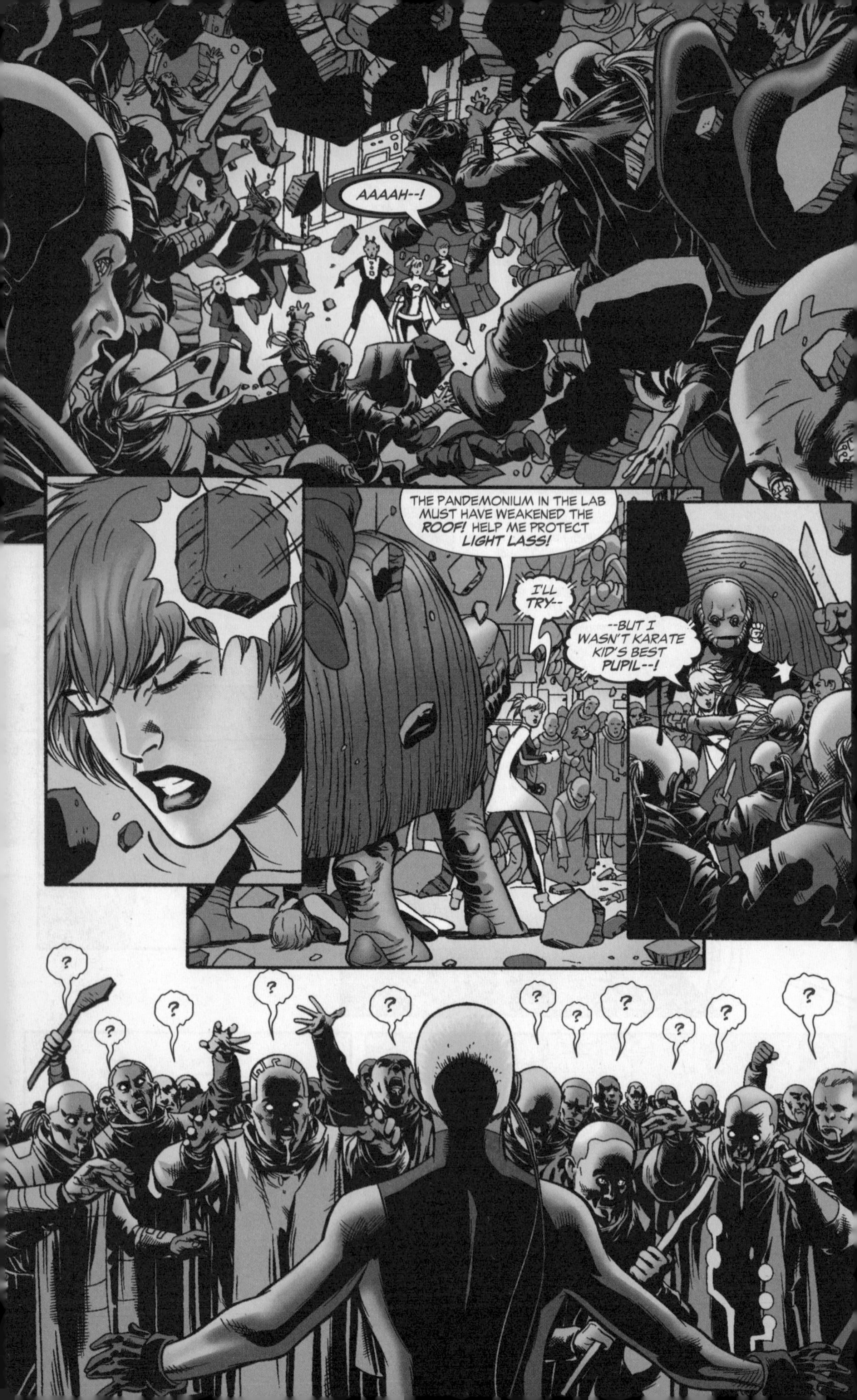
AAAAH--!
THE PANDEMONIUM IN THE LAB MUST HAVE WEAKENED THE ROOF! HELP ME PROTECT LIGHT LASS!
I'LL TRY--
--BUT I WASN'T KARATE KID'S BEST PUPIL--!
?
?
?
?
?
?
?
?
?
?
?
?

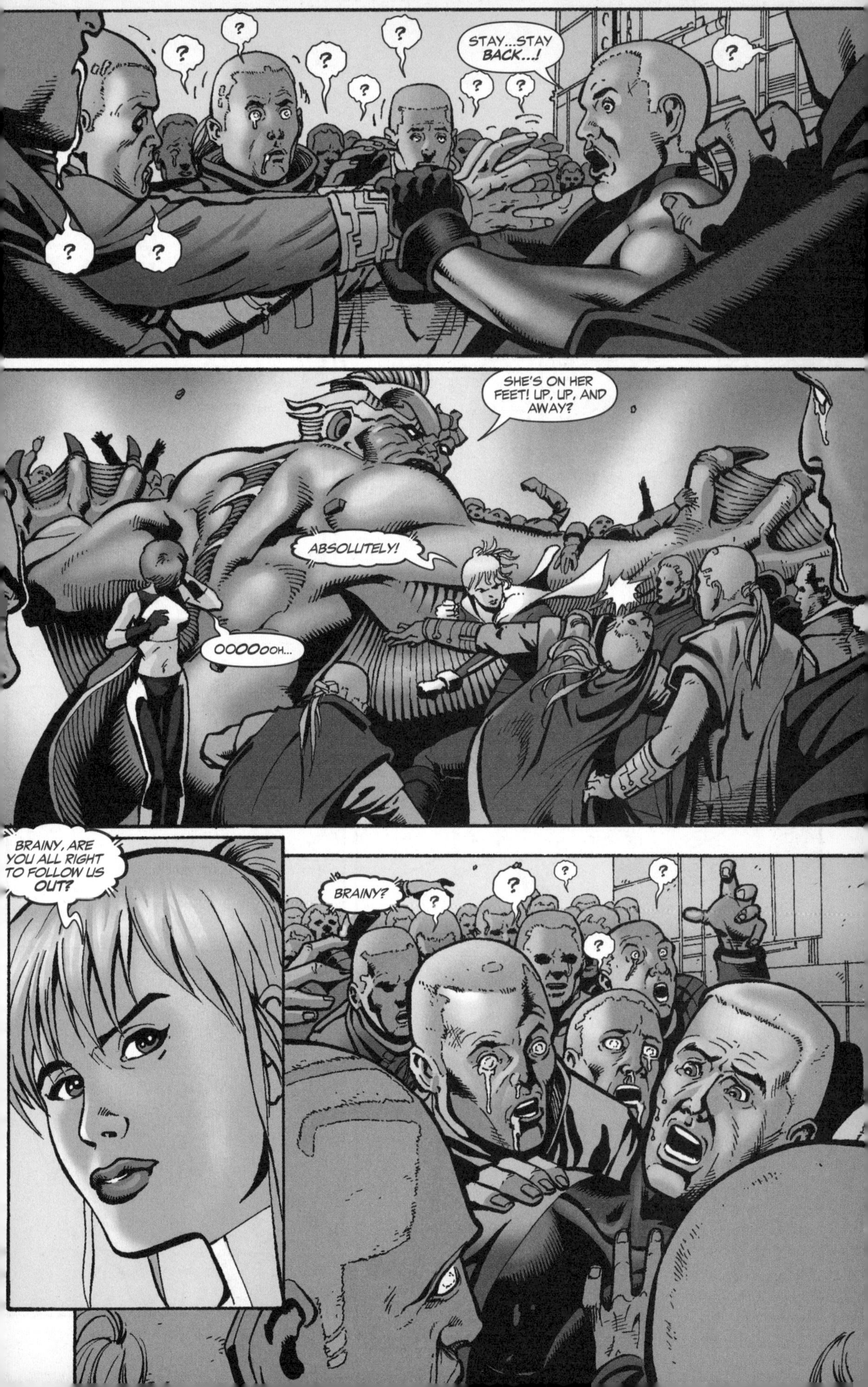
?
?
?
?
STAY...STAY BACK...!
?
?
?
?
?
?
SHE'S ON HER FEET! UP, UP, AND AWAY?
ABSOLUTELY!
OOOOOOH...
BRAINY, ARE YOU ALL RIGHT TO FOLLOW US OUT?
BRAINY?
?
?
?
?
?

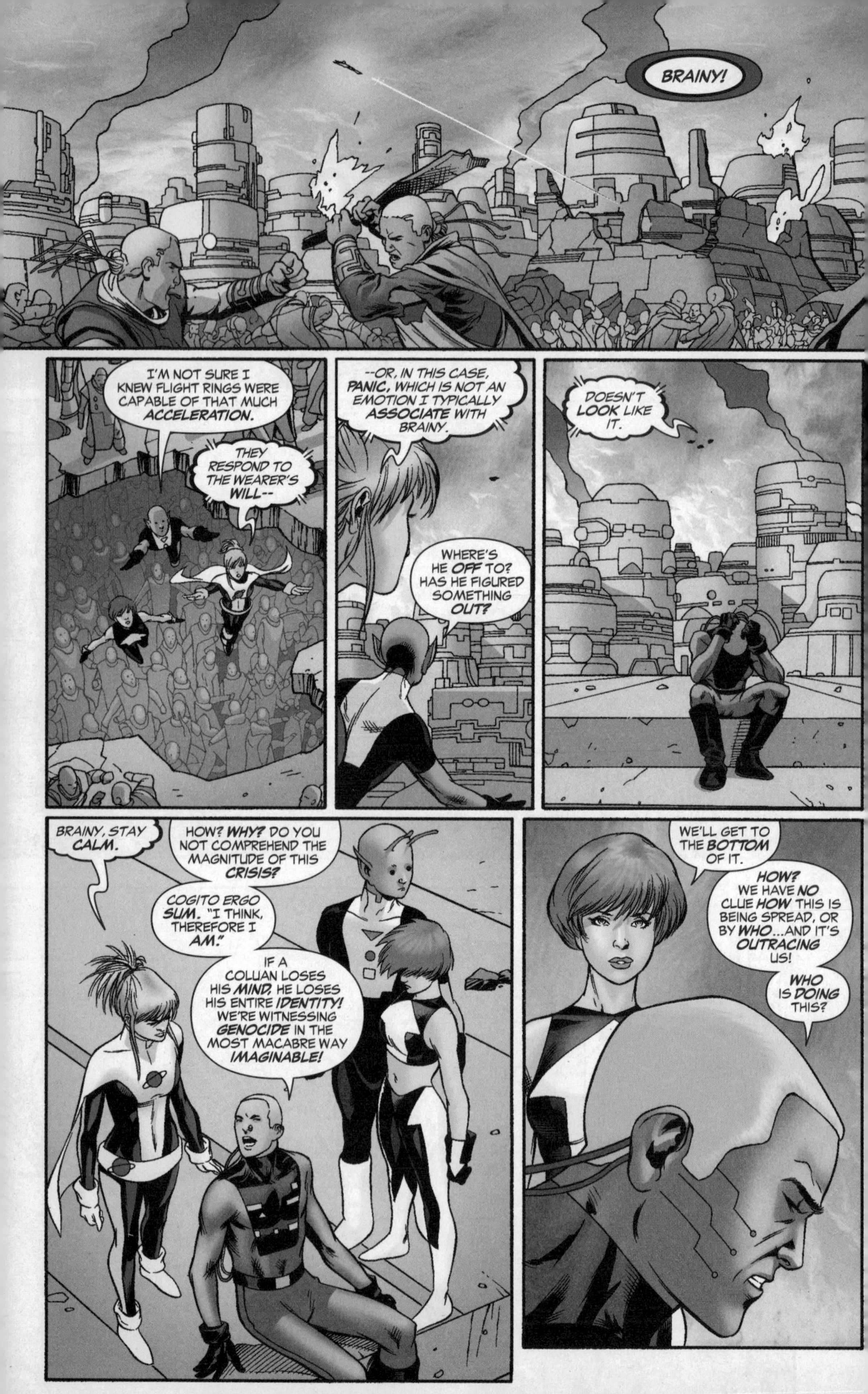
BRAINY!
I'M NOT SURE I KNEW FLIGHT RINGS WERE CAPABLE OF THAT MUCH ACCELERATION.
THEY RESPOND TO THE WEARER'S WILL--
--OR, IN THIS CASE, PANIC, WHICH IS NOT AN EMOTION I TYPICALLY ASSOCIATE WITH BRAINY.
WHERE'S HE OFF TO? HAS HE FIGURED SOMETHING OUT?
DOESN'T LOOK LIKE IT.
BRAINY, STAY CALM.
HOW? WHY? DO YOU NOT COMPREHEND THE MAGNITUDE OF THIS CRISIS?
COGITO ERGO SUM. "I THINK, THEREFORE I AM."
IF A COLUAN LOSES HIS MIND, HE LOSES HIS ENTIRE IDENTITY! WE'RE WITNESSING GENOCIDE IN THE MOST MACABRE WAY IMAGINABLE!
WE'LL GET TO THE BOTTOM OF IT.
HOW? WE HAVE NO CLUE HOW THIS IS BEING SPREAD, OR BY WHO...AND IT'S OUTRACING US!
WHO IS DOING THIS?

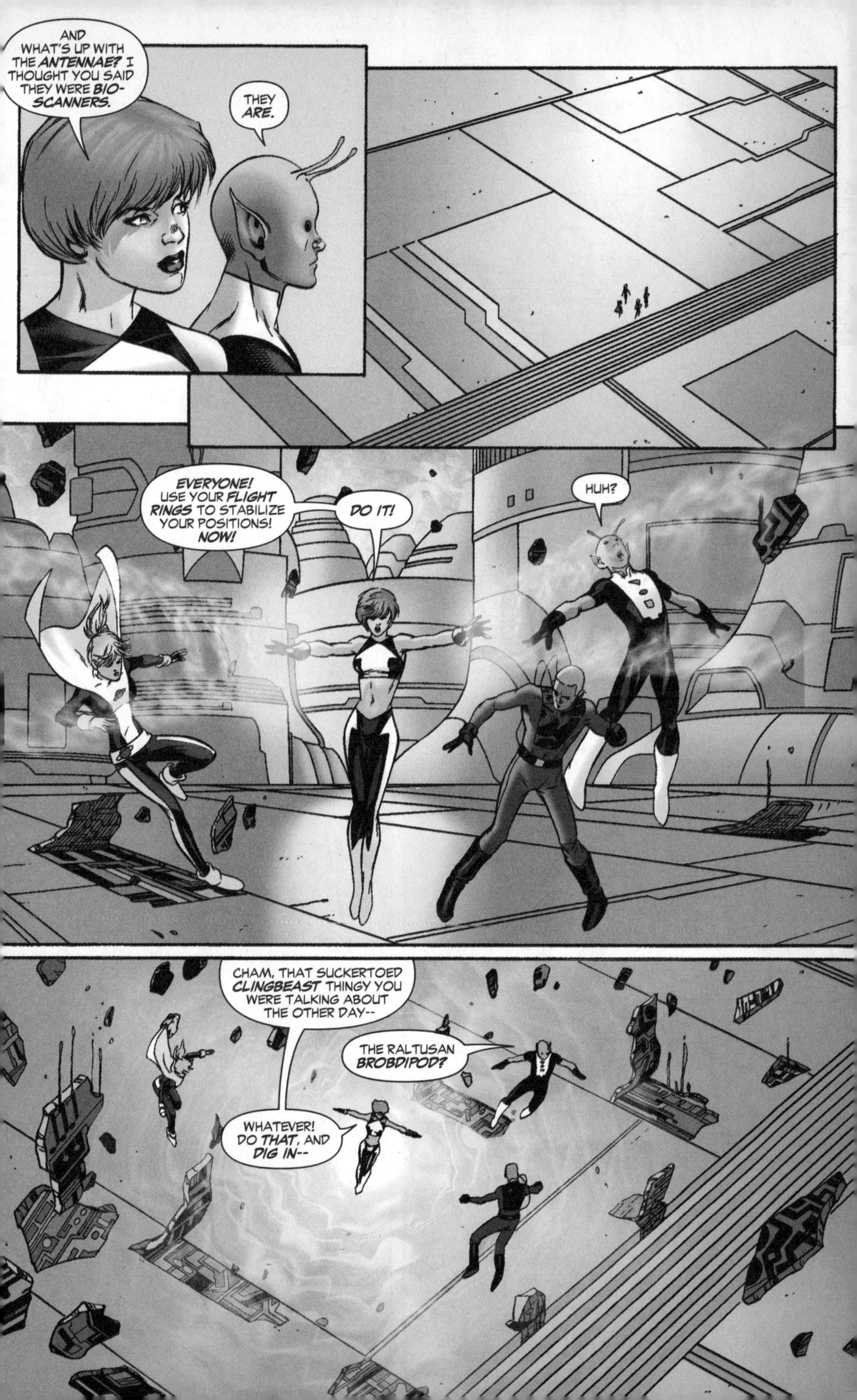
AND WHAT'S UP WITH THE ANTENNAE? I THOUGHT YOU SAID THEY WERE BIO-SCANNERS.
THEY ARE.
EVERYONE! USE YOUR FLIGHT RINGS TO STABILIZE YOUR POSITIONS! NOW!
DO IT!
HUH?
CHAM, THAT SUCKERTOED CLINGBEAST THINGY YOU WERE TALKING ABOUT THE OTHER DAY--
THE RALTUSAN BROBDIPOD?
WHATEVER! DO THAT, AND DIG IN--

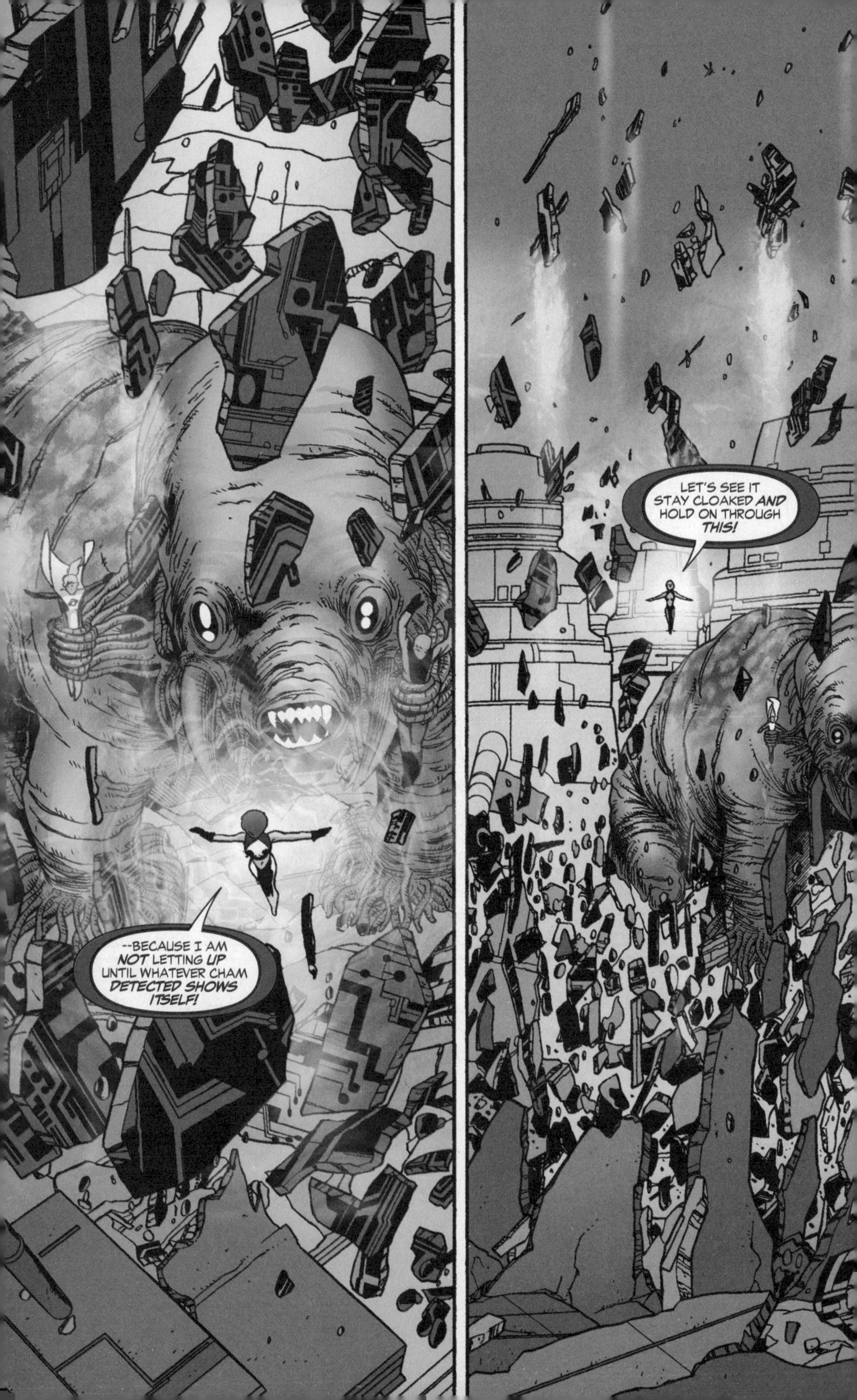
--BECAUSE I AM NOT LETTING UP UNTIL WHATEVER CHAM DETECTED SHOWS ITSELF!
LET'S SEE IT STAY CLOAKED AND HOLD ON THROUGH THIS!

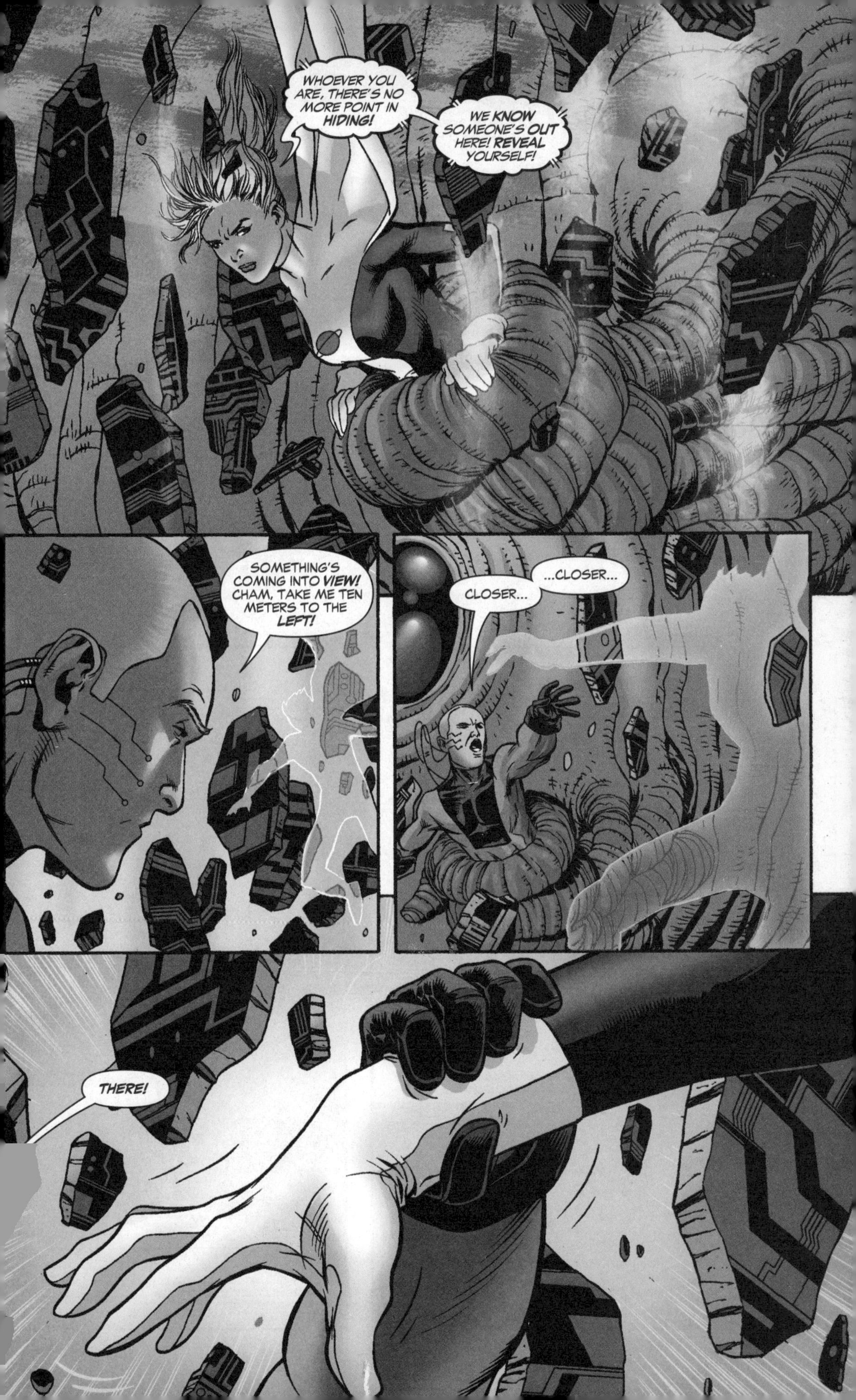
WHOEVER YOU ARE, THERE'S NO MORE POINT IN HIDING!
WE KNOW SOMEONE'S OUT HERE! REVEAL YOURSELF!
SOMETHING'S COMING INTO VIEW! CHAM, TAKE ME TEN METERS TO THE LEFT!
CLOSER...
...CLOSER...
THERE!

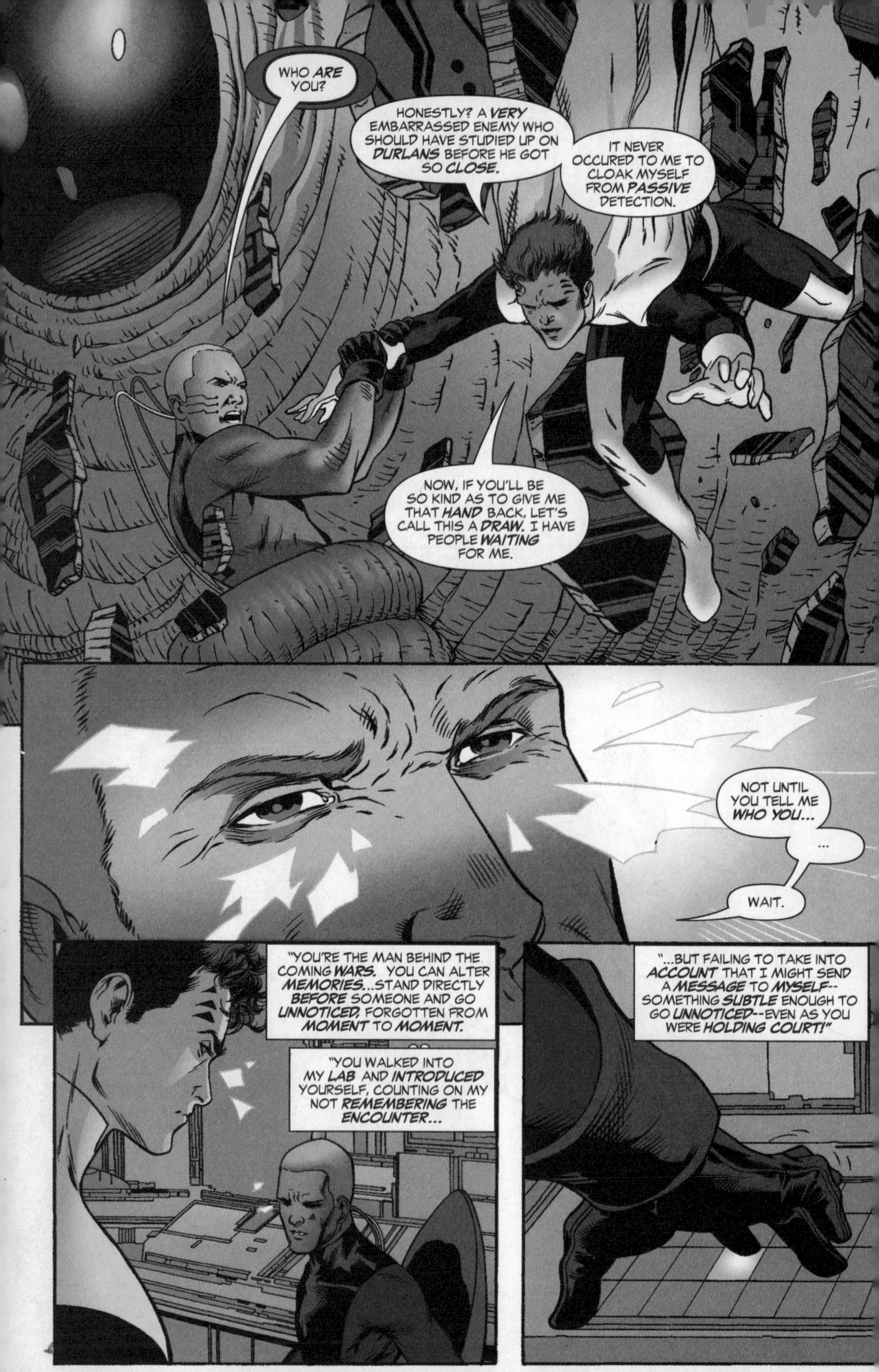
WHO ARE YOU?
HONESTLY? A VERY EMBARRASSED ENEMY WHO SHOULD HAVE STUDIED UP ON DURLANS BEFORE HE GOT SO CLOSE.
IT NEVER OCCURED TO ME TO CLOAK MYSELF FROM PASSIVE DETECTION.
NOW, IF YOU'LL BE SO KIND AS TO GIVE ME THAT HAND BACK, LET'S CALL THIS A DRAW. I HAVE PEOPLE WAITING FOR ME.
NOT UNTIL YOU TELL ME WHO YOU...
...
WAIT.
"YOU'RE THE MAN BEHIND THE COMING WARS. YOU CAN ALTER MEMORIES...STAND DIRECTLY BEFORE SOMEONE AND GO UNNOTICED, FORGOTTEN FROM MOMENT TO MOMENT.
"YOU WALKED INTO MY LAB AND INTRODUCED YOURSELF, COUNTING ON MY NOT REMEMBERING THE ENCOUNTER...
"...BUT FAILING TO TAKE INTO ACCOUNT THAT I MIGHT SEND A MESSAGE TO MYSELF--SOMETHING SUBTLE ENOUGH TO GO UNNOTICED--EVEN AS YOU WERE HOLDING COURT!"

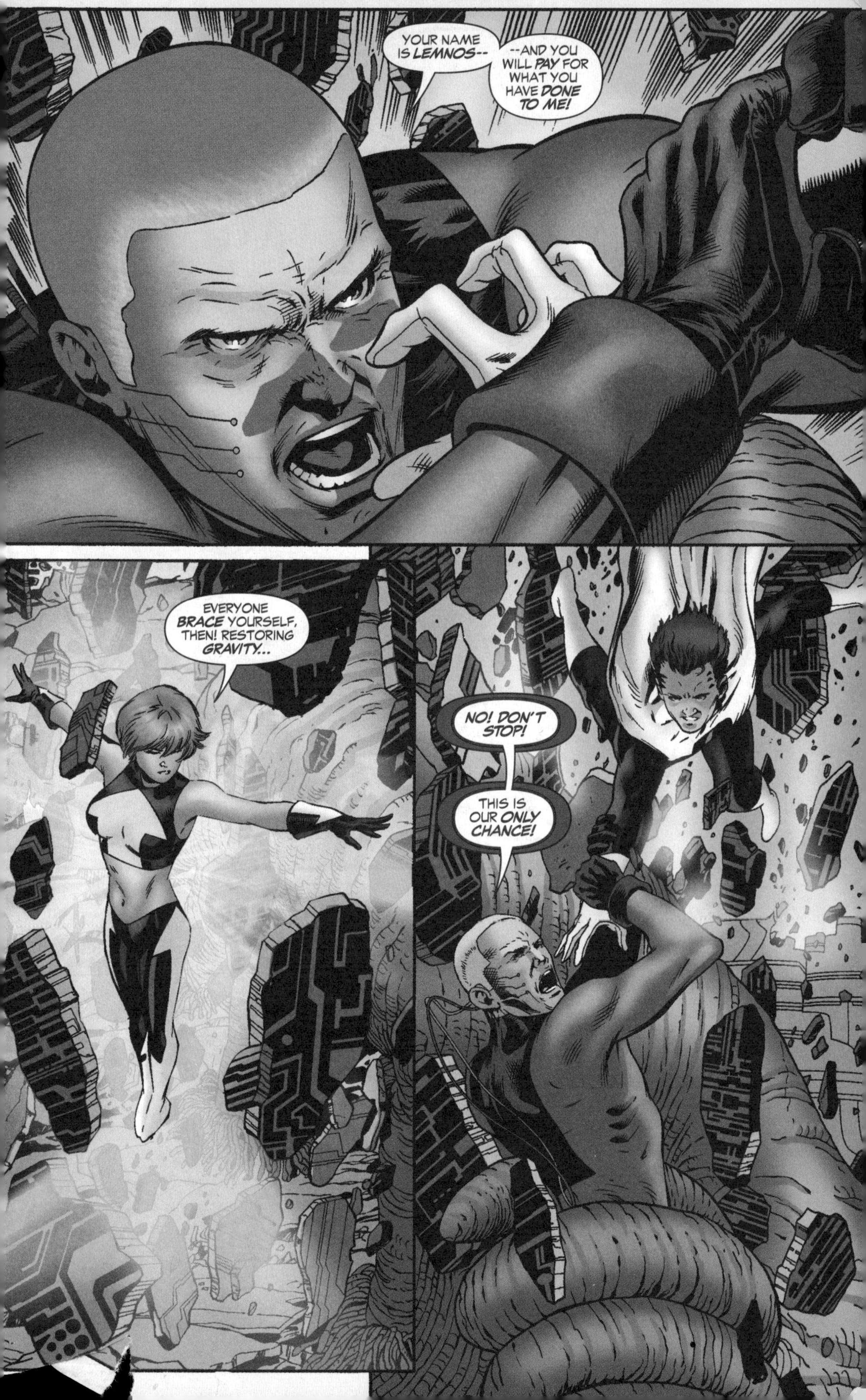
YOUR NAME IS LEMNOS--
--AND YOU WILL PAY FOR WHAT YOU HAVE DONE TO ME!
EVERYONE BRACE YOURSELF, THEN! RESTORING GRAVITY...
NO! DON'T STOP!
THIS IS OUR ONLY CHANCE!

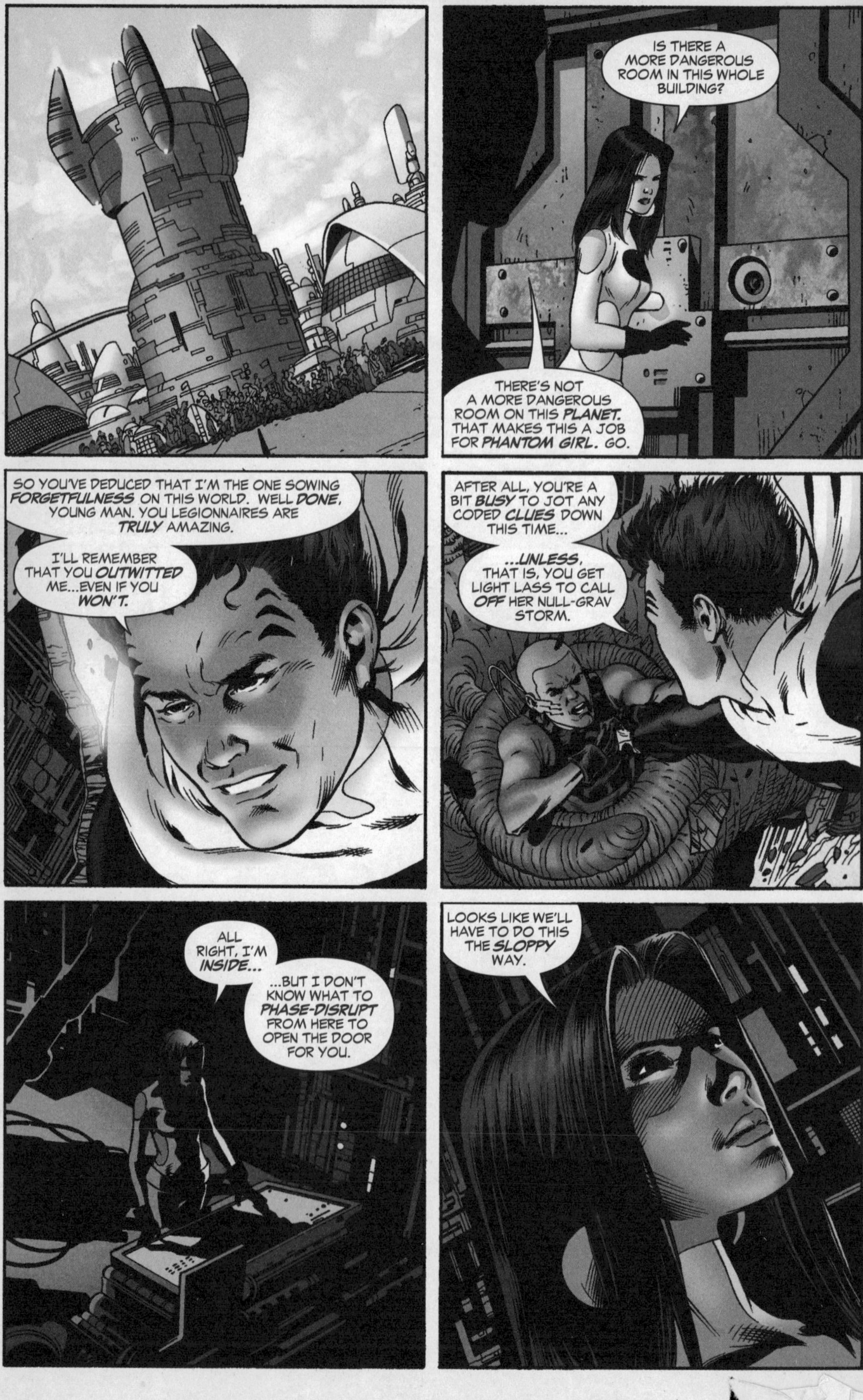
IS THERE A MORE DANGEROUS ROOM IN THIS WHOLE BUILDING?
THERE'S NOT A MORE DANGEROUS ROOM ON THIS *PLANET.* THAT MAKES THIS A JOB FOR *PHANTOM GIRL.* GO.
SO YOU'VE DEDUCED THAT I'M THE ONE SOWING *FORGETFULNESS* ON THIS WORLD. WELL *DONE,* YOUNG MAN. YOU LEGIONNAIRES ARE *TRULY* AMAZING.
I'LL REMEMBER THAT YOU *OUTWITTED* ME...EVEN IF YOU *WON'T.*
AFTER ALL, YOU'RE A BIT *BUSY* TO JOT ANY CODED *CLUES* DOWN THIS TIME...
...UNLESS, THAT IS, YOU GET LIGHT LASS TO CALL *OFF* HER NULL-GRAV STORM.
ALL RIGHT, I'M *INSIDE...*
...BUT I DON'T KNOW WHAT TO *PHASE-DISRUPT* FROM HERE TO OPEN THE DOOR FOR YOU.
LOOKS LIKE WE'LL HAVE TO DO THIS THE *SLOPPY* WAY.

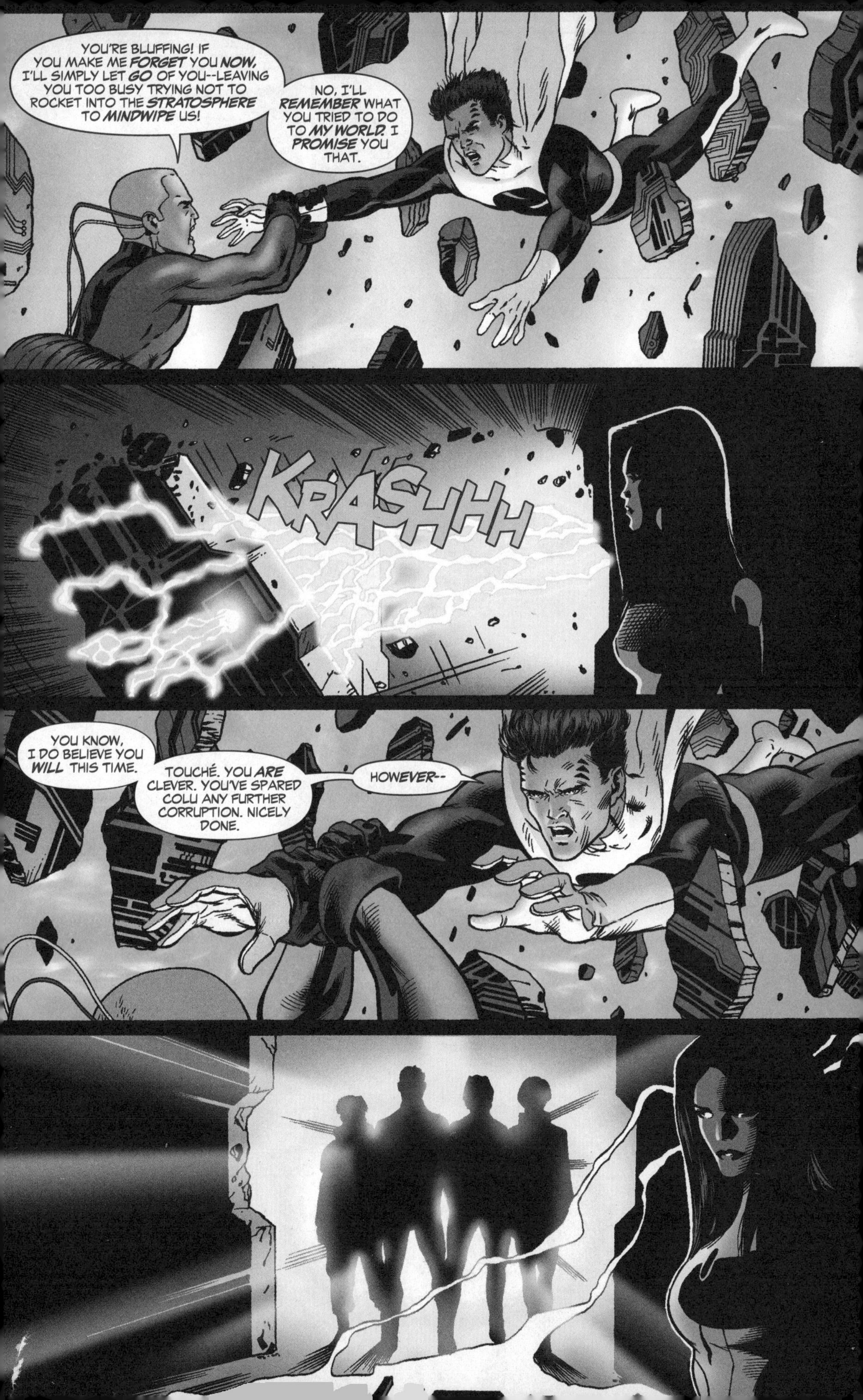
YOU'RE BLUFFING! IF YOU MAKE ME FORGET YOU NOW, I'LL SIMPLY LET GO OF YOU--LEAVING YOU TOO BUSY TRYING NOT TO ROCKET INTO THE STRATOSPHERE TO MINDWIPE US!
NO, I'LL REMEMBER WHAT YOU TRIED TO DO TO MY WORLD. I PROMISE YOU THAT.
KRASHHH
YOU KNOW, I DO BELIEVE YOU WILL THIS TIME.
TOUCHÉ. YOU ARE CLEVER. YOU'VE SPARED COLU ANY FURTHER CORRUPTION. NICELY DONE.
HOWEVER--

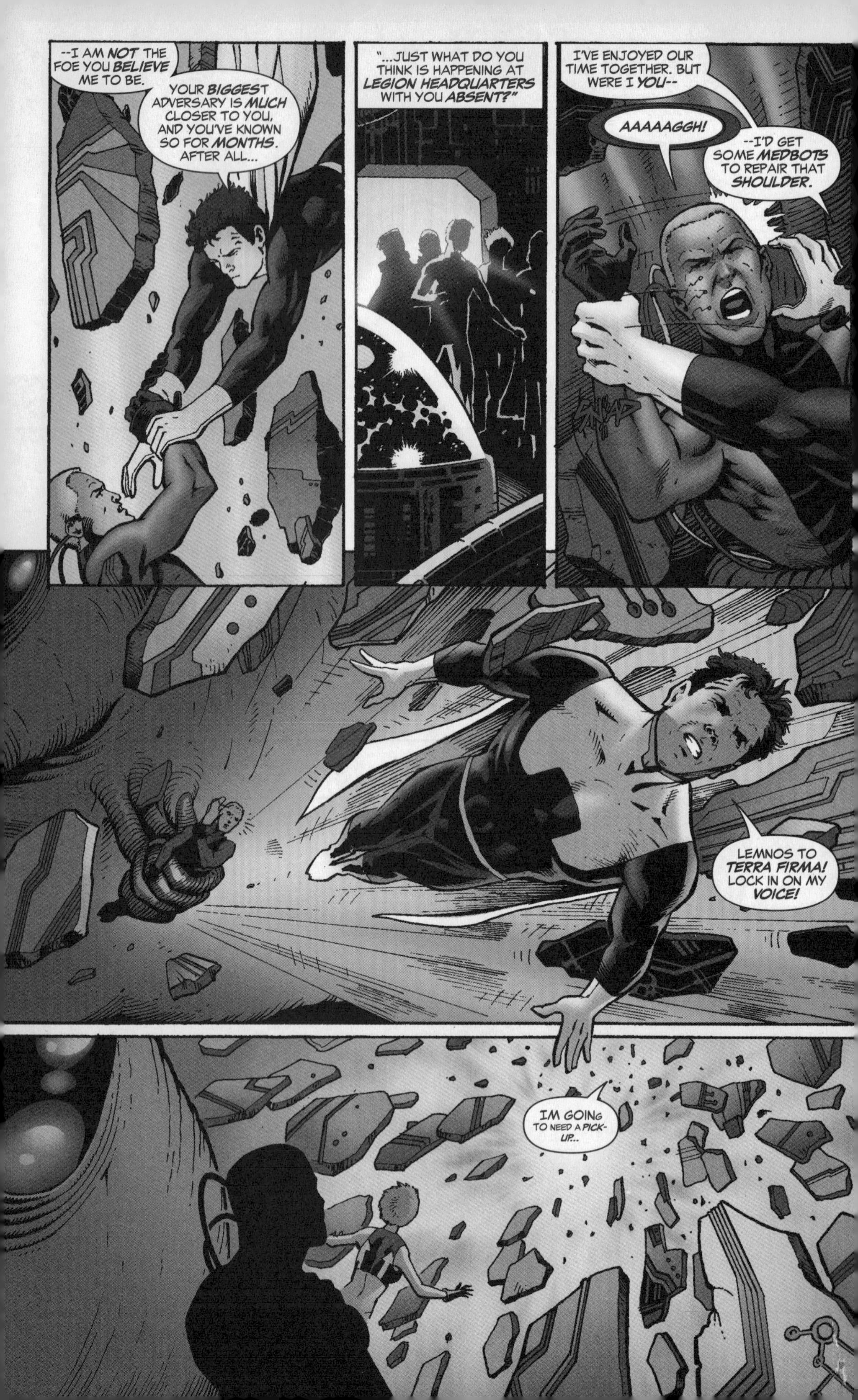
--I AM NOT THE FOE YOU BELIEVE ME TO BE.
YOUR BIGGEST ADVERSARY IS MUCH CLOSER TO YOU, AND YOU'VE KNOWN SO FOR MONTHS. AFTER ALL...
"...JUST WHAT DO YOU THINK IS HAPPENING AT LEGION HEADQUARTERS WITH YOU ABSENT?"
I'VE ENJOYED OUR TIME TOGETHER. BUT WERE I YOU--
AAAAAAGGH!
--I'D GET SOME MEDBOTS TO REPAIR THAT SHOULDER.
SNAP
LEMNOS TO TERRA FIRMA! LOCK IN ON MY VOICE!
IM GOING TO NEED A PICK-UP...

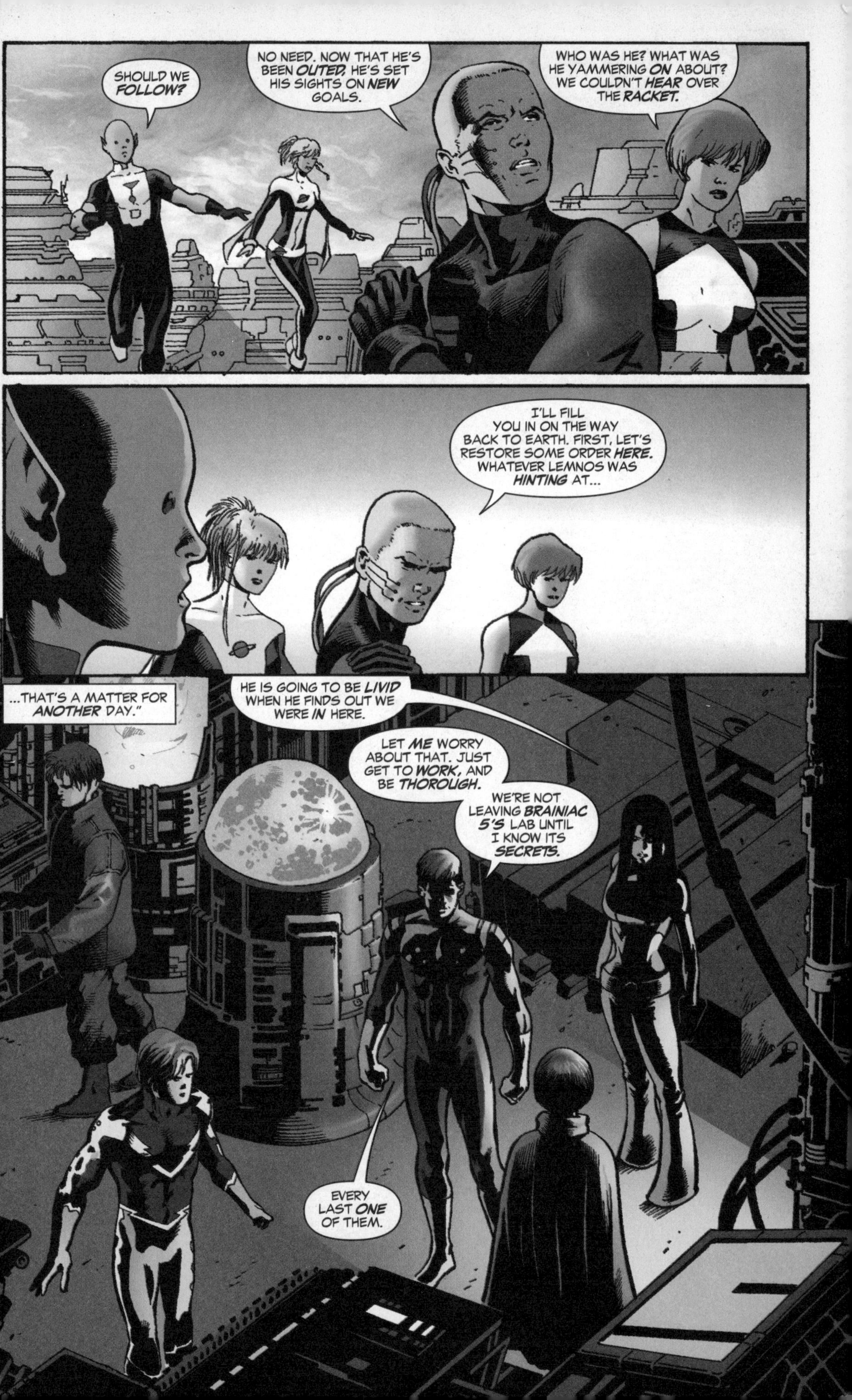
SHOULD WE FOLLOW?
NO NEED. NOW THAT HE'S BEEN OUTED, HE'S SET HIS SIGHTS ON NEW GOALS.
WHO WAS HE? WHAT WAS HE YAMMERING ON ABOUT? WE COULDN'T HEAR OVER THE RACKET.
I'LL FILL YOU IN ON THE WAY BACK TO EARTH. FIRST, LET'S RESTORE SOME ORDER HERE. WHATEVER LEMNOS WAS HINTING AT...
...THAT'S A MATTER FOR ANOTHER DAY."
HE IS GOING TO BE LIVID WHEN HE FINDS OUT WE WERE IN HERE.
LET ME WORRY ABOUT THAT. JUST GET TO WORK, AND BE THOROUGH.
WE'RE NOT LEAVING BRAINIAC 5'S LAB UNTIL I KNOW ITS SECRETS.
EVERY LAST ONE OF THEM.

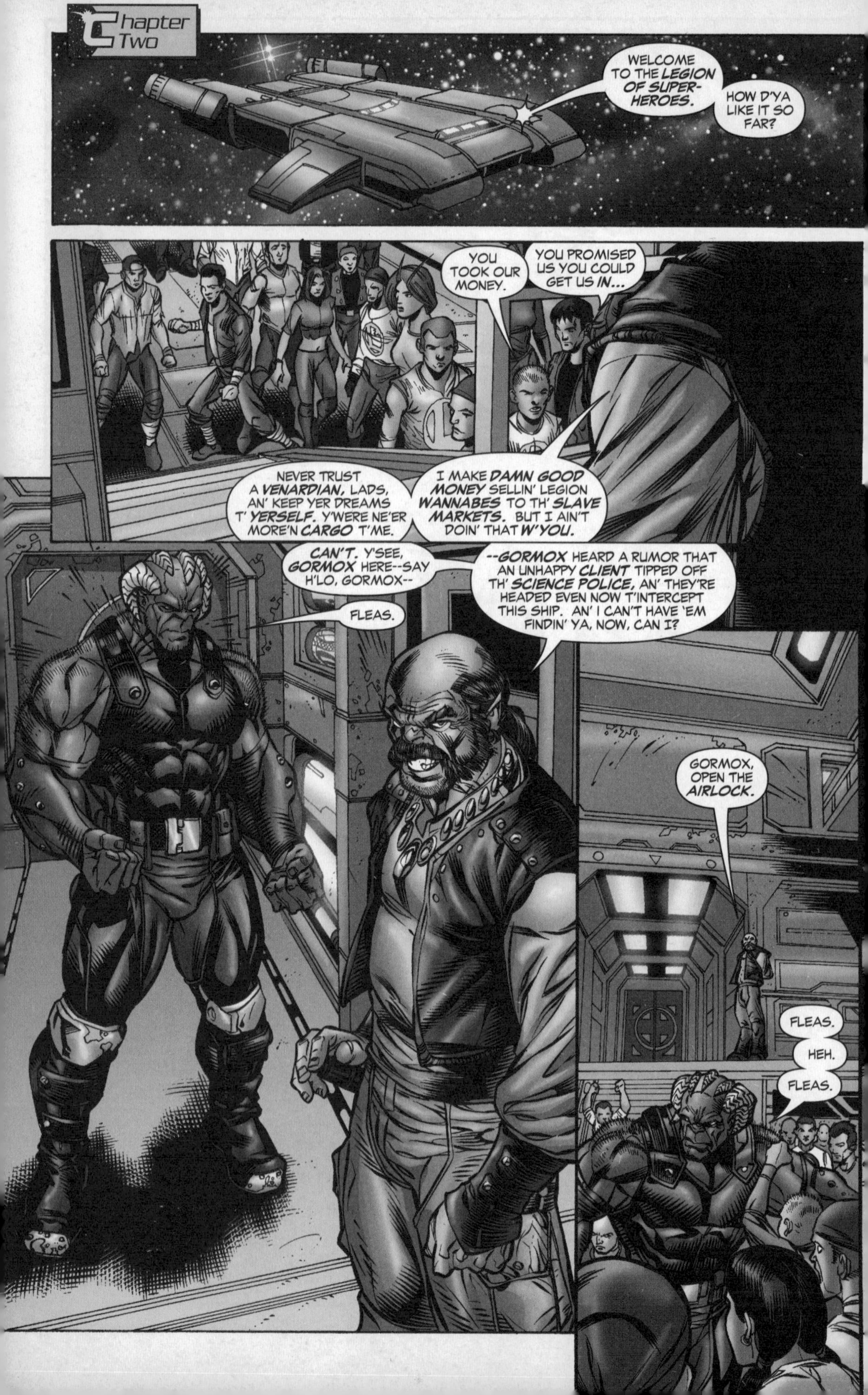
Chapter Two
WELCOME TO THE LEGION OF SUPER-HEROES.
HOW D'YA LIKE IT SO FAR?
YOU TOOK OUR MONEY.
YOU PROMISED US YOU COULD GET US IN...
I MAKE DAMN GOOD MONEY SELLIN' LEGION WANNABES TO TH' SLAVE MARKETS. BUT I AIN'T DOIN' THAT W'YOU.
NEVER TRUST A VENARDIAN, LADS, AN' KEEP YER DREAMS T' YERSELF. Y'WERE NE'ER MORE'N CARGO T'ME.
CAN'T. Y'SEE, GORMOX HERE--SAY H'LO, GORMOX--
FLEAS.
--GORMOX HEARD A RUMOR THAT AN UNHAPPY CLIENT TIPPED OFF TH' SCIENCE POLICE, AN' THEY'RE HEADED EVEN NOW T'INTERCEPT THIS SHIP. AN' I CAN'T HAVE 'EM FINDIN' YA, NOW, CAN I?
GORMOX, OPEN THE AIRLOCK.
FLEAS.
HEH.
FLEAS.

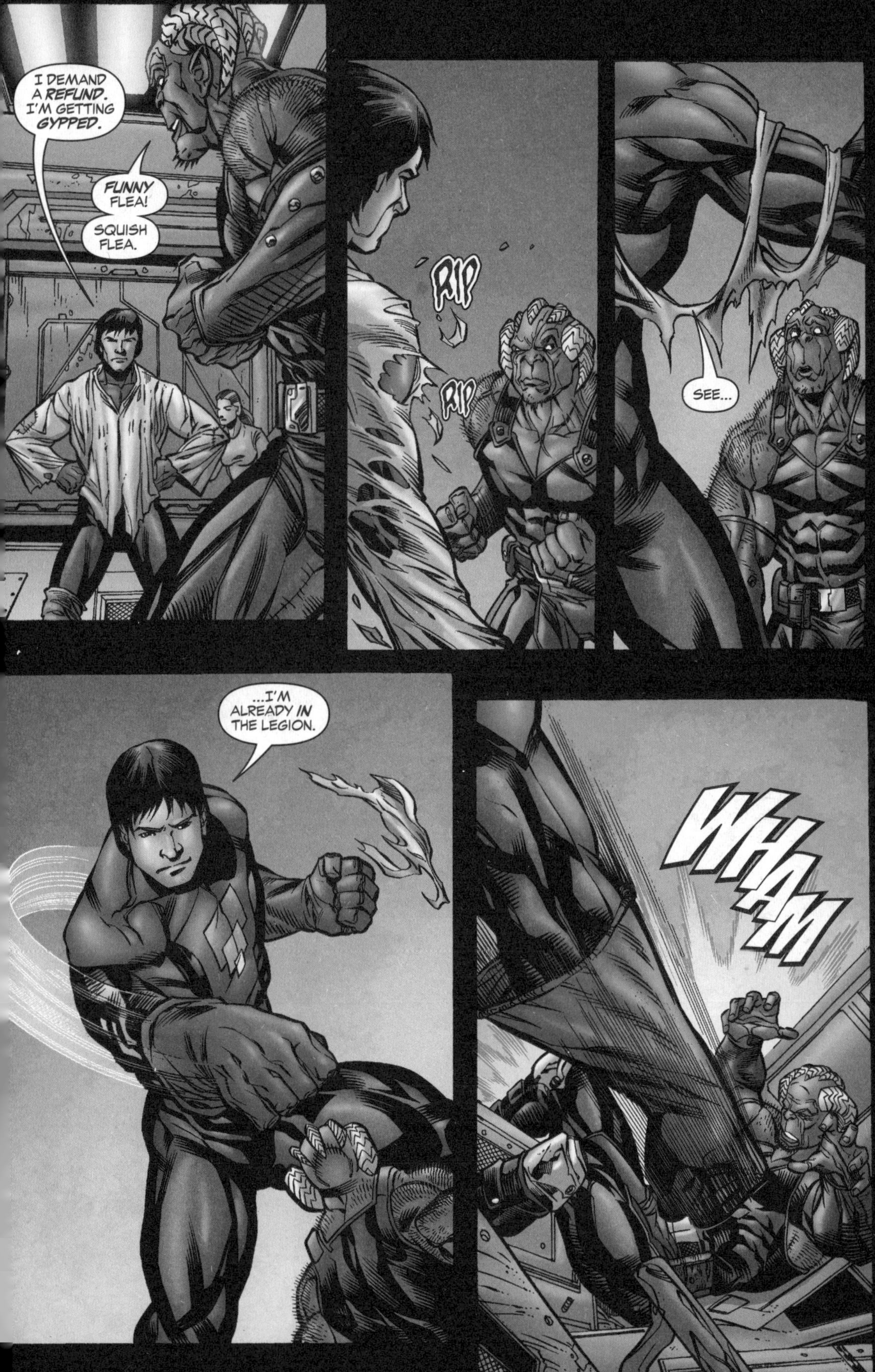
I DEMAND A REFUND. I'M GETTING GYPPED.
FUNNY FLEA!
SQUISH FLEA.
RIP
RIP
SEE...
...I'M ALREADY IN THE LEGION.
WHAM

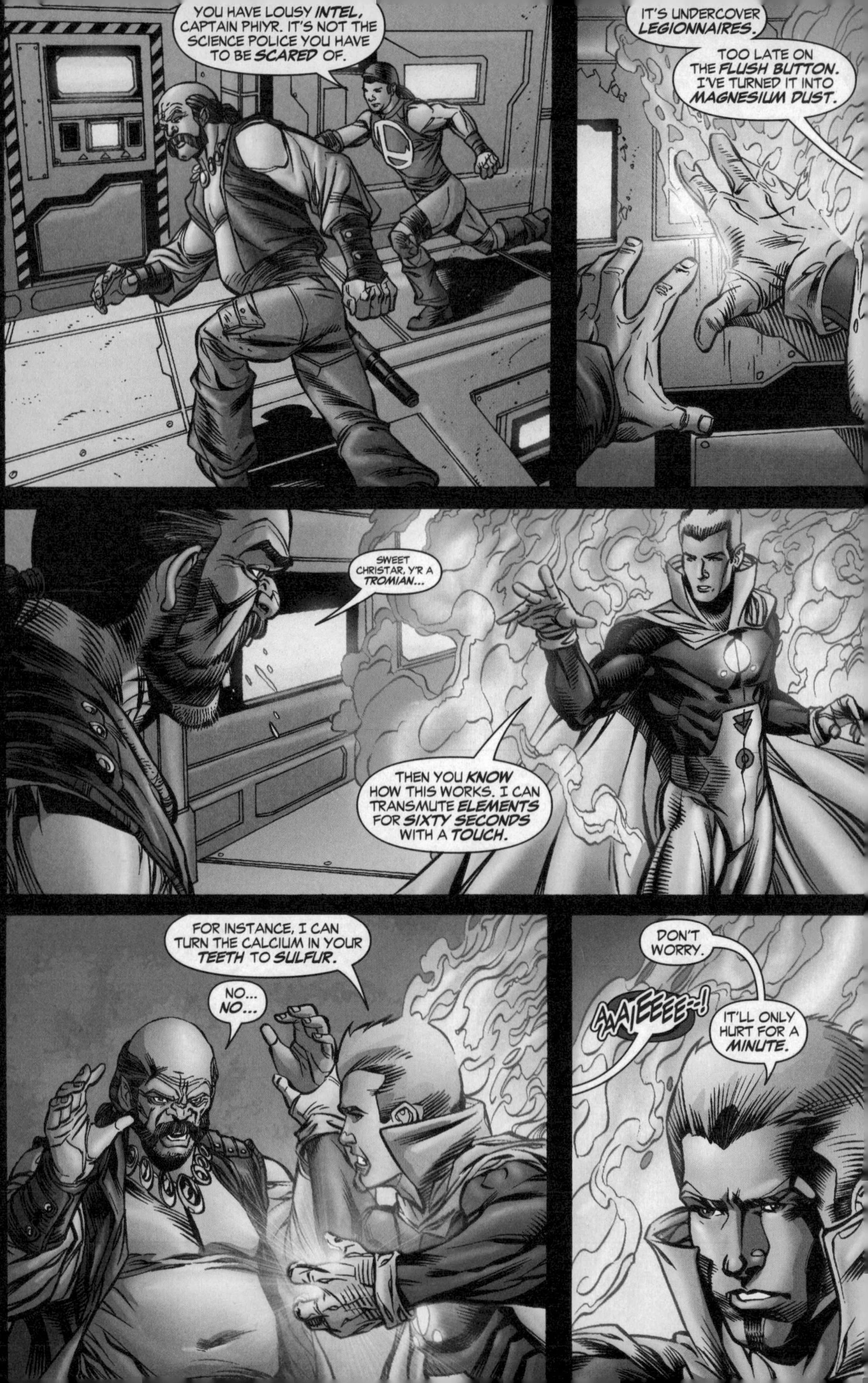
YOU HAVE LOUSY INTEL, CAPTAIN PHIYR. IT'S NOT THE SCIENCE POLICE YOU HAVE TO BE SCARED OF.
IT'S UNDERCOVER LEGIONNAIRES.
TOO LATE ON THE FLUSH BUTTON. I'VE TURNED IT INTO MAGNESIUM DUST.
SWEET CHRISTAR, Y'R A TROMIAN...
THEN YOU KNOW HOW THIS WORKS. I CAN TRANSMUTE ELEMENTS FOR SIXTY SECONDS WITH A TOUCH.
FOR INSTANCE, I CAN TURN THE CALCIUM IN YOUR TEETH TO SULFUR.
NO... NO...
DON'T WORRY.
AAAIEEEE--!
IT'LL ONLY HURT FOR A MINUTE.

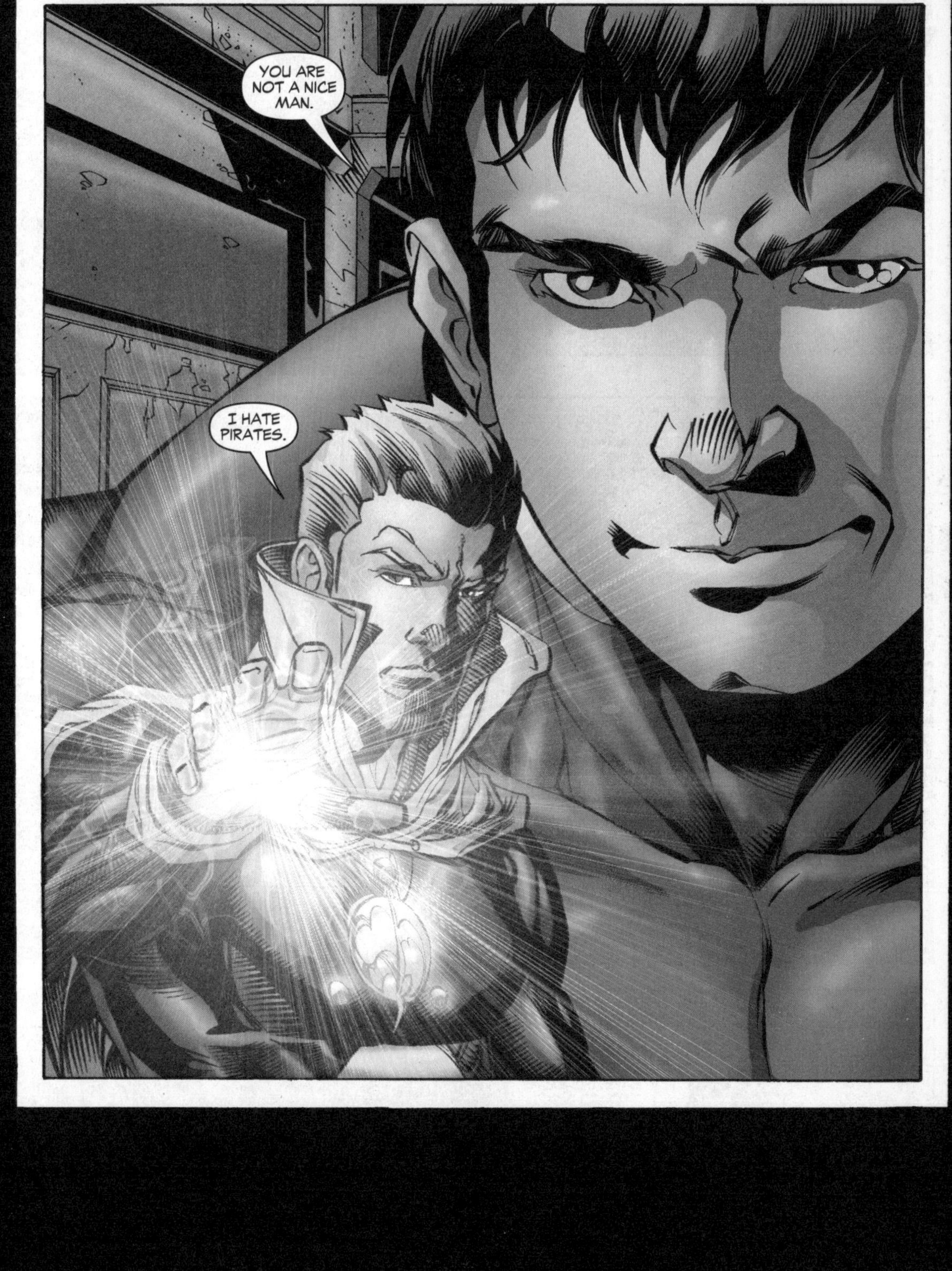

YOU ARE NOT A NICE MAN.
I HATE PIRATES.

COS DID **WHAT?**

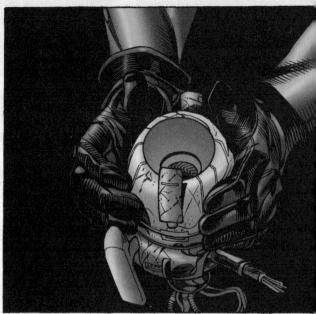

APPARENTLY, HE FORCED HIS WAY INTO BRAINIAC 5'S **LAB** WHILE BRAINY WAS **OFF-WORLD.**

BRAINY TOOK ONE LOOK AROUND, SEALED THE **DOOR** WITH A **FORCE-FIELD,** AND ALL STAR BOY AND I HAVE HEARD FROM INSIDE FOR THE LAST **TWENTY MINUTES** IS THE SOUND OF THINGS SMASHING.

KSSH

BRAINY MUST BE **HOMICIDAL.** OR COSMIC BOY IS **SUICIDAL.** OR **BOTH.** WHAT WAS COS **LOOKING** FOR?

DOES HE EVEN HAVE THE **RIGHT** TO GO INSIDE WITHOUT PERMISSION?

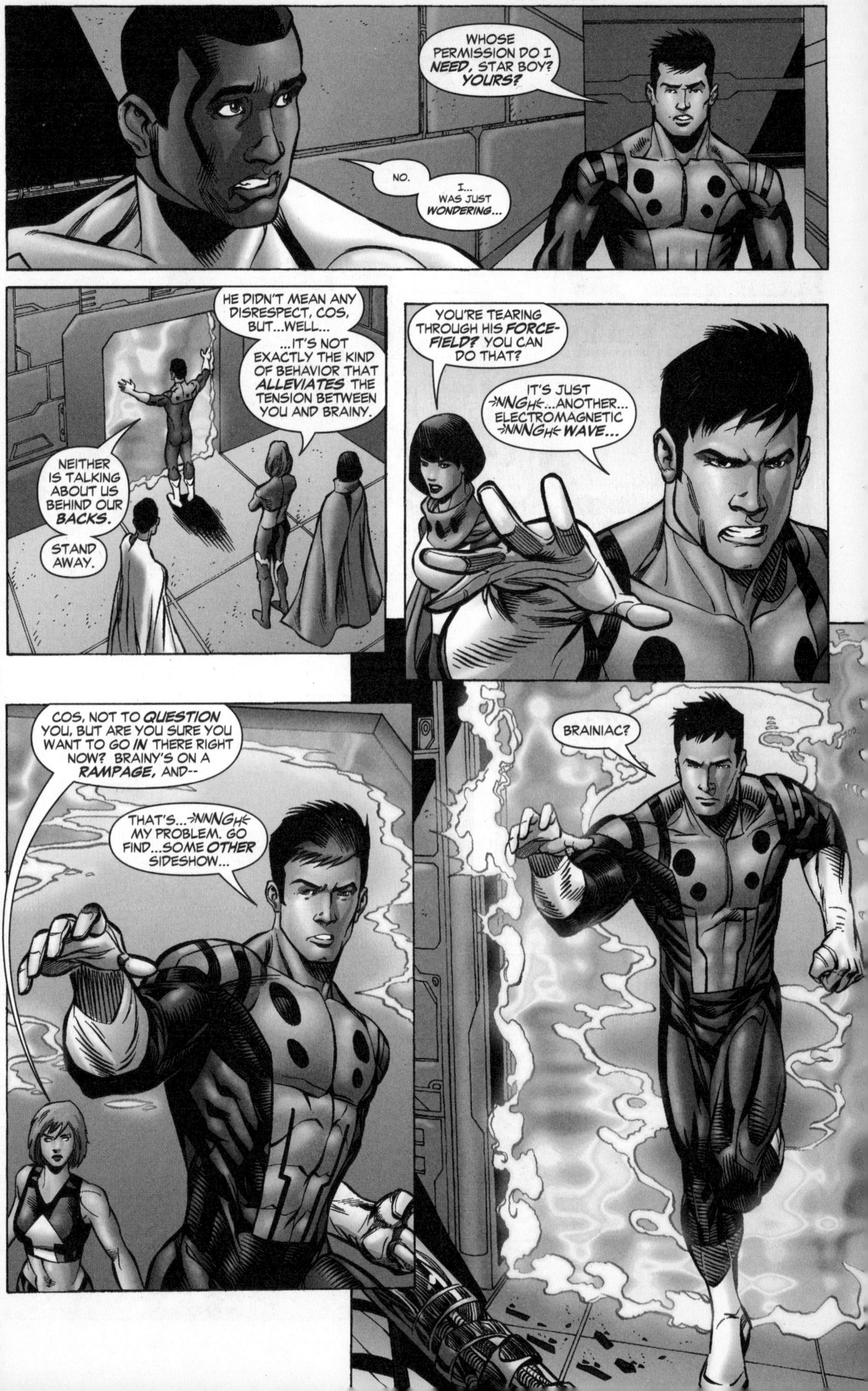
WHOSE PERMISSION DO I NEED, STAR BOY? YOURS?
NO.
I... WAS JUST WONDERING...
HE DIDN'T MEAN ANY DISRESPECT, COS, BUT...WELL...
...IT'S NOT EXACTLY THE KIND OF BEHAVIOR THAT ALLEVIATES THE TENSION BETWEEN YOU AND BRAINY.
NEITHER IS TALKING ABOUT US BEHIND OUR BACKS.
STAND AWAY.
YOU'RE TEARING THROUGH HIS FORCE-FIELD? YOU CAN DO THAT?
IT'S JUST NNGH...ANOTHER... ELECTROMAGNETIC NNNGH WAVE...
COS, NOT TO QUESTION YOU, BUT ARE YOU SURE YOU WANT TO GO IN THERE RIGHT NOW? BRAINY'S ON A RAMPAGE, AND--
THAT'S...NNNGH MY PROBLEM. GO FIND...SOME OTHER SIDESHOW...
BRAINIAC?

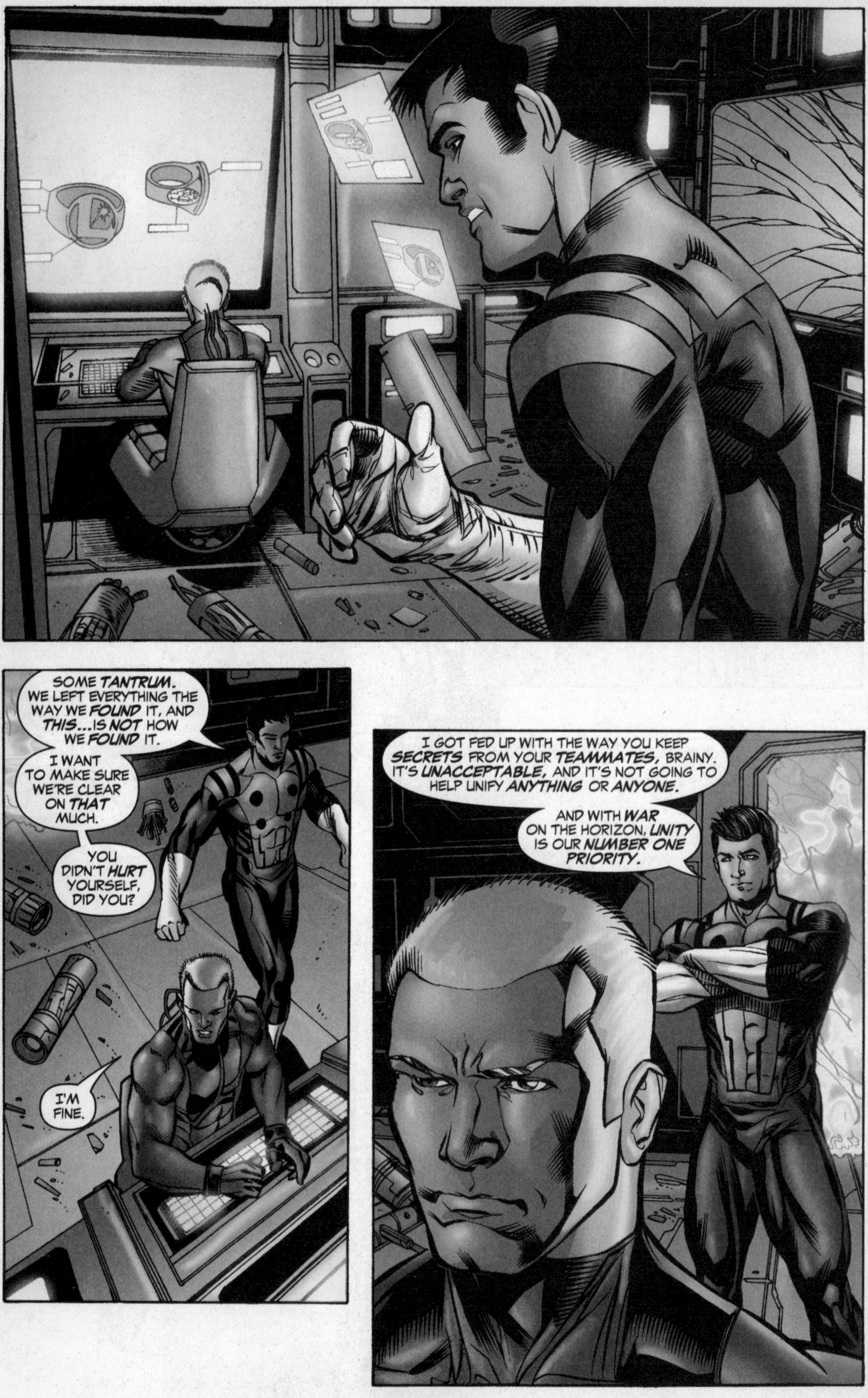
SOME TANTRUM. WE LEFT EVERYTHING THE WAY WE FOUND IT, AND THIS...IS NOT HOW WE FOUND IT.
I WANT TO MAKE SURE WE'RE CLEAR ON THAT MUCH.
YOU DIDN'T HURT YOURSELF, DID YOU?
I'M FINE.
I GOT FED UP WITH THE WAY YOU KEEP SECRETS FROM YOUR TEAMMATES, BRAINY. IT'S UNACCEPTABLE, AND IT'S NOT GOING TO HELP UNIFY ANYTHING OR ANYONE.
AND WITH WAR ON THE HORIZON, UNITY IS OUR NUMBER ONE PRIORITY.

BRAINY, ARE YOU LISTENING? ARE YOU EVEN *HERE?*

I'M FINE.

DID YOU FIND WHAT YOU WERE *LOOKING* FOR?

THAT DEPENDS ON WHAT COMES OUT OF *THIS.* FROM HERE ON OUT, I WANT *TOTAL COMMUNICATION* BETWEEN *ALL* LEGIONNAIRES AT *ALL TIMES.*

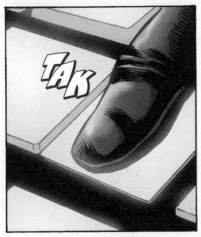

TAK

FINE.

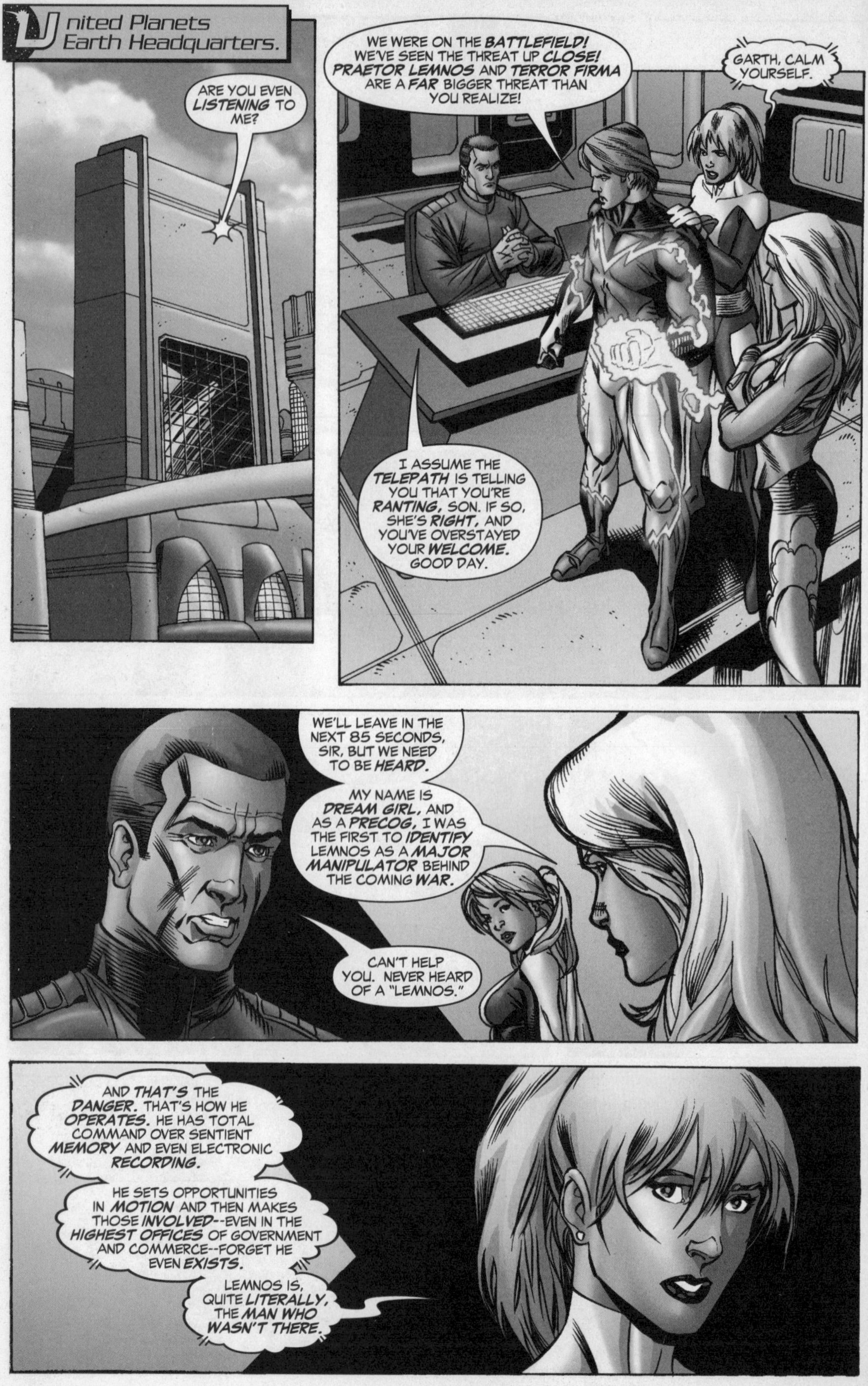
United Planets Earth Headquarters.
ARE YOU EVEN LISTENING TO ME?
WE WERE ON THE BATTLEFIELD! WE'VE SEEN THE THREAT UP CLOSE! PRAETOR LEMNOS AND TERROR FIRMA ARE A FAR BIGGER THREAT THAN YOU REALIZE!
GARTH, CALM YOURSELF.
I ASSUME THE TELEPATH IS TELLING YOU THAT YOU'RE RANTING, SON. IF SO, SHE'S RIGHT, AND YOU'VE OVERSTAYED YOUR WELCOME. GOOD DAY.
WE'LL LEAVE IN THE NEXT 85 SECONDS, SIR, BUT WE NEED TO BE HEARD.
MY NAME IS DREAM GIRL, AND AS A PRECOG, I WAS THE FIRST TO IDENTIFY LEMNOS AS A MAJOR MANIPULATOR BEHIND THE COMING WAR.
CAN'T HELP YOU. NEVER HEARD OF A "LEMNOS."
AND THAT'S THE DANGER. THAT'S HOW HE OPERATES. HE HAS TOTAL COMMAND OVER SENTIENT MEMORY AND EVEN ELECTRONIC RECORDING.
HE SETS OPPORTUNITIES IN MOTION AND THEN MAKES THOSE INVOLVED--EVEN IN THE HIGHEST OFFICES OF GOVERNMENT AND COMMERCE--FORGET HE EVEN EXISTS.
LEMNOS IS, QUITE LITERALLY, THE MAN WHO WASN'T THERE.

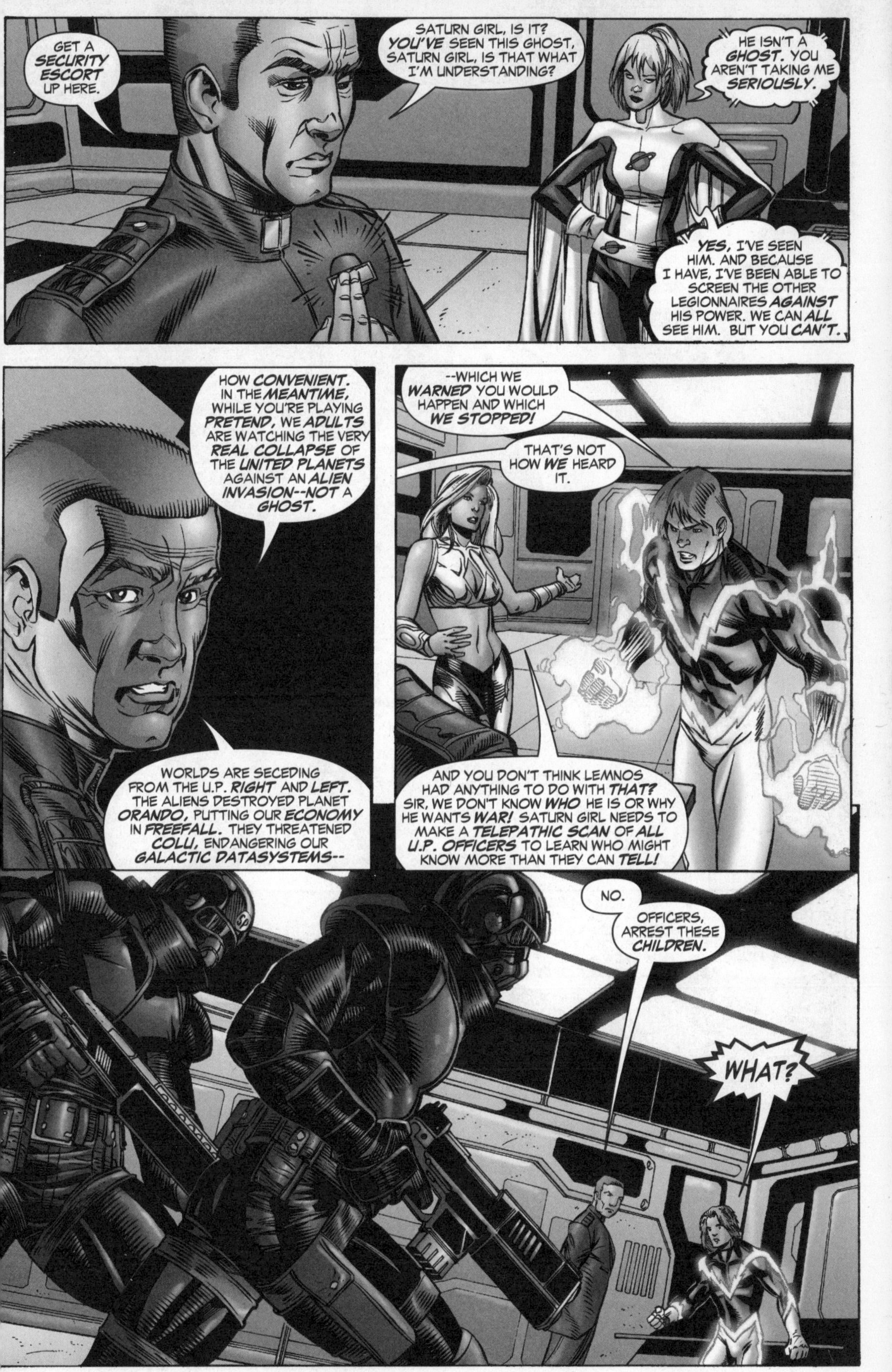
GET A SECURITY ESCORT UP HERE.
SATURN GIRL, IS IT? YOU'VE SEEN THIS GHOST, SATURN GIRL, IS THAT WHAT I'M UNDERSTANDING?
HE ISN'T A GHOST. YOU AREN'T TAKING ME SERIOUSLY.
YES, I'VE SEEN HIM. AND BECAUSE I HAVE, I'VE BEEN ABLE TO SCREEN THE OTHER LEGIONNAIRES AGAINST HIS POWER. WE CAN ALL SEE HIM. BUT YOU CAN'T.
HOW CONVENIENT. IN THE MEANTIME, WHILE YOU'RE PLAYING PRETEND, WE ADULTS ARE WATCHING THE VERY REAL COLLAPSE OF THE UNITED PLANETS AGAINST AN ALIEN INVASION--NOT A GHOST.
WORLDS ARE SECEDING FROM THE U.P. RIGHT AND LEFT. THE ALIENS DESTROYED PLANET ORANDO, PUTTING OUR ECONOMY IN FREEFALL. THEY THREATENED COLU, ENDANGERING OUR GALACTIC DATASYSTEMS--
--WHICH WE WARNED YOU WOULD HAPPEN AND WHICH WE STOPPED!
THAT'S NOT HOW WE HEARD IT.
AND YOU DON'T THINK LEMNOS HAD ANYTHING TO DO WITH THAT? SIR, WE DON'T KNOW WHO HE IS OR WHY HE WANTS WAR! SATURN GIRL NEEDS TO MAKE A TELEPATHIC SCAN OF ALL U.P. OFFICERS TO LEARN WHO MIGHT KNOW MORE THAN THEY CAN TELL!
NO.
OFFICERS, ARREST THESE CHILDREN.
WHAT?

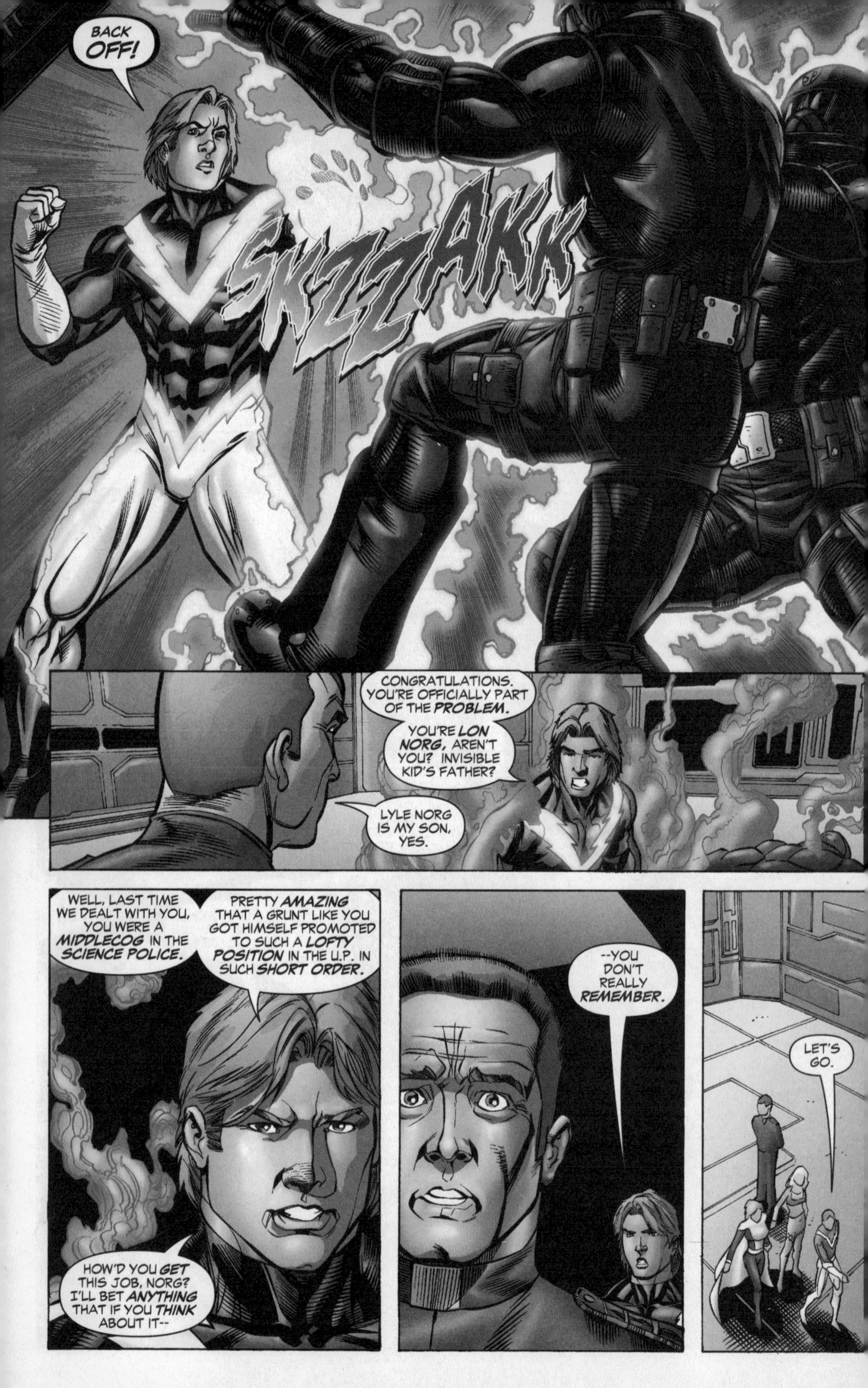
BACK OFF!
SKZZAKK
CONGRATULATIONS. YOU'RE OFFICIALLY PART OF THE PROBLEM.
YOU'RE LON NORG, AREN'T YOU? INVISIBLE KID'S FATHER?
LYLE NORG IS MY SON, YES.
WELL, LAST TIME WE DEALT WITH YOU, YOU WERE A MIDDLECOG IN THE SCIENCE POLICE.
PRETTY AMAZING THAT A GRUNT LIKE YOU GOT HIMSELF PROMOTED TO SUCH A LOFTY POSITION IN THE U.P. IN SUCH SHORT ORDER.
HOW'D YOU GET THIS JOB, NORG? I'LL BET ANYTHING THAT IF YOU THINK ABOUT IT--
--YOU DON'T REALLY REMEMBER.
...
LET'S GO.
..

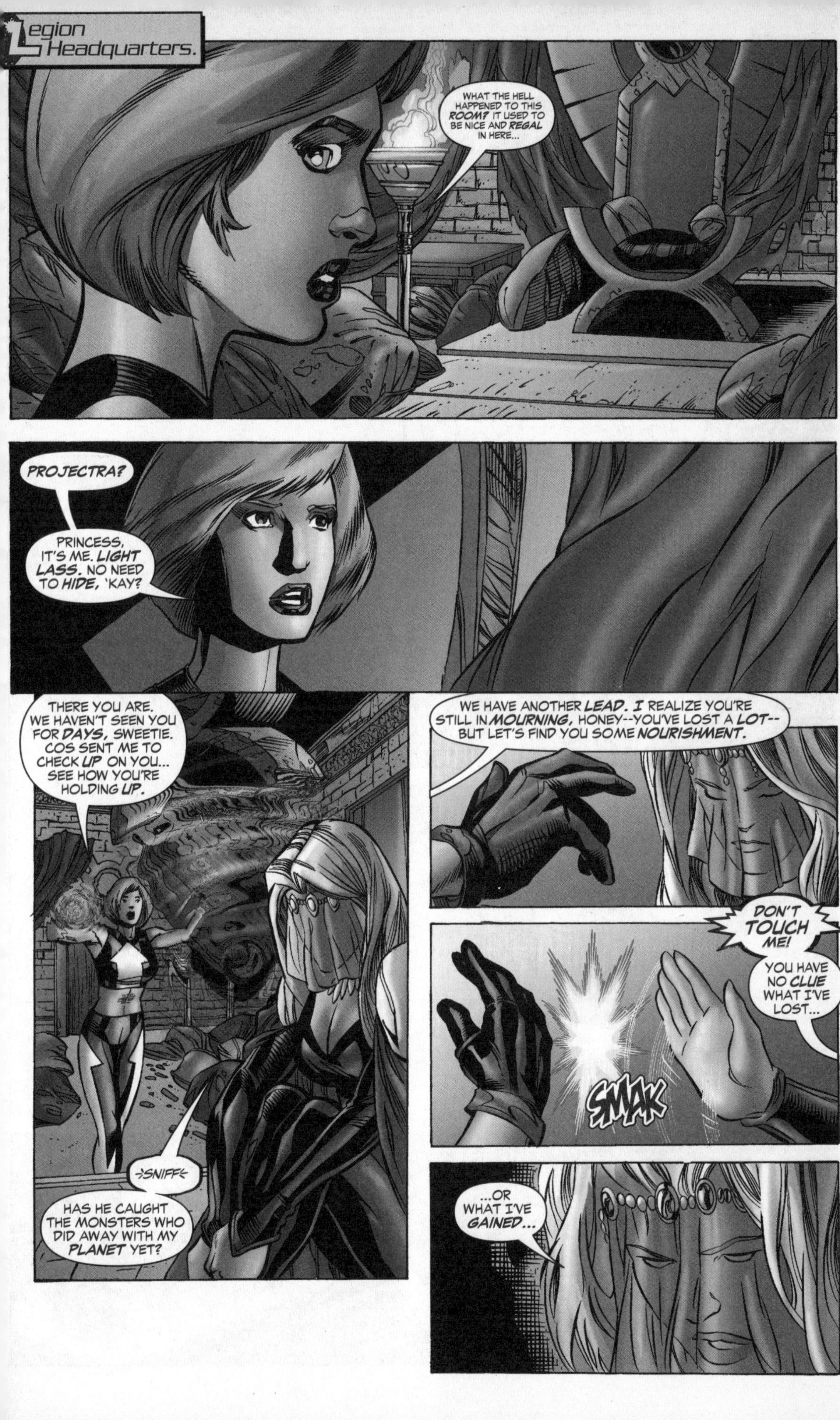
Legion Headquarters.
WHAT THE HELL HAPPENED TO THIS ROOM? IT USED TO BE NICE AND REGAL IN HERE...
PROJECTRA?
PRINCESS, IT'S ME. LIGHT LASS. NO NEED TO HIDE, 'KAY?
THERE YOU ARE. WE HAVEN'T SEEN YOU FOR DAYS, SWEETIE. COS SENT ME TO CHECK UP ON YOU... SEE HOW YOU'RE HOLDING UP.
<SNIFF>
HAS HE CAUGHT THE MONSTERS WHO DID AWAY WITH MY PLANET YET?
WE HAVE ANOTHER LEAD. I REALIZE YOU'RE STILL IN MOURNING, HONEY--YOU'VE LOST A LOT--BUT LET'S FIND YOU SOME NOURISHMENT.
DON'T TOUCH ME!
YOU HAVE NO CLUE WHAT I'VE LOST...
SMAK
...OR WHAT I'VE GAINED...

THERE SHOULDN'T BE ANY *GAIN* AT *ALL*, SHOULD THERE?

I PUT YOU IN CHARGE OF THE *LEGION TREASURY* ELEMENT LAD. YOU TELL *ME. I* ASSUME WE'RE *BANKRUPT.*

THAT'S THE *THING.* THE COFFERS ARE ACTUALLY REMARKABLY *FULL,* EVEN *WITHOUT* PROJECTRA'S FORTUNE. WAS THERE AN *INHERITANCE* OF SOME SORT?

FROM A *CHARRED PLANET?* I DOUBT IT. SOLVE THIS *MYSTERY,* ALL RIGHT? IT'S ONE OF THE *NINE THOUSAND PINS* I'M JUGGLING, AND MY PATIENCE IS *EXHAUSTED.*

COS...

...WE HAVE TO *TALK.* PRIVATELY.

NINE THOUSAND AND *ONE.* WHAT IS IT, SUN BOY?

I'VE MADE MY *DECISION,* COS.

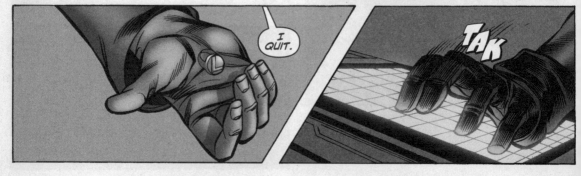

I QUIT.

TAK

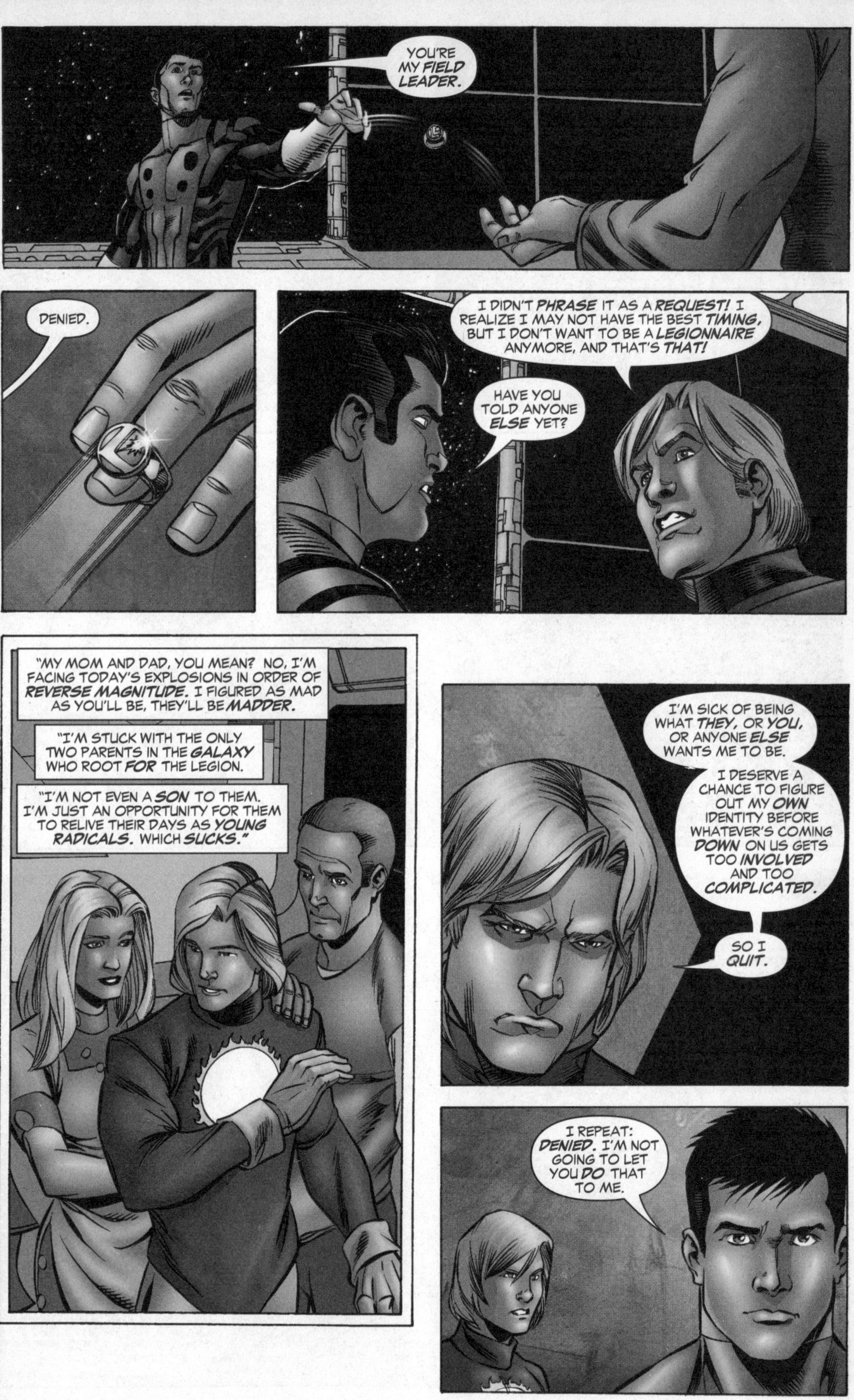
YOU'RE MY FIELD LEADER.
DENIED.
I DIDN'T PHRASE IT AS A REQUEST! I REALIZE I MAY NOT HAVE THE BEST TIMING, BUT I DON'T WANT TO BE A LEGIONNAIRE ANYMORE, AND THAT'S THAT!
HAVE YOU TOLD ANYONE ELSE YET?
"MY MOM AND DAD, YOU MEAN? NO, I'M FACING TODAY'S EXPLOSIONS IN ORDER OF REVERSE MAGNITUDE. I FIGURED AS MAD AS YOU'LL BE, THEY'LL BE MADDER.
"I'M STUCK WITH THE ONLY TWO PARENTS IN THE GALAXY WHO ROOT FOR THE LEGION.
"I'M NOT EVEN A SON TO THEM. I'M JUST AN OPPORTUNITY FOR THEM TO RELIVE THEIR DAYS AS YOUNG RADICALS. WHICH SUCKS."
I'M SICK OF BEING WHAT THEY, OR YOU, OR ANYONE ELSE WANTS ME TO BE.
I DESERVE A CHANCE TO FIGURE OUT MY OWN IDENTITY BEFORE WHATEVER'S COMING DOWN ON US GETS TOO INVOLVED AND TOO COMPLICATED.
SO I QUIT.
I REPEAT: DENIED. I'M NOT GOING TO LET YOU DO THAT TO ME.

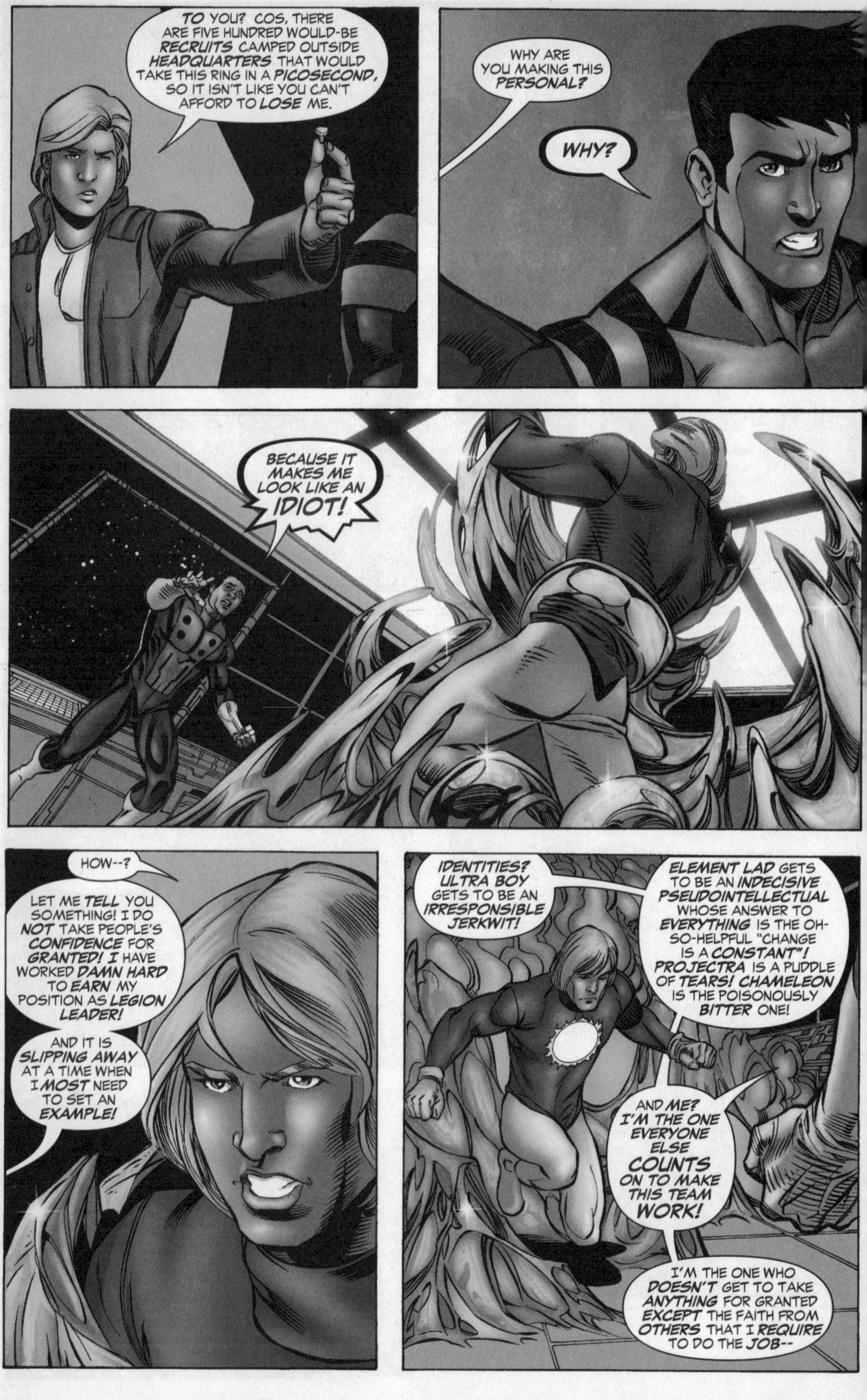
TO YOU? COS, THERE ARE FIVE HUNDRED WOULD-BE RECRUITS CAMPED OUTSIDE HEADQUARTERS THAT WOULD TAKE THIS RING IN A PICOSECOND, SO IT ISN'T LIKE YOU CAN'T AFFORD TO LOSE ME.
WHY ARE YOU MAKING THIS PERSONAL?
WHY?
BECAUSE IT MAKES ME LOOK LIKE AN IDIOT!
HOW--?
LET ME TELL YOU SOMETHING! I DO NOT TAKE PEOPLE'S CONFIDENCE FOR GRANTED! I HAVE WORKED DAMN HARD TO EARN MY POSITION AS LEGION LEADER!
AND IT IS SLIPPING AWAY AT A TIME WHEN I MOST NEED TO SET AN EXAMPLE!
IDENTITIES? ULTRA BOY GETS TO BE AN IRRESPONSIBLE JERKWIT!
ELEMENT LAD GETS TO BE AN INDECISIVE PSEUDOINTELLECTUAL WHOSE ANSWER TO EVERYTHING IS THE OH-SO-HELPFUL "CHANGE IS A CONSTANT"! PROJECTRA IS A PUDDLE OF TEARS! CHAMELEON IS THE POISONOUSLY BITTER ONE!
AND ME? I'M THE ONE EVERYONE ELSE COUNTS ON TO MAKE THIS TEAM WORK!
I'M THE ONE WHO DOESN'T GET TO TAKE ANYTHING FOR GRANTED EXCEPT THE FAITH FROM OTHERS THAT I REQUIRE TO DO THE JOB--

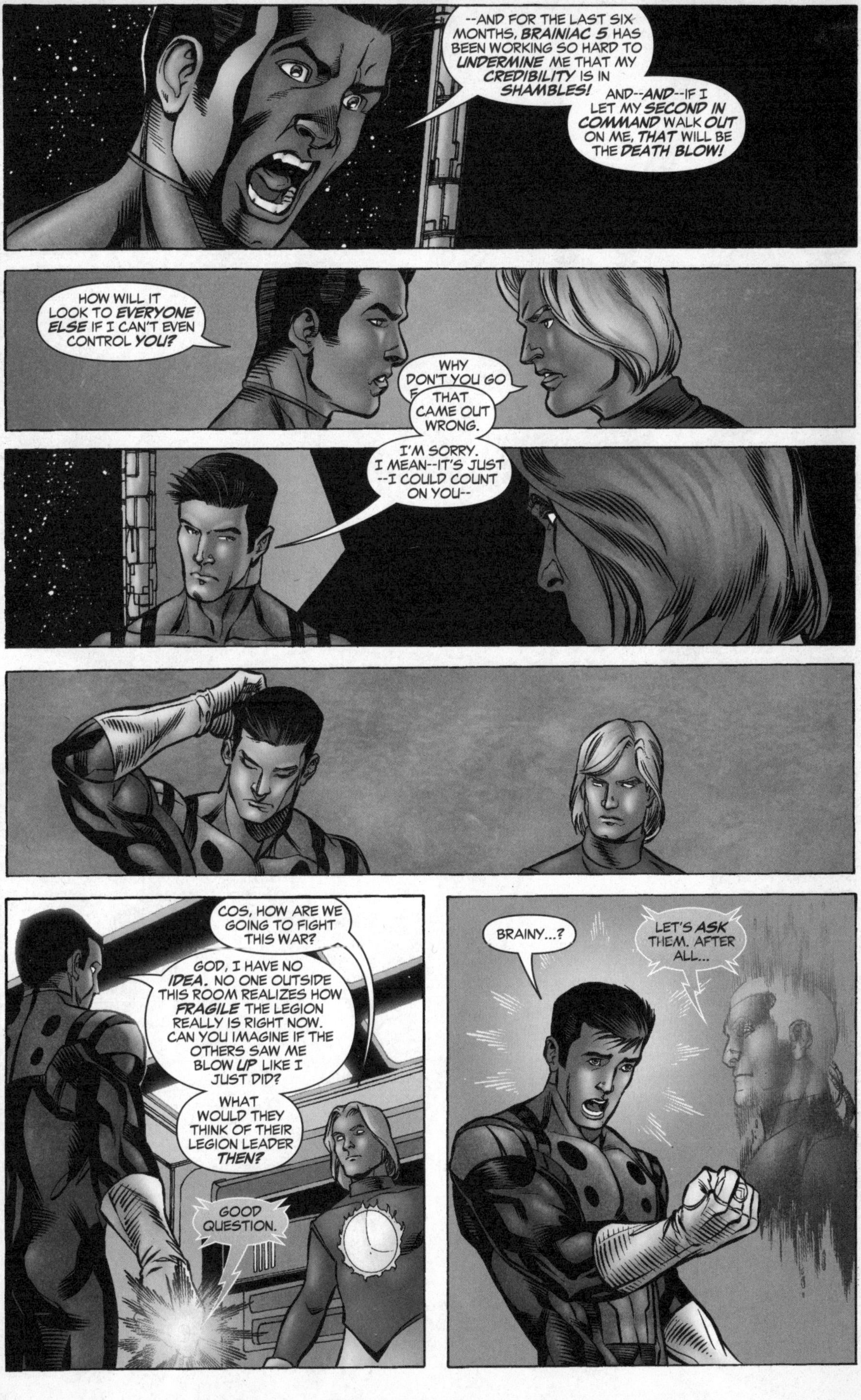
--AND FOR THE LAST SIX MONTHS, BRAINIAC 5 HAS BEEN WORKING SO HARD TO UNDERMINE ME THAT MY CREDIBILITY IS IN SHAMBLES!
AND--AND--IF I LET MY SECOND IN COMMAND WALK OUT ON ME, THAT WILL BE THE DEATH BLOW!
HOW WILL IT LOOK TO EVERYONE ELSE IF I CAN'T EVEN CONTROL YOU?
WHY DON'T YOU GO
THAT CAME OUT WRONG.
I'M SORRY. I MEAN--IT'S JUST --I COULD COUNT ON YOU--
COS, HOW ARE WE GOING TO FIGHT THIS WAR?
GOD, I HAVE NO IDEA. NO ONE OUTSIDE THIS ROOM REALIZES HOW FRAGILE THE LEGION REALLY IS RIGHT NOW. CAN YOU IMAGINE IF THE OTHERS SAW ME BLOW UP LIKE I JUST DID?
WHAT WOULD THEY THINK OF THEIR LEGION LEADER THEN?
GOOD QUESTION.
BRAINY...?
LET'S ASK THEM. AFTER ALL...

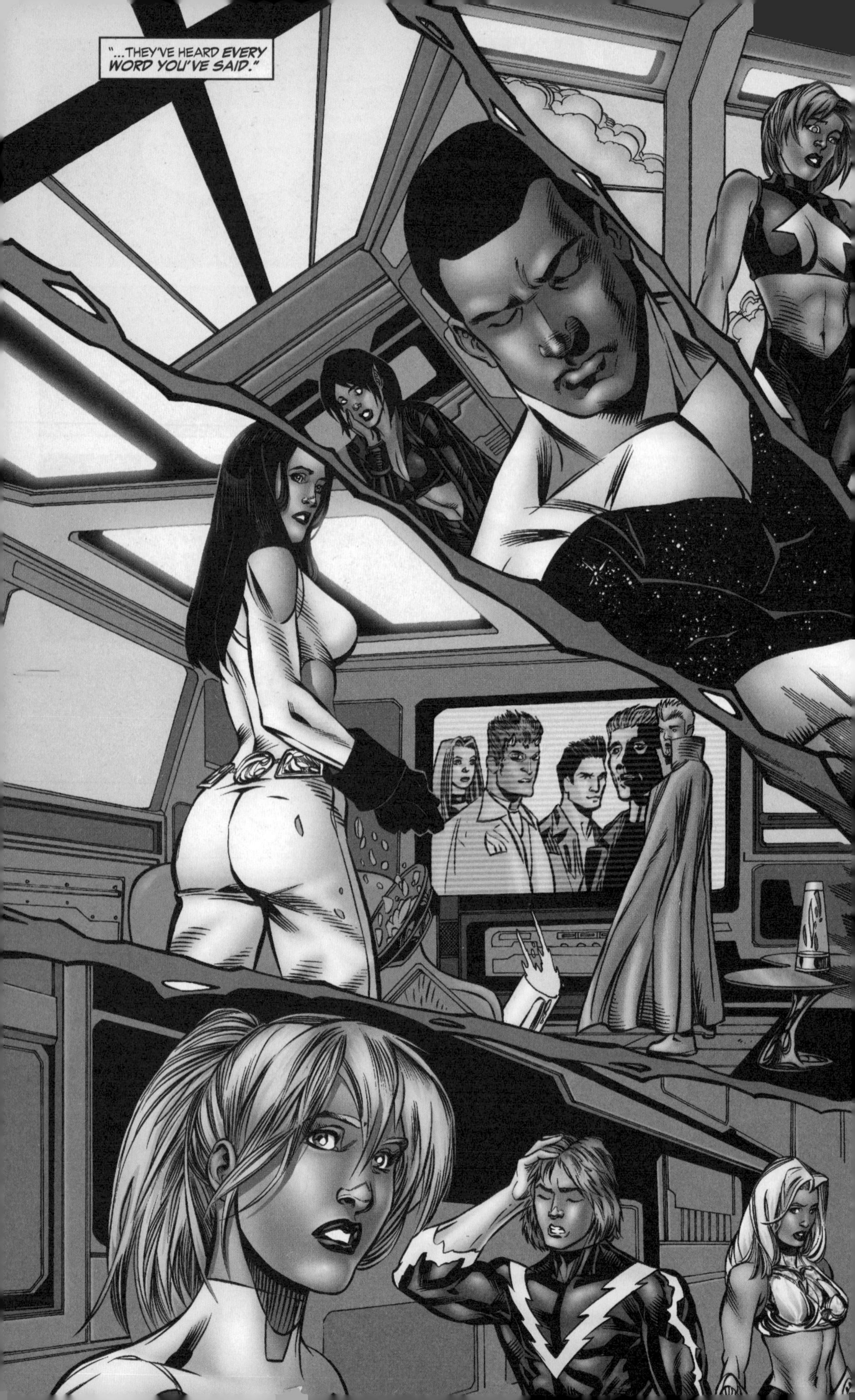
"...THEY'VE HEARD EVERY WORD YOU'VE SAID."

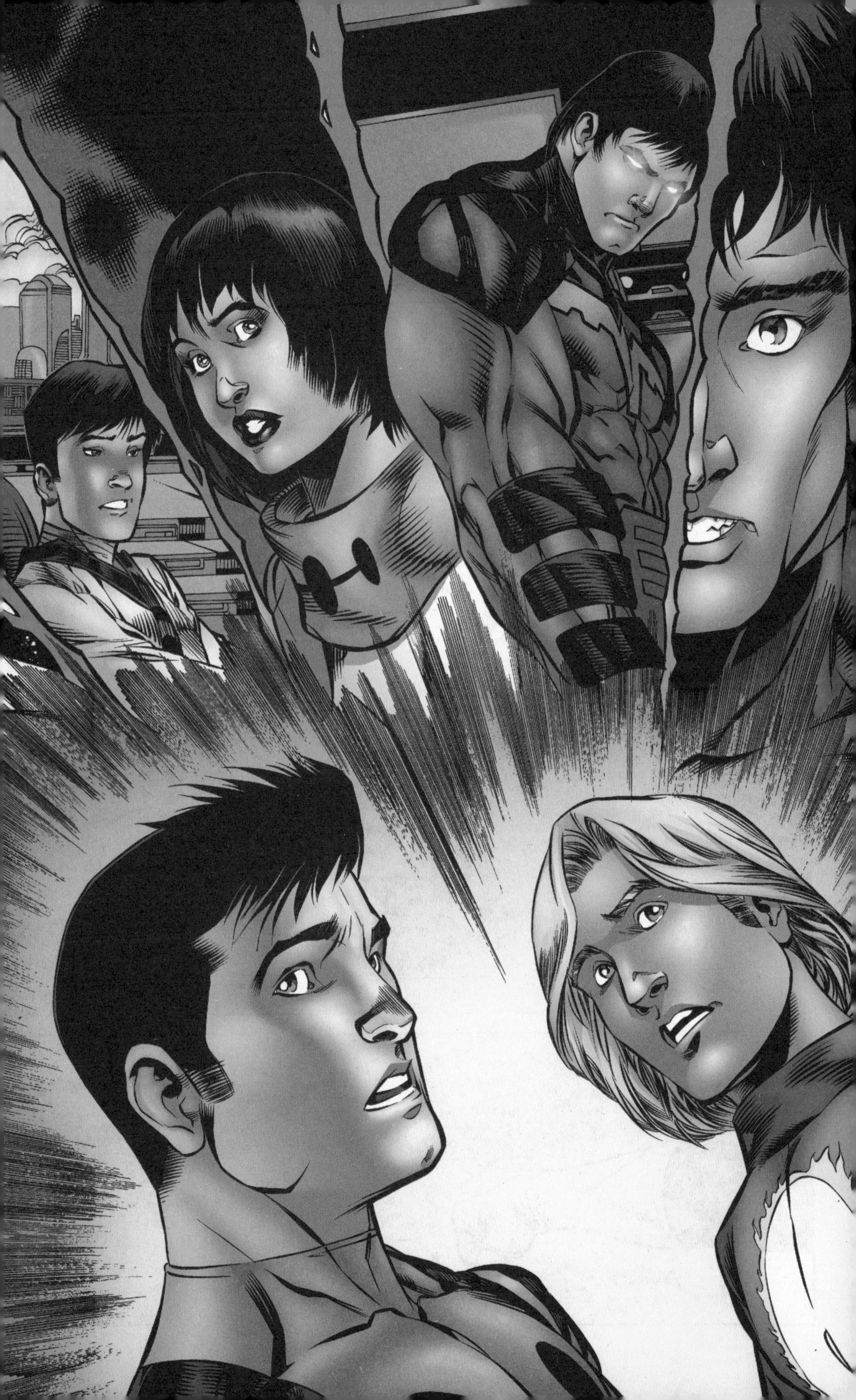

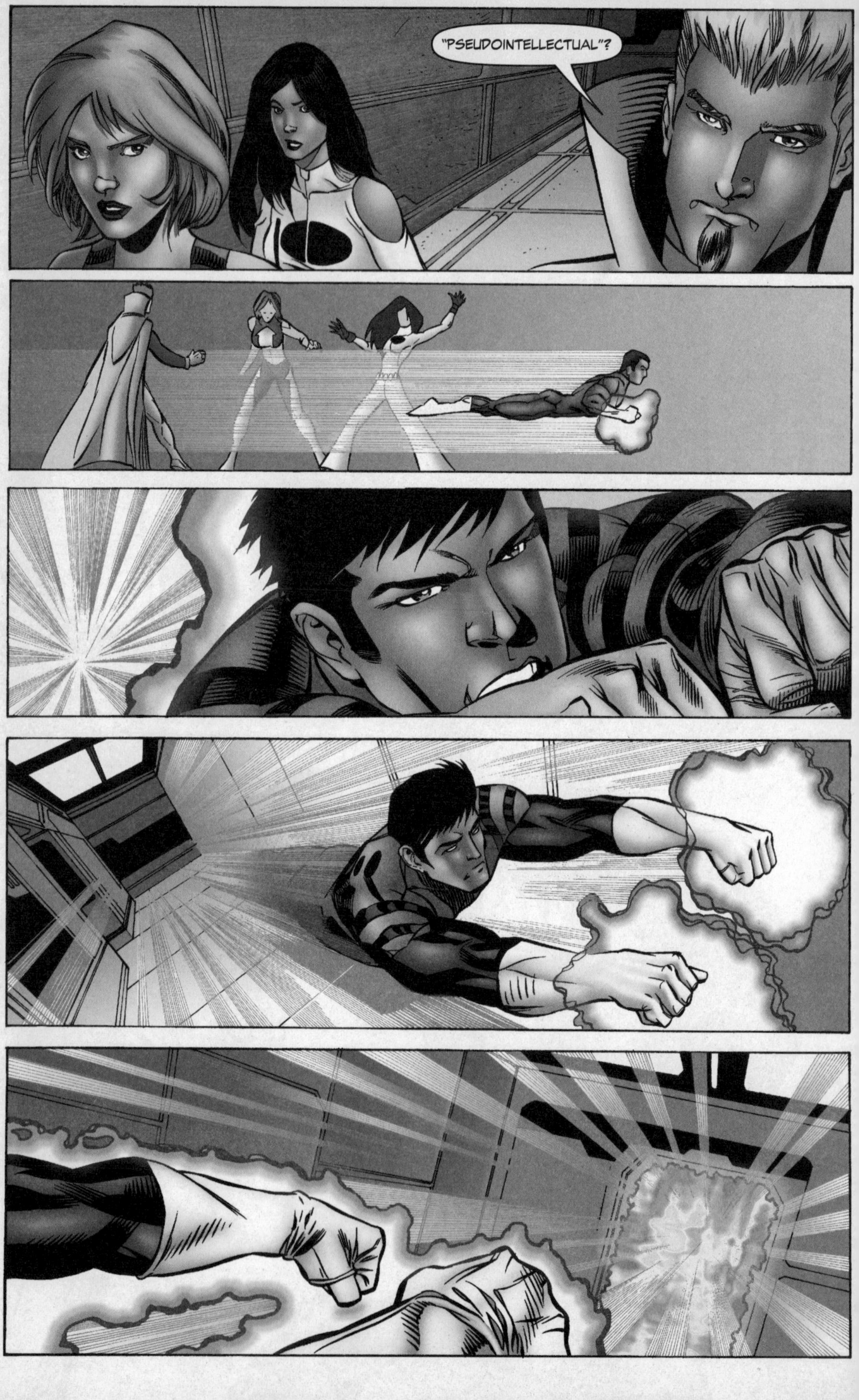
"PSEUDOINTELLECTUAL"?

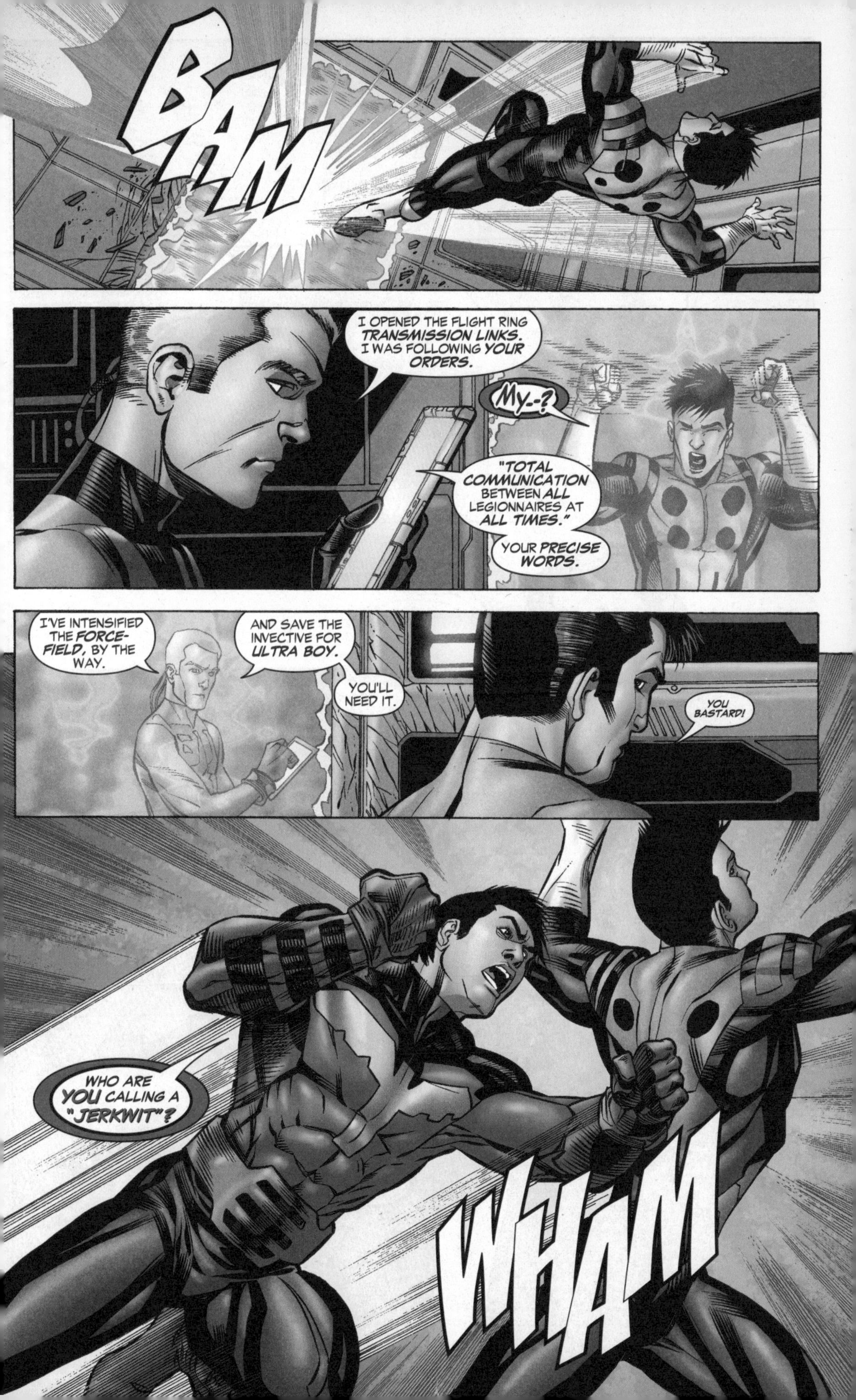
BAM
I OPENED THE FLIGHT RING TRANSMISSION LINKS. I WAS FOLLOWING YOUR ORDERS.
My--?
"TOTAL COMMUNICATION BETWEEN ALL LEGIONNAIRES AT ALL TIMES."
YOUR PRECISE WORDS.
I'VE INTENSIFIED THE FORCE-FIELD, BY THE WAY.
AND SAVE THE INVECTIVE FOR ULTRA BOY.
YOU'LL NEED IT.
YOU BASTARD!
WHO ARE YOU CALLING A "JERKWIT"?
WHAM

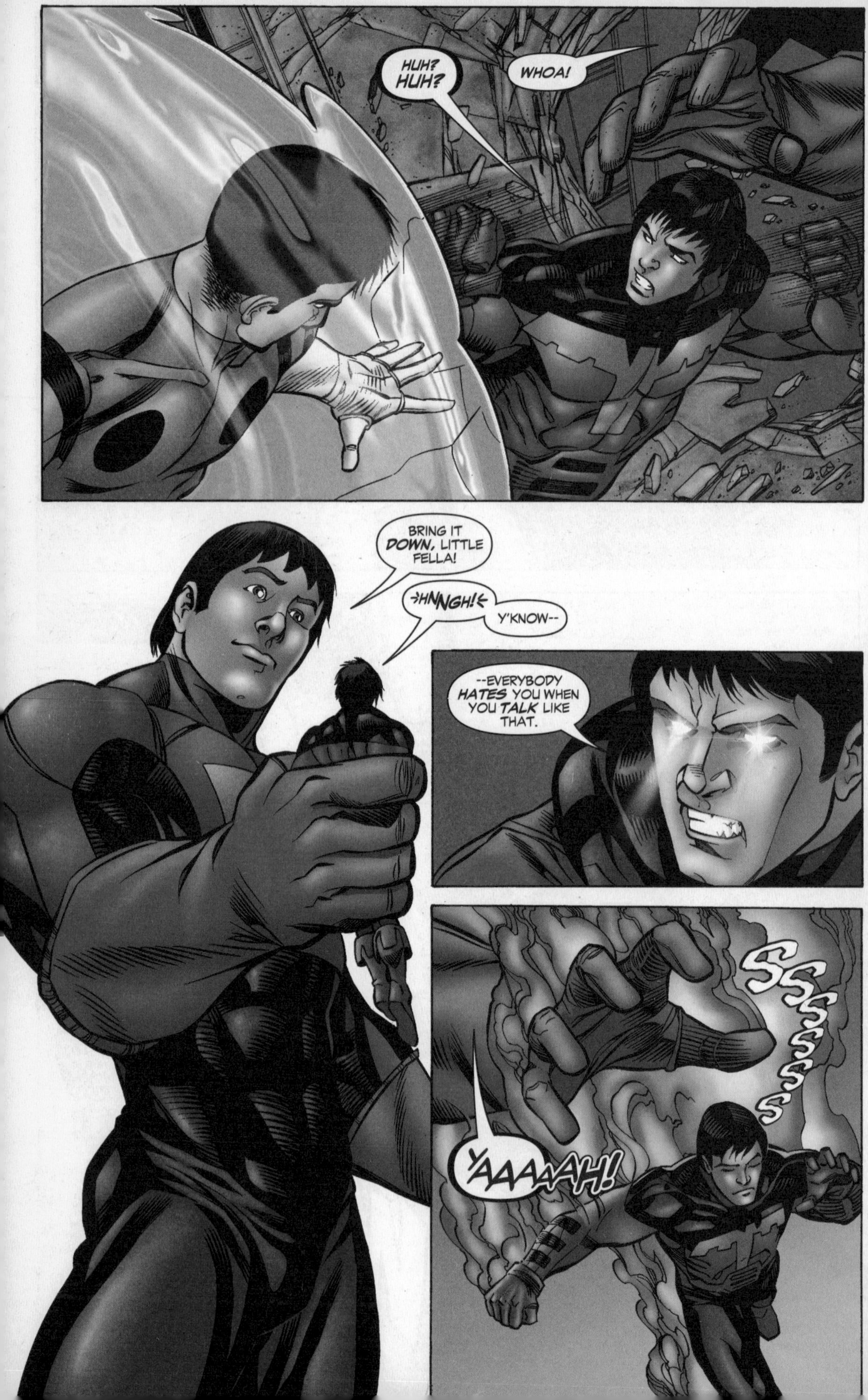
HUH? HUH?
WHOA!
BRING IT DOWN, LITTLE FELLA!
HNNGH! Y'KNOW--
--EVERYBODY HATES YOU WHEN YOU TALK LIKE THAT.
SSSSSSSS
YAAAAAH!

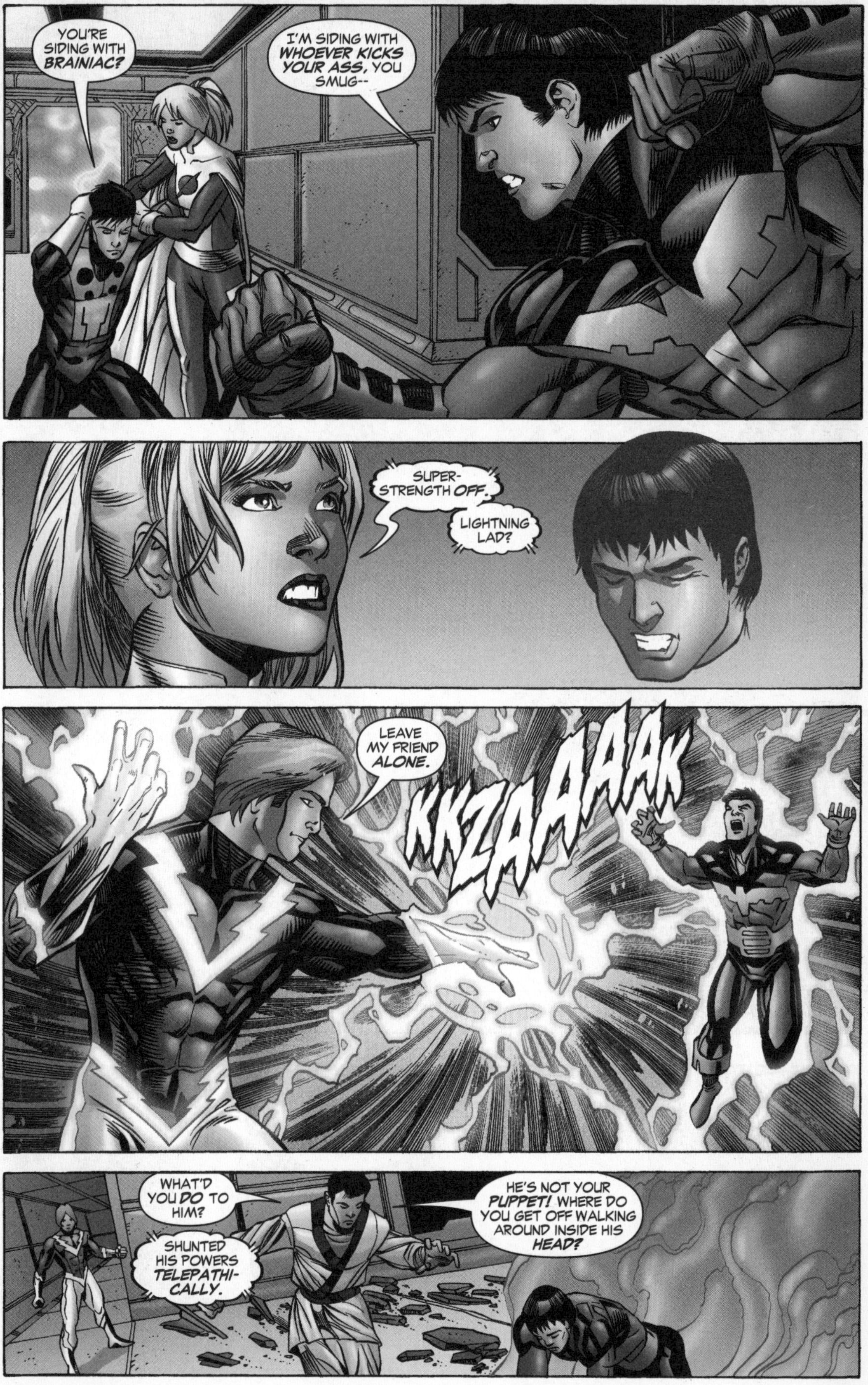
YOU'RE SIDING WITH BRAINIAC?
I'M SIDING WITH WHOEVER KICKS YOUR ASS, YOU SMUG--
SUPER-STRENGTH OFF.
LIGHTNING LAD?
LEAVE MY FRIEND ALONE.
KKZAAAAAK
WHAT'D YOU DO TO HIM?
SHUNTED HIS POWERS TELEPATHICALLY.
HE'S NOT YOUR PUPPET! WHERE DO YOU GET OFF WALKING AROUND INSIDE HIS HEAD?

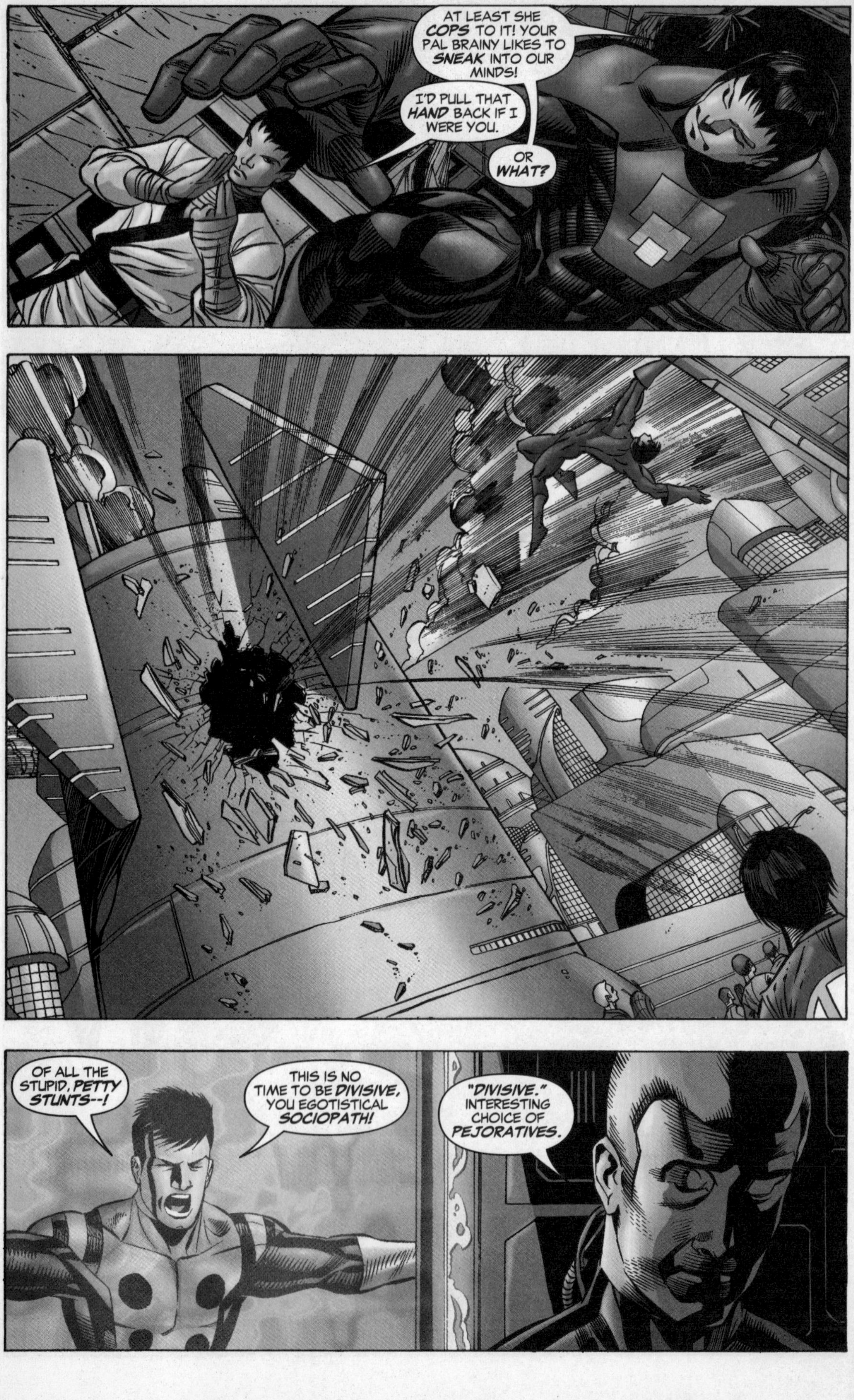
AT LEAST SHE COPS TO IT! YOUR PAL BRAINY LIKES TO SNEAK INTO OUR MINDS!
I'D PULL THAT HAND BACK IF I WERE YOU.
OR WHAT?
OF ALL THE STUPID, PETTY STUNTS--!
THIS IS NO TIME TO BE DIVISIVE, YOU EGOTISTICAL SOCIOPATH!
"DIVISIVE." INTERESTING CHOICE OF PEJORATIVES.

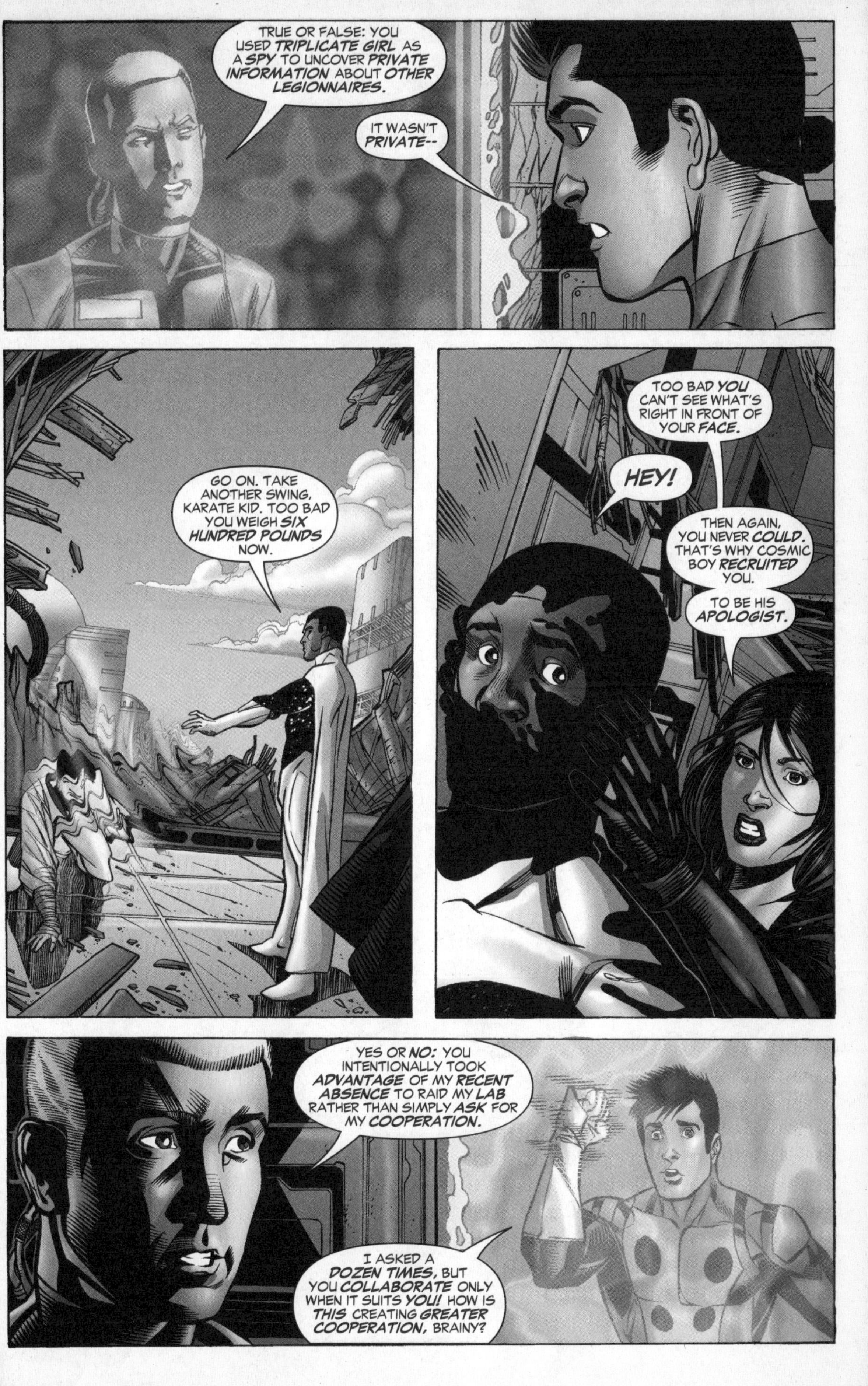
TRUE OR FALSE: YOU USED TRIPLICATE GIRL AS A SPY TO UNCOVER PRIVATE INFORMATION ABOUT OTHER LEGIONNAIRES.
IT WASN'T PRIVATE--
GO ON. TAKE ANOTHER SWING, KARATE KID. TOO BAD YOU WEIGH SIX HUNDRED POUNDS NOW.
TOO BAD YOU CAN'T SEE WHAT'S RIGHT IN FRONT OF YOUR FACE.
HEY!
THEN AGAIN, YOU NEVER COULD. THAT'S WHY COSMIC BOY RECRUITED YOU.
TO BE HIS APOLOGIST.
YES OR NO: YOU INTENTIONALLY TOOK ADVANTAGE OF MY RECENT ABSENCE TO RAID MY LAB RATHER THAN SIMPLY ASK FOR MY COOPERATION.
I ASKED A DOZEN TIMES, BUT YOU COLLABORATE ONLY WHEN IT SUITS YOU! HOW IS THIS CREATING GREATER COOPERATION, BRAINY?

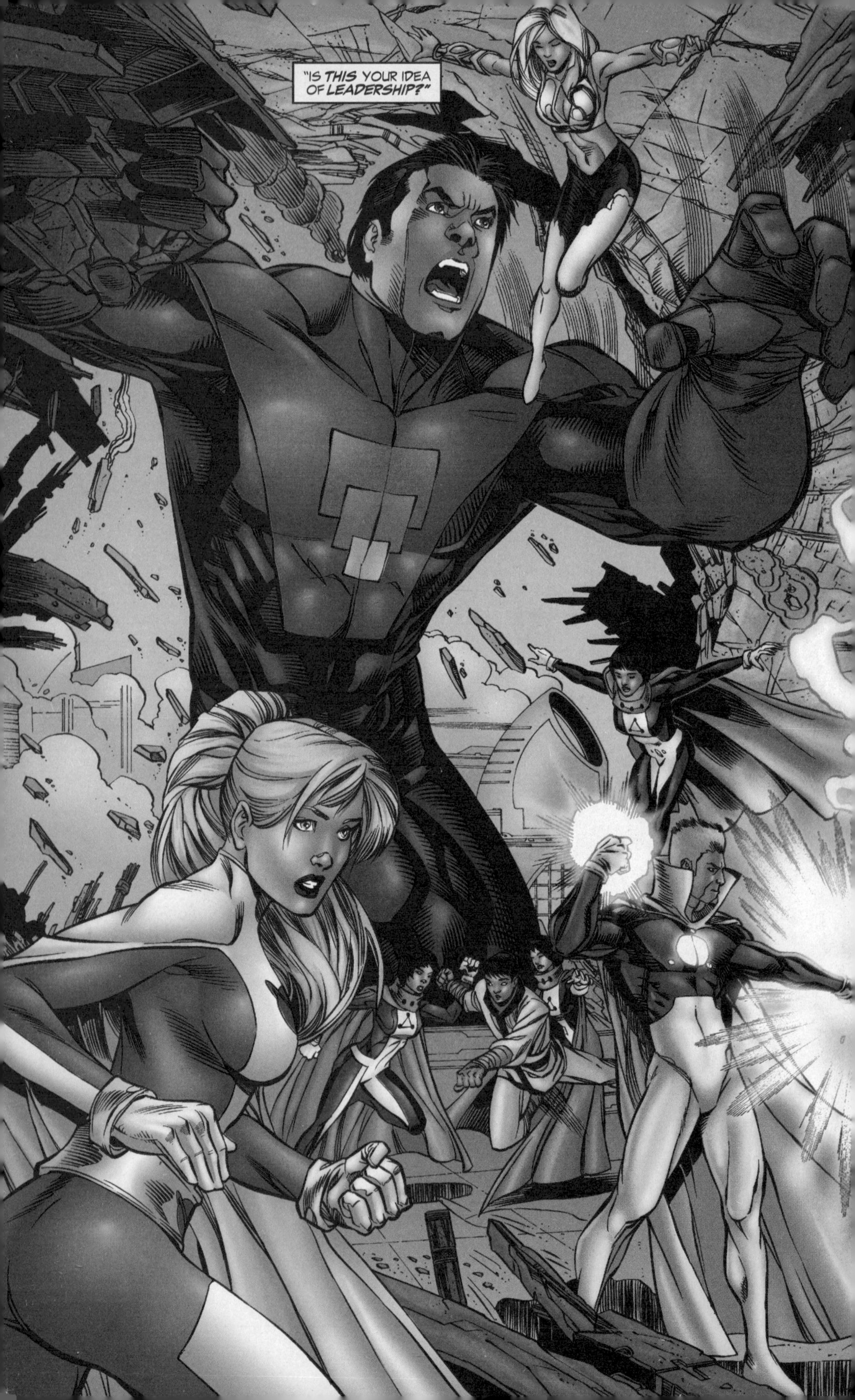
"IS THIS YOUR IDEA OF LEADERSHIP?"

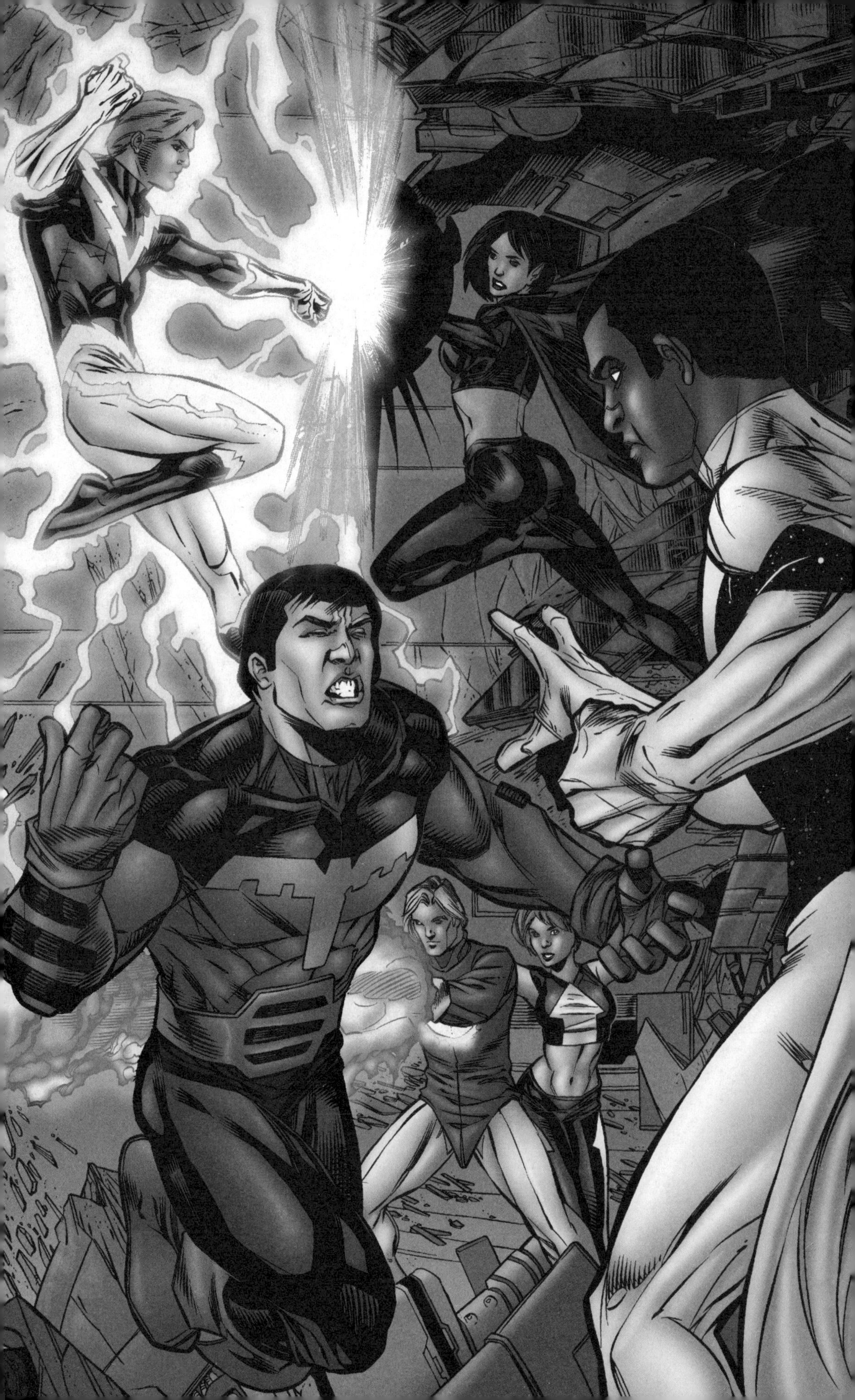

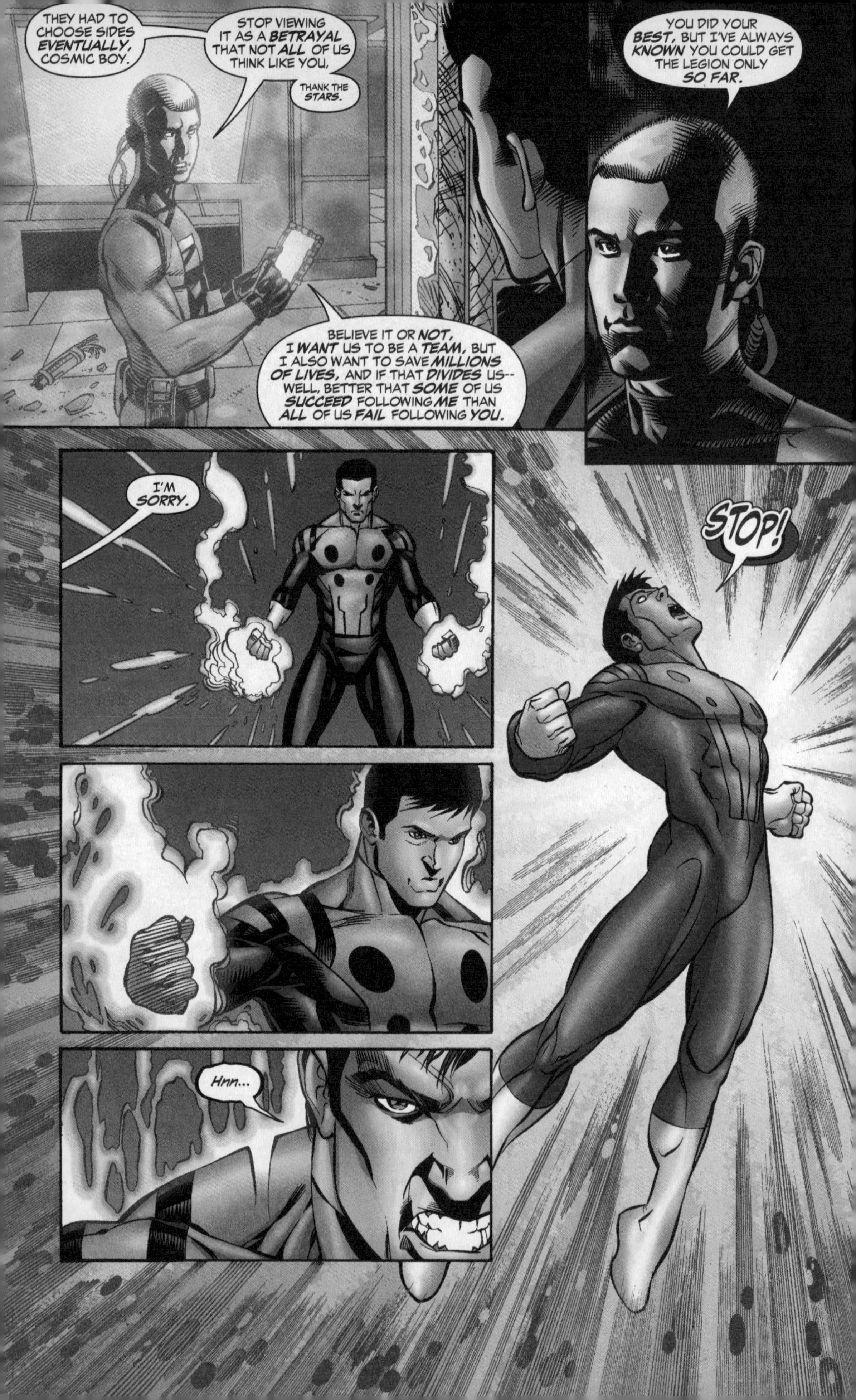
THEY HAD TO CHOOSE SIDES EVENTUALLY, COSMIC BOY.
STOP VIEWING IT AS A BETRAYAL THAT NOT ALL OF US THINK LIKE YOU,
THANK THE STARS.
BELIEVE IT OR NOT, I WANT US TO BE A TEAM, BUT I ALSO WANT TO SAVE MILLIONS OF LIVES, AND IF THAT DIVIDES US--WELL, BETTER THAT SOME OF US SUCCEED FOLLOWING ME THAN ALL OF US FAIL FOLLOWING YOU.
YOU DID YOUR BEST, BUT I'VE ALWAYS KNOWN YOU COULD GET THE LEGION ONLY SO FAR.
I'M SORRY.
STOP!
Hnn...

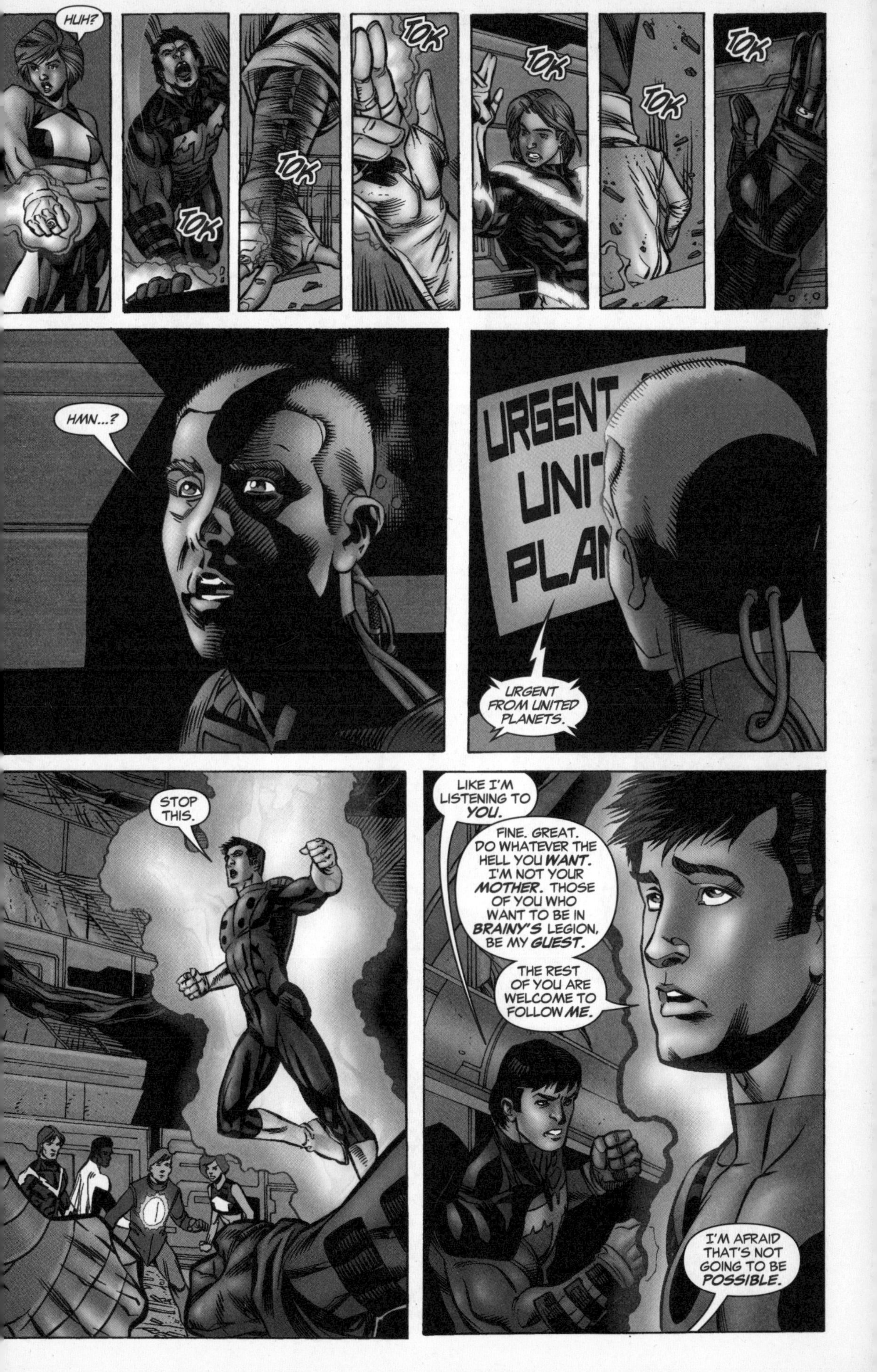
HUH?
TOK
TOK
TOK
TOK
TOK
TOK
TOK
HMN...?
URGENT UNIT PLAN
URGENT FROM UNITED PLANETS.
STOP THIS.
LIKE I'M LISTENING TO YOU.
FINE. GREAT. DO WHATEVER THE HELL YOU WANT. I'M NOT YOUR MOTHER. THOSE OF YOU WHO WANT TO BE IN BRAINY'S LEGION, BE MY GUEST.
THE REST OF YOU ARE WELCOME TO FOLLOW ME.
I'M AFRAID THAT'S NOT GOING TO BE POSSIBLE.

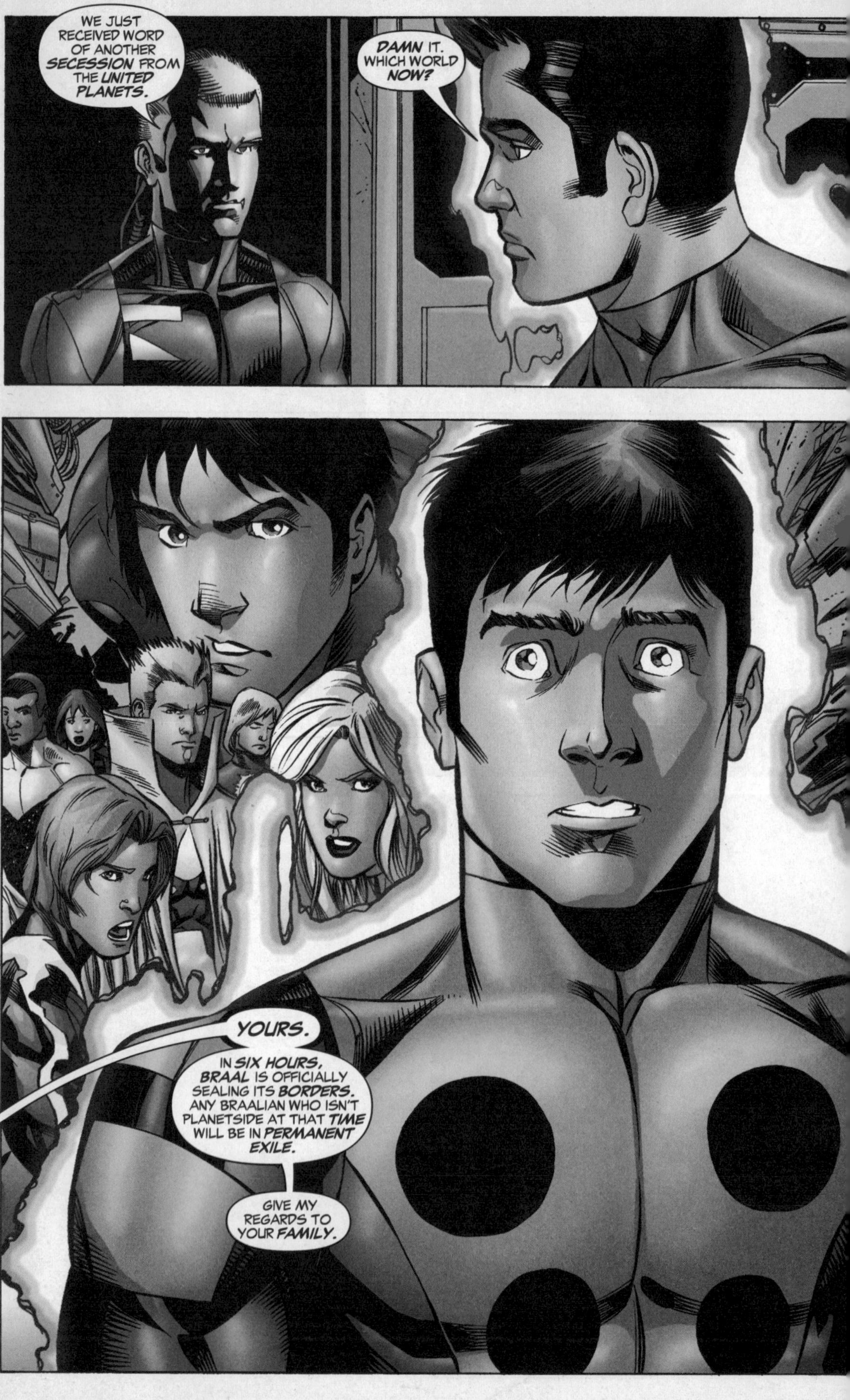
WE JUST RECEIVED WORD OF ANOTHER SECESSION FROM THE UNITED PLANETS.
DAMN IT. WHICH WORLD NOW?
YOURS.
IN SIX HOURS, BRAAL IS OFFICIALLY SEALING ITS BORDERS. ANY BRAALIAN WHO ISN'T PLANETSIDE AT THAT TIME WILL BE IN PERMANENT EXILE.
GIVE MY REGARDS TO YOUR FAMILY.

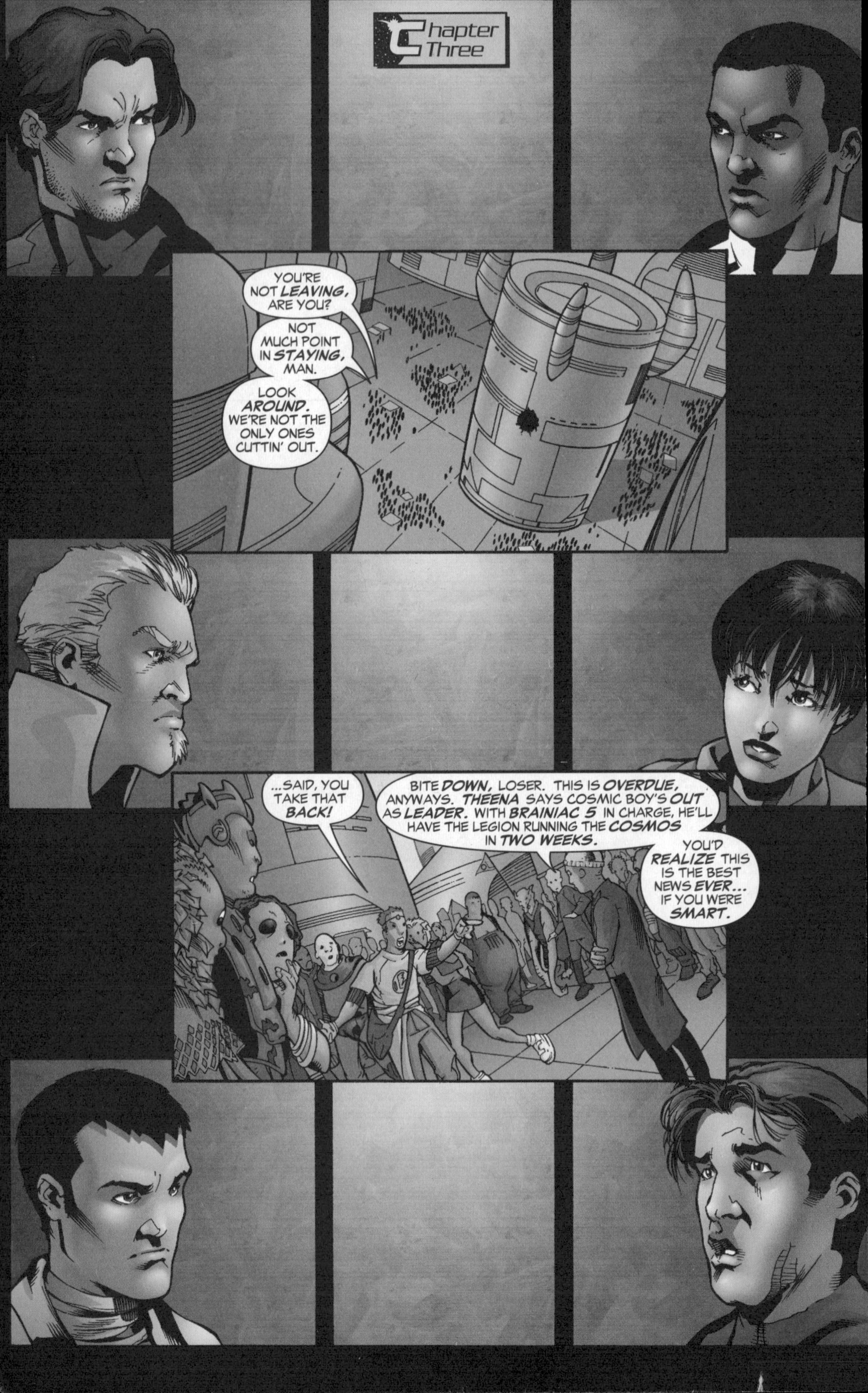
Chapter Three
YOU'RE NOT LEAVING, ARE YOU?
NOT MUCH POINT IN STAYING, MAN.
LOOK AROUND. WE'RE NOT THE ONLY ONES CUTTIN' OUT.
...SAID, YOU TAKE THAT BACK!
BITE DOWN, LOSER. THIS IS OVERDUE, ANYWAYS. THEENA SAYS COSMIC BOY'S OUT AS LEADER. WITH BRAINIAC 5 IN CHARGE, HE'LL HAVE THE LEGION RUNNING THE COSMOS IN TWO WEEKS.
YOU'D REALIZE THIS IS THE BEST NEWS EVER... IF YOU WERE SMART.

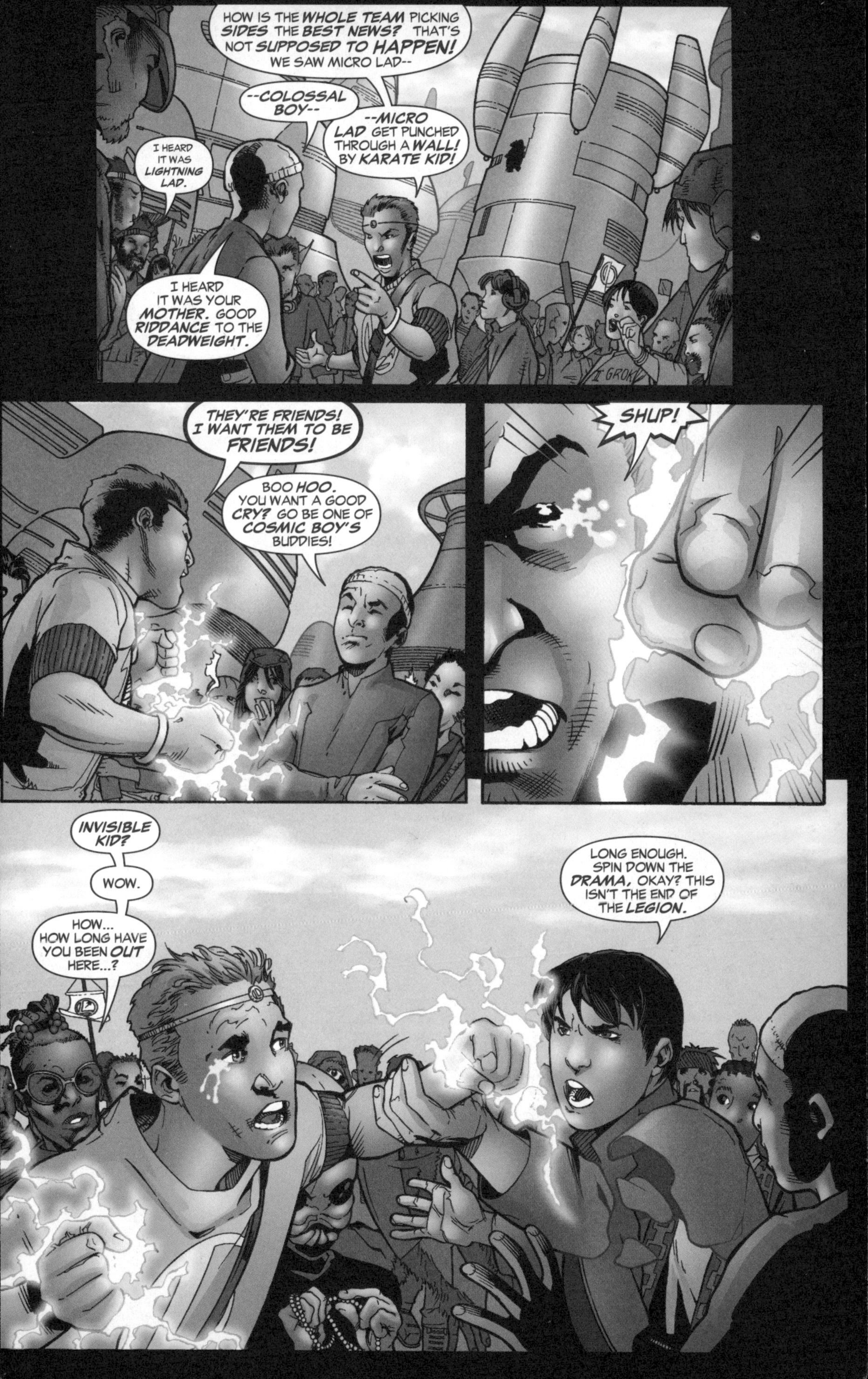
HOW IS THE WHOLE TEAM PICKING SIDES THE BEST NEWS? THAT'S NOT SUPPOSED TO HAPPEN! WE SAW MICRO LAD--
--COLOSSAL BOY--
--MICRO LAD GET PUNCHED THROUGH A WALL! BY KARATE KID!
I HEARD IT WAS LIGHTNING LAD.
I HEARD IT WAS YOUR MOTHER. GOOD RIDDANCE TO THE DEADWEIGHT.
THEY'RE FRIENDS! I WANT THEM TO BE FRIENDS!
BOO HOO. YOU WANT A GOOD CRY? GO BE ONE OF COSMIC BOY'S BUDDIES!
SHUP!
INVISIBLE KID?
WOW.
HOW... HOW LONG HAVE YOU BEEN OUT HERE...?
LONG ENOUGH. SPIN DOWN THE DRAMA, OKAY? THIS ISN'T THE END OF THE LEGION.

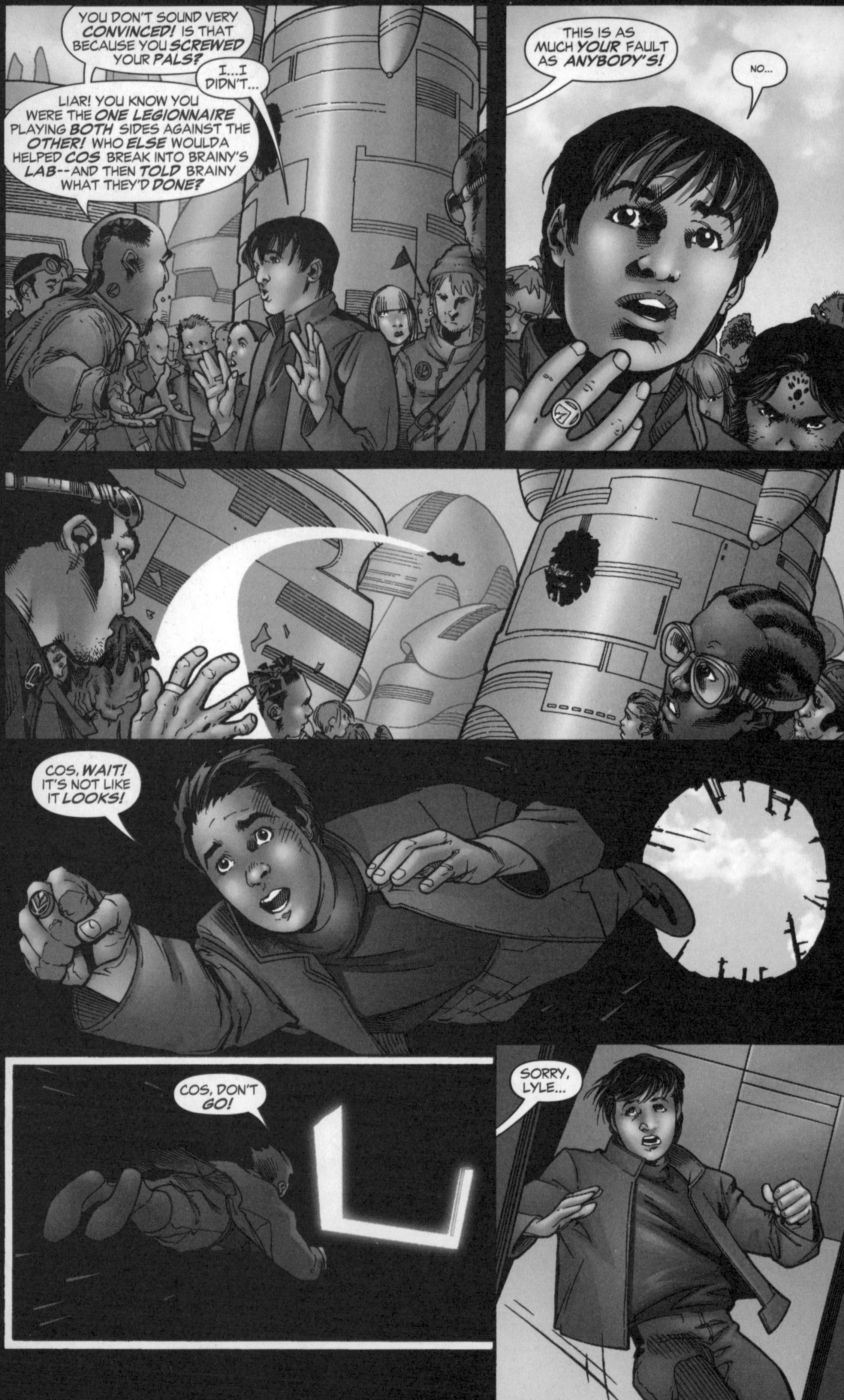
YOU DON'T SOUND VERY CONVINCED! IS THAT BECAUSE YOU SCREWED YOUR PALS?
I...I DIDN'T...
LIAR! YOU KNOW YOU WERE THE ONE LEGIONNAIRE PLAYING BOTH SIDES AGAINST THE OTHER! WHO ELSE WOULDA HELPED COS BREAK INTO BRAINY'S LAB--AND THEN TOLD BRAINY WHAT THEY'D DONE?
THIS IS AS MUCH YOUR FAULT AS ANYBODY'S!
NO...
COS, WAIT! IT'S NOT LIKE IT LOOKS!
COS, DON'T GO!
SORRY, LYLE...

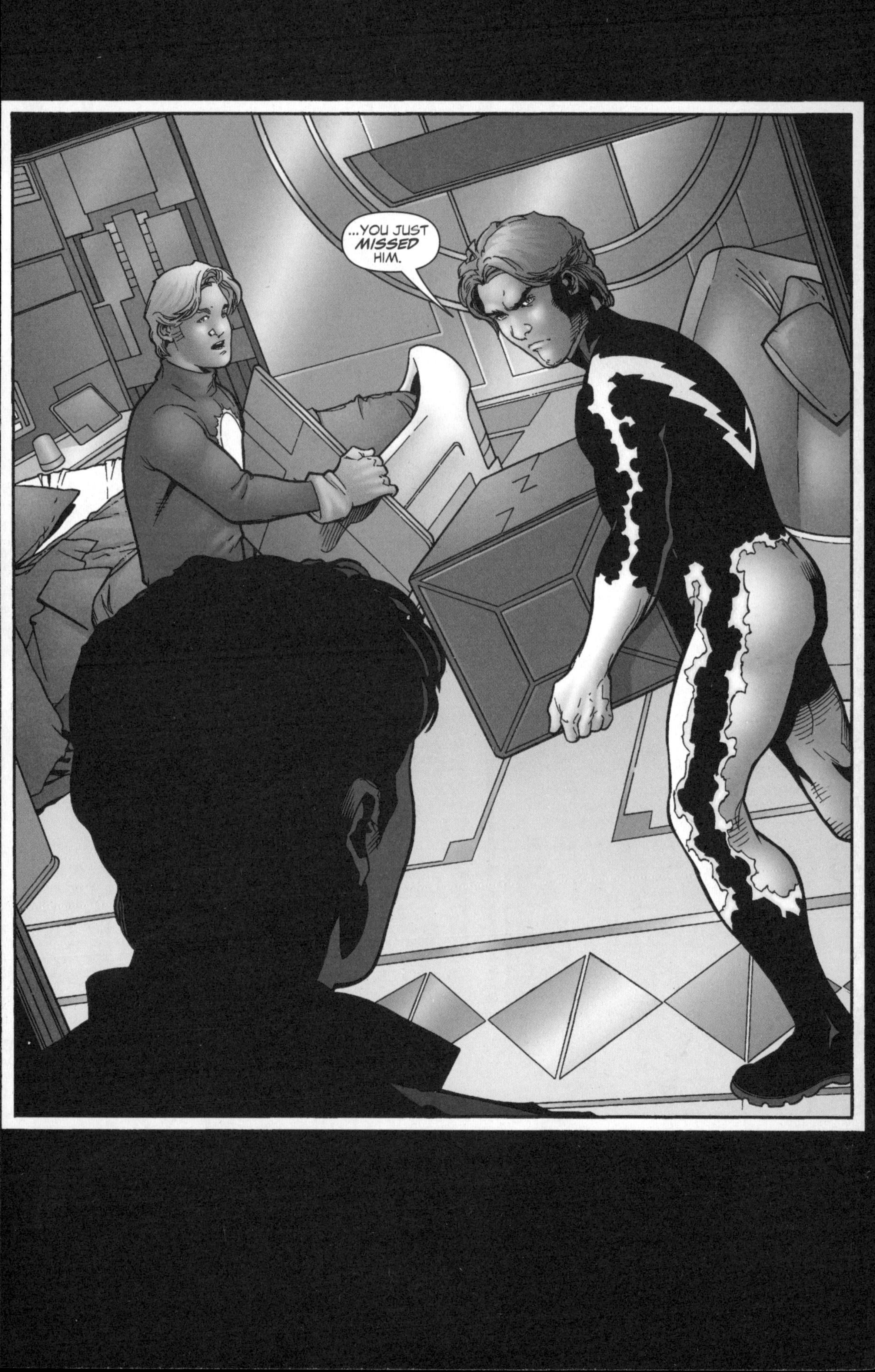
...YOU JUST MISSED HIM.

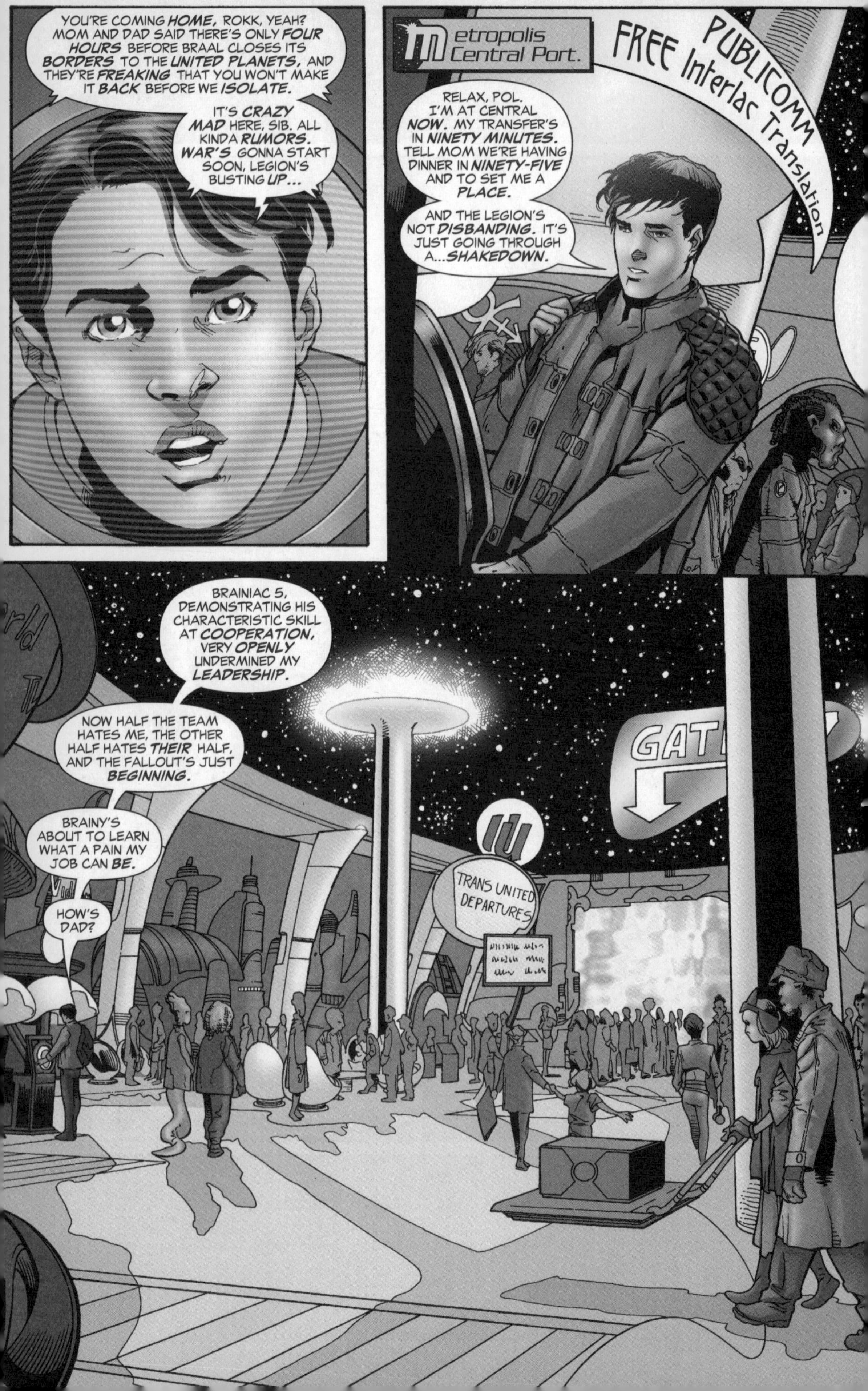
YOU'RE COMING HOME, ROKK, YEAH? MOM AND DAD SAID THERE'S ONLY FOUR HOURS BEFORE BRAAL CLOSES ITS BORDERS TO THE UNITED PLANETS, AND THEY'RE FREAKING THAT YOU WON'T MAKE IT BACK BEFORE WE ISOLATE.
IT'S CRAZY MAD HERE, SIB. ALL KINDA RUMORS. WAR'S GONNA START SOON, LEGION'S BUSTING UP...
Metropolis Central Port.
PUBLICOMM FREE Interlac Translation
RELAX, POL. I'M AT CENTRAL NOW. MY TRANSFER'S IN NINETY MINUTES. TELL MOM WE'RE HAVING DINNER IN NINETY-FIVE AND TO SET ME A PLACE.
AND THE LEGION'S NOT DISBANDING. IT'S JUST GOING THROUGH A...SHAKEDOWN.
BRAINIAC 5, DEMONSTRATING HIS CHARACTERISTIC SKILL AT COOPERATION, VERY OPENLY UNDERMINED MY LEADERSHIP.
NOW HALF THE TEAM HATES ME, THE OTHER HALF HATES THEIR HALF, AND THE FALLOUT'S JUST BEGINNING.
BRAINY'S ABOUT TO LEARN WHAT A PAIN MY JOB CAN BE.
HOW'S DAD?
TRANS UNITED DEPARTURES
GAT

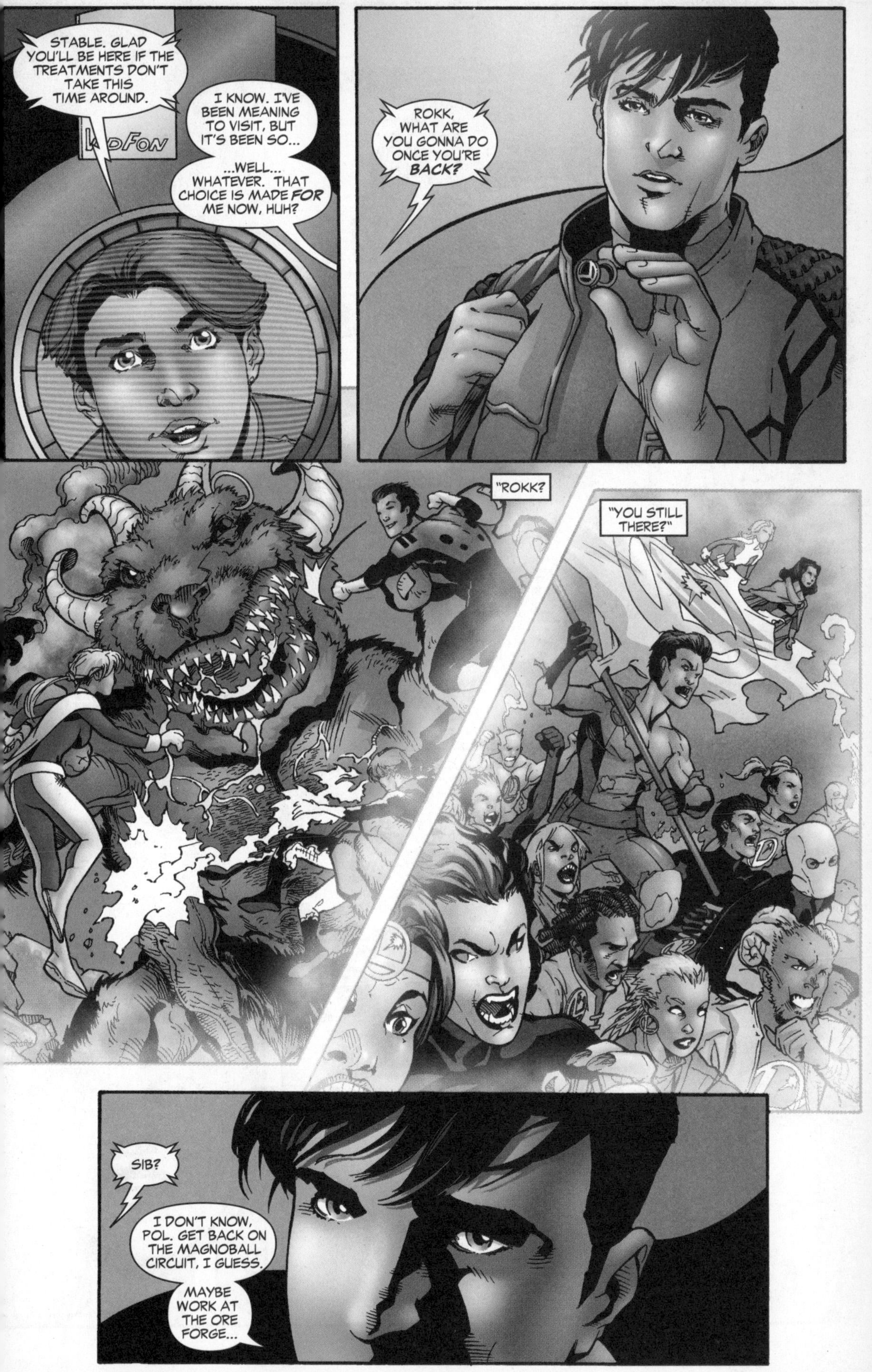
STABLE. GLAD YOU'LL BE HERE IF THE TREATMENTS DON'T TAKE THIS TIME AROUND.
I KNOW. I'VE BEEN MEANING TO VISIT, BUT IT'S BEEN SO...
...WELL... WHATEVER. THAT CHOICE IS MADE FOR ME NOW, HUH?
LADFON
ROKK, WHAT ARE YOU GONNA DO ONCE YOU'RE BACK?
"ROKK?
"YOU STILL THERE?"
SIB?
I DON'T KNOW, POL. GET BACK ON THE MAGNOBALL CIRCUIT, I GUESS.
MAYBE WORK AT THE ORE FORGE...

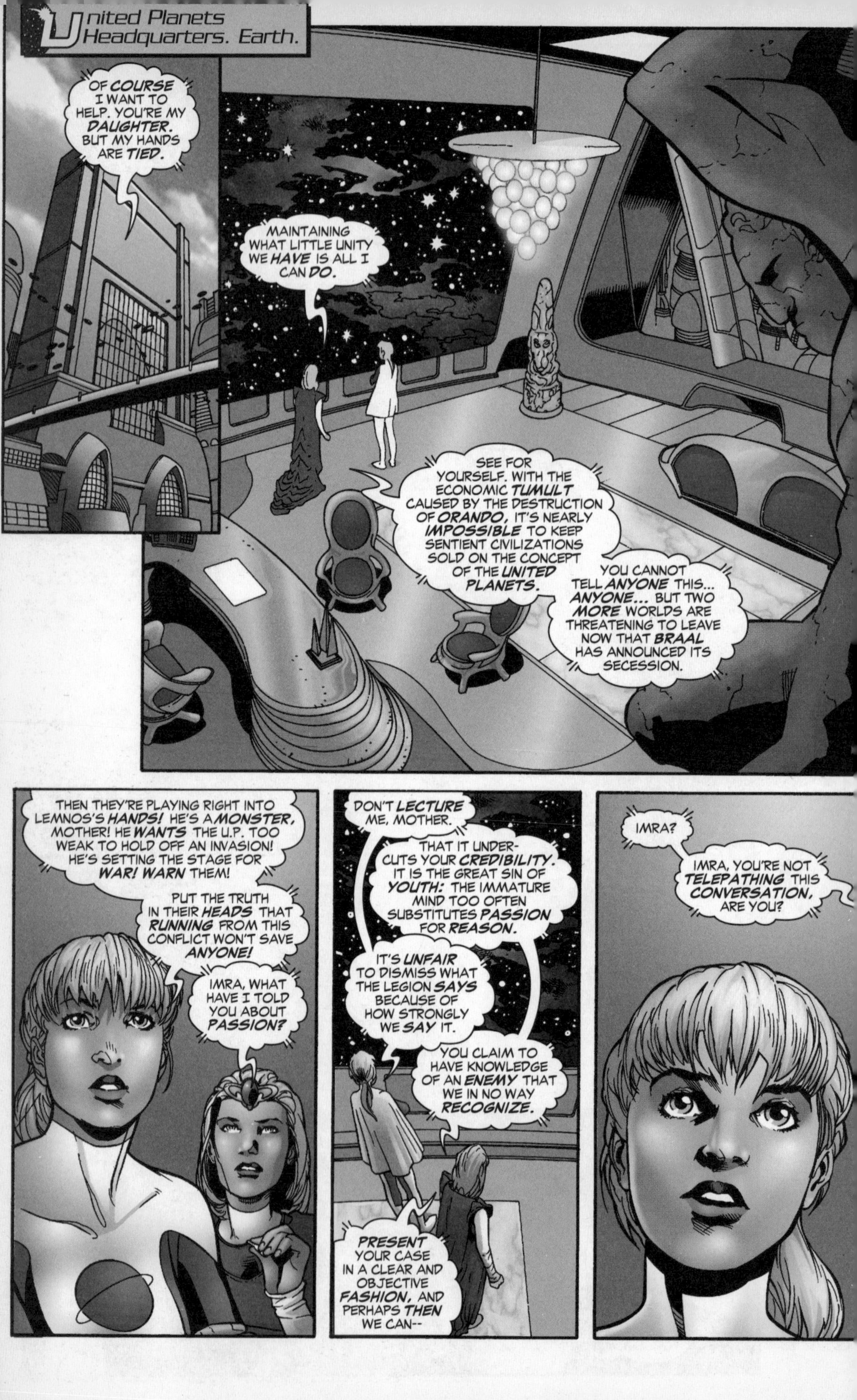
United Planets Headquarters. Earth.
OF COURSE I WANT TO HELP. YOU'RE MY DAUGHTER. BUT MY HANDS ARE TIED.
MAINTAINING WHAT LITTLE UNITY WE HAVE IS ALL I CAN DO.
SEE FOR YOURSELF. WITH THE ECONOMIC TUMULT CAUSED BY THE DESTRUCTION OF ORANDO, IT'S NEARLY IMPOSSIBLE TO KEEP SENTIENT CIVILIZATIONS SOLD ON THE CONCEPT OF THE UNITED PLANETS.
YOU CANNOT TELL ANYONE THIS... ANYONE... BUT TWO MORE WORLDS ARE THREATENING TO LEAVE NOW THAT BRAAL HAS ANNOUNCED ITS SECESSION.
THEN THEY'RE PLAYING RIGHT INTO LEMNOS'S HANDS! HE'S A MONSTER, MOTHER! HE WANTS THE U.P. TOO WEAK TO HOLD OFF AN INVASION! HE'S SETTING THE STAGE FOR WAR! WARN THEM!
PUT THE TRUTH IN THEIR HEADS THAT RUNNING FROM THIS CONFLICT WON'T SAVE ANYONE!
IMRA, WHAT HAVE I TOLD YOU ABOUT PASSION?
DON'T LECTURE ME, MOTHER.
THAT IT UNDERCUTS YOUR CREDIBILITY. IT IS THE GREAT SIN OF YOUTH: THE IMMATURE MIND TOO OFTEN SUBSTITUTES PASSION FOR REASON.
IT'S UNFAIR TO DISMISS WHAT THE LEGION SAYS BECAUSE OF HOW STRONGLY WE SAY IT.
YOU CLAIM TO HAVE KNOWLEDGE OF AN ENEMY THAT WE IN NO WAY RECOGNIZE.
PRESENT YOUR CASE IN A CLEAR AND OBJECTIVE FASHION, AND PERHAPS THEN WE CAN--
IMRA?
IMRA, YOU'RE NOT TELEPATHING THIS CONVERSATION, ARE YOU?

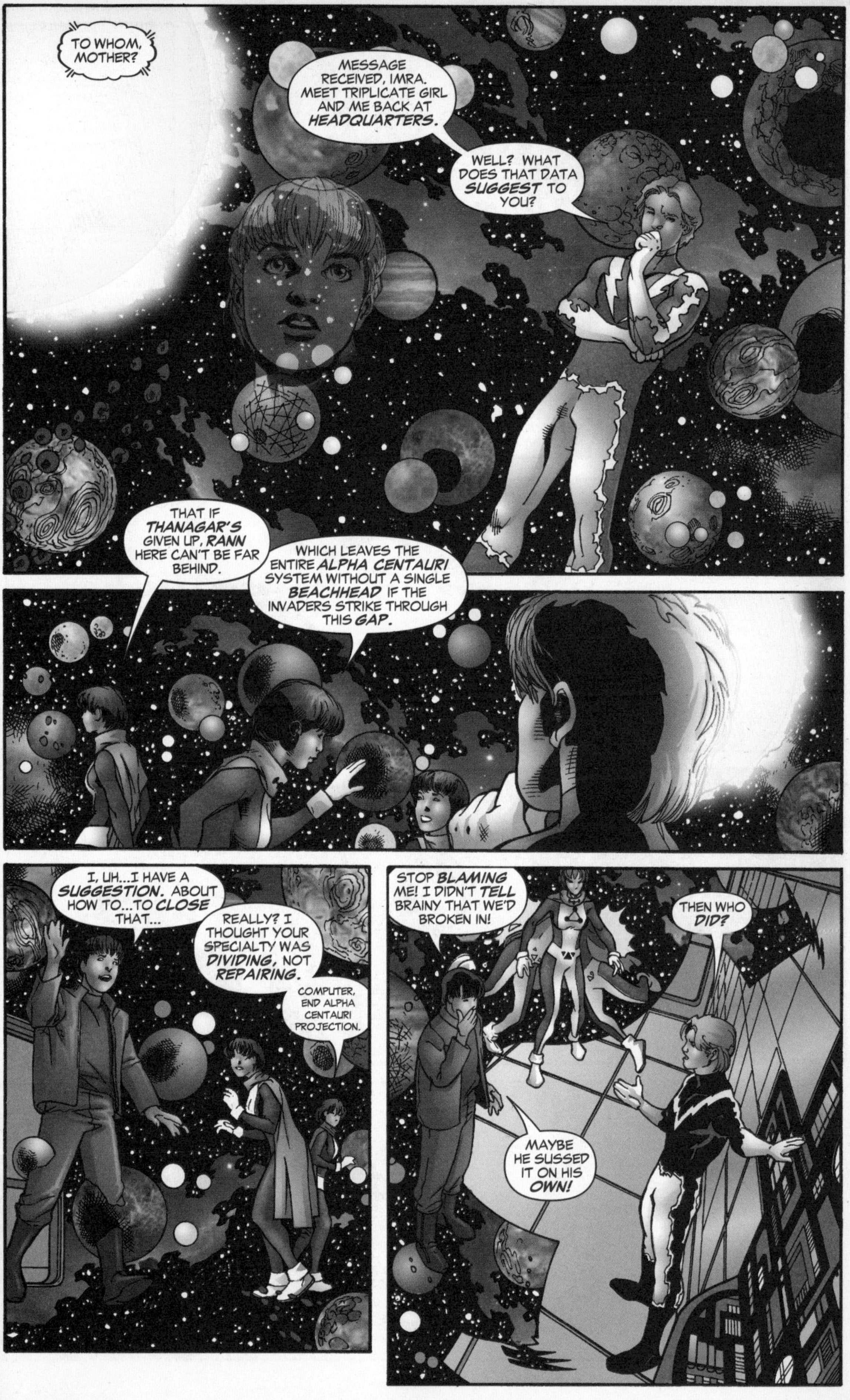
TO WHOM, MOTHER?
MESSAGE RECEIVED, IMRA. MEET TRIPLICATE GIRL AND ME BACK AT HEADQUARTERS.
WELL? WHAT DOES THAT DATA SUGGEST TO YOU?
THAT IF THANAGAR'S GIVEN UP, RANN HERE CAN'T BE FAR BEHIND.
WHICH LEAVES THE ENTIRE ALPHA CENTAURI SYSTEM WITHOUT A SINGLE BEACHHEAD IF THE INVADERS STRIKE THROUGH THIS GAP.
I, UH...I HAVE A SUGGESTION. ABOUT HOW TO...TO CLOSE THAT...
REALLY? I THOUGHT YOUR SPECIALTY WAS DIVIDING, NOT REPAIRING.
COMPUTER, END ALPHA CENTAURI PROJECTION.
STOP BLAMING ME! I DIDN'T TELL BRAINY THAT WE'D BROKEN IN!
THEN WHO DID?
MAYBE HE SUSSED IT ON HIS OWN!

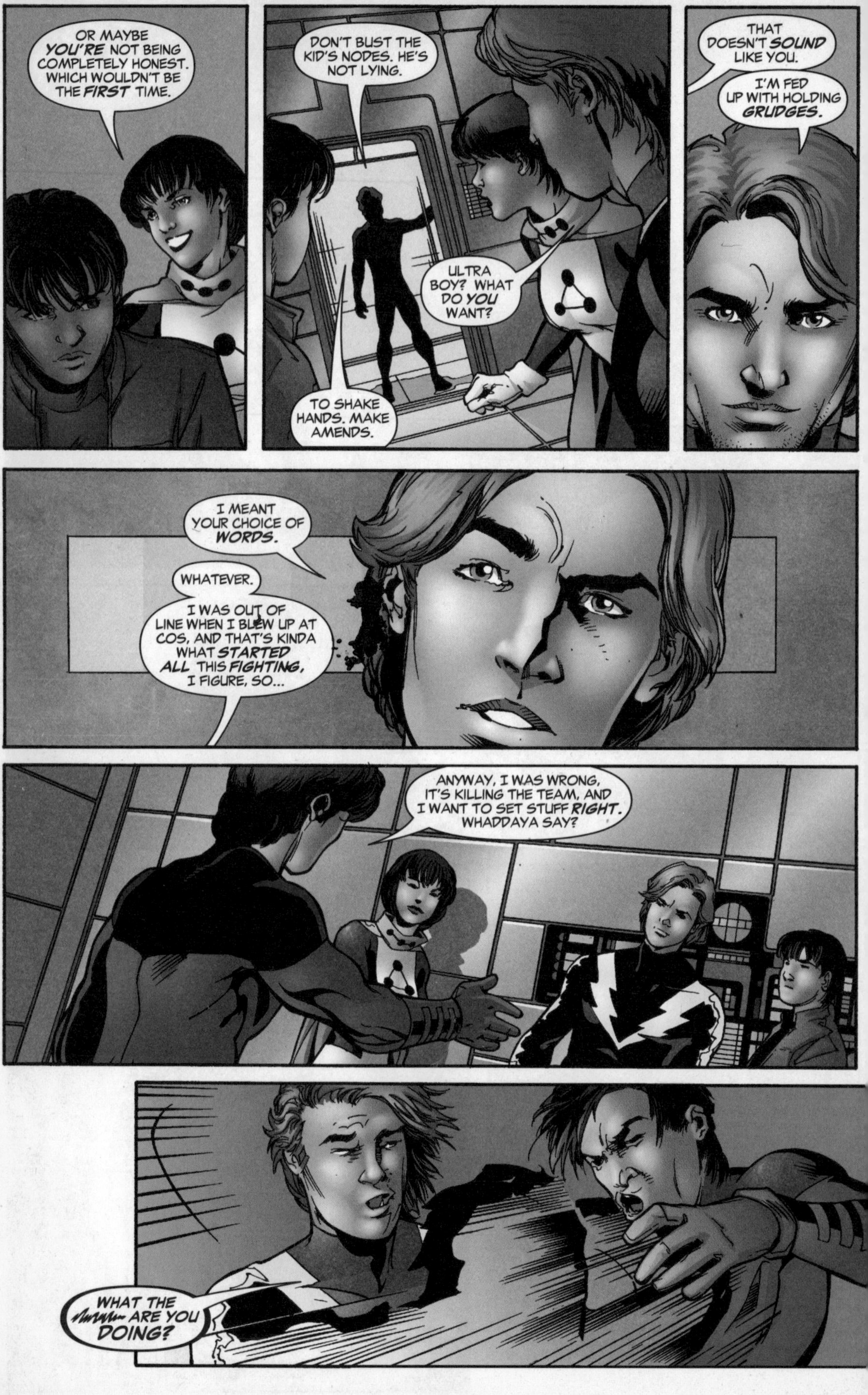
OR MAYBE YOU'RE NOT BEING COMPLETELY HONEST. WHICH WOULDN'T BE THE FIRST TIME.
DON'T BUST THE KID'S NODES. HE'S NOT LYING.
ULTRA BOY? WHAT DO YOU WANT?
TO SHAKE HANDS. MAKE AMENDS.
THAT DOESN'T SOUND LIKE YOU.
I'M FED UP WITH HOLDING GRUDGES.
I MEANT YOUR CHOICE OF WORDS.
WHATEVER.
I WAS OUT OF LINE WHEN I BLEW UP AT COS, AND THAT'S KINDA WHAT STARTED ALL THIS FIGHTING, I FIGURE, SO...
ANYWAY, I WAS WRONG, IT'S KILLING THE TEAM, AND I WANT TO SET STUFF RIGHT. WHADDAYA SAY?
WHAT THE ARE YOU DOING?

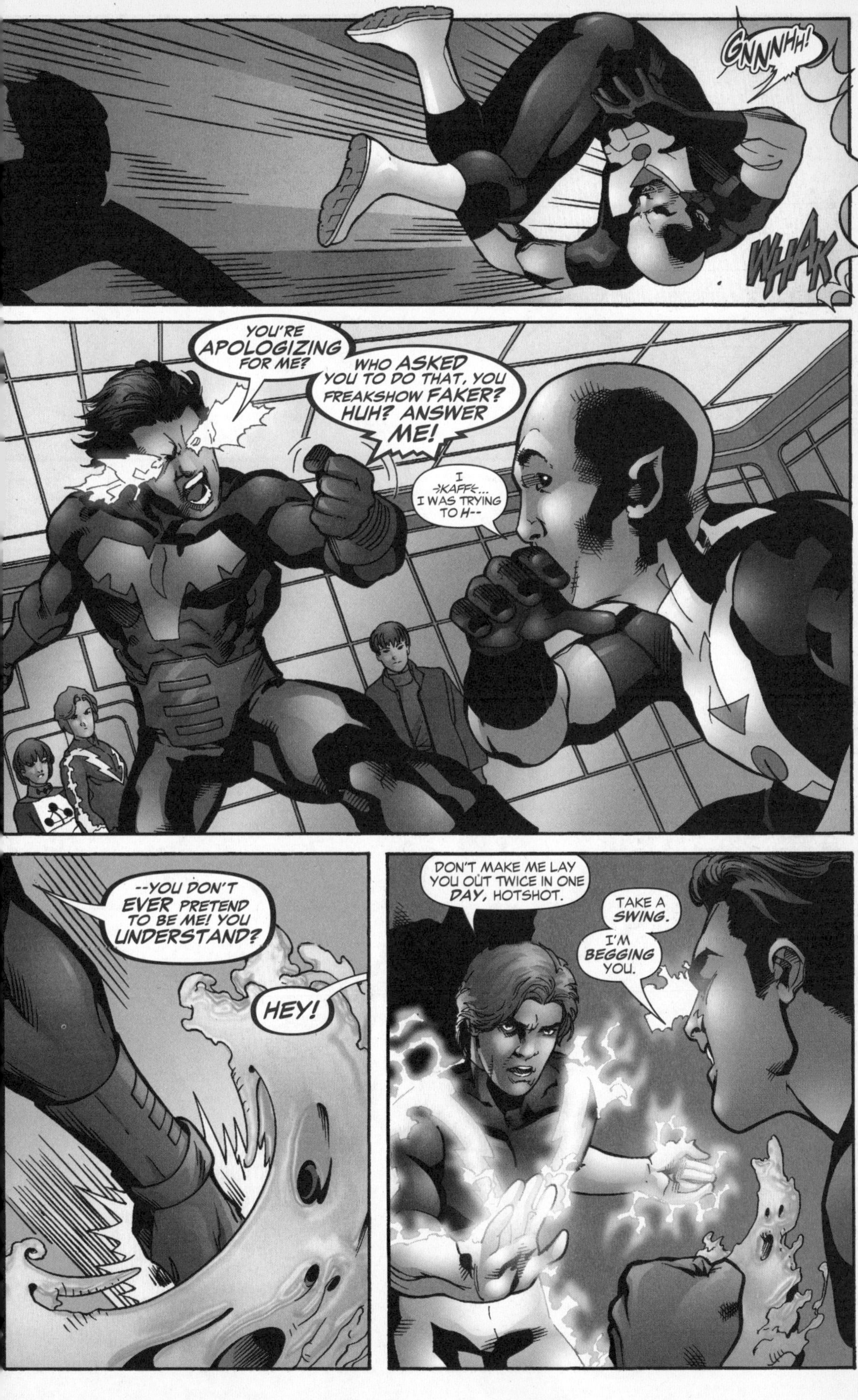
GNNNHH!
WHAK
YOU'RE APOLOGIZING FOR ME?
WHO ASKED YOU TO DO THAT, YOU FREAKSHOW FAKER? HUH? ANSWER ME!
I KAFF... I WAS TRYING TO H--
--YOU DON'T EVER PRETEND TO BE ME! YOU UNDERSTAND?
HEY!
DON'T MAKE ME LAY YOU OUT TWICE IN ONE DAY, HOTSHOT.
TAKE A SWING.
I'M BEGGING YOU.

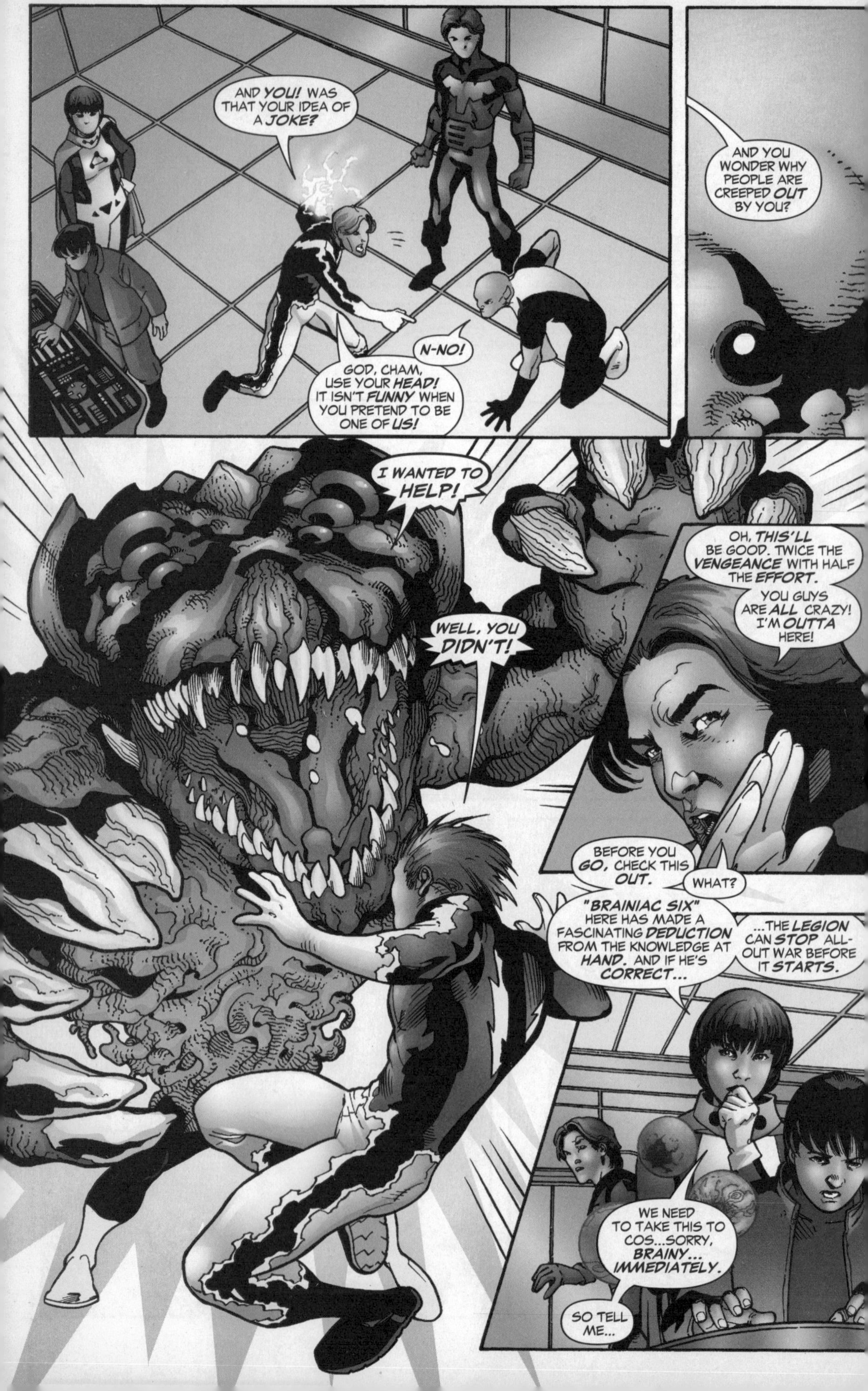

AND YOU! WAS THAT YOUR IDEA OF A JOKE?
N-NO!
GOD, CHAM, USE YOUR HEAD! IT ISN'T FUNNY WHEN YOU PRETEND TO BE ONE OF US!
AND YOU WONDER WHY PEOPLE ARE CREEPED OUT BY YOU?
I WANTED TO HELP!
WELL, YOU DIDN'T!
OH, THIS'LL BE GOOD. TWICE THE VENGEANCE WITH HALF THE EFFORT.
YOU GUYS ARE ALL CRAZY! I'M OUTTA HERE!
BEFORE YOU GO, CHECK THIS OUT.
WHAT?
"BRAINIAC SIX" HERE HAS MADE A FASCINATING DEDUCTION FROM THE KNOWLEDGE AT HAND. AND IF HE'S CORRECT...
...THE LEGION CAN STOP ALL-OUT WAR BEFORE IT STARTS.
SO TELL ME...
WE NEED TO TAKE THIS TO COS...SORRY, BRAINY... IMMEDIATELY.

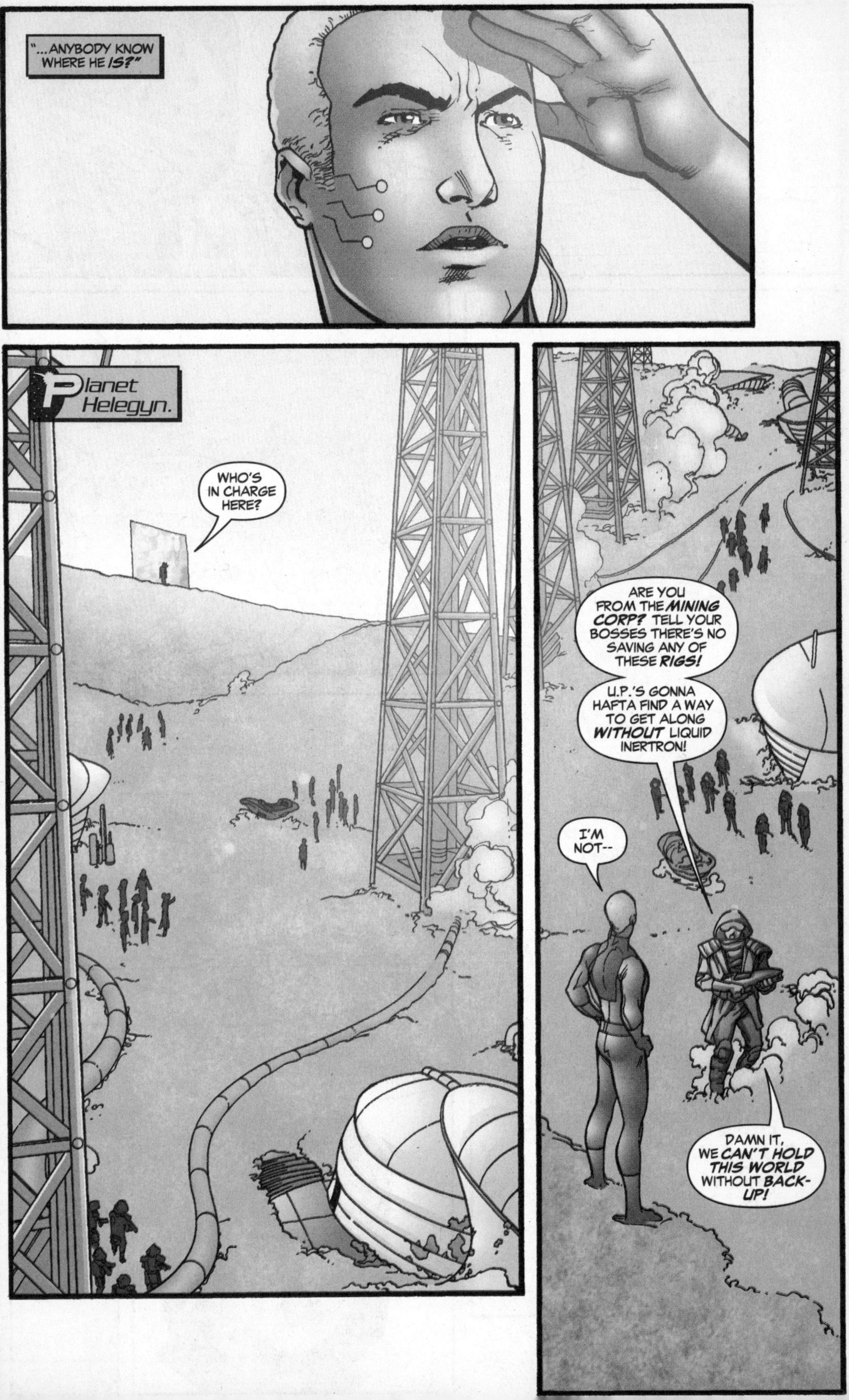
"...ANYBODY KNOW WHERE HE IS?"
Planet Helegyn.
WHO'S IN CHARGE HERE?
ARE YOU FROM THE MINING CORP? TELL YOUR BOSSES THERE'S NO SAVING ANY OF THESE RIGS!
U.P.'S GONNA HAFTA FIND A WAY TO GET ALONG WITHOUT LIQUID INERTRON!
I'M NOT--
DAMN IT, WE CAN'T HOLD THIS WORLD WITHOUT BACK-UP!

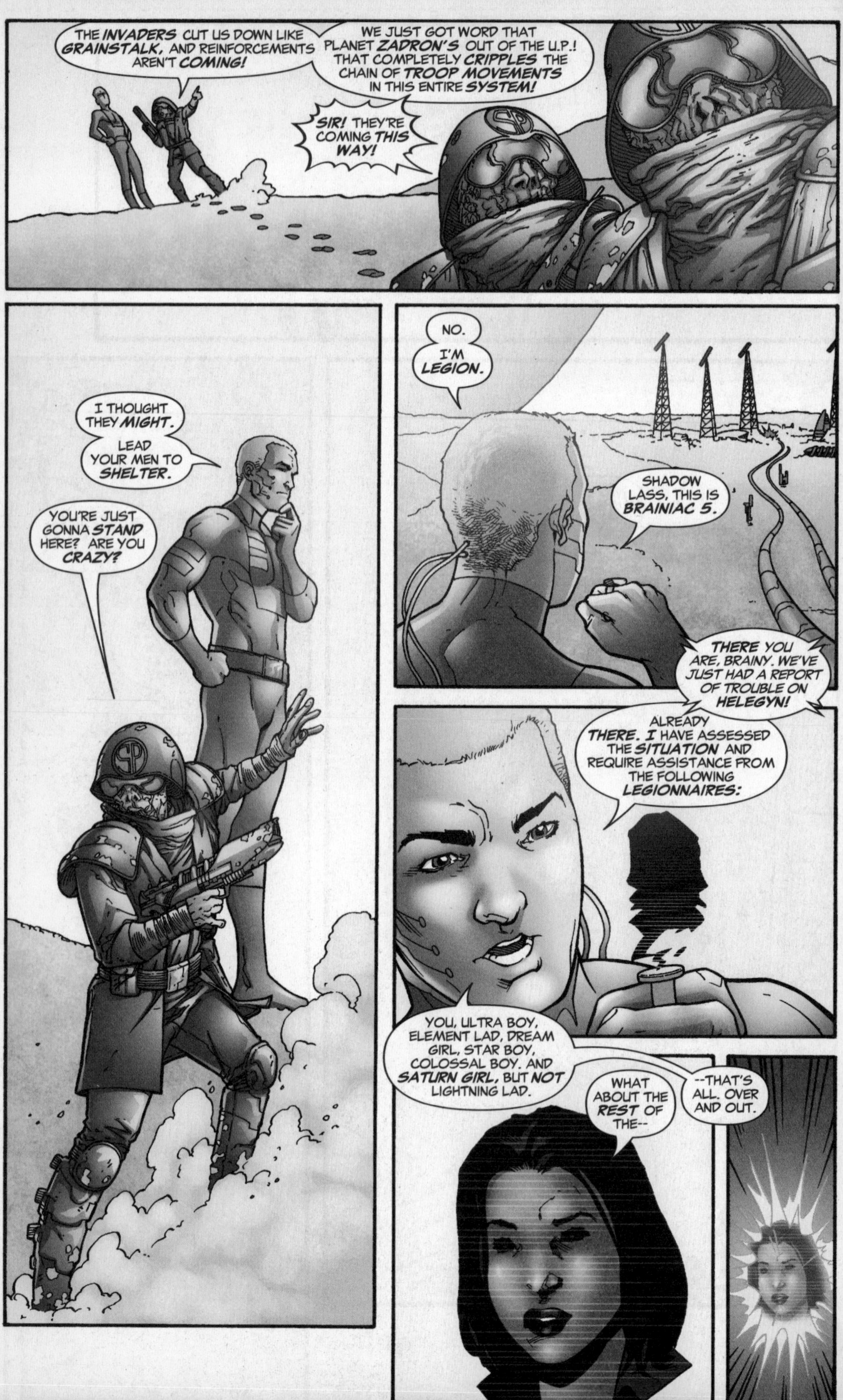
THE INVADERS CUT US DOWN LIKE GRAINSTALK, AND REINFORCEMENTS AREN'T COMING!
WE JUST GOT WORD THAT PLANET ZADRON'S OUT OF THE U.P.! THAT COMPLETELY CRIPPLES THE CHAIN OF TROOP MOVEMENTS IN THIS ENTIRE SYSTEM!
SIR! THEY'RE COMING THIS WAY!
I THOUGHT THEY MIGHT.
LEAD YOUR MEN TO SHELTER.
YOU'RE JUST GONNA STAND HERE? ARE YOU CRAZY?
NO.
I'M LEGION.
SHADOW LASS, THIS IS BRAINIAC 5.
THERE YOU ARE, BRAINY. WE'VE JUST HAD A REPORT OF TROUBLE ON HELEGYN!
ALREADY THERE. I HAVE ASSESSED THE SITUATION AND REQUIRE ASSISTANCE FROM THE FOLLOWING LEGIONNAIRES:
YOU, ULTRA BOY, ELEMENT LAD, DREAM GIRL, STAR BOY, COLOSSAL BOY. AND SATURN GIRL, BUT NOT LIGHTNING LAD.
WHAT ABOUT THE REST OF THE--
--THAT'S ALL. OVER AND OUT.

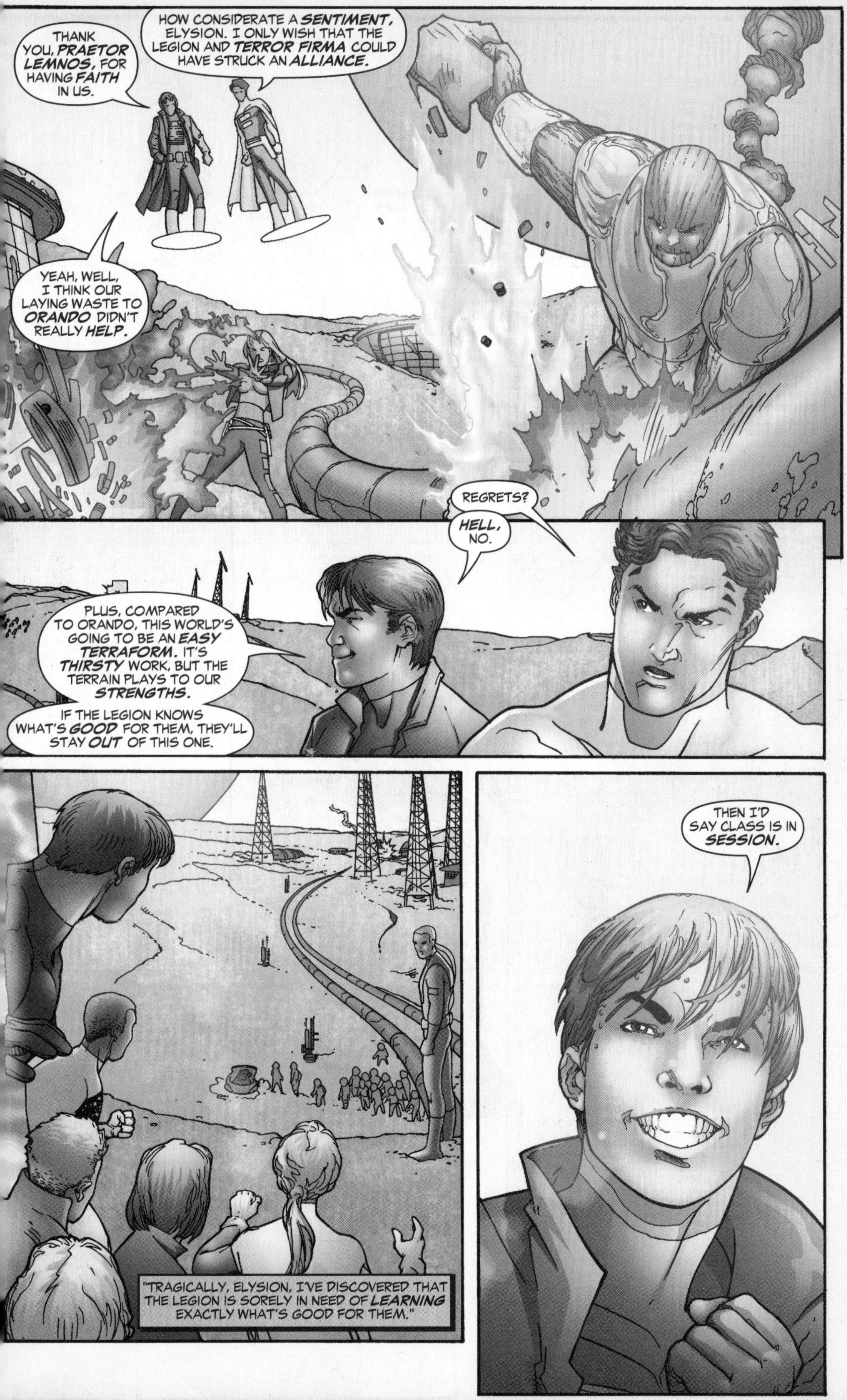
THANK YOU, PRAETOR LEMNOS, FOR HAVING FAITH IN US.
HOW CONSIDERATE A SENTIMENT, ELYSION. I ONLY WISH THAT THE LEGION AND TERROR FIRMA COULD HAVE STRUCK AN ALLIANCE.
YEAH, WELL, I THINK OUR LAYING WASTE TO ORANDO DIDN'T REALLY HELP.
REGRETS?
HELL, NO.
PLUS, COMPARED TO ORANDO, THIS WORLD'S GOING TO BE AN EASY TERRAFORM. IT'S THIRSTY WORK, BUT THE TERRAIN PLAYS TO OUR STRENGTHS.
IF THE LEGION KNOWS WHAT'S GOOD FOR THEM, THEY'LL STAY OUT OF THIS ONE.
"TRAGICALLY, ELYSION, I'VE DISCOVERED THAT THE LEGION IS SORELY IN NEED OF LEARNING EXACTLY WHAT'S GOOD FOR THEM."
THEN I'D SAY CLASS IS IN SESSION.

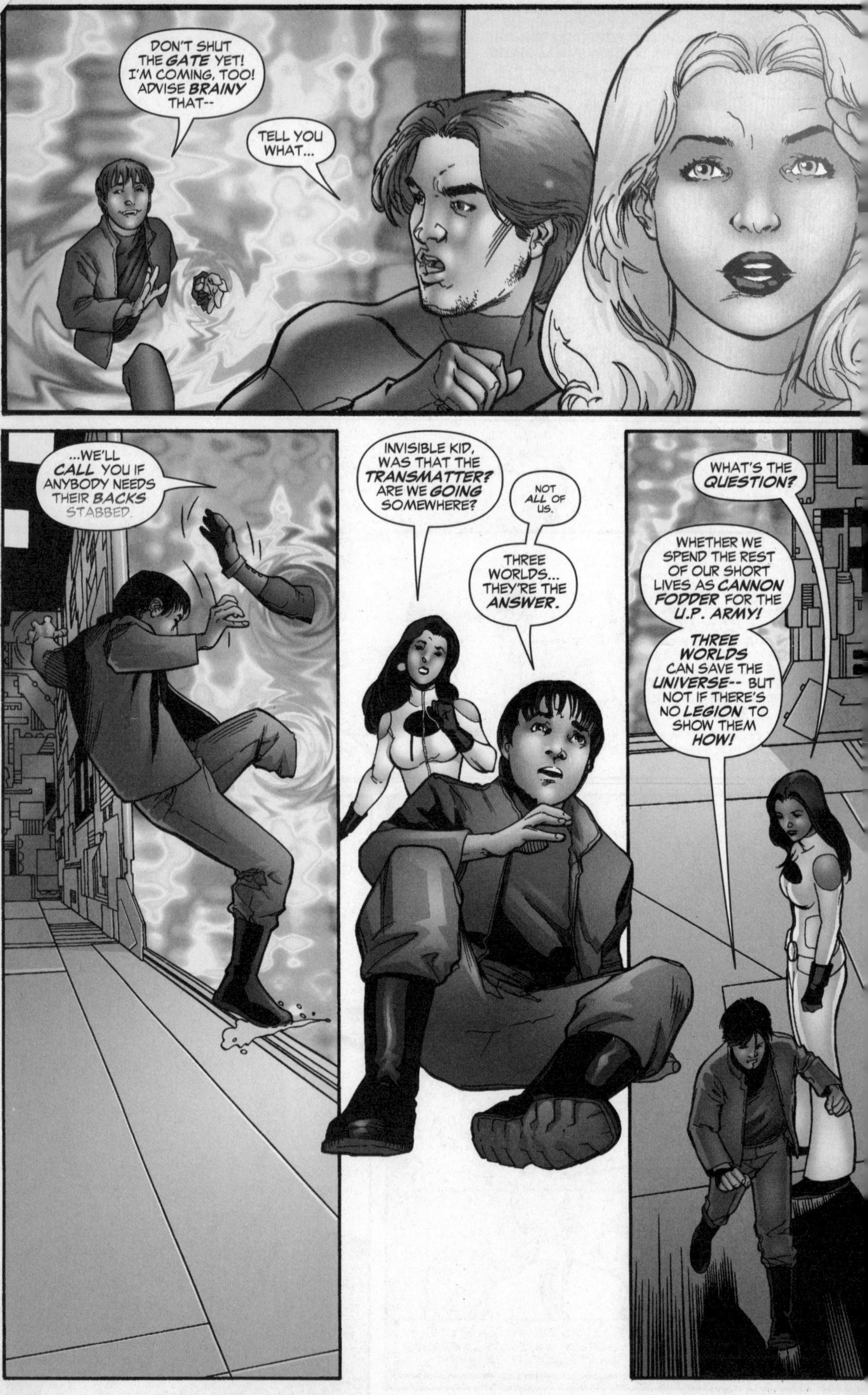
DON'T SHUT THE GATE YET! I'M COMING, TOO! ADVISE BRAINY THAT--
TELL YOU WHAT...
...WE'LL CALL YOU IF ANYBODY NEEDS THEIR BACKS STABBED.
INVISIBLE KID, WAS THAT THE TRANSMATTER? ARE WE GOING SOMEWHERE?
NOT ALL OF US.
THREE WORLDS... THEY'RE THE ANSWER.
WHAT'S THE QUESTION?
WHETHER WE SPEND THE REST OF OUR SHORT LIVES AS CANNON FODDER FOR THE U.P. ARMY!
THREE WORLDS CAN SAVE THE UNIVERSE-- BUT NOT IF THERE'S NO LEGION TO SHOW THEM HOW!

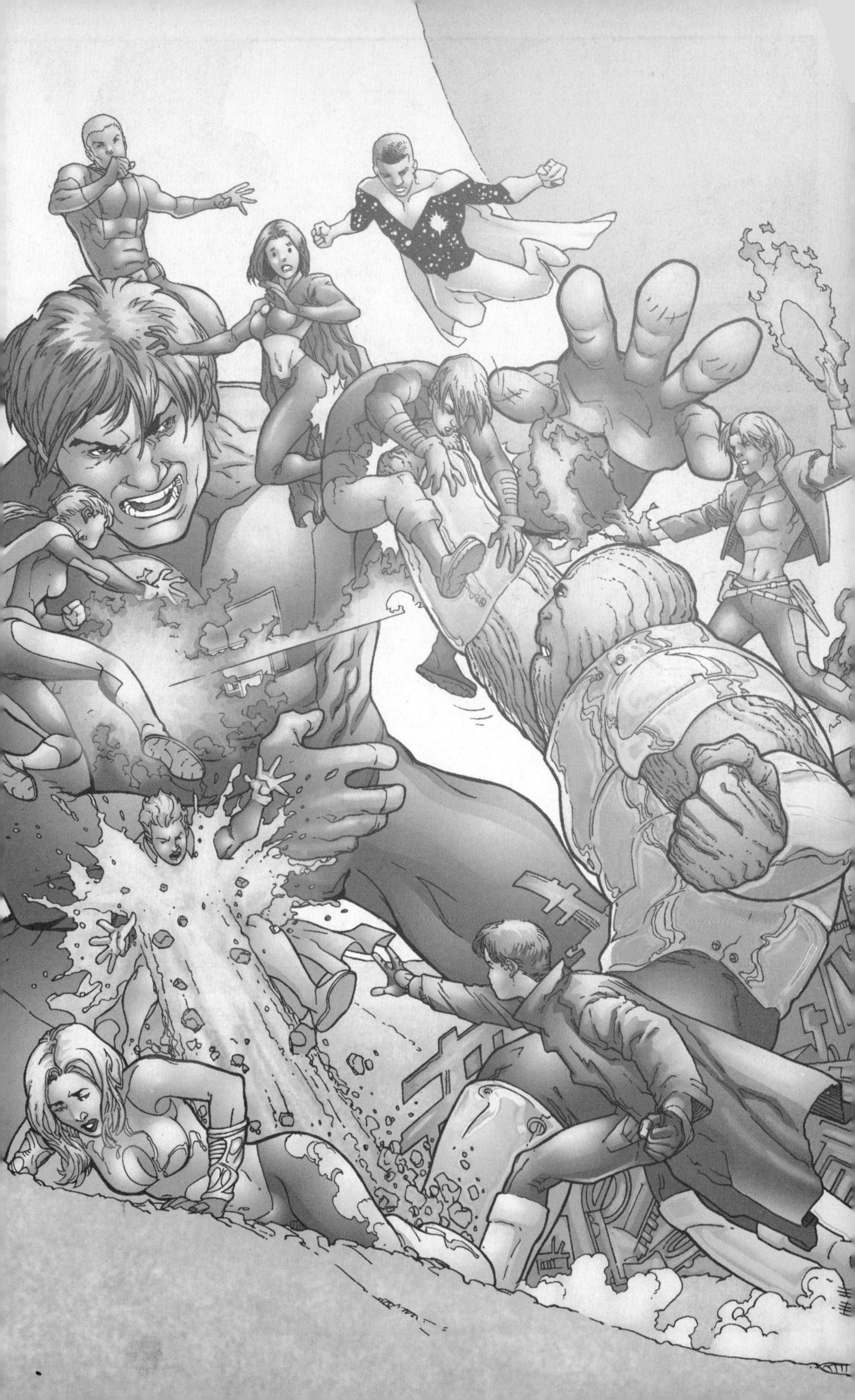

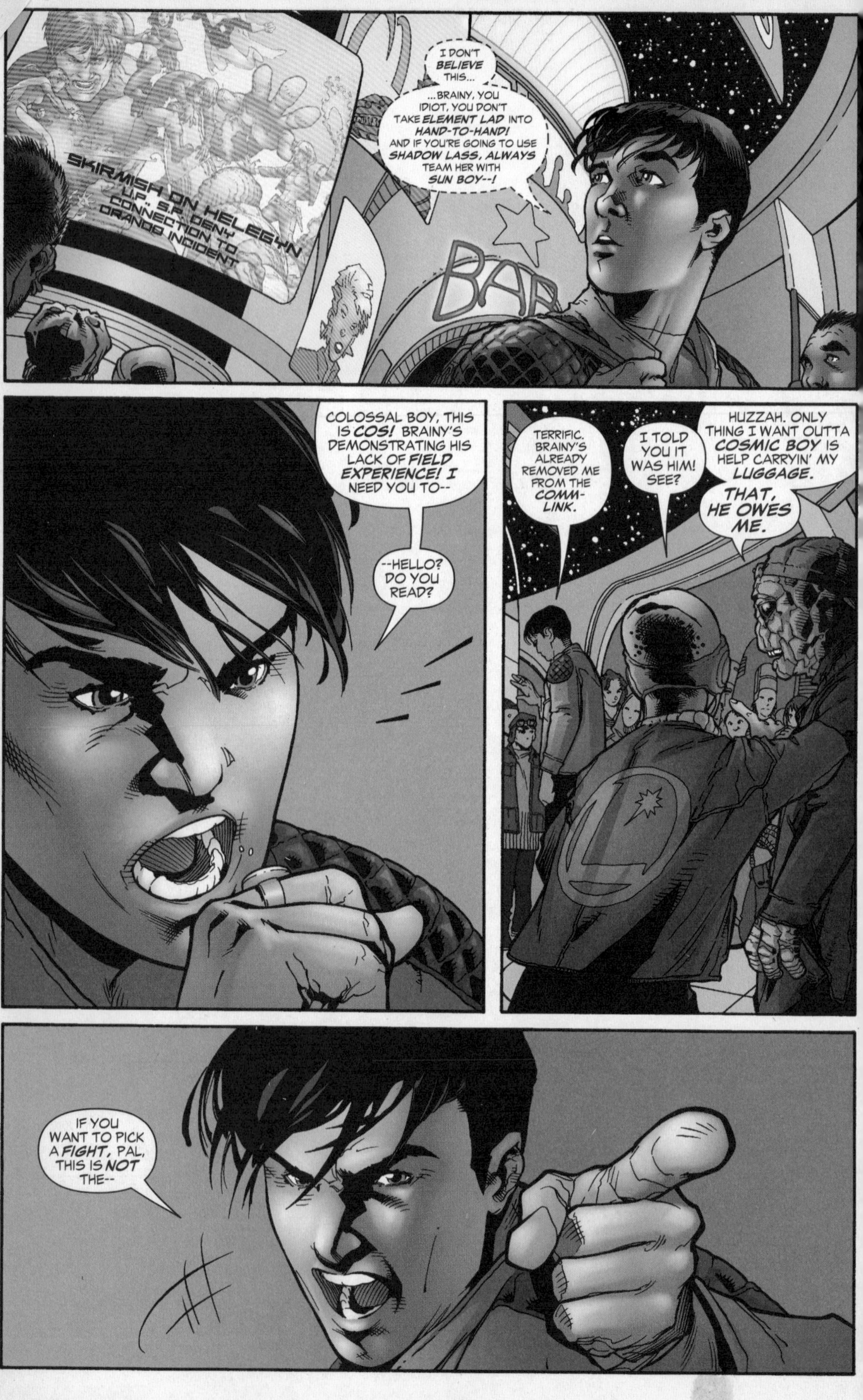
SKIRMISH ON HELEGYN
U.P., S.P. DENY CONNECTION TO ORANDO INCIDENT
BAR
I DON'T BELIEVE THIS...
...BRAINY, YOU IDIOT, YOU DON'T TAKE ELEMENT LAD INTO HAND-TO-HAND! AND IF YOU'RE GOING TO USE SHADOW LASS, ALWAYS TEAM HER WITH SUN BOY--!
COLOSSAL BOY, THIS IS COS! BRAINY'S DEMONSTRATING HIS LACK OF FIELD EXPERIENCE! I NEED YOU TO--
--HELLO? DO YOU READ?
TERRIFIC. BRAINY'S ALREADY REMOVED ME FROM THE COMM-LINK.
I TOLD YOU IT WAS HIM! SEE?
HUZZAH. ONLY THING I WANT OUTTA COSMIC BOY IS HELP CARRYIN' MY LUGGAGE.
THAT, HE OWES ME.
IF YOU WANT TO PICK A FIGHT, PAL, THIS IS NOT THE--

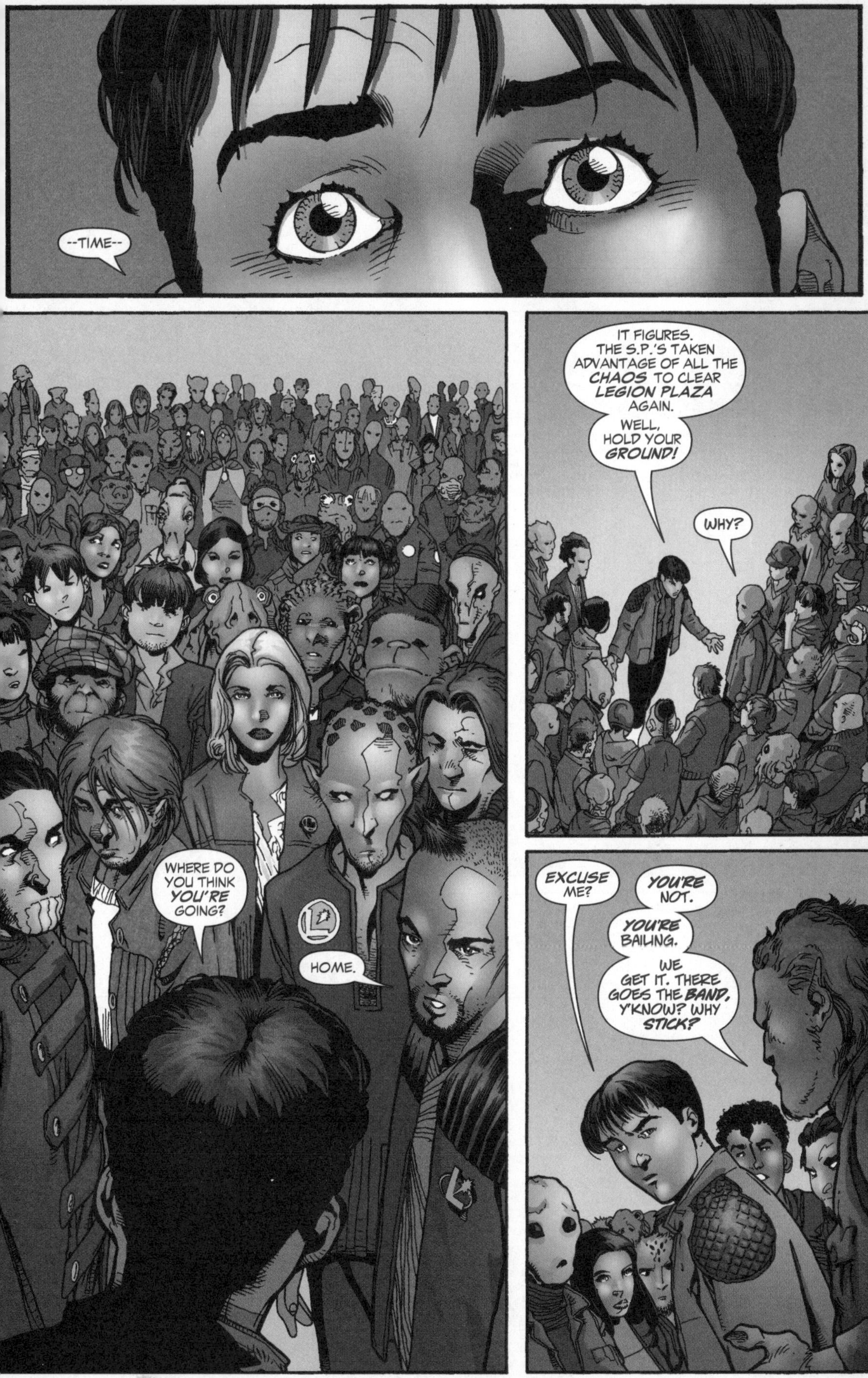
--TIME--
IT FIGURES. THE S.P.'S TAKEN ADVANTAGE OF ALL THE CHAOS TO CLEAR LEGION PLAZA AGAIN.
WELL, HOLD YOUR GROUND!
WHY?
WHERE DO YOU THINK YOU'RE GOING?
HOME.
EXCUSE ME?
YOU'RE NOT.
YOU'RE BAILING.
WE GET IT. THERE GOES THE BAND, Y'KNOW? WHY STICK?

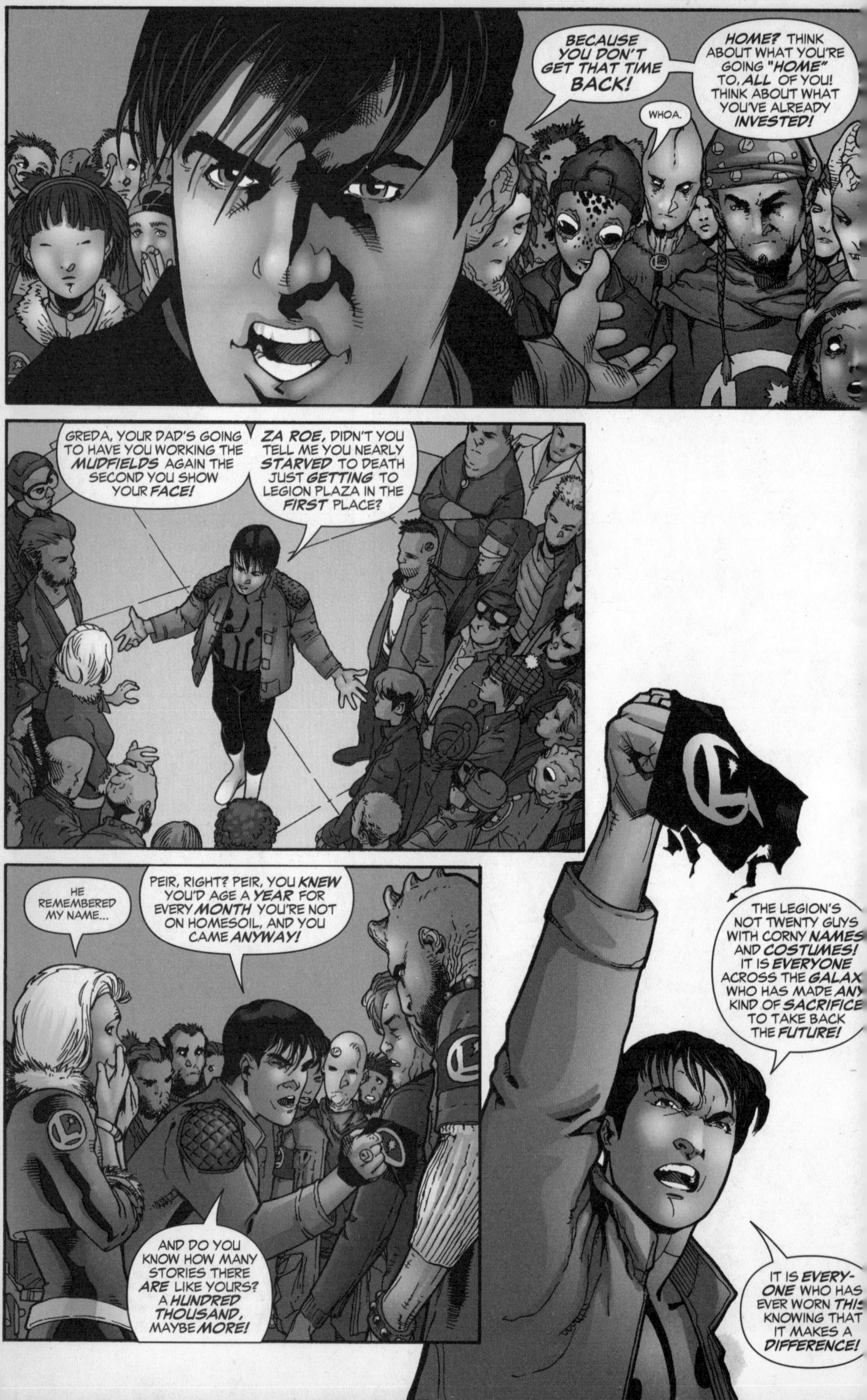
BECAUSE YOU DON'T GET THAT TIME BACK!
HOME? THINK ABOUT WHAT YOU'RE GOING "HOME" TO, ALL OF YOU! THINK ABOUT WHAT YOU'VE ALREADY INVESTED!
WHOA.
GREDA, YOUR DAD'S GOING TO HAVE YOU WORKING THE MUDFIELDS AGAIN THE SECOND YOU SHOW YOUR FACE!
ZA ROE, DIDN'T YOU TELL ME YOU NEARLY STARVED TO DEATH JUST GETTING TO LEGION PLAZA IN THE FIRST PLACE?
HE REMEMBERED MY NAME...
PEIR, RIGHT? PEIR, YOU KNEW YOU'D AGE A YEAR FOR EVERY MONTH YOU'RE NOT ON HOMESOIL, AND YOU CAME ANYWAY!
AND DO YOU KNOW HOW MANY STORIES THERE ARE LIKE YOURS? A HUNDRED THOUSAND, MAYBE MORE!
THE LEGION'S NOT TWENTY GUYS WITH CORNY NAMES AND COSTUMES! IT IS EVERYONE ACROSS THE GALAX WHO HAS MADE ANY KIND OF SACRIFICE TO TAKE BACK THE FUTURE!
IT IS EVERY-ONE WHO HAS EVER WORN THIS KNOWING THAT IT MAKES A DIFFERENCE!

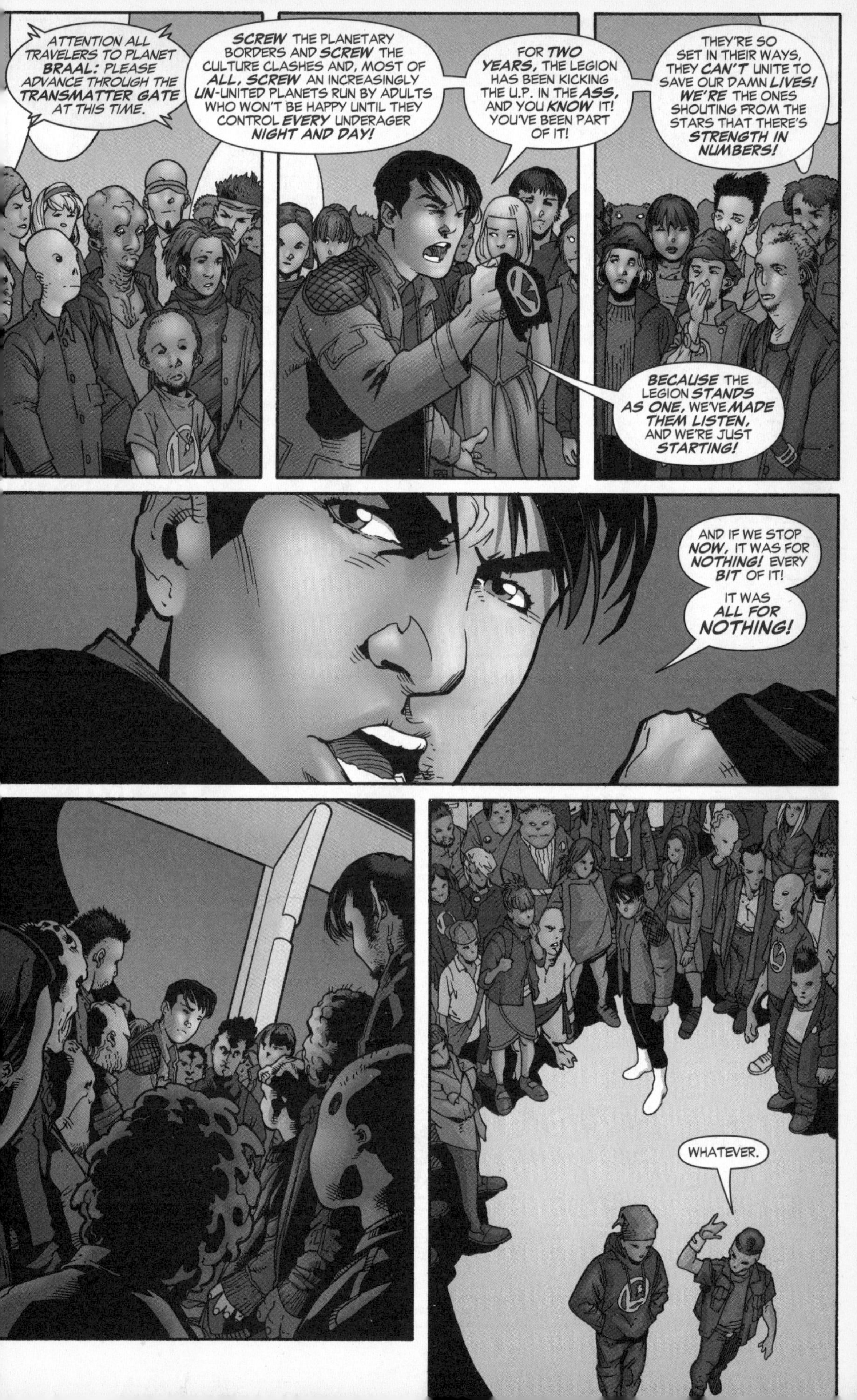
ATTENTION ALL TRAVELERS TO PLANET BRAAL: PLEASE ADVANCE THROUGH THE TRANSMATTER GATE AT THIS TIME.
SCREW THE PLANETARY BORDERS AND SCREW THE CULTURE CLASHES AND, MOST OF ALL, SCREW AN INCREASINGLY UN-UNITED PLANETS RUN BY ADULTS WHO WON'T BE HAPPY UNTIL THEY CONTROL EVERY UNDERAGER NIGHT AND DAY!
FOR TWO YEARS, THE LEGION HAS BEEN KICKING THE U.P. IN THE ASS, AND YOU KNOW IT! YOU'VE BEEN PART OF IT!
THEY'RE SO SET IN THEIR WAYS, THEY CAN'T UNITE TO SAVE OUR DAMN LIVES! WE'RE THE ONES SHOUTING FROM THE STARS THAT THERE'S STRENGTH IN NUMBERS!
BECAUSE THE LEGION STANDS AS ONE, WE'VE MADE THEM LISTEN, AND WE'RE JUST STARTING!
AND IF WE STOP NOW, IT WAS FOR NOTHING! EVERY BIT OF IT!
IT WAS ALL FOR NOTHING!
WHATEVER.

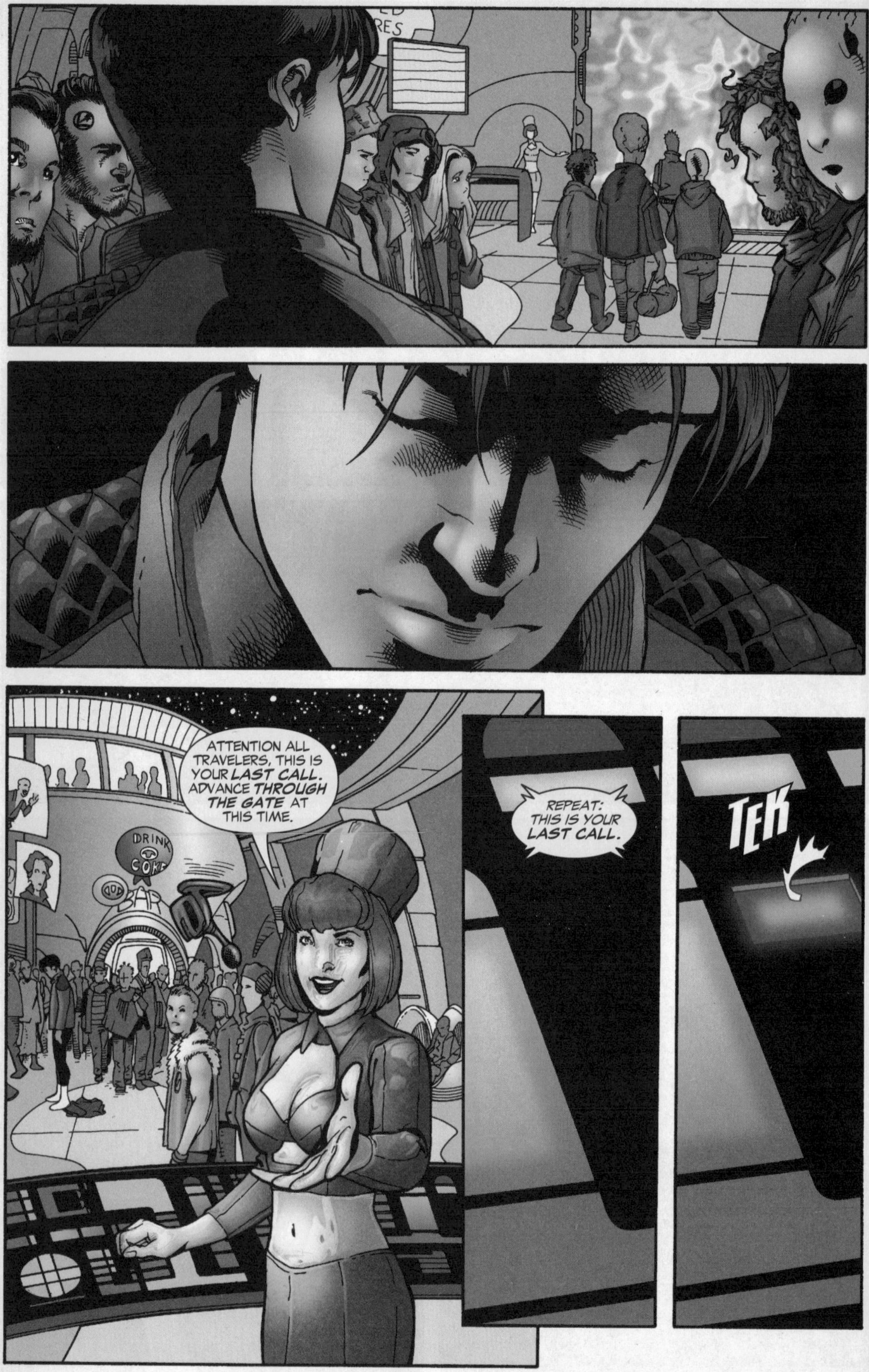
ATTENTION ALL TRAVELERS, THIS IS YOUR LAST CALL. ADVANCE THROUGH THE GATE AT THIS TIME.
DRINK COKE
BAR
REPEAT: THIS IS YOUR LAST CALL.
TEK

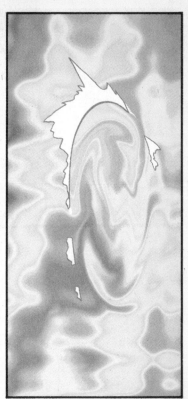

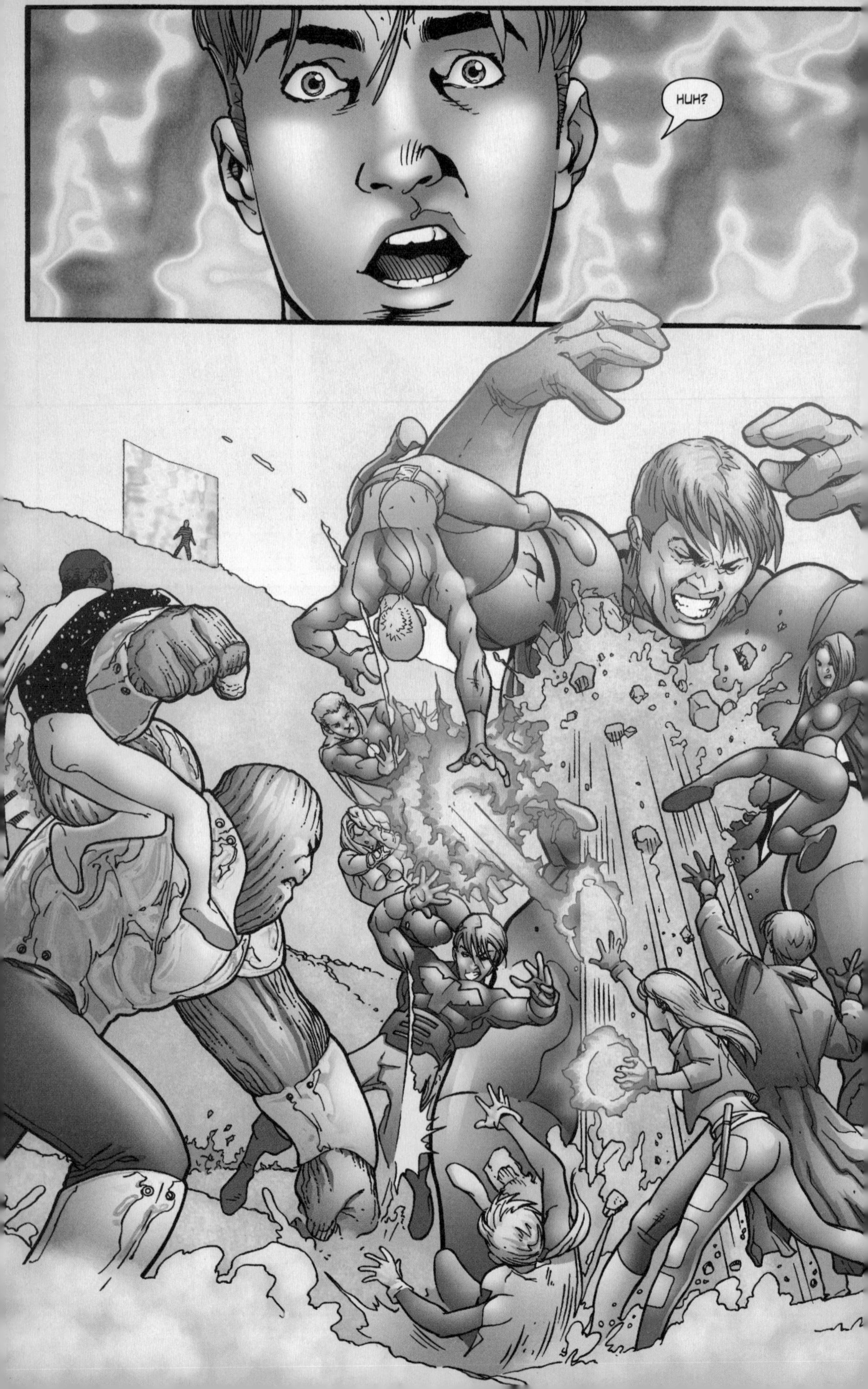
HUH?

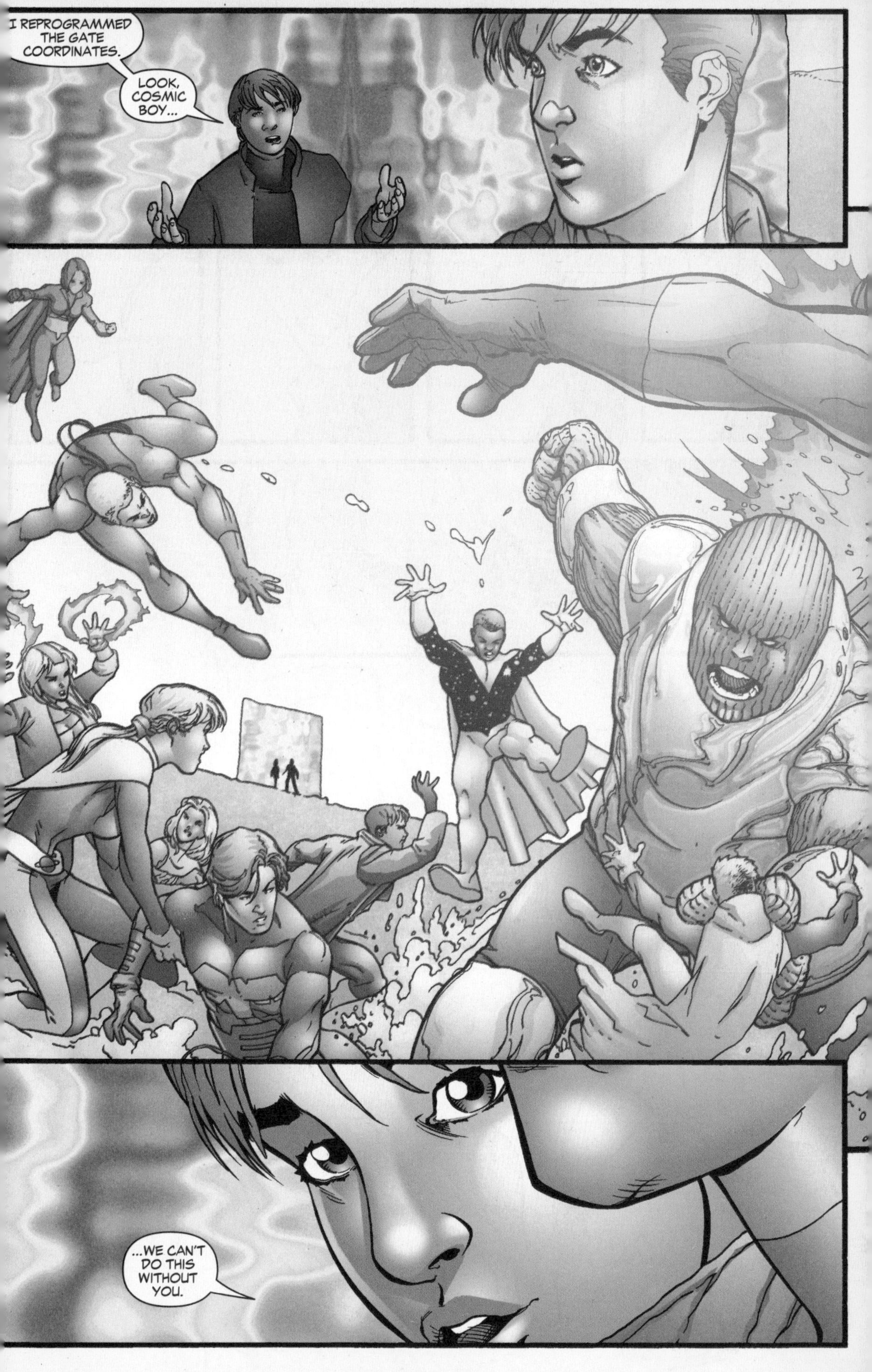
I REPROGRAMMED THE GATE COORDINATES.
LOOK, COSMIC BOY...
...WE CAN'T DO THIS WITHOUT YOU.

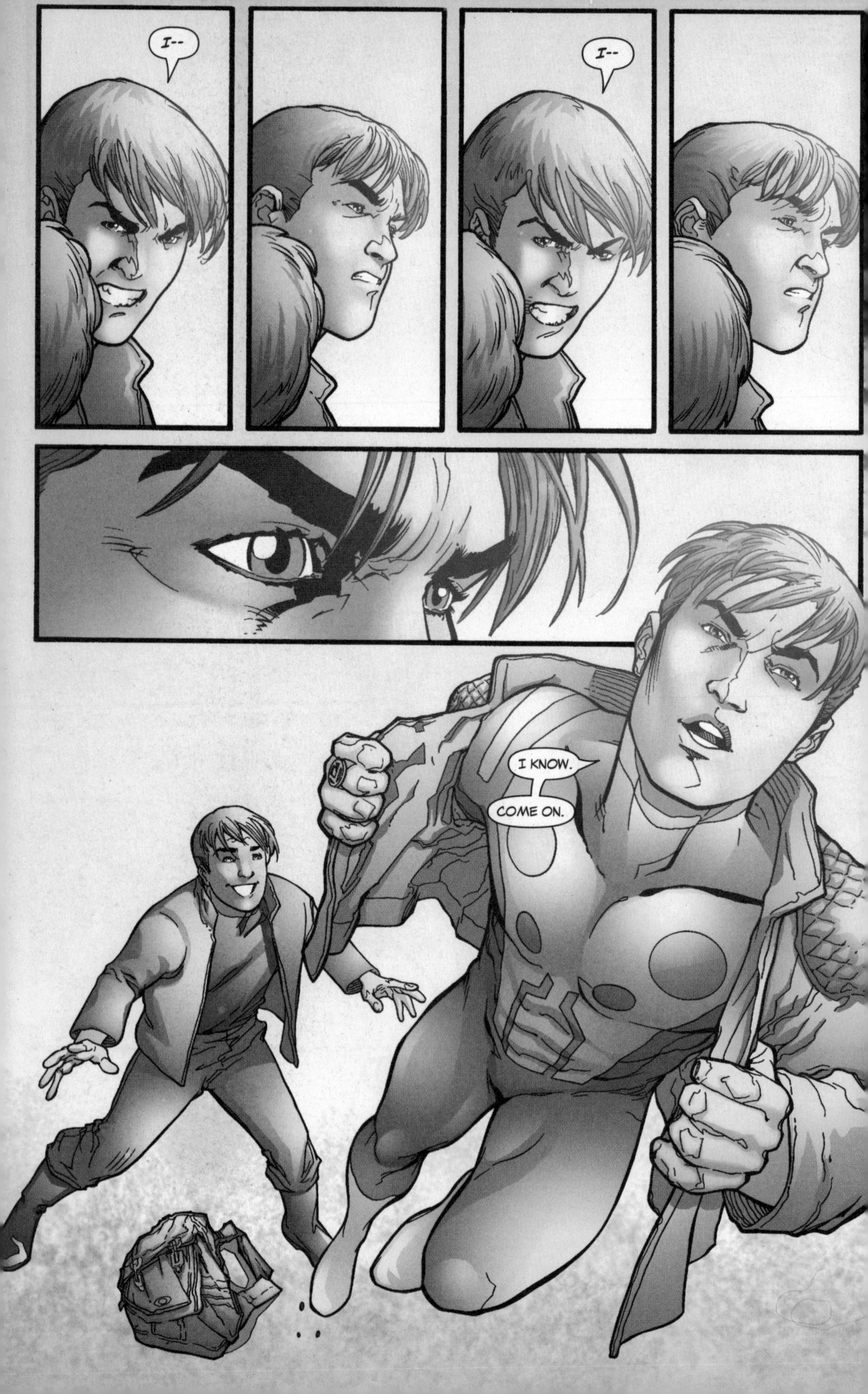
I--
I--
I KNOW.
COME ON.

Braal. The Krinn family.

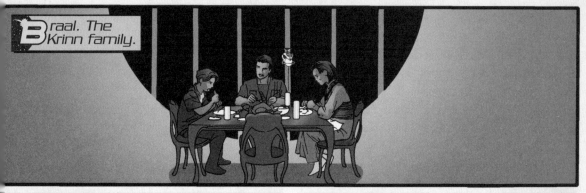

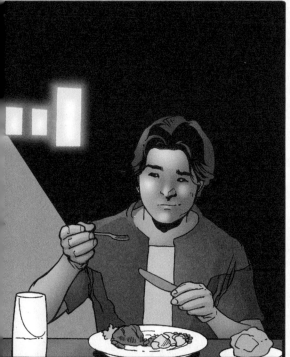

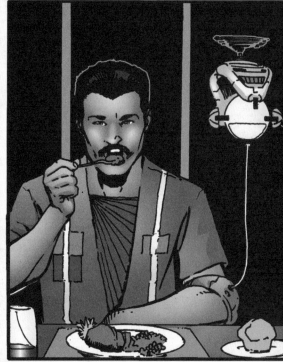

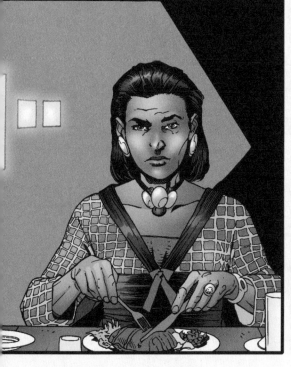

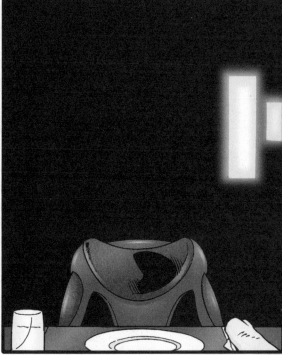

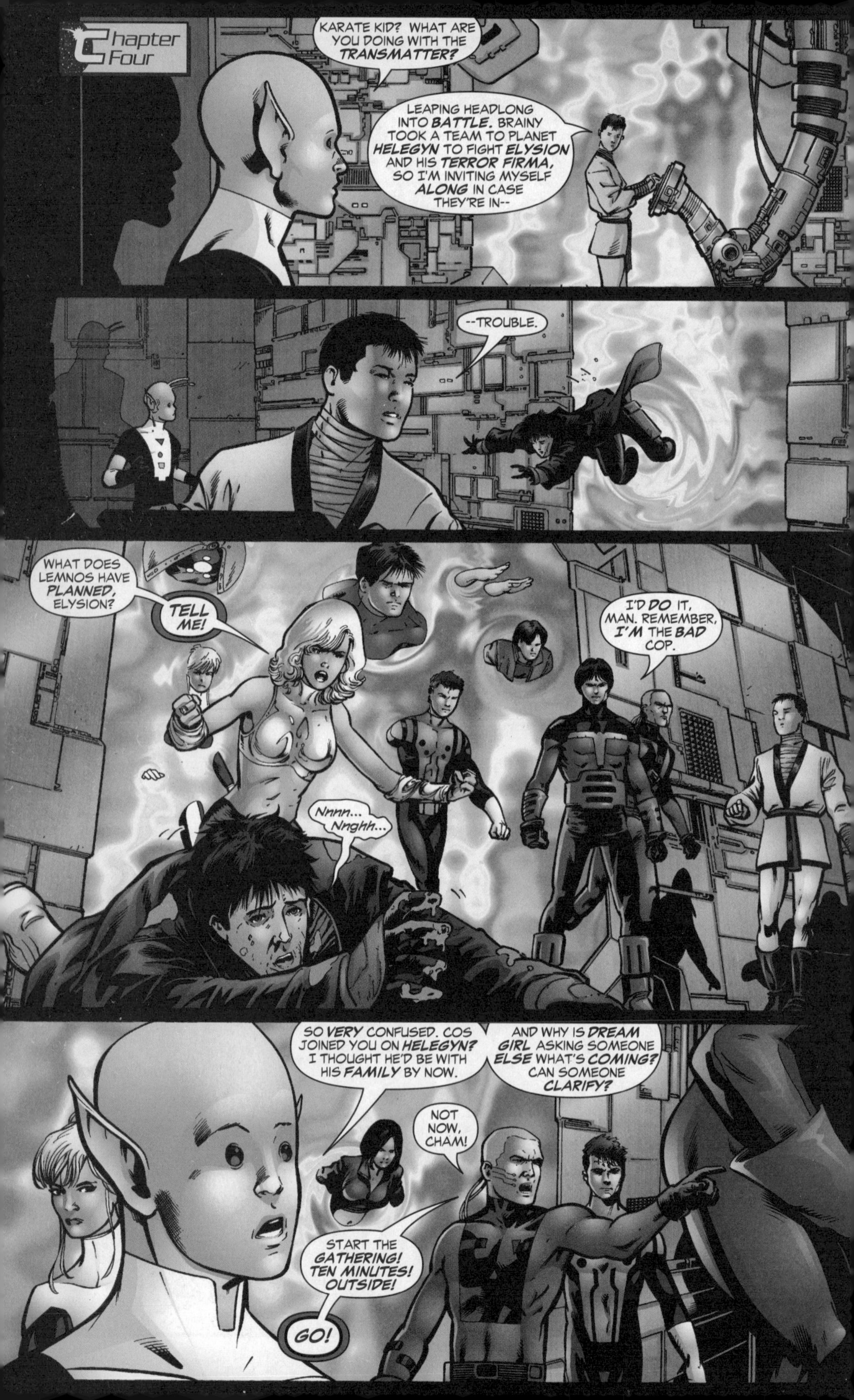
Chapter Four
KARATE KID? WHAT ARE YOU DOING WITH THE TRANSMATTER?
LEAPING HEADLONG INTO BATTLE. BRAINY TOOK A TEAM TO PLANET HELEGYN TO FIGHT ELYSION AND HIS TERROR FIRMA, SO I'M INVITING MYSELF ALONG IN CASE THEY'RE IN--
--TROUBLE.
WHAT DOES LEMNOS HAVE PLANNED, ELYSION?
TELL ME!
I'D DO IT, MAN. REMEMBER, I'M THE BAD COP.
Nnnn... Nnghh...
SO VERY CONFUSED. COS JOINED YOU ON HELEGYN? I THOUGHT HE'D BE WITH HIS FAMILY BY NOW.
AND WHY IS DREAM GIRL ASKING SOMEONE ELSE WHAT'S COMING? CAN SOMEONE CLARIFY?
NOT NOW, CHAM!
START THE GATHERING! TEN MINUTES! OUTSIDE!
GO!

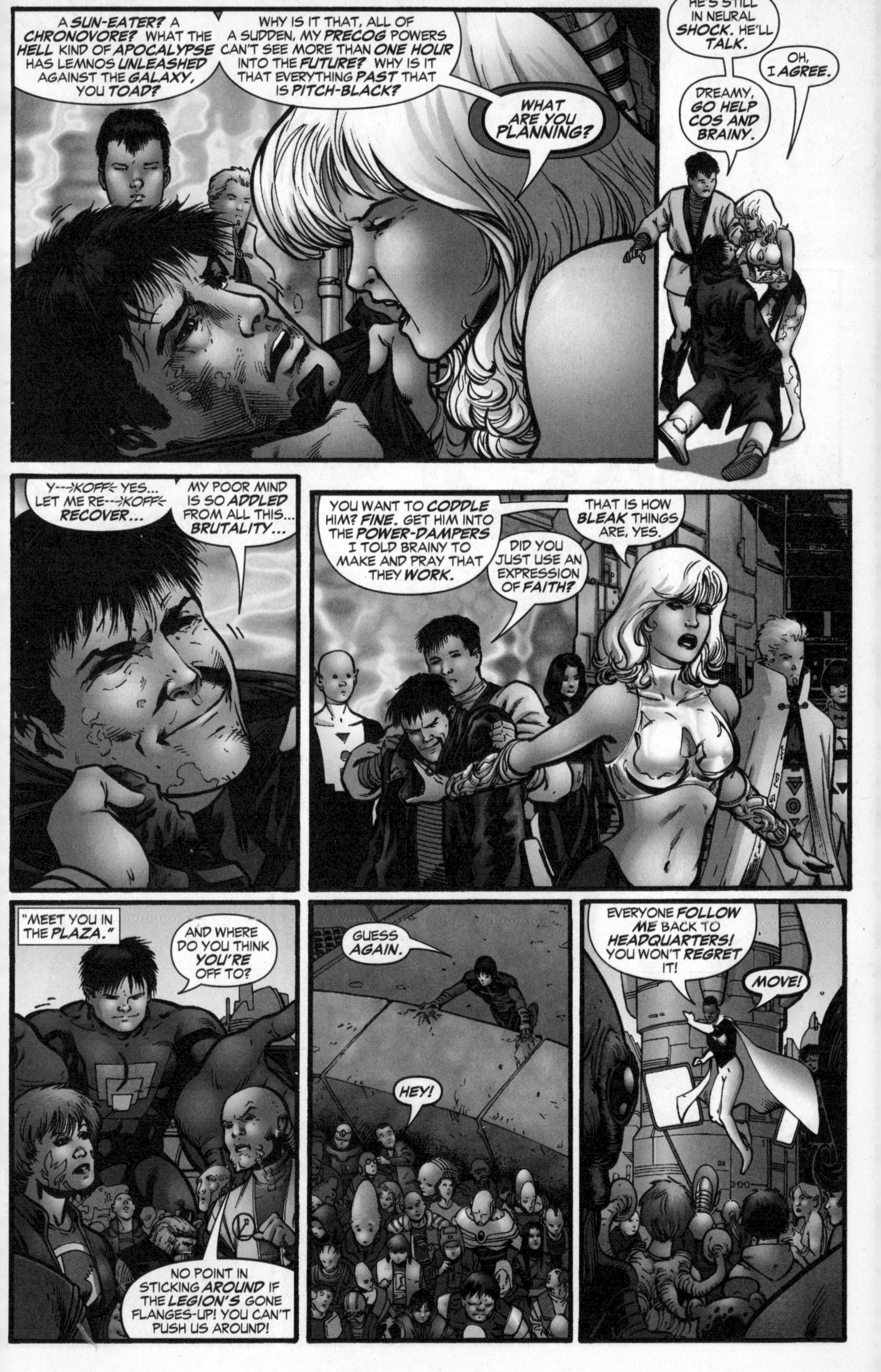
A SUN-EATER? A CHRONOVORE? WHAT THE HELL KIND OF APOCALYPSE HAS LEMNOS UNLEASHED AGAINST THE GALAXY, YOU TOAD?
WHY IS IT THAT, ALL OF A SUDDEN, MY PRECOG POWERS CAN'T SEE MORE THAN ONE HOUR INTO THE FUTURE? WHY IS IT THAT EVERYTHING PAST THAT IS PITCH-BLACK?
WHAT ARE YOU PLANNING?
HE'S STILL IN NEURAL SHOCK. HE'LL TALK.
OH, I AGREE.
DREAMY, GO HELP COS AND BRAINY.
Y-->KOFF< YES... LET ME RE-->KOFF< RECOVER...
MY POOR MIND IS SO ADDLED FROM ALL THIS... BRUTALITY...
YOU WANT TO CODDLE HIM? FINE. GET HIM INTO THE POWER-DAMPERS I TOLD BRAINY TO MAKE AND PRAY THAT THEY WORK.
DID YOU JUST USE AN EXPRESSION OF FAITH?
THAT IS HOW BLEAK THINGS ARE, YES.
"MEET YOU IN THE PLAZA."
AND WHERE DO YOU THINK YOU'RE OFF TO?
NO POINT IN STICKING AROUND IF THE LEGION'S GONE FLANGES-UP! YOU CAN'T PUSH US AROUND!
GUESS AGAIN.
HEY!
EVERYONE FOLLOW ME BACK TO HEADQUARTERS! YOU WON'T REGRET IT!
MOVE!

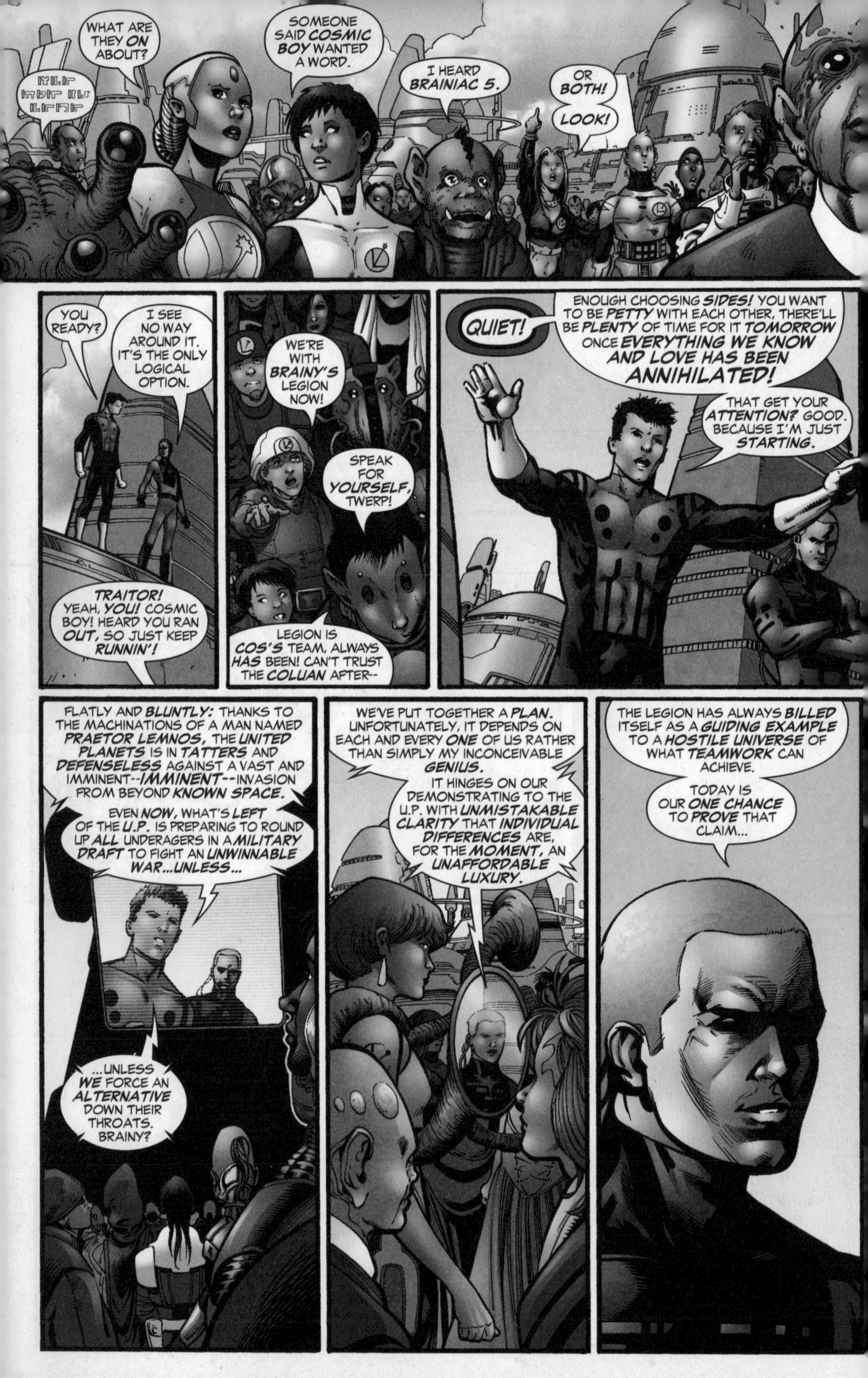
WHAT ARE THEY ON ABOUT?
SOMEONE SAID COSMIC BOY WANTED A WORD.
I HEARD BRAINIAC 5.
OR BOTH!
LOOK!
YOU READY?
I SEE NO WAY AROUND IT. IT'S THE ONLY LOGICAL OPTION.
TRAITOR! YEAH, YOU! COSMIC BOY! HEARD YOU RAN OUT, SO JUST KEEP RUNNIN'!
WE'RE WITH BRAINY'S LEGION NOW!
SPEAK FOR YOURSELF, TWERP!
LEGION IS COS'S TEAM, ALWAYS HAS BEEN! CAN'T TRUST THE COLUAN AFTER--
QUIET!
ENOUGH CHOOSING SIDES! YOU WANT TO BE PETTY WITH EACH OTHER, THERE'LL BE PLENTY OF TIME FOR IT TOMORROW ONCE EVERYTHING WE KNOW AND LOVE HAS BEEN ANNIHILATED!
THAT GET YOUR ATTENTION? GOOD. BECAUSE I'M JUST STARTING.
FLATLY AND BLUNTLY: THANKS TO THE MACHINATIONS OF A MAN NAMED PRAETOR LEMNOS, THE UNITED PLANETS IS IN TATTERS AND DEFENSELESS AGAINST A VAST AND IMMINENT--IMMINENT--INVASION FROM BEYOND KNOWN SPACE.
EVEN NOW, WHAT'S LEFT OF THE U.P. IS PREPARING TO ROUND UP ALL UNDERAGERS IN A MILITARY DRAFT TO FIGHT AN UNWINNABLE WAR...UNLESS...
...UNLESS WE FORCE AN ALTERNATIVE DOWN THEIR THROATS. BRAINY?
WE'VE PUT TOGETHER A PLAN. UNFORTUNATELY, IT DEPENDS ON EACH AND EVERY ONE OF US RATHER THAN SIMPLY MY INCONCEIVABLE GENIUS.
IT HINGES ON OUR DEMONSTRATING TO THE U.P. WITH UNMISTAKABLE CLARITY THAT INDIVIDUAL DIFFERENCES ARE, FOR THE MOMENT, AN UNAFFORDABLE LUXURY.
THE LEGION HAS ALWAYS BILLED ITSELF AS A GUIDING EXAMPLE TO A HOSTILE UNIVERSE OF WHAT TEAMWORK CAN ACHIEVE.
TODAY IS OUR ONE CHANCE TO PROVE THAT CLAIM...

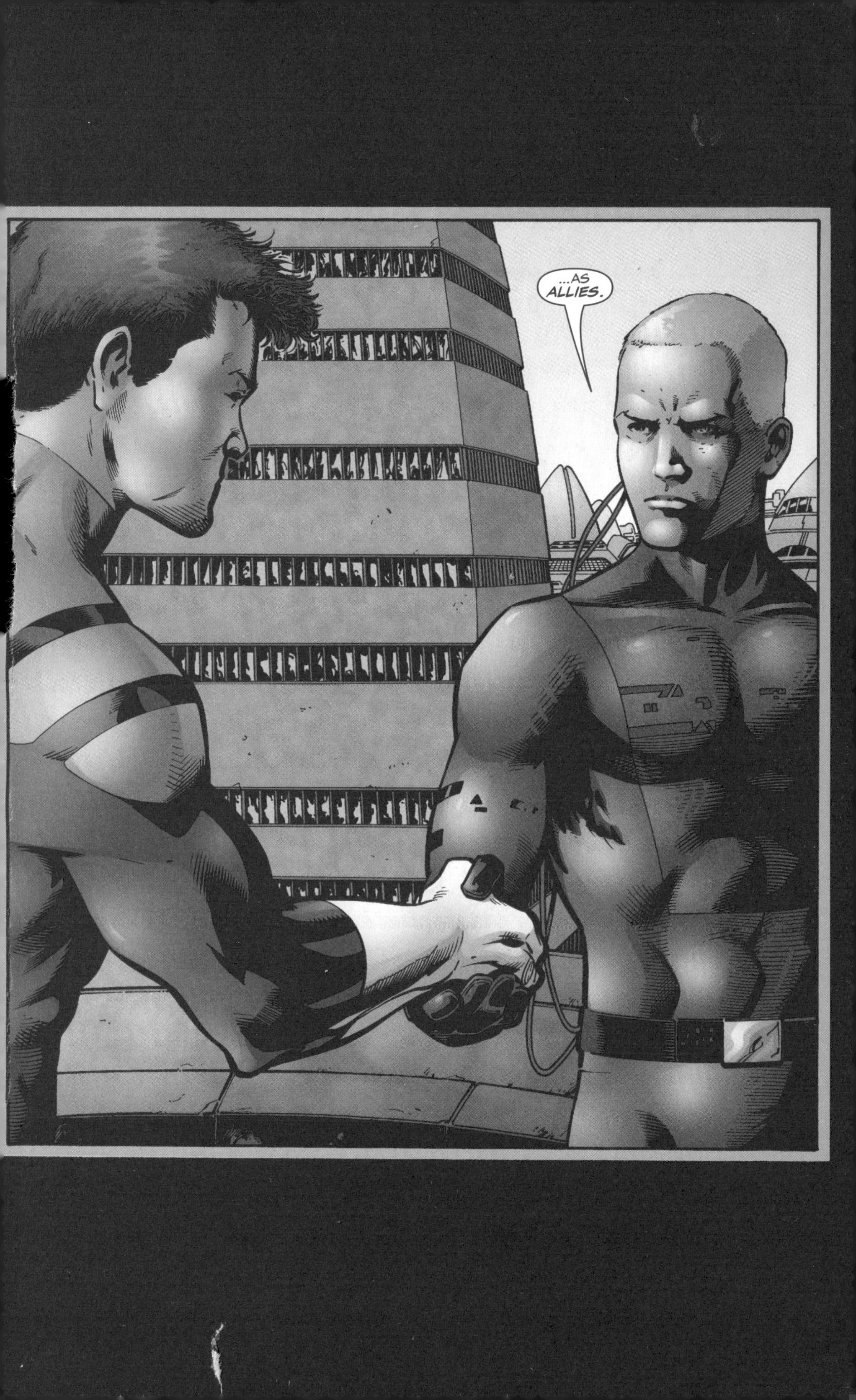
...AS ALLIES.

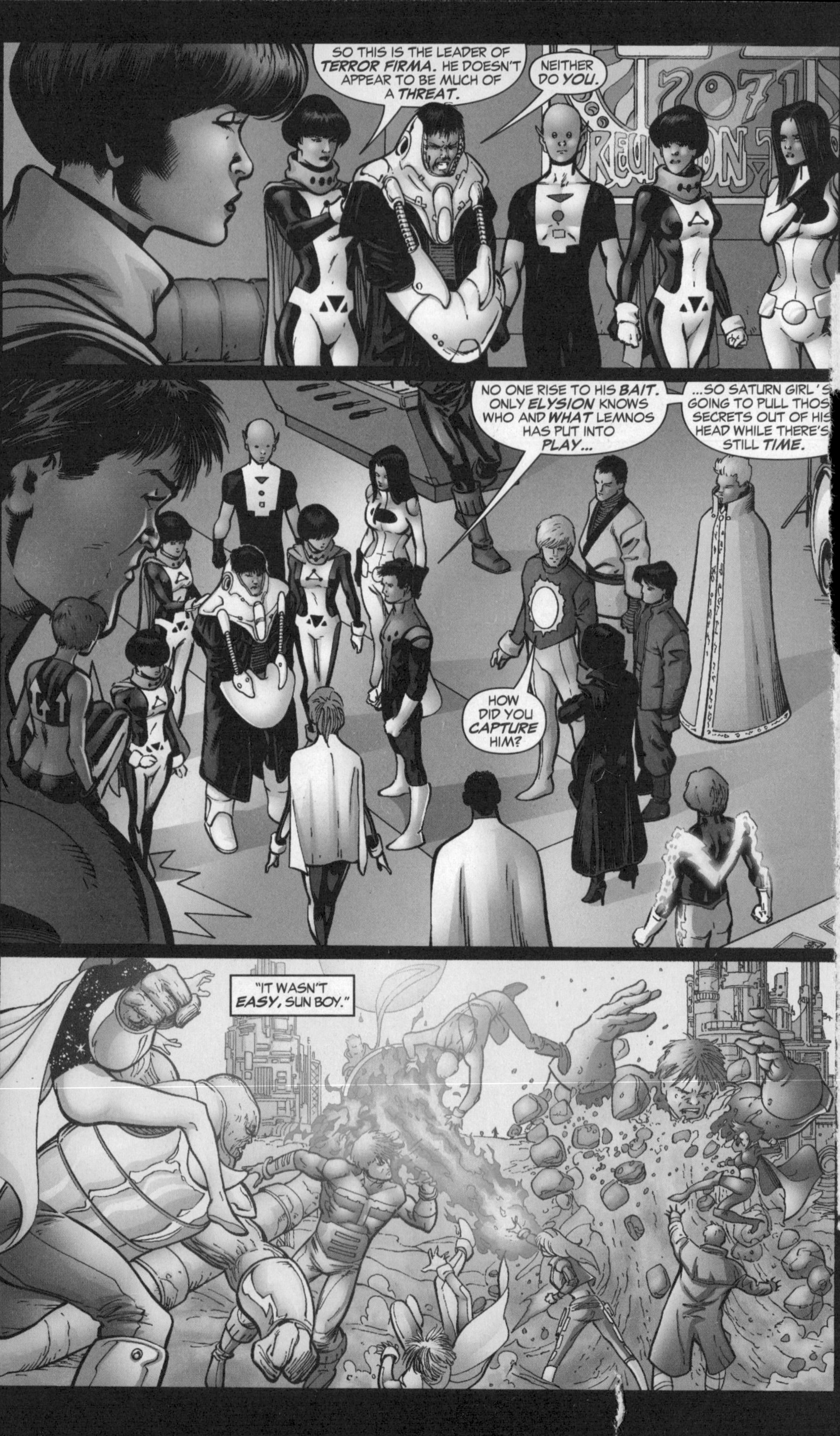
SO THIS IS THE LEADER OF TERROR FIRMA. HE DOESN'T APPEAR TO BE MUCH OF A THREAT.
NEITHER DO YOU.
NO ONE RISE TO HIS BAIT. ONLY ELYSION KNOWS WHO AND WHAT LEMNOS HAS PUT INTO PLAY...
...SO SATURN GIRL'S GOING TO PULL THOS SECRETS OUT OF HIS HEAD WHILE THERE'S STILL TIME.
HOW DID YOU CAPTURE HIM?
"IT WASN'T EASY, SUN BOY."

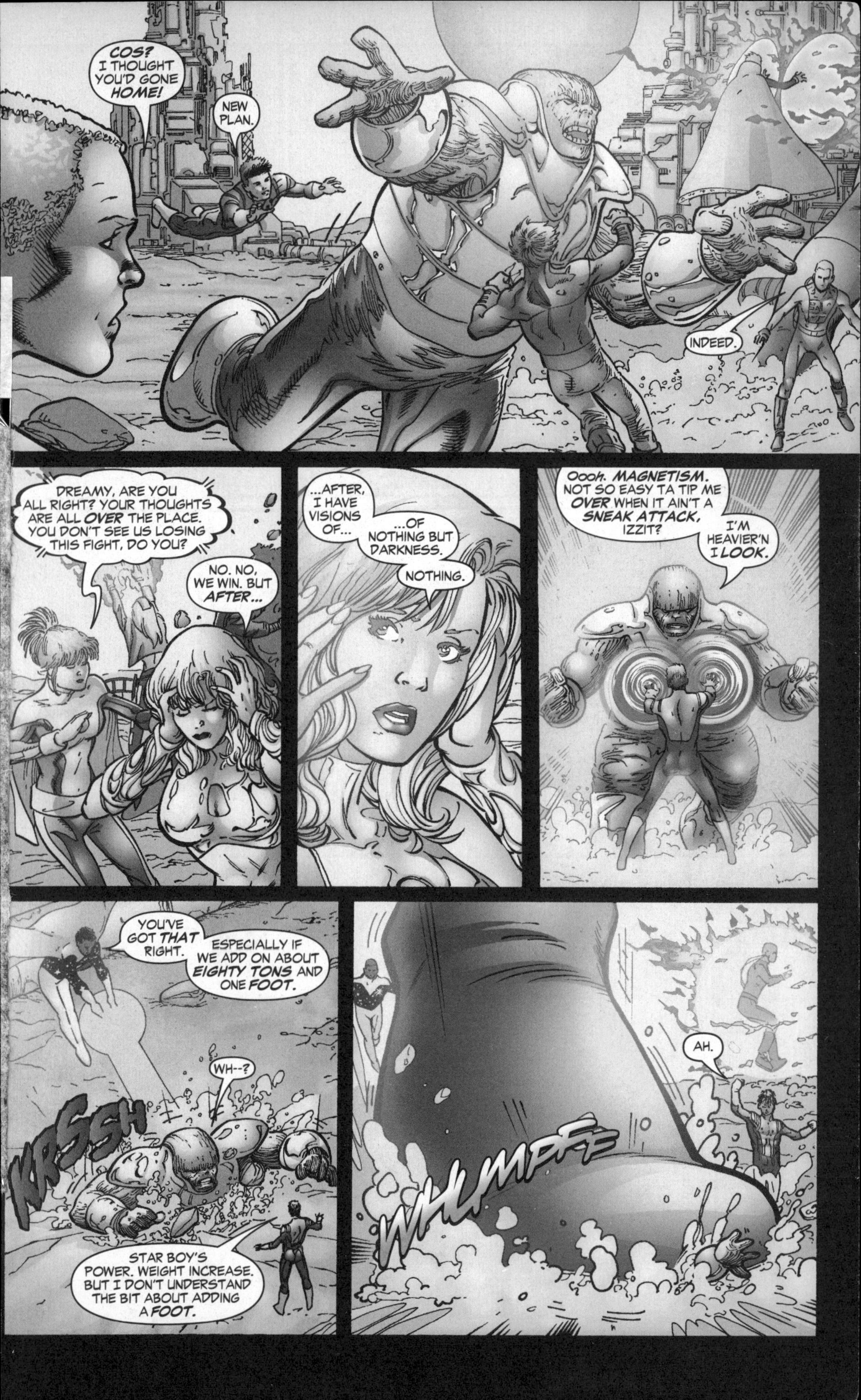
COS? I THOUGHT YOU'D GONE HOME!
NEW PLAN.
INDEED.
DREAMY, ARE YOU ALL RIGHT? YOUR THOUGHTS ARE ALL OVER THE PLACE. YOU DON'T SEE US LOSING THIS FIGHT, DO YOU?
NO. NO, WE WIN. BUT AFTER...
...AFTER, I HAVE VISIONS OF...
...OF NOTHING BUT DARKNESS.
NOTHING.
Oooh. MAGNETISM. NOT SO EASY TA TIP ME OVER WHEN IT AIN'T A SNEAK ATTACK, IZZIT?
I'M HEAVIER'N I LOOK.
YOU'VE GOT THAT RIGHT.
ESPECIALLY IF WE ADD ON ABOUT EIGHTY TONS AND ONE FOOT.
WH--?
KRSSH
STAR BOY'S POWER. WEIGHT INCREASE. BUT I DON'T UNDERSTAND THE BIT ABOUT ADDING A FOOT.
AH.
WHUMPFF

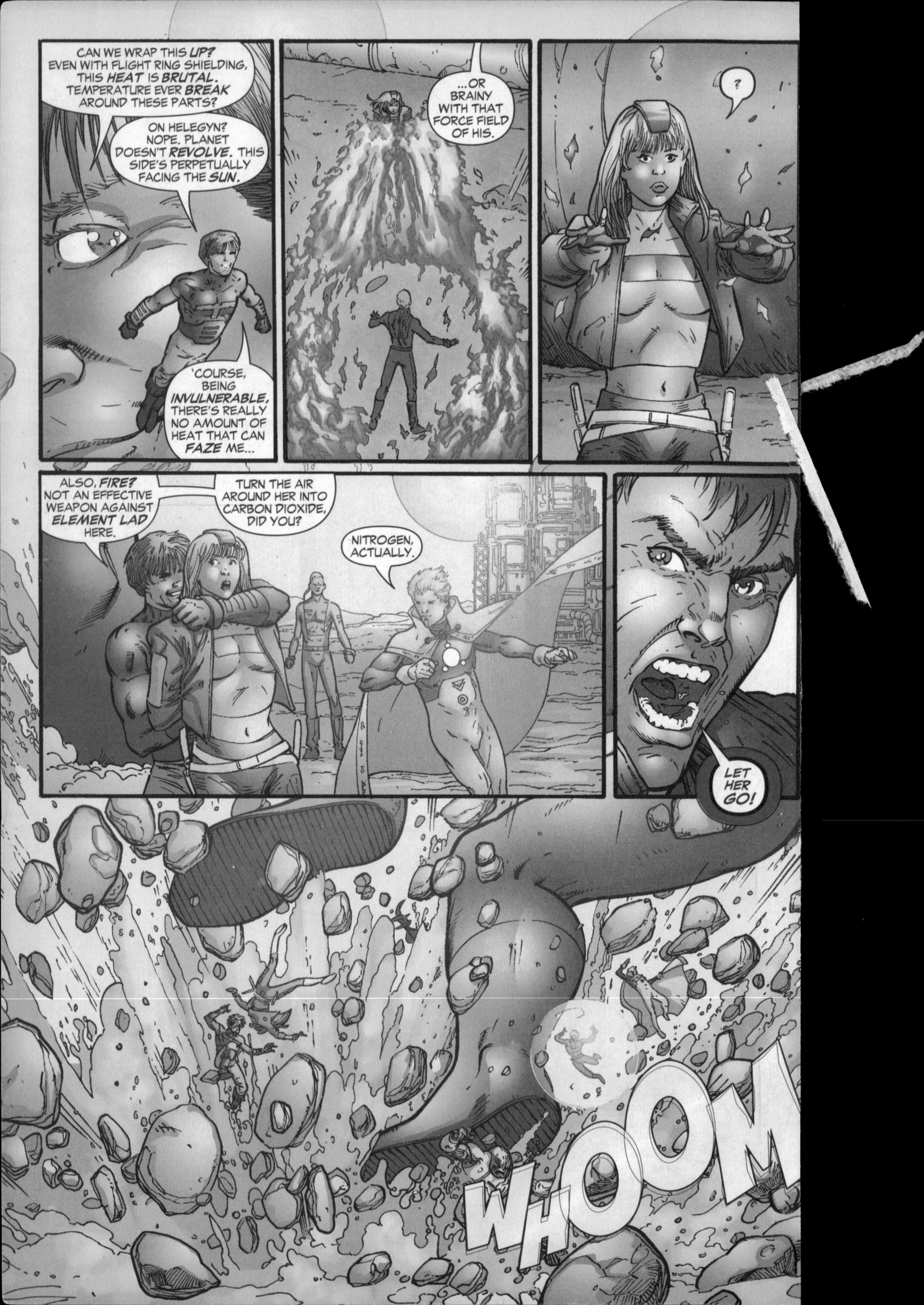
CAN WE WRAP THIS UP? EVEN WITH FLIGHT RING SHIELDING, THIS HEAT IS BRUTAL. TEMPERATURE EVER BREAK AROUND THESE PARTS?
ON HELEGYN? NOPE. PLANET DOESN'T REVOLVE. THIS SIDE'S PERPETUALLY FACING THE SUN.
'COURSE, BEING INVULNERABLE, THERE'S REALLY NO AMOUNT OF HEAT THAT CAN FAZE ME...
...OR BRAINY WITH THAT FORCE FIELD OF HIS.
?
ALSO, FIRE? NOT AN EFFECTIVE WEAPON AGAINST ELEMENT LAD HERE.
TURN THE AIR AROUND HER INTO CARBON DIOXIDE, DID YOU?
NITROGEN, ACTUALLY.
LET HER GO!
WHOOOM

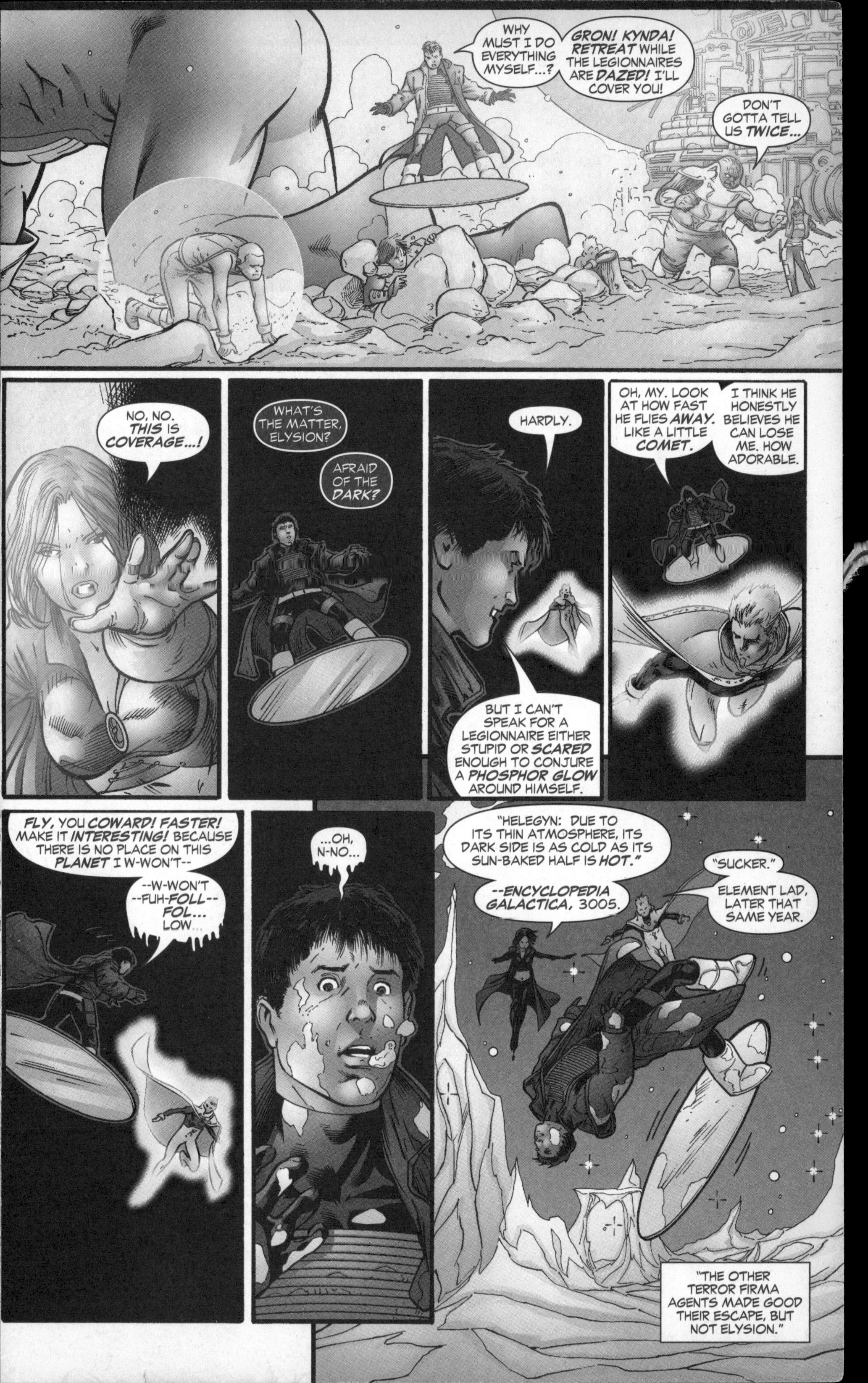

WHY MUST I DO EVERYTHING MYSELF...?
GRON! KYNDA! RETREAT WHILE THE LEGIONNAIRES ARE DAZED! I'LL COVER YOU!
DON'T GOTTA TELL US TWICE...
NO, NO. THIS IS COVERAGE...!
WHAT'S THE MATTER, ELYSION?
AFRAID OF THE DARK?
HARDLY.
BUT I CAN'T SPEAK FOR A LEGIONNAIRE EITHER STUPID OR SCARED ENOUGH TO CONJURE A PHOSPHOR GLOW AROUND HIMSELF.
OH, MY. LOOK AT HOW FAST HE FLIES AWAY. LIKE A LITTLE COMET.
I THINK HE HONESTLY BELIEVES HE CAN LOSE ME. HOW ADORABLE.
FLY, YOU COWARD! FASTER! MAKE IT INTERESTING! BECAUSE THERE IS NO PLACE ON THIS PLANET I W-WON'T--
--W-WON'T --FUH-FOLL-- FOL... LOW...
...OH, N-NO...
"HELEGYN: DUE TO ITS THIN ATMOSPHERE, ITS DARK SIDE IS AS COLD AS ITS SUN-BAKED HALF IS HOT."
--ENCYCLOPEDIA GALACTICA, 3005.
"SUCKER."
ELEMENT LAD, LATER THAT SAME YEAR.
"THE OTHER TERROR FIRMA AGENTS MADE GOOD THEIR ESCAPE, BUT NOT ELYSION."

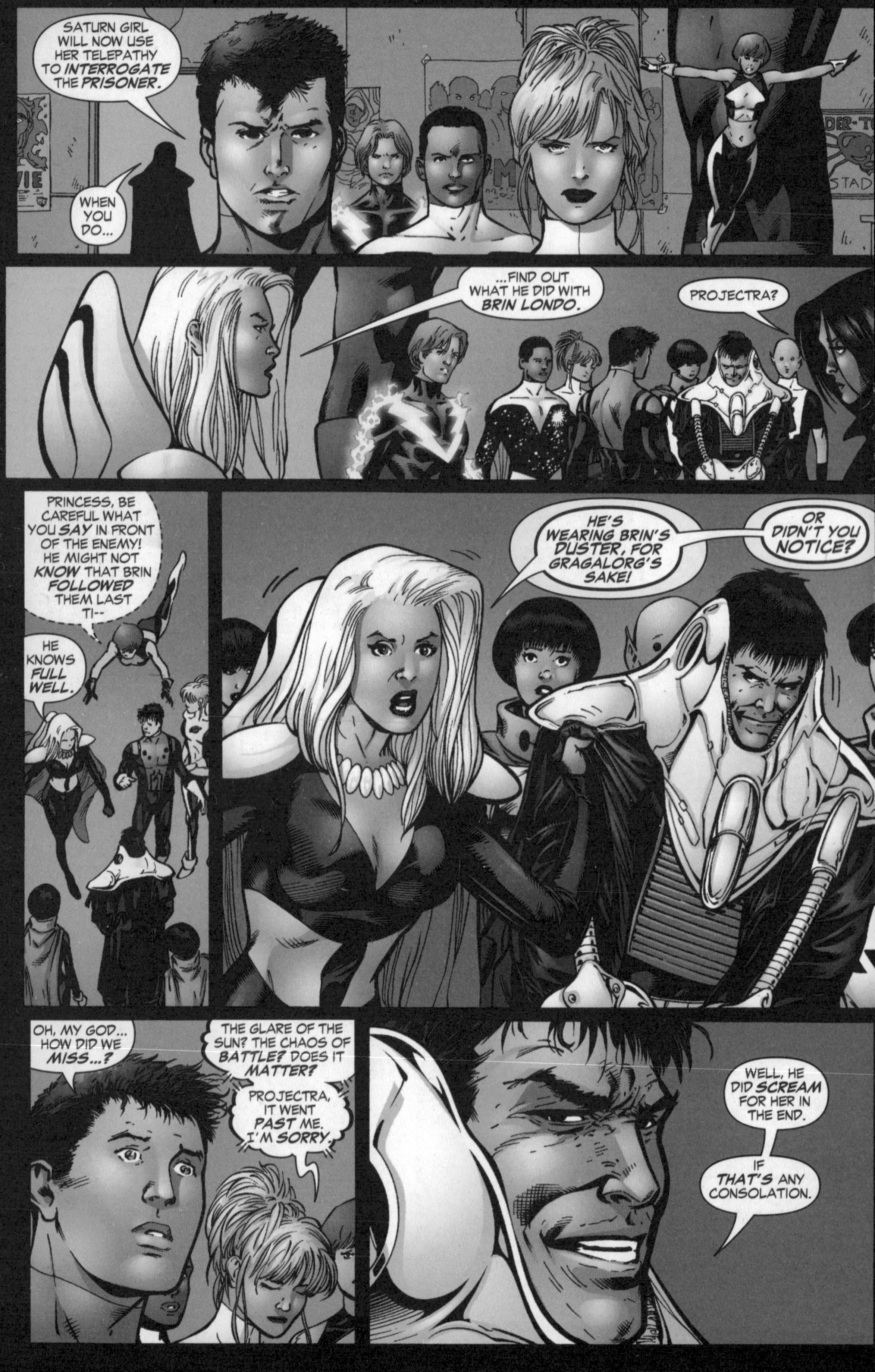

SATURN GIRL WILL NOW USE HER TELEPATHY TO INTERROGATE THE PRISONER.
WHEN YOU DO...
...FIND OUT WHAT HE DID WITH BRIN LONDO.
PROJECTRA?
PRINCESS, BE CAREFUL WHAT YOU SAY IN FRONT OF THE ENEMY! HE MIGHT NOT KNOW THAT BRIN FOLLOWED THEM LAST TI--
HE KNOWS FULL WELL.
HE'S WEARING BRIN'S DUSTER, FOR GRAGALORG'S SAKE!
OR DIDN'T YOU NOTICE?
OH, MY GOD... HOW DID WE MISS...?
THE GLARE OF THE SUN? THE CHAOS OF BATTLE? DOES IT MATTER?
PROJECTRA, IT WENT PAST ME. I'M SORRY.
WELL, HE DID SCREAM FOR HER IN THE END.
IF THAT'S ANY CONSOLATION.

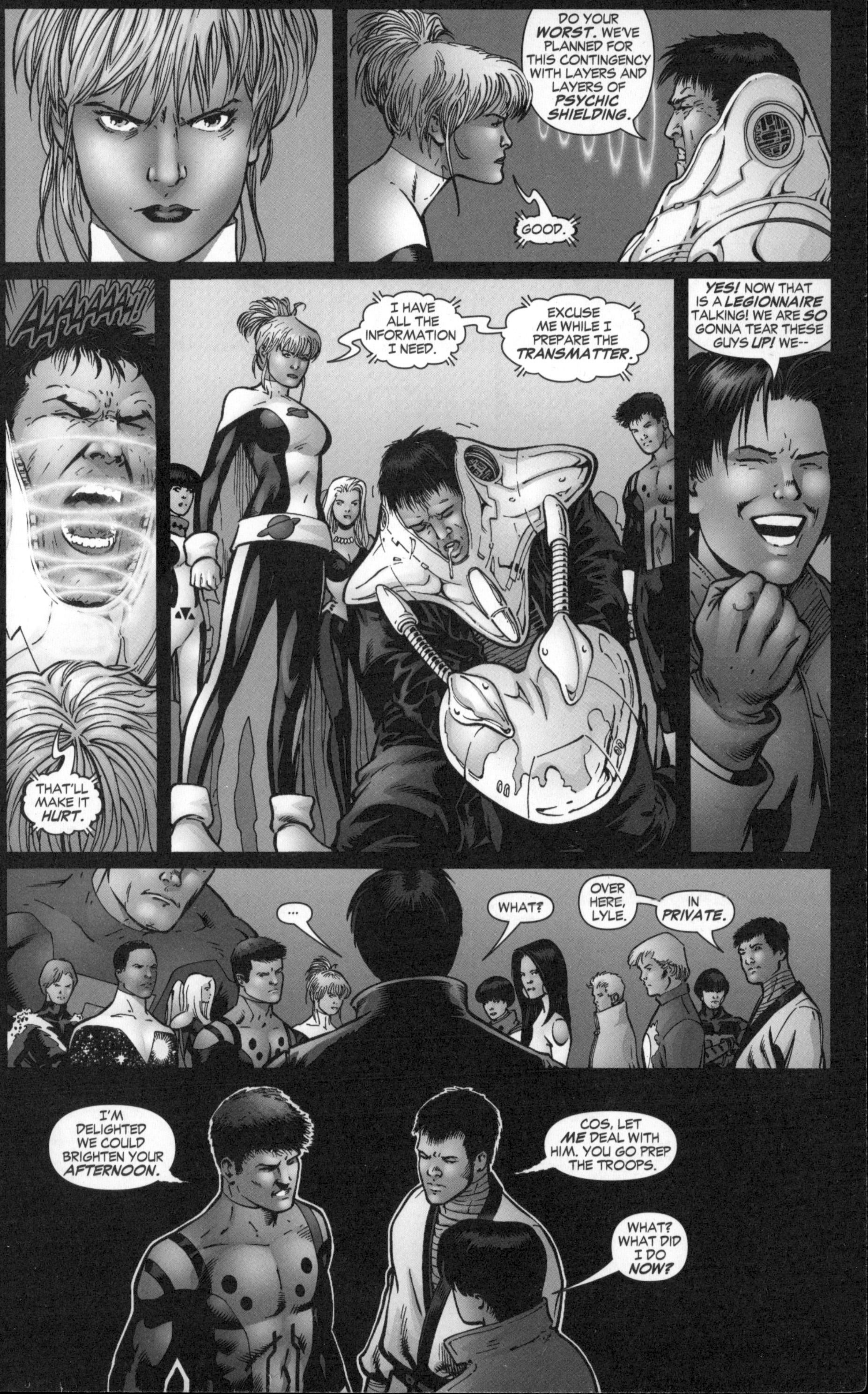
DO YOUR WORST. WE'VE PLANNED FOR THIS CONTINGENCY WITH LAYERS AND LAYERS OF PSYCHIC SHIELDING.
GOOD.
AAAAAAH!
THAT'LL MAKE IT HURT.
I HAVE ALL THE INFORMATION I NEED.
EXCUSE ME WHILE I PREPARE THE TRANSMATTER.
YES! NOW THAT IS A LEGIONNAIRE TALKING! WE ARE SO GONNA TEAR THESE GUYS UP! WE--
...
WHAT?
OVER HERE, LYLE.
IN PRIVATE.
I'M DELIGHTED WE COULD BRIGHTEN YOUR AFTERNOON.
COS, LET ME DEAL WITH HIM. YOU GO PREP THE TROOPS.
WHAT? WHAT DID I DO NOW?

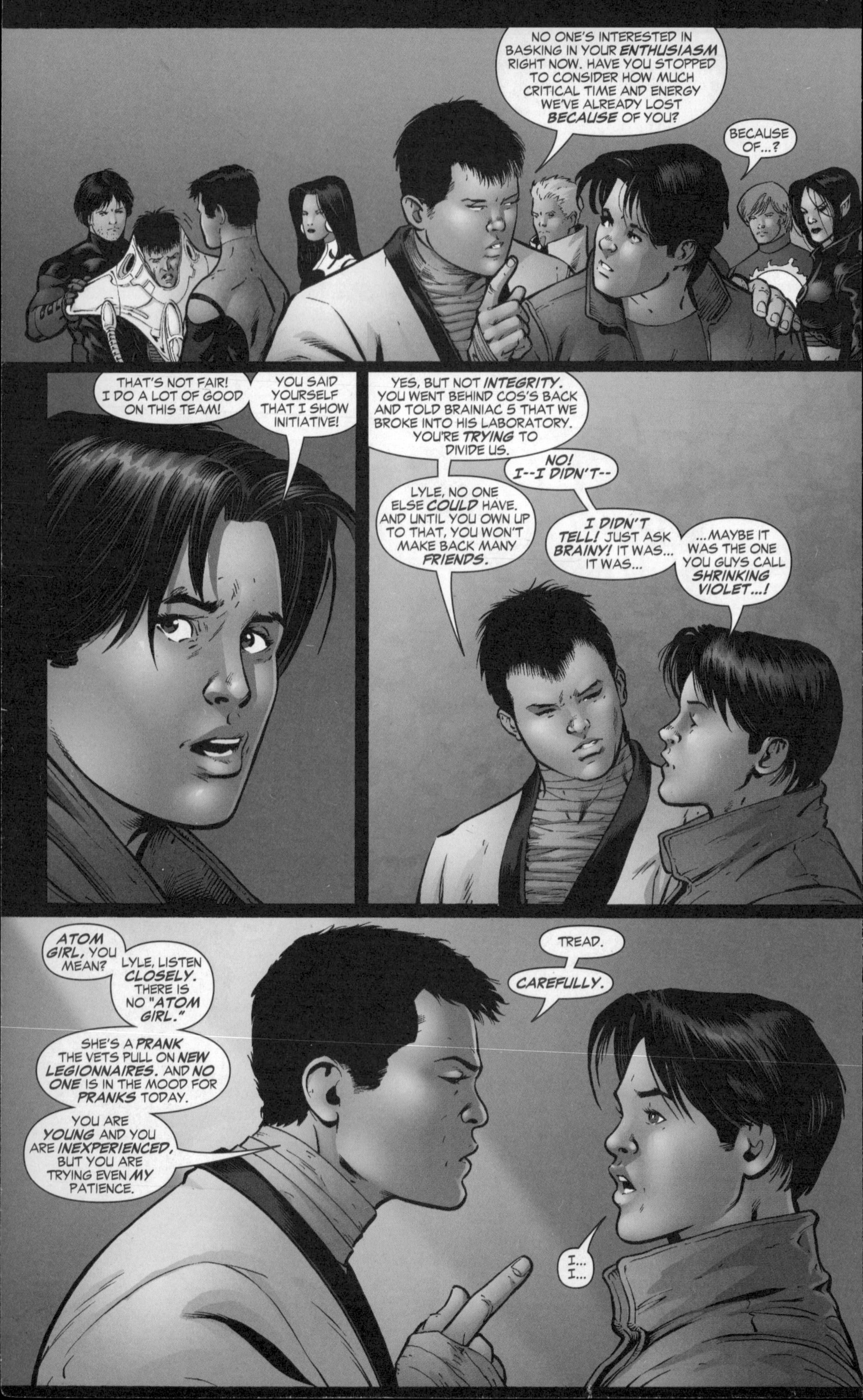
NO ONE'S INTERESTED IN BASKING IN YOUR ENTHUSIASM RIGHT NOW. HAVE YOU STOPPED TO CONSIDER HOW MUCH CRITICAL TIME AND ENERGY WE'VE ALREADY LOST BECAUSE OF YOU?
BECAUSE OF...?
THAT'S NOT FAIR! I DO A LOT OF GOOD ON THIS TEAM!
YOU SAID YOURSELF THAT I SHOW INITIATIVE!
YES, BUT NOT INTEGRITY. YOU WENT BEHIND COS'S BACK AND TOLD BRAINIAC 5 THAT WE BROKE INTO HIS LABORATORY. YOU'RE TRYING TO DIVIDE US.
NO! I--I DIDN'T--
LYLE, NO ONE ELSE COULD HAVE. AND UNTIL YOU OWN UP TO THAT, YOU WON'T MAKE BACK MANY FRIENDS.
I DIDN'T TELL! JUST ASK BRAINY! IT WAS... IT WAS...
...MAYBE IT WAS THE ONE YOU GUYS CALL SHRINKING VIOLET...!
ATOM GIRL, YOU MEAN?
LYLE, LISTEN CLOSELY. THERE IS NO "ATOM GIRL."
SHE'S A PRANK THE VETS PULL ON NEW LEGIONNAIRES. AND NO ONE IS IN THE MOOD FOR PRANKS TODAY.
YOU ARE YOUNG AND YOU ARE INEXPERIENCED, BUT YOU ARE TRYING EVEN MY PATIENCE.
TREAD.
CAREFULLY.
I... I...

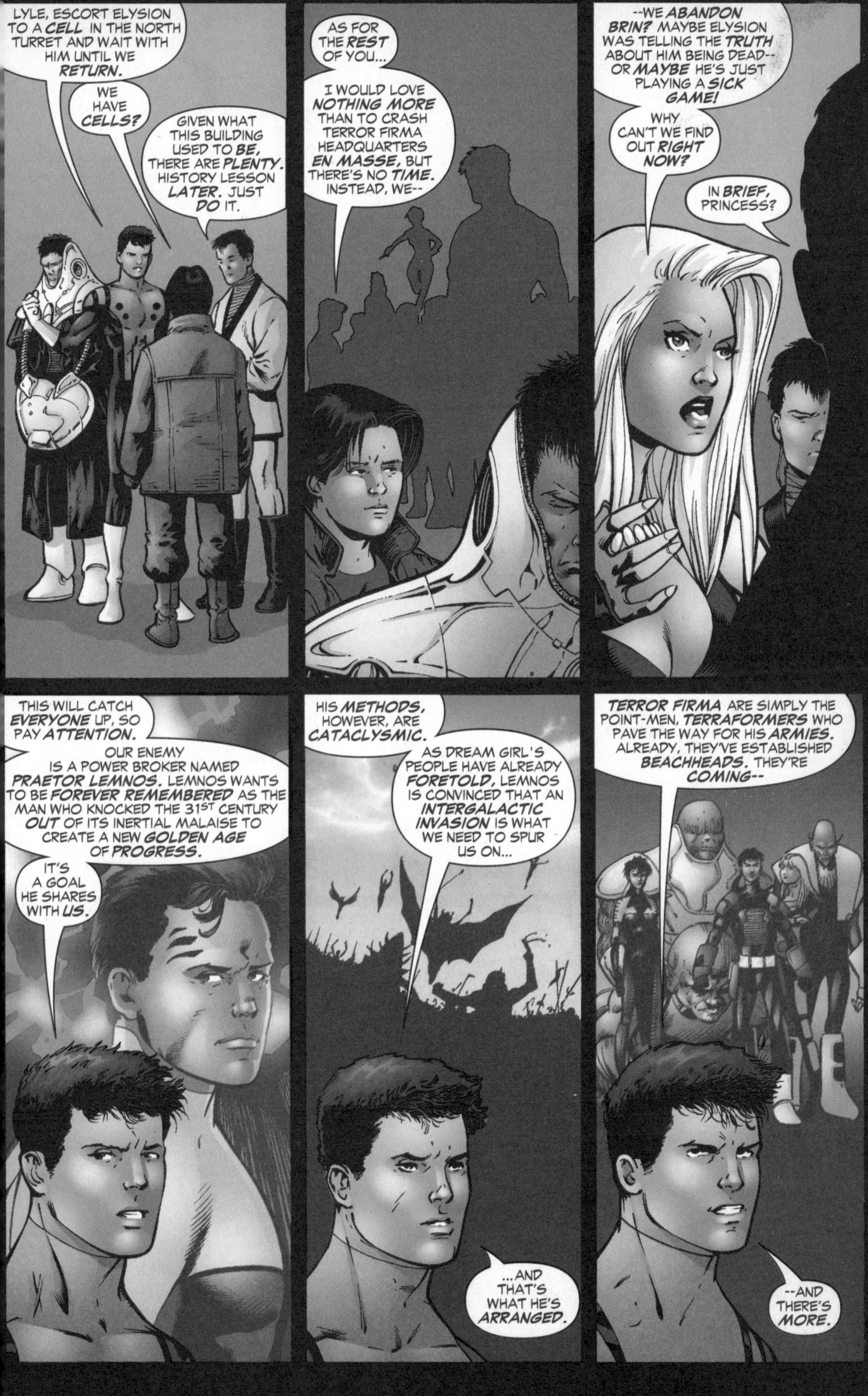

LYLE, ESCORT ELYSION TO A CELL IN THE NORTH TURRET AND WAIT WITH HIM UNTIL WE RETURN.
WE HAVE CELLS?
GIVEN WHAT THIS BUILDING USED TO BE, THERE ARE PLENTY. HISTORY LESSON LATER. JUST DO IT.
AS FOR THE REST OF YOU...
I WOULD LOVE NOTHING MORE THAN TO CRASH TERROR FIRMA HEADQUARTERS EN MASSE, BUT THERE'S NO TIME. INSTEAD, WE--
--WE ABANDON BRIN? MAYBE ELYSION WAS TELLING THE TRUTH ABOUT HIM BEING DEAD--OR MAYBE HE'S JUST PLAYING A SICK GAME!
WHY CAN'T WE FIND OUT RIGHT NOW?
IN BRIEF, PRINCESS?
THIS WILL CATCH EVERYONE UP, SO PAY ATTENTION.
OUR ENEMY IS A POWER BROKER NAMED PRAETOR LEMNOS. LEMNOS WANTS TO BE FOREVER REMEMBERED AS THE MAN WHO KNOCKED THE 31ST CENTURY OUT OF ITS INERTIAL MALAISE TO CREATE A NEW GOLDEN AGE OF PROGRESS.
IT'S A GOAL HE SHARES WITH US.
HIS METHODS, HOWEVER, ARE CATACLYSMIC.
AS DREAM GIRL'S PEOPLE HAVE ALREADY FORETOLD, LEMNOS IS CONVINCED THAT AN INTERGALACTIC INVASION IS WHAT WE NEED TO SPUR US ON...
...AND THAT'S WHAT HE'S ARRANGED.
TERROR FIRMA ARE SIMPLY THE POINT-MEN, TERRAFORMERS WHO PAVE THE WAY FOR HIS ARMIES. ALREADY, THEY'VE ESTABLISHED BEACHHEADS. THEY'RE COMING--
--AND THERE'S MORE.

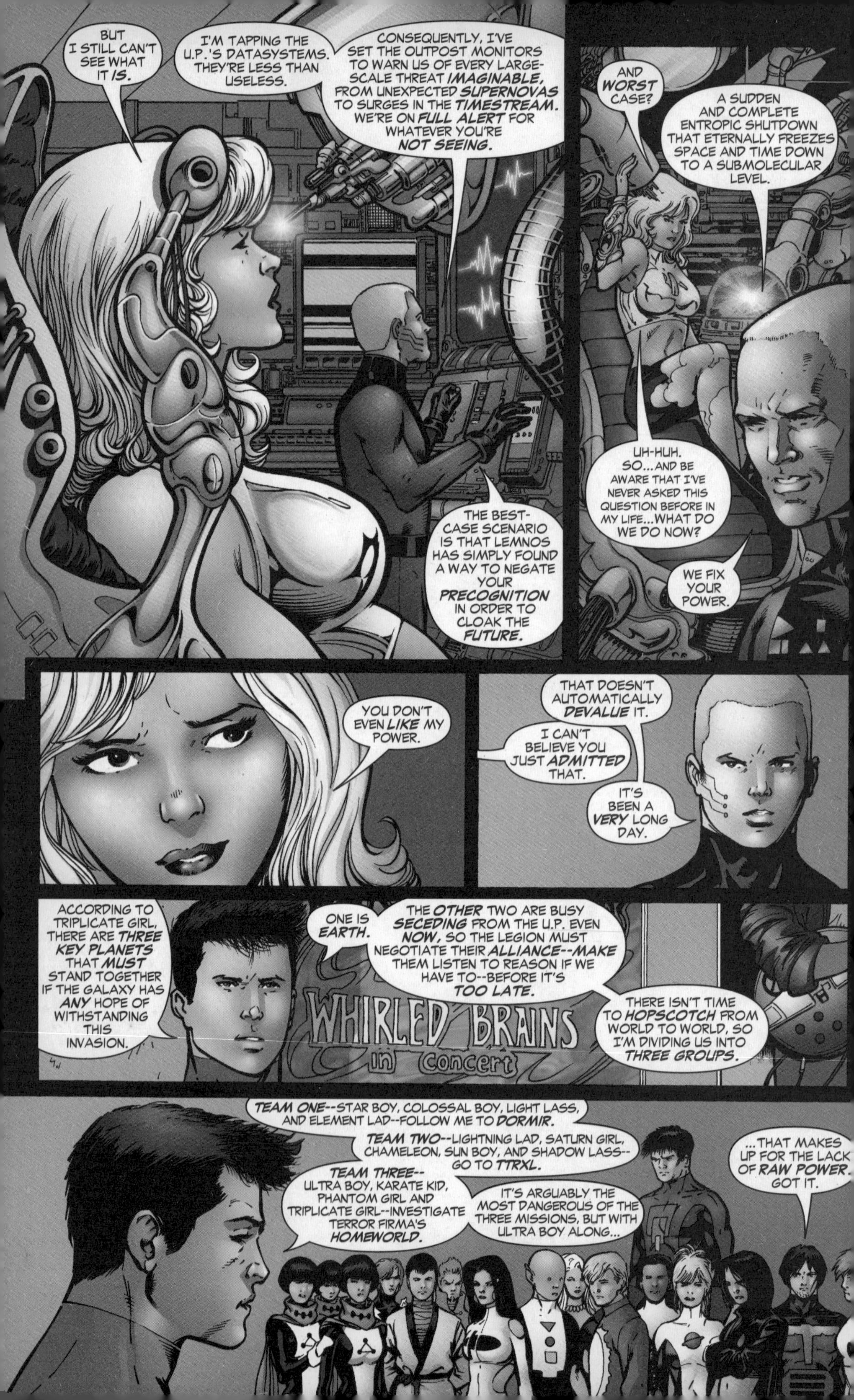

BUT I STILL CAN'T SEE WHAT IT IS.
I'M TAPPING THE U.P.'S DATASYSTEMS. THEY'RE LESS THAN USELESS.
CONSEQUENTLY, I'VE SET THE OUTPOST MONITORS TO WARN US OF EVERY LARGE-SCALE THREAT IMAGINABLE, FROM UNEXPECTED SUPERNOVAS TO SURGES IN THE TIMESTREAM. WE'RE ON FULL ALERT FOR WHATEVER YOU'RE NOT SEEING.
THE BEST-CASE SCENARIO IS THAT LEMNOS HAS SIMPLY FOUND A WAY TO NEGATE YOUR PRECOGNITION IN ORDER TO CLOAK THE FUTURE.
AND WORST CASE?
A SUDDEN AND COMPLETE ENTROPIC SHUTDOWN THAT ETERNALLY FREEZES SPACE AND TIME DOWN TO A SUBMOLECULAR LEVEL.
UH-HUH. SO...AND BE AWARE THAT I'VE NEVER ASKED THIS QUESTION BEFORE IN MY LIFE...WHAT DO WE DO NOW?
WE FIX YOUR POWER.
YOU DON'T EVEN LIKE MY POWER.
THAT DOESN'T AUTOMATICALLY DEVALUE IT.
I CAN'T BELIEVE YOU JUST ADMITTED THAT.
IT'S BEEN A VERY LONG DAY.
ACCORDING TO TRIPLICATE GIRL, THERE ARE THREE KEY PLANETS THAT MUST STAND TOGETHER IF THE GALAXY HAS ANY HOPE OF WITHSTANDING THIS INVASION.
ONE IS EARTH.
THE OTHER TWO ARE BUSY SECEDING FROM THE U.P. EVEN NOW, SO THE LEGION MUST NEGOTIATE THEIR ALLIANCE--MAKE THEM LISTEN TO REASON IF WE HAVE TO--BEFORE IT'S TOO LATE.
WHIRLED BRAINS in concert
THERE ISN'T TIME TO HOPSCOTCH FROM WORLD TO WORLD, SO I'M DIVIDING US INTO THREE GROUPS.
TEAM ONE--STAR BOY, COLOSSAL BOY, LIGHT LASS, AND ELEMENT LAD--FOLLOW ME TO DORMIR.
TEAM TWO--LIGHTNING LAD, SATURN GIRL, CHAMELEON, SUN BOY, AND SHADOW LASS--GO TO TTRXL.
TEAM THREE--ULTRA BOY, KARATE KID, PHANTOM GIRL AND TRIPLICATE GIRL--INVESTIGATE TERROR FIRMA'S HOMEWORLD.
IT'S ARGUABLY THE MOST DANGEROUS OF THE THREE MISSIONS, BUT WITH ULTRA BOY ALONG...
...THAT MAKES UP FOR THE LACK OF RAW POWER. GOT IT.

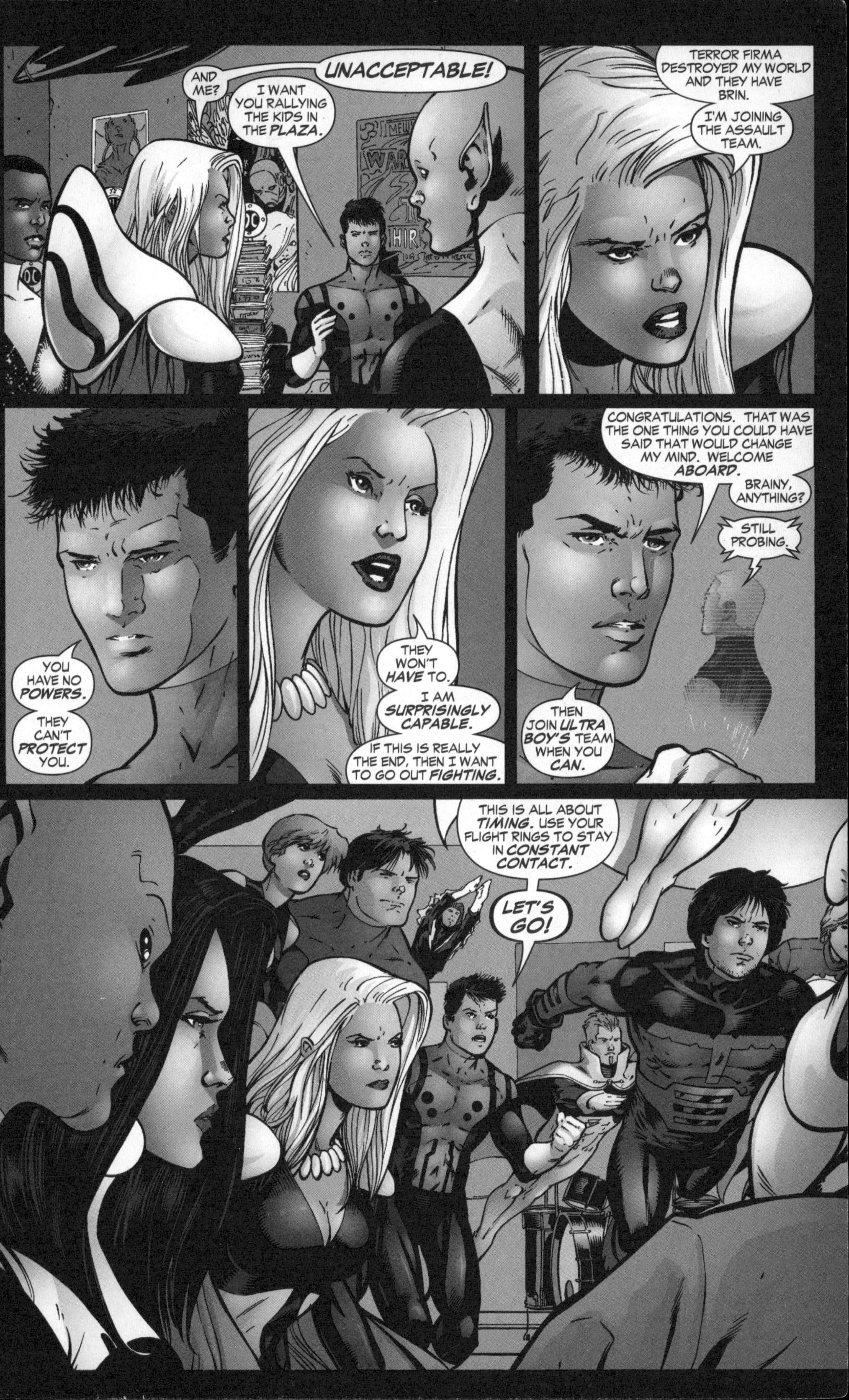
AND ME?
UNACCEPTABLE!
I WANT YOU RALLYING THE KIDS IN THE PLAZA.
TERROR FIRMA DESTROYED MY WORLD AND THEY HAVE BRIN.
I'M JOINING THE ASSAULT TEAM.
YOU HAVE NO POWERS.
THEY CAN'T PROTECT YOU.
THEY WON'T HAVE TO.
I AM SURPRISINGLY CAPABLE.
IF THIS IS REALLY THE END, THEN I WANT TO GO OUT FIGHTING.
CONGRATULATIONS. THAT WAS THE ONE THING YOU COULD HAVE SAID THAT WOULD CHANGE MY MIND. WELCOME ABOARD.
BRAINY, ANYTHING?
STILL PROBING.
THEN JOIN ULTRA BOY'S TEAM WHEN YOU CAN.
THIS IS ALL ABOUT TIMING. USE YOUR FLIGHT RINGS TO STAY IN CONSTANT CONTACT.
LET'S GO!

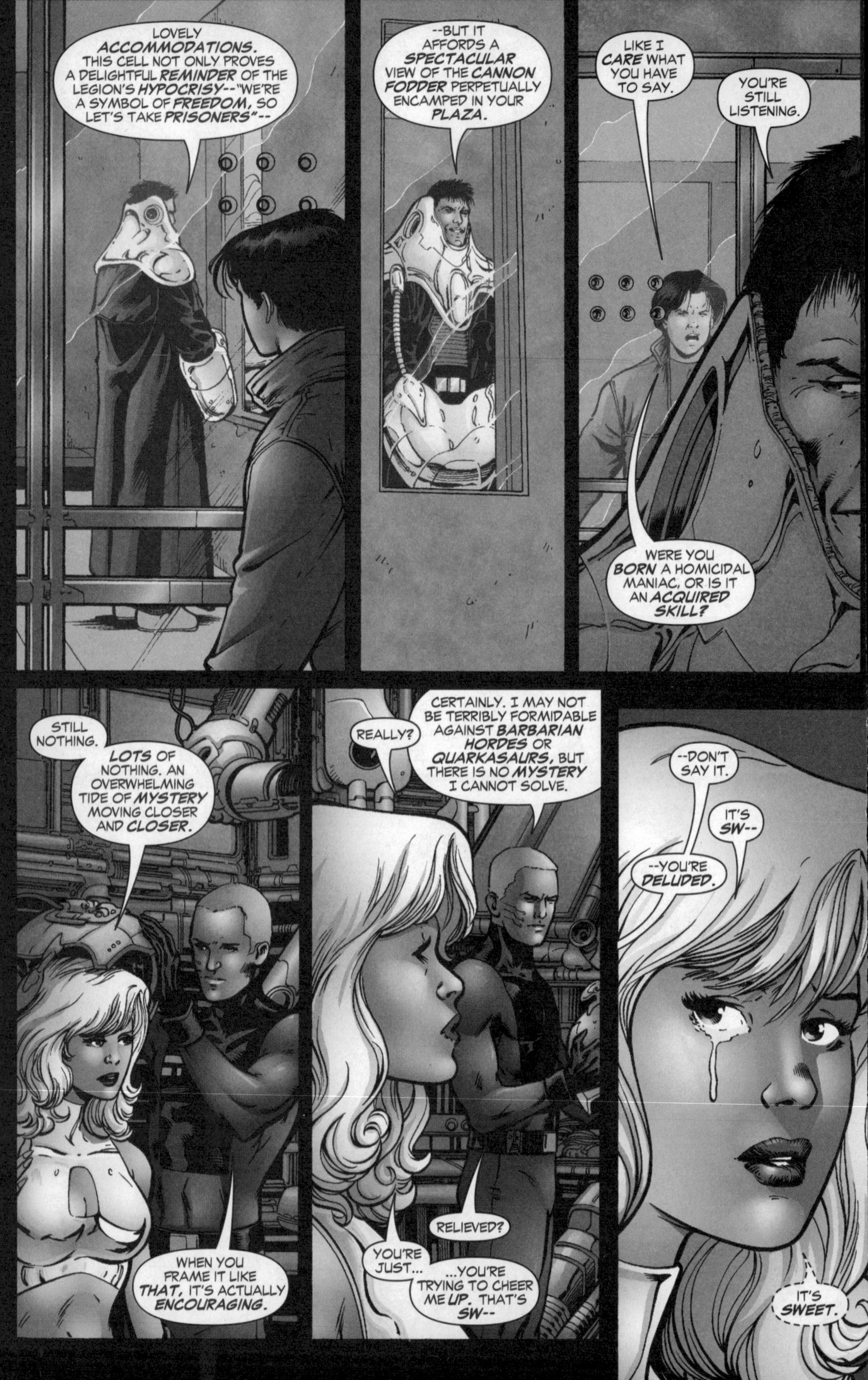
LOVELY ACCOMMODATIONS. THIS CELL NOT ONLY PROVES A DELIGHTFUL REMINDER OF THE LEGION'S HYPOCRISY--"WE'RE A SYMBOL OF FREEDOM, SO LET'S TAKE PRISONERS"--
--BUT IT AFFORDS A SPECTACULAR VIEW OF THE CANNON FODDER PERPETUALLY ENCAMPED IN YOUR PLAZA.
LIKE I CARE WHAT YOU HAVE TO SAY.
YOU'RE STILL LISTENING.
WERE YOU BORN A HOMICIDAL MANIAC, OR IS IT AN ACQUIRED SKILL?
STILL NOTHING.
LOTS OF NOTHING. AN OVERWHELMING TIDE OF MYSTERY MOVING CLOSER AND CLOSER.
WHEN YOU FRAME IT LIKE THAT, IT'S ACTUALLY ENCOURAGING.
REALLY?
CERTAINLY. I MAY NOT BE TERRIBLY FORMIDABLE AGAINST BARBARIAN HORDES OR QUARKASAURS, BUT THERE IS NO MYSTERY I CANNOT SOLVE.
RELIEVED?
YOU'RE JUST...
...YOU'RE TRYING TO CHEER ME UP. THAT'S SW--
--DON'T SAY IT.
IT'S SW--
--YOU'RE DELUDED.
IT'S SWEET.

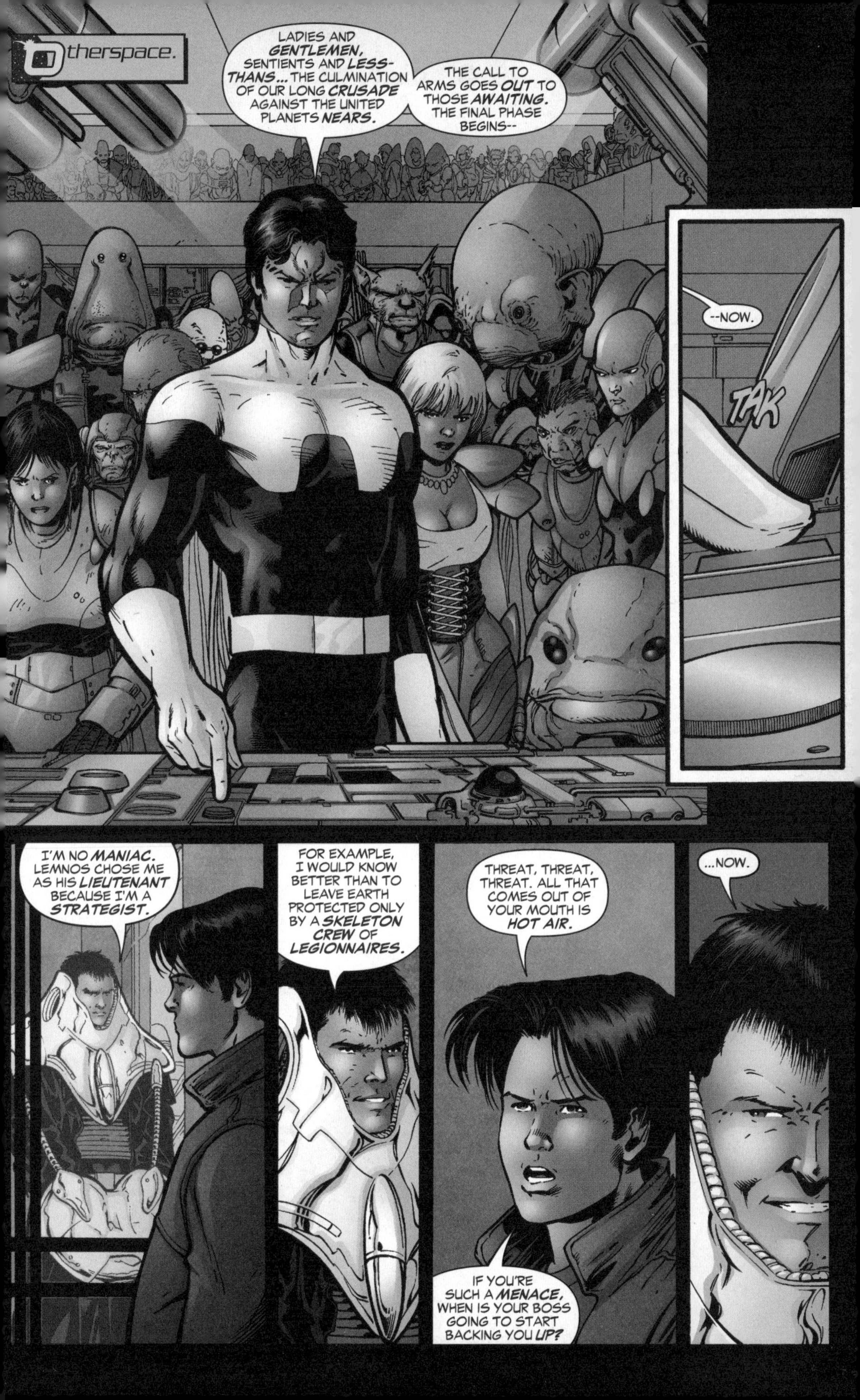
Otherspace.
LADIES AND GENTLEMEN, SENTIENTS AND LESS-THANS... THE CULMINATION OF OUR LONG CRUSADE AGAINST THE UNITED PLANETS NEARS.
THE CALL TO ARMS GOES OUT TO THOSE AWAITING. THE FINAL PHASE BEGINS--
--NOW.
TAK
I'M NO MANIAC. LEMNOS CHOSE ME AS HIS LIEUTENANT BECAUSE I'M A STRATEGIST.
FOR EXAMPLE, I WOULD KNOW BETTER THAN TO LEAVE EARTH PROTECTED ONLY BY A SKELETON CREW OF LEGIONNAIRES.
THREAT, THREAT, THREAT. ALL THAT COMES OUT OF YOUR MOUTH IS HOT AIR.
IF YOU'RE SUCH A MENACE, WHEN IS YOUR BOSS GOING TO START BACKING YOU UP?
...NOW.

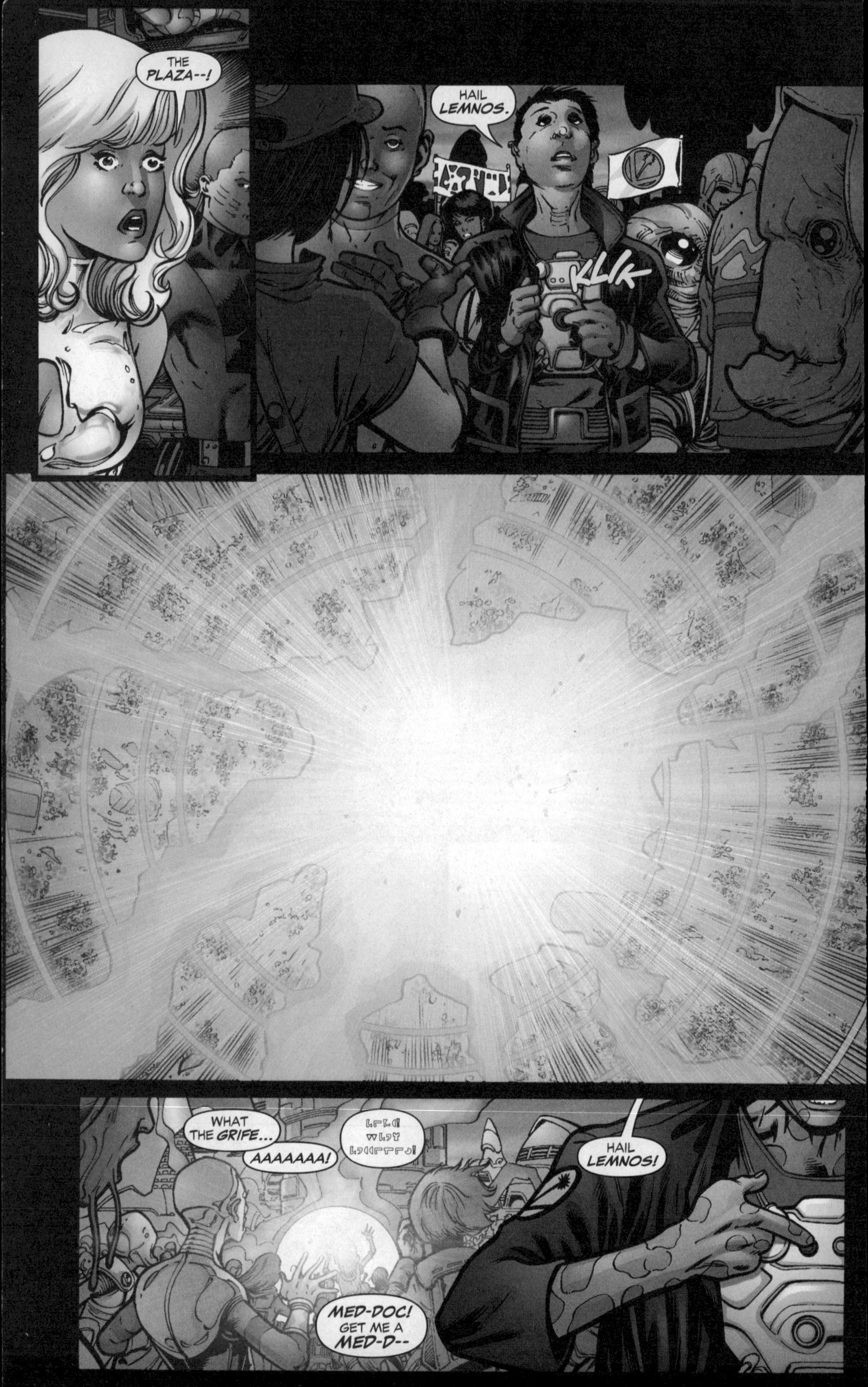
THE PLAZA--!
HAIL LEMNOS.
KLIK
WHAT THE GRIFE...
AAAAAAA!
HAIL LEMNOS!
MED-DOC! GET ME A MED-D--

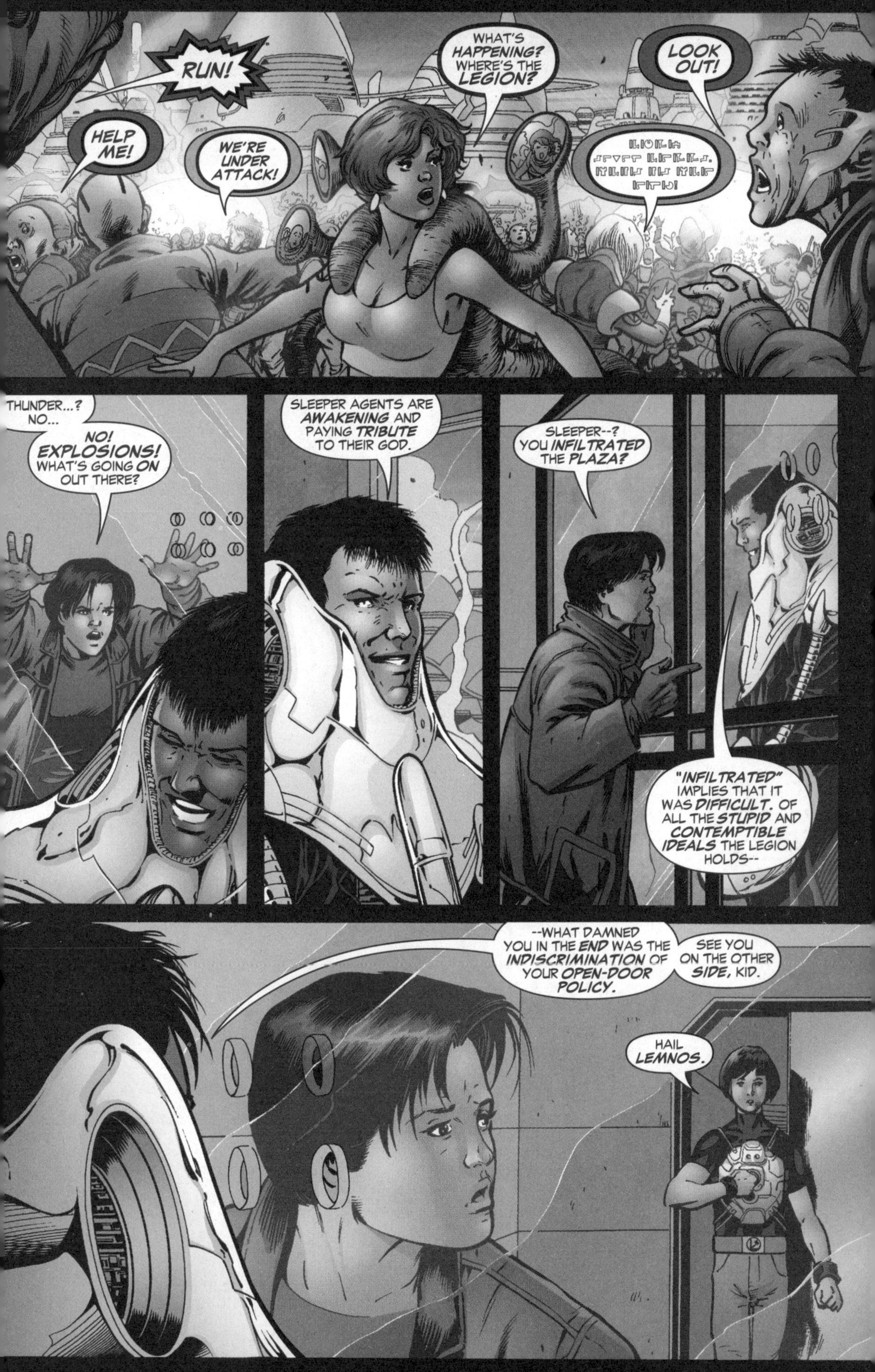
RUN!
HELP ME!
WE'RE UNDER ATTACK!
WHAT'S HAPPENING? WHERE'S THE LEGION?
LOOK OUT!
THUNDER...? NO... NO! EXPLOSIONS! WHAT'S GOING ON OUT THERE?
SLEEPER AGENTS ARE AWAKENING AND PAYING TRIBUTE TO THEIR GOD.
SLEEPER--? YOU INFILTRATED THE PLAZA?
"INFILTRATED" IMPLIES THAT IT WAS DIFFICULT. OF ALL THE STUPID AND CONTEMPTIBLE IDEALS THE LEGION HOLDS--
--WHAT DAMNED YOU IN THE END WAS THE INDISCRIMINATION OF YOUR OPEN-DOOR POLICY.
SEE YOU ON THE OTHER SIDE, KID.
HAIL LEMNOS.

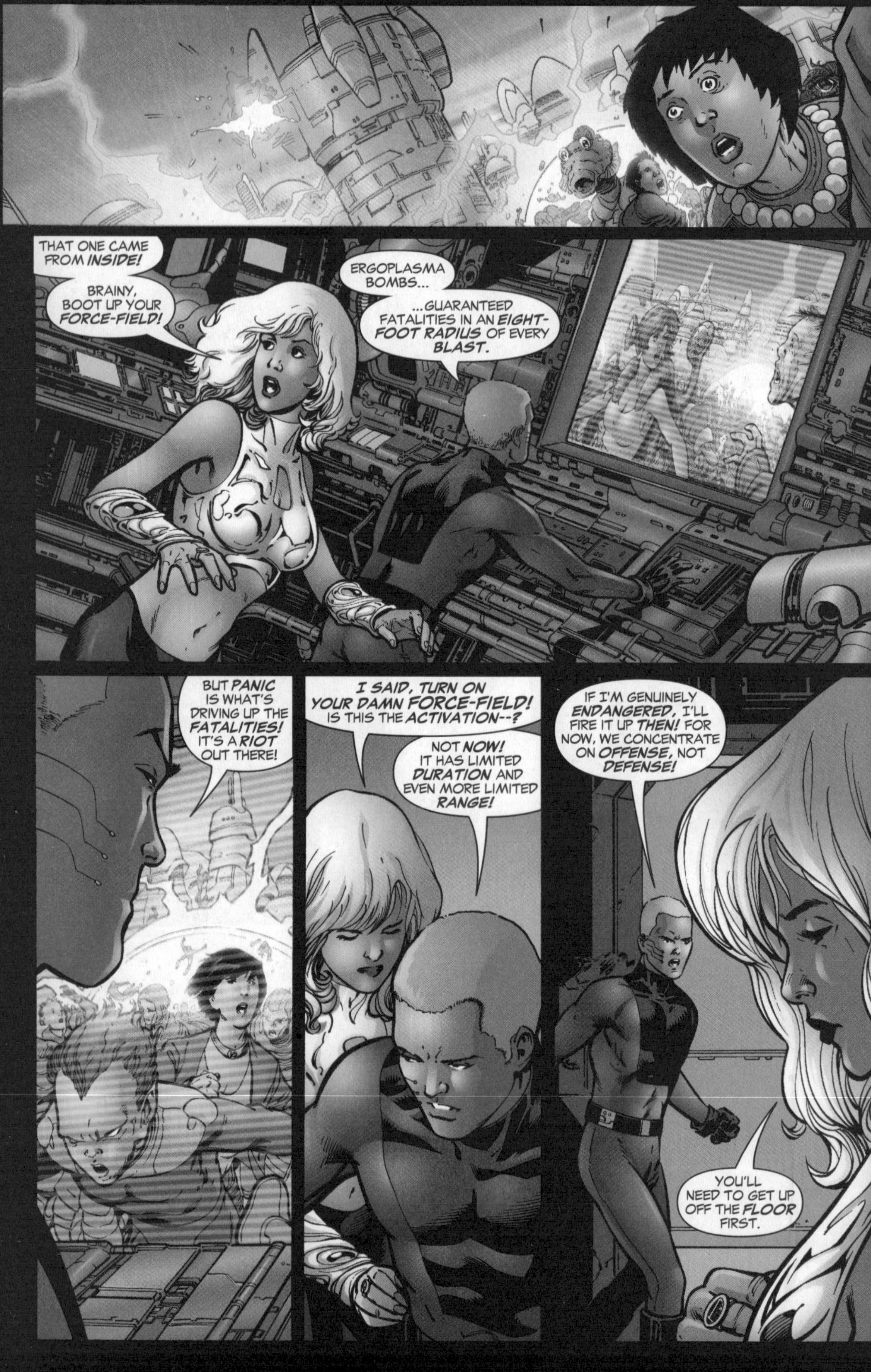
THAT ONE CAME FROM INSIDE!
BRAINY, BOOT UP YOUR FORCE-FIELD!
ERGOPLASMA BOMBS...
...GUARANTEED FATALITIES IN AN EIGHT-FOOT RADIUS OF EVERY BLAST.
BUT PANIC IS WHAT'S DRIVING UP THE FATALITIES! IT'S A RIOT OUT THERE!
I SAID, TURN ON YOUR DAMN FORCE-FIELD! IS THIS THE ACTIVATION--?
NOT NOW! IT HAS LIMITED DURATION AND EVEN MORE LIMITED RANGE!
IF I'M GENUINELY ENDANGERED, I'LL FIRE IT UP THEN! FOR NOW, WE CONCENTRATE ON OFFENSE, NOT DEFENSE!
YOU'LL NEED TO GET UP OFF THE FLOOR FIRST.

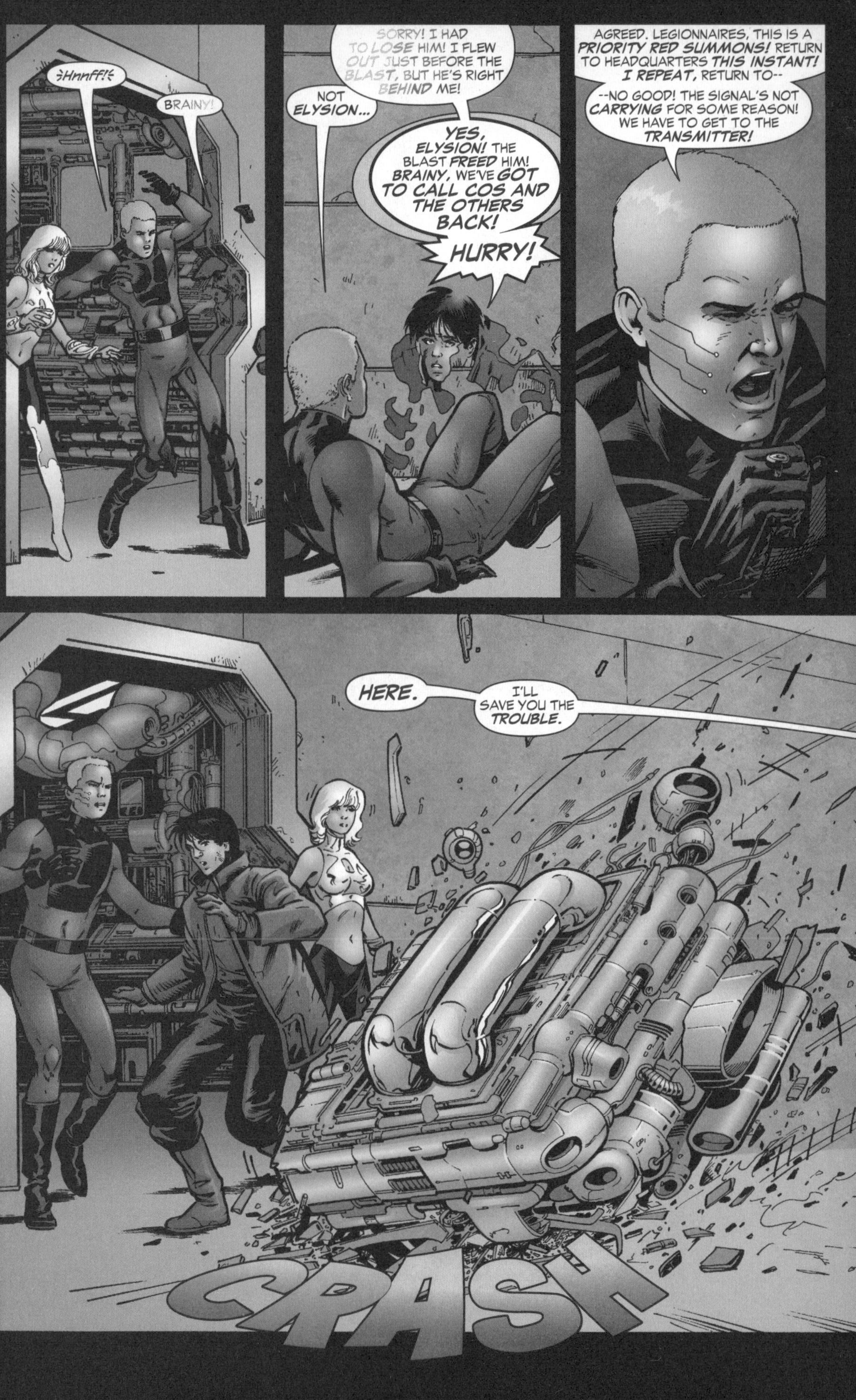

;Hnnff!;
BRAINY!
SORRY! I HAD TO LOSE HIM! I FLEW OUT JUST BEFORE THE BLAST, BUT HE'S RIGHT BEHIND ME!
NOT ELYSION...
YES, ELYSION! THE BLAST FREED HIM! BRAINY, WE'VE GOT TO CALL COS AND THE OTHERS BACK!
HURRY!
AGREED. LEGIONNAIRES, THIS IS A PRIORITY RED SUMMONS! RETURN TO HEADQUARTERS THIS INSTANT! I REPEAT, RETURN TO--
--NO GOOD! THE SIGNAL'S NOT CARRYING FOR SOME REASON! WE HAVE TO GET TO THE TRANSMITTER!
HERE.
I'LL SAVE YOU THE TROUBLE.
CRASH

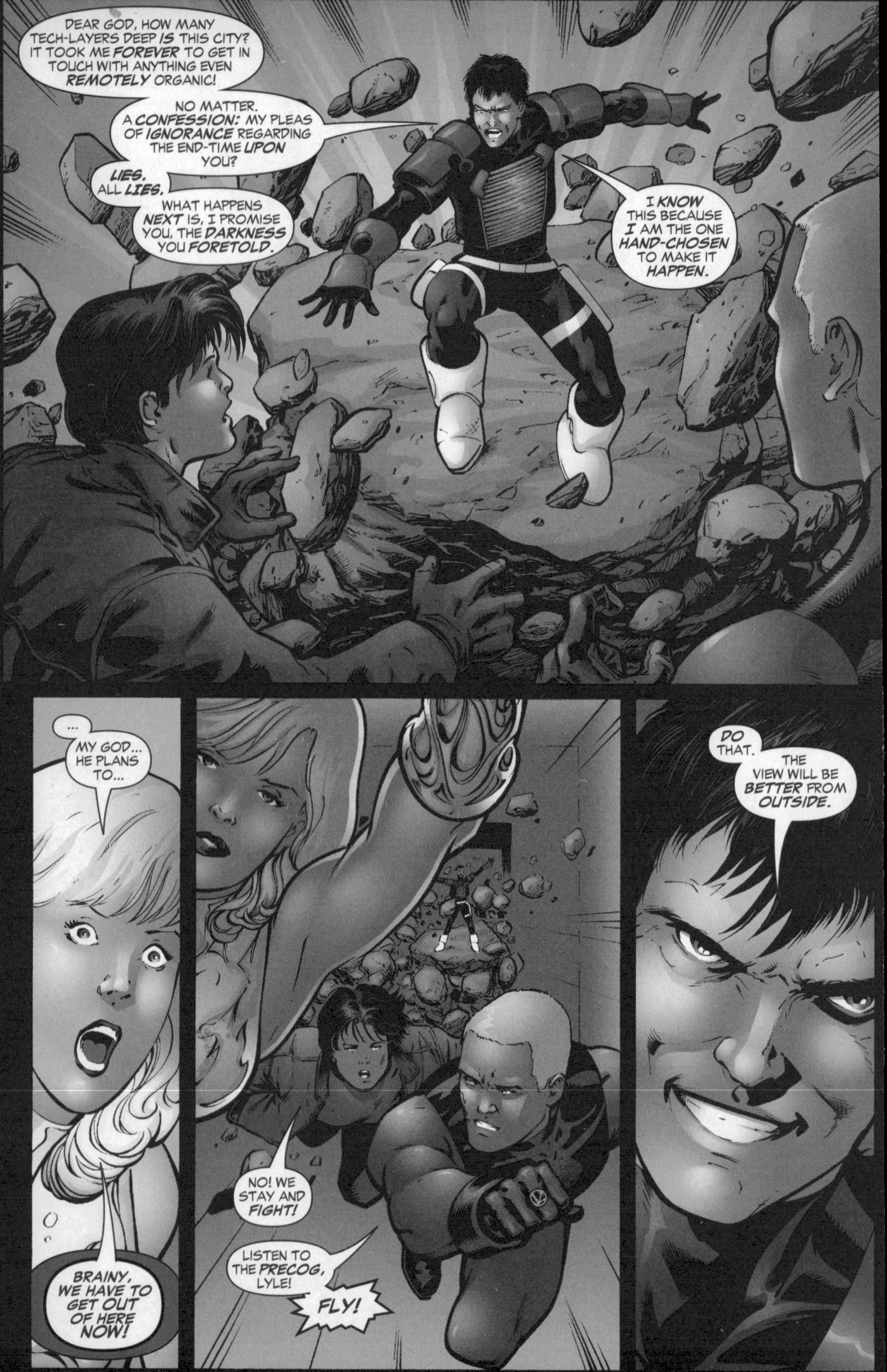

DEAR GOD, HOW MANY TECH-LAYERS DEEP IS THIS CITY? IT TOOK ME FOREVER TO GET IN TOUCH WITH ANYTHING EVEN REMOTELY ORGANIC!
NO MATTER. A CONFESSION: MY PLEAS OF IGNORANCE REGARDING THE END-TIME UPON YOU?
LIES. ALL LIES.
WHAT HAPPENS NEXT IS, I PROMISE YOU, THE DARKNESS YOU FORETOLD.
I KNOW THIS BECAUSE I AM THE ONE HAND-CHOSEN TO MAKE IT HAPPEN.
... MY GOD... HE PLANS TO...
BRAINY, WE HAVE TO GET OUT OF HERE NOW!
NO! WE STAY AND FIGHT!
LISTEN TO THE PRECOG, LYLE!
FLY!
DO THAT.
THE VIEW WILL BE BETTER FROM OUTSIDE.

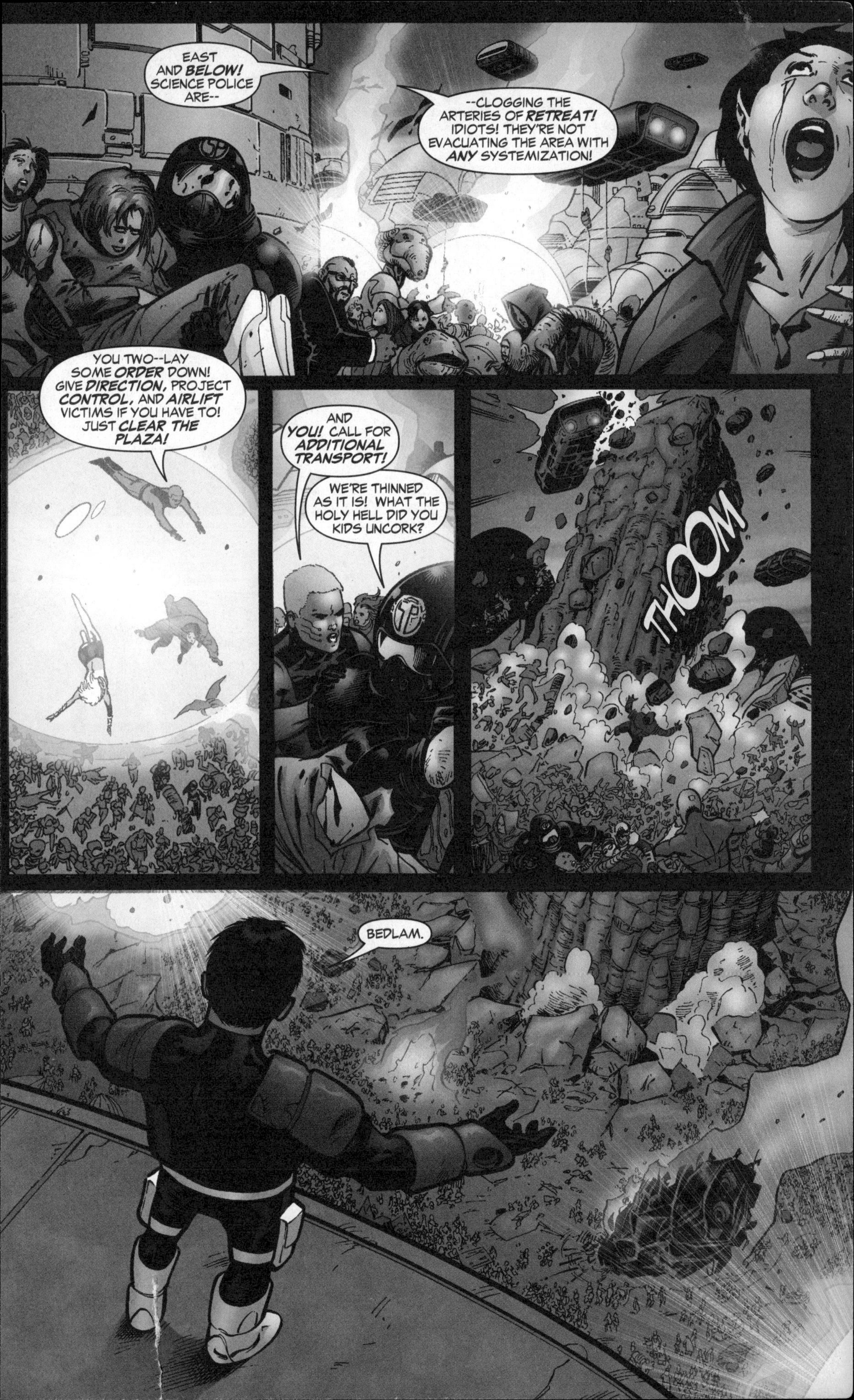
EAST AND BELOW! SCIENCE POLICE ARE--
--CLOGGING THE ARTERIES OF RETREAT! IDIOTS! THEY'RE NOT EVACUATING THE AREA WITH ANY SYSTEMIZATION!
YOU TWO--LAY SOME ORDER DOWN! GIVE DIRECTION, PROJECT CONTROL, AND AIRLIFT VICTIMS IF YOU HAVE TO! JUST CLEAR THE PLAZA!
AND YOU! CALL FOR ADDITIONAL TRANSPORT!
WE'RE THINNED AS IT IS! WHAT THE HOLY HELL DID YOU KIDS UNCORK?
THOOM
BEDLAM.

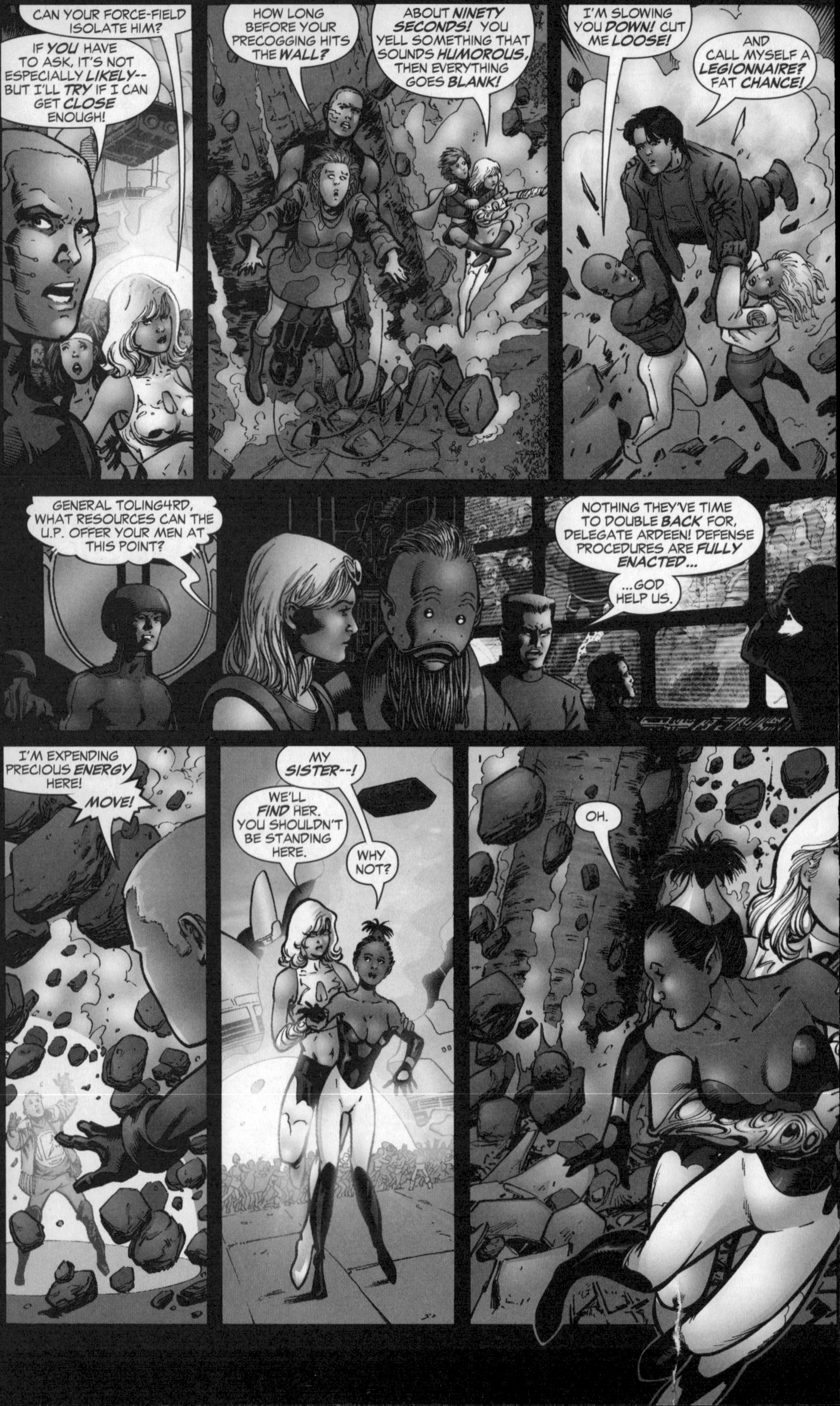
CAN YOUR FORCE-FIELD ISOLATE HIM?
IF YOU HAVE TO ASK, IT'S NOT ESPECIALLY LIKELY-- BUT I'LL TRY IF I CAN GET CLOSE ENOUGH!
HOW LONG BEFORE YOUR PRECOGGING HITS THE WALL?
ABOUT NINETY SECONDS! YOU YELL SOMETHING THAT SOUNDS HUMOROUS, THEN EVERYTHING GOES BLANK!
I'M SLOWING YOU DOWN! CUT ME LOOSE!
AND CALL MYSELF A LEGIONNAIRE? FAT CHANCE!
GENERAL TOLING4RD, WHAT RESOURCES CAN THE U.P. OFFER YOUR MEN AT THIS POINT?
NOTHING THEY'VE TIME TO DOUBLE BACK FOR, DELEGATE ARDEEN! DEFENSE PROCEDURES ARE FULLY ENACTED...
...GOD HELP US.
I'M EXPENDING PRECIOUS ENERGY HERE!
MOVE!
MY SISTER--!
WE'LL FIND HER. YOU SHOULDN'T BE STANDING HERE.
WHY NOT?
OH.

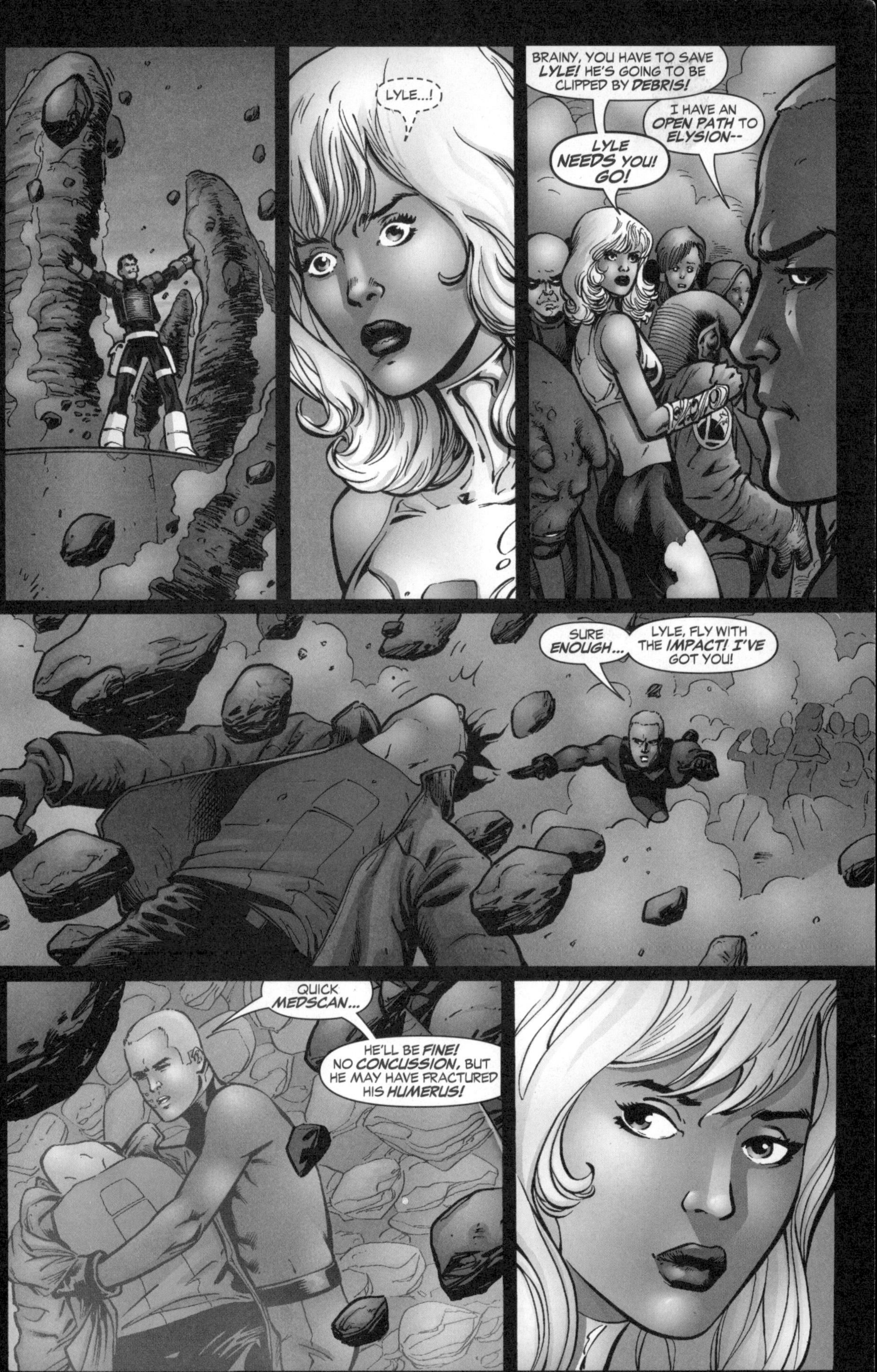
LYLE...!
BRAINY, YOU HAVE TO SAVE LYLE! HE'S GOING TO BE CLIPPED BY DEBRIS!
I HAVE AN OPEN PATH TO ELYSION--
LYLE NEEDS YOU! GO!
SURE ENOUGH...
LYLE, FLY WITH THE IMPACT! I'VE GOT YOU!
QUICK MEDSCAN...
HE'LL BE FINE! NO CONCUSSION, BUT HE MAY HAVE FRACTURED HIS HUMERUS!

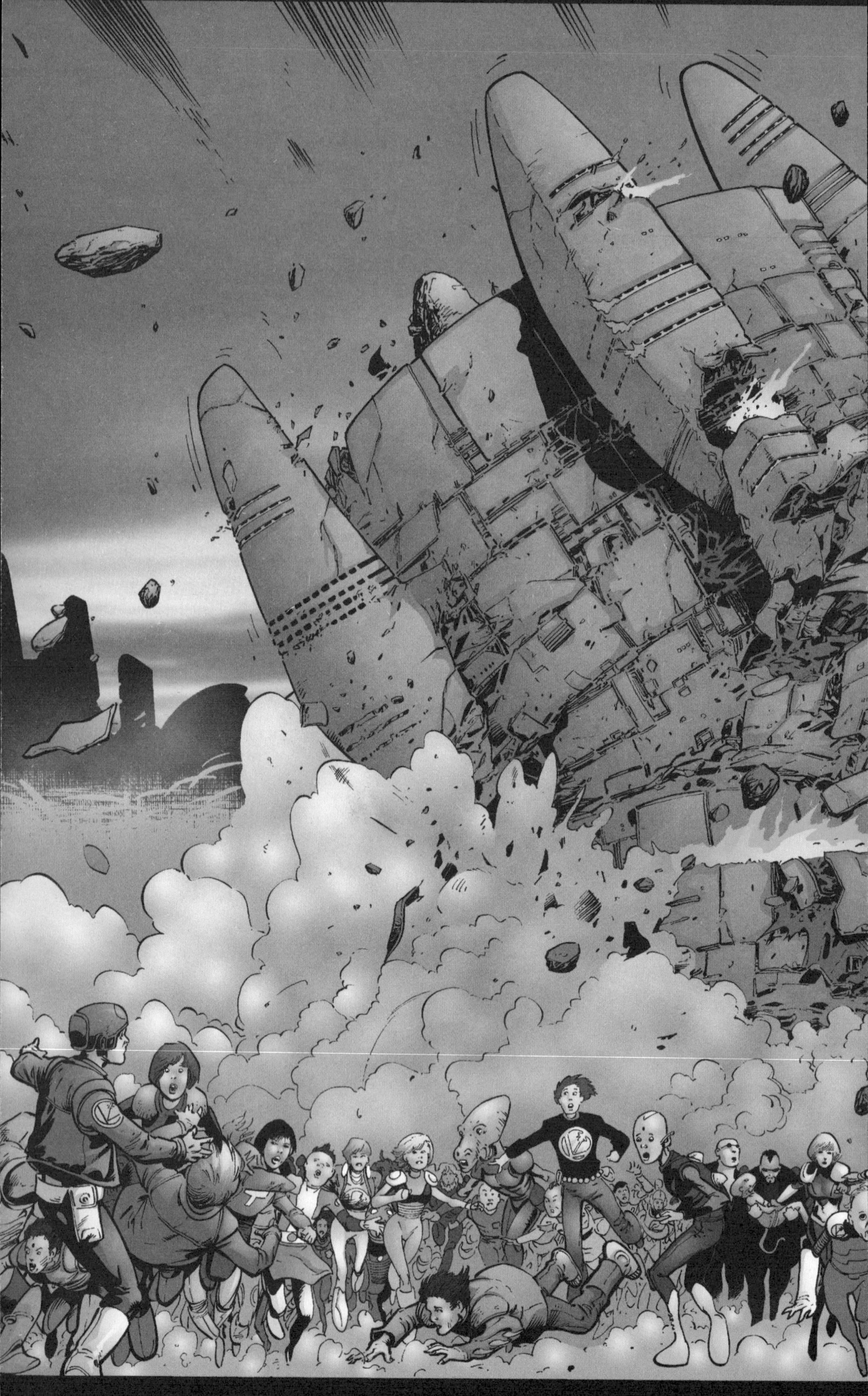

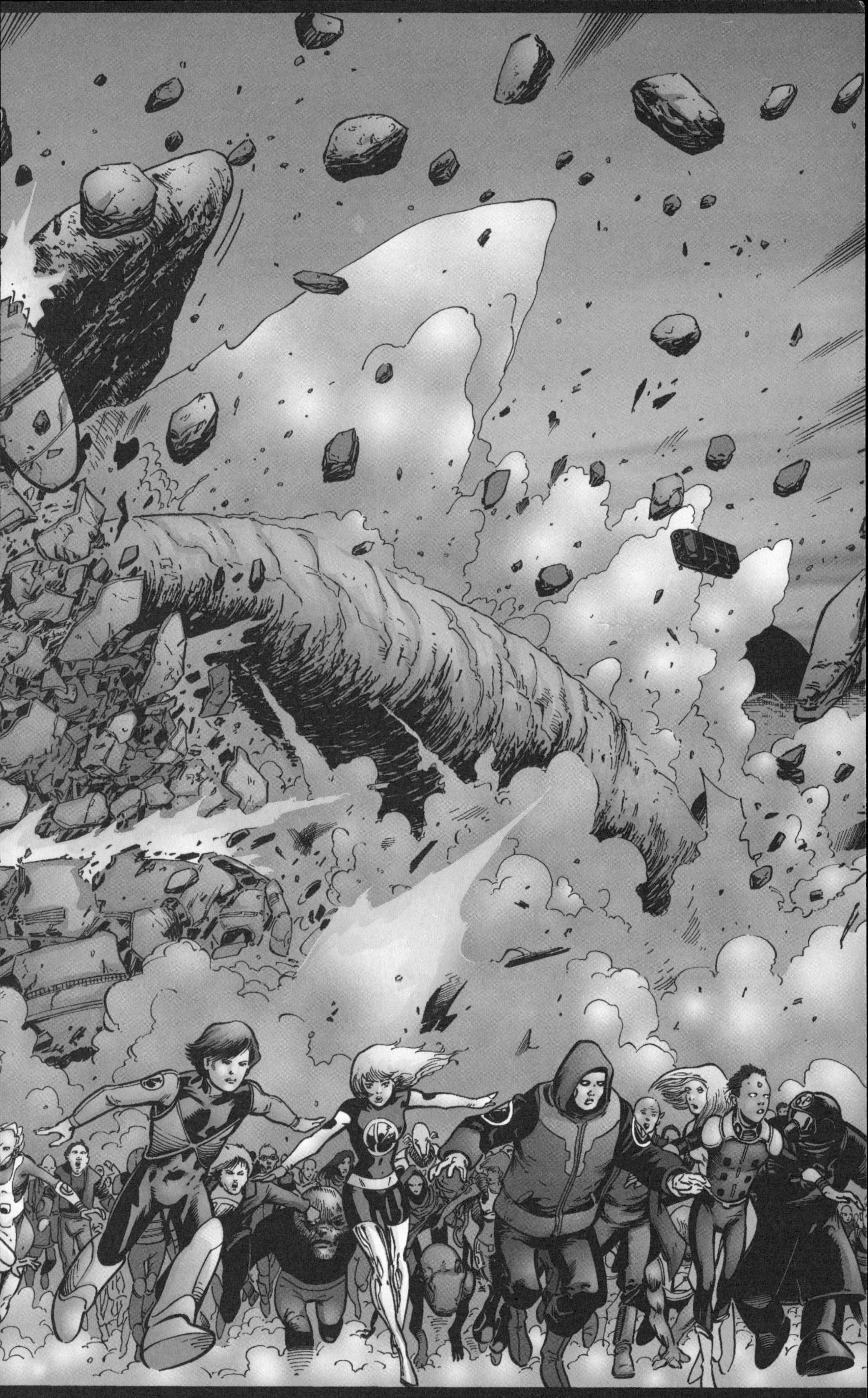

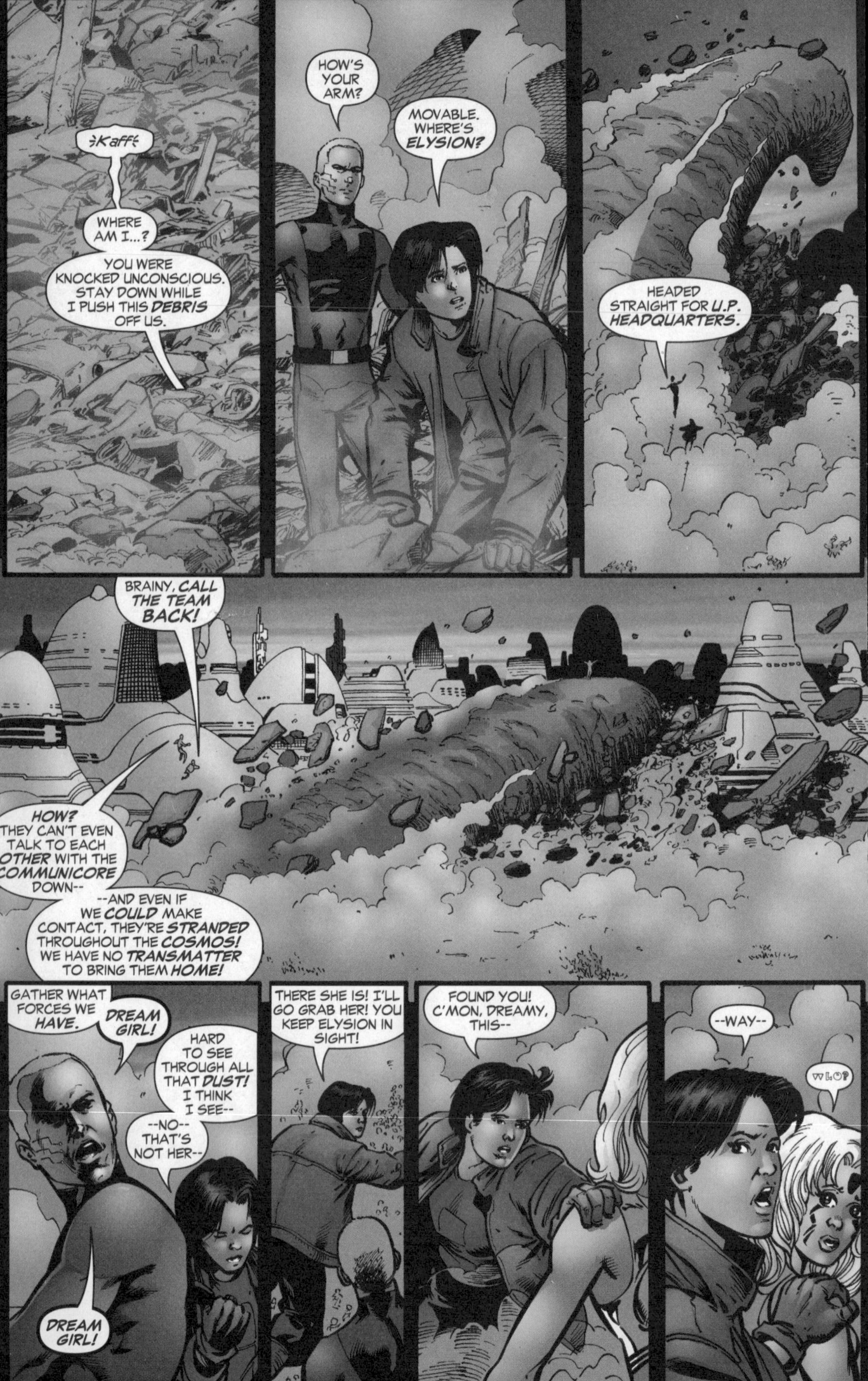
Kaff
WHERE AM I...?
YOU WERE KNOCKED UNCONSCIOUS. STAY DOWN WHILE I PUSH THIS DEBRIS OFF US.
HOW'S YOUR ARM?
MOVABLE. WHERE'S ELYSION?
HEADED STRAIGHT FOR U.P. HEADQUARTERS.
BRAINY, CALL THE TEAM BACK!
HOW? THEY CAN'T EVEN TALK TO EACH OTHER WITH THE COMMUNICORE DOWN--
--AND EVEN IF WE COULD MAKE CONTACT, THEY'RE STRANDED THROUGHOUT THE COSMOS! WE HAVE NO TRANSMATTER TO BRING THEM HOME!
GATHER WHAT FORCES WE HAVE.
DREAM GIRL!
HARD TO SEE THROUGH ALL THAT DUST! I THINK I SEE--
--NO-- THAT'S NOT HER--
DREAM GIRL!
THERE SHE IS! I'LL GO GRAB HER! YOU KEEP ELYSION IN SIGHT!
FOUND YOU! C'MON, DREAMY, THIS--
--WAY--
WLO?

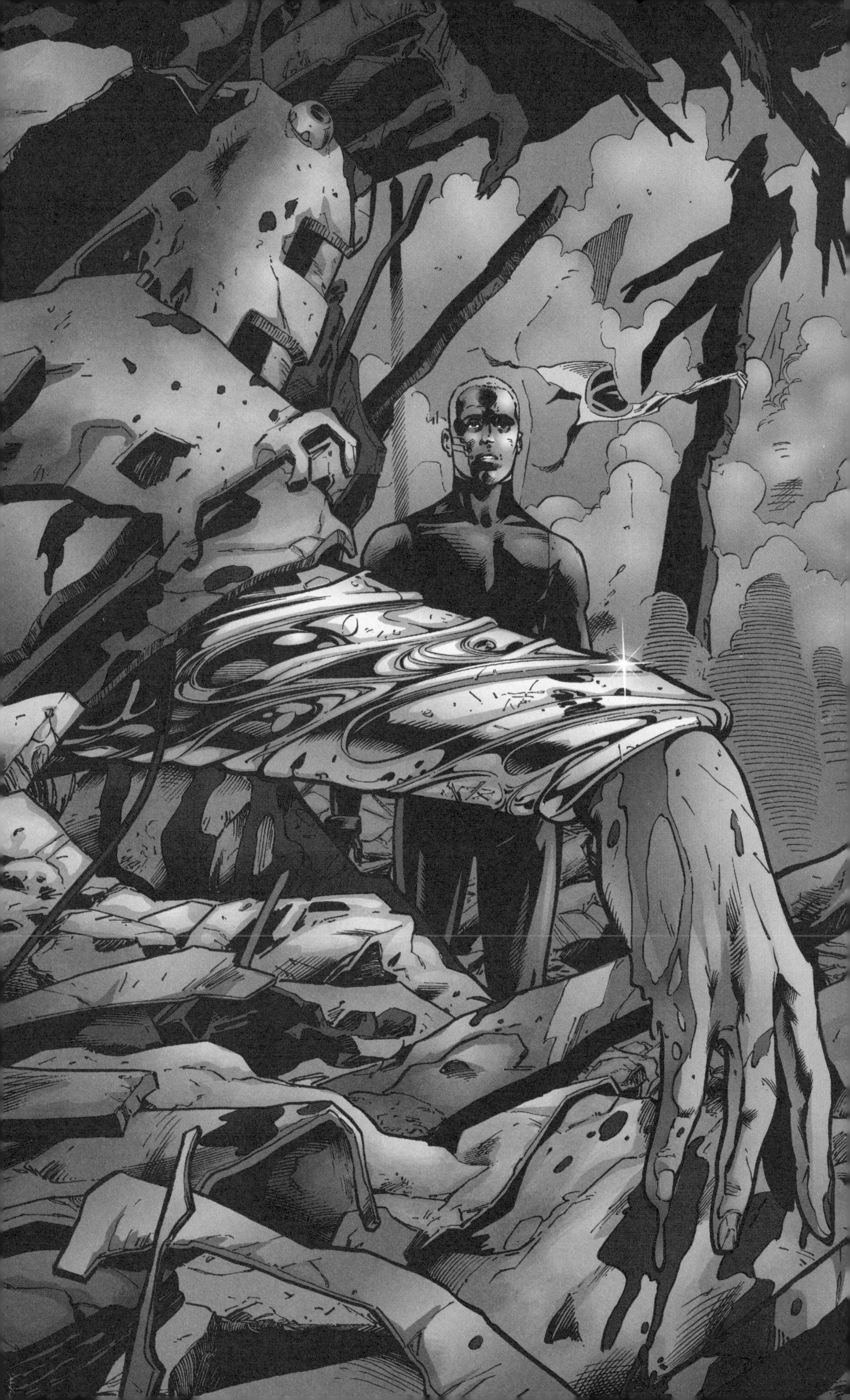

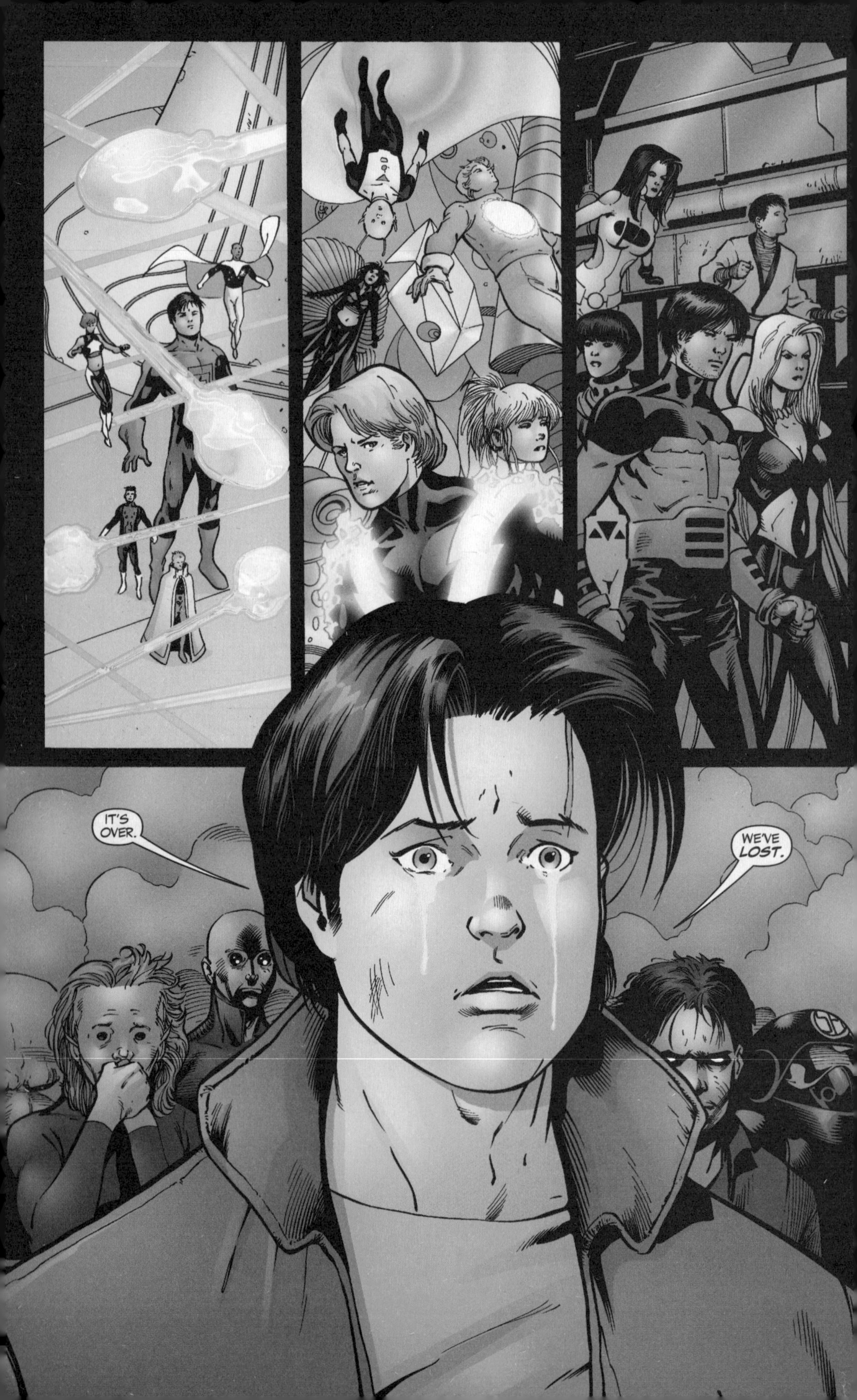
IT'S OVER.
WE'VE LOST.

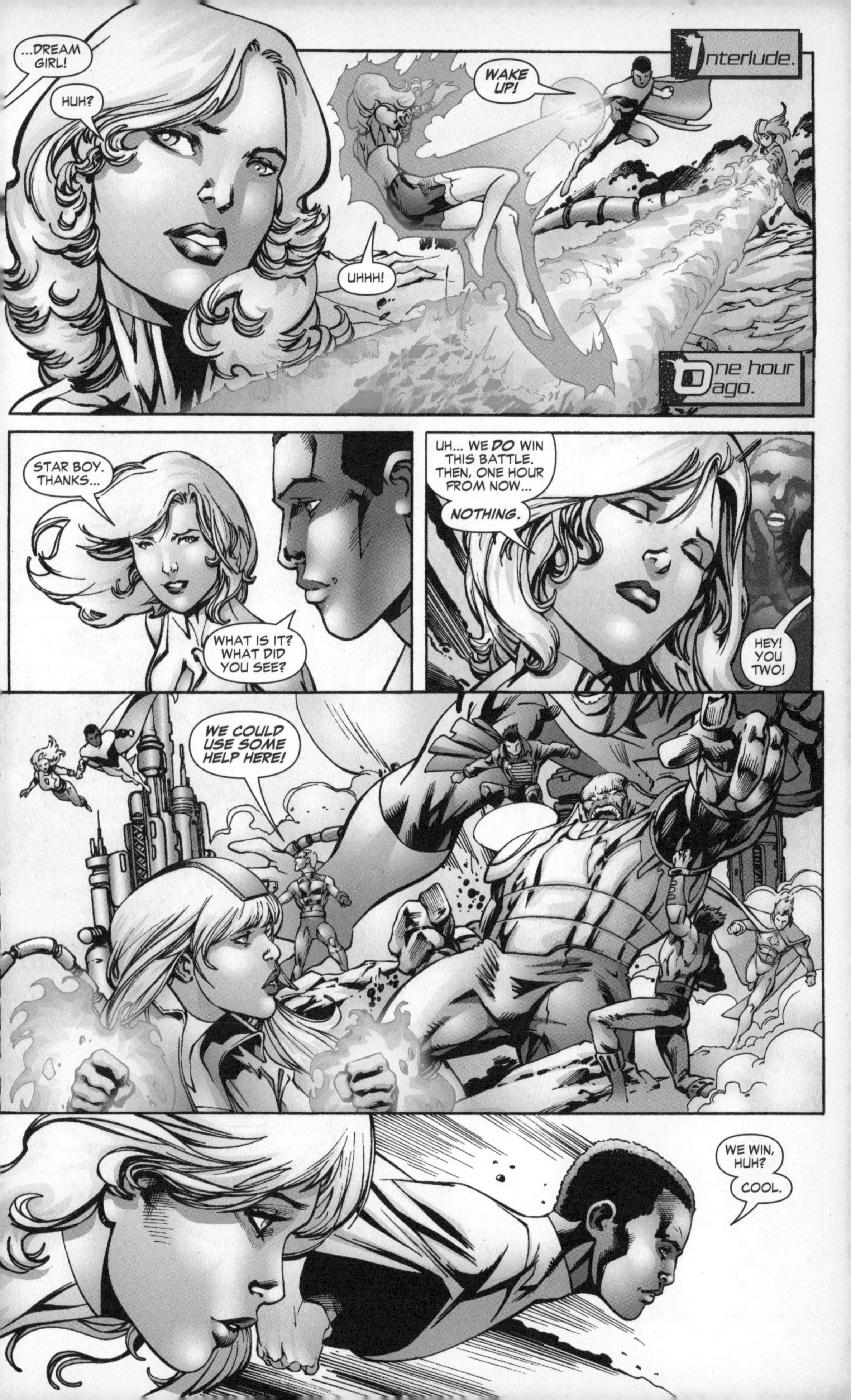
...DREAM GIRL!
HUH?
Interlude.
WAKE UP!
UHHH!
One hour ago.
STAR BOY. THANKS...
WHAT IS IT? WHAT DID YOU SEE?
UH... WE DO WIN THIS BATTLE. THEN, ONE HOUR FROM NOW...
NOTHING.
HEY! YOU TWO!
WE COULD USE SOME HELP HERE!
WE WIN, HUH?
COOL.

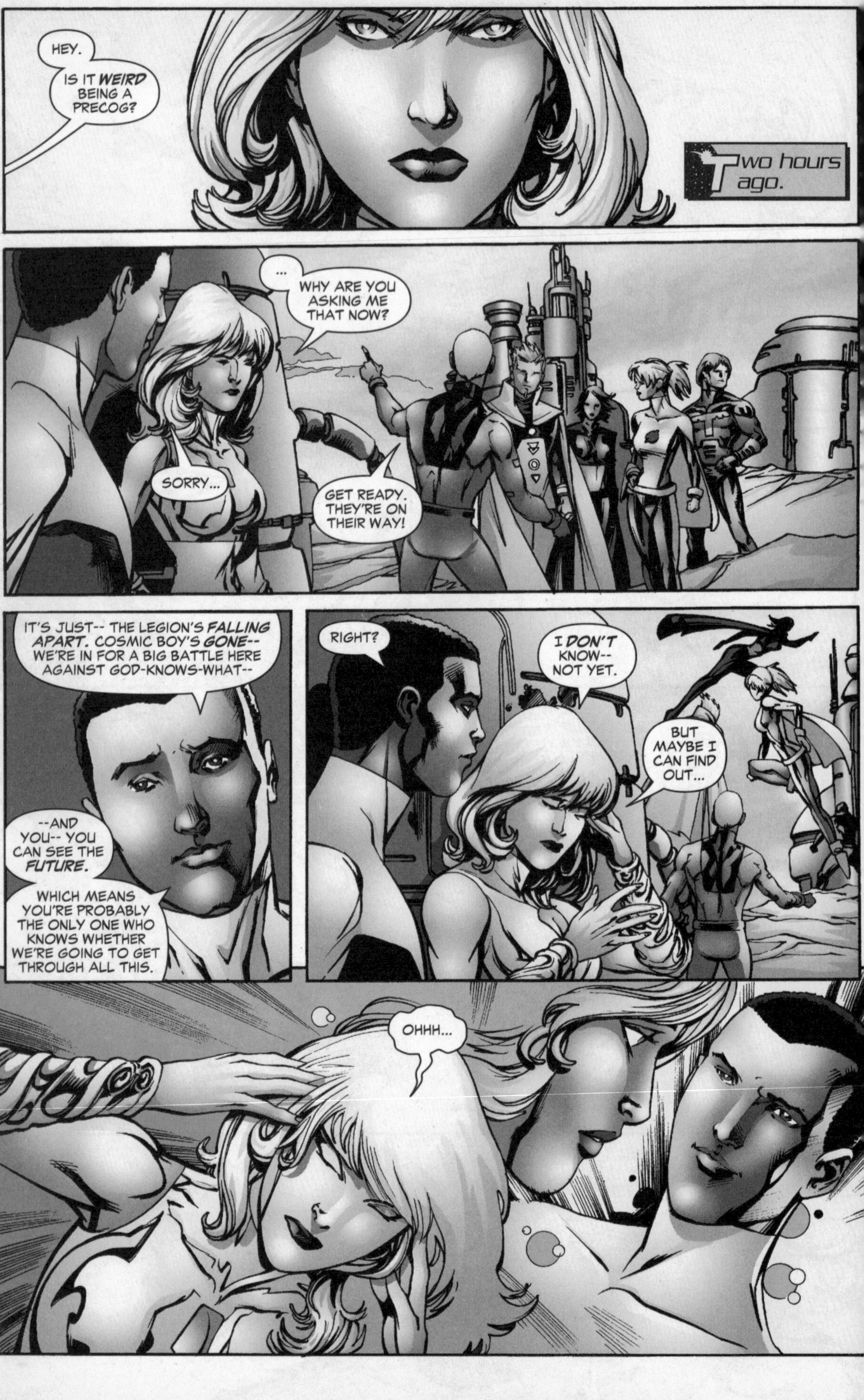
HEY.
IS IT WEIRD BEING A PRECOG?
Two hours ago.
...
WHY ARE YOU ASKING ME THAT NOW?
SORRY...
GET READY. THEY'RE ON THEIR WAY!
IT'S JUST-- THE LEGION'S FALLING APART. COSMIC BOY'S GONE-- WE'RE IN FOR A BIG BATTLE HERE AGAINST GOD-KNOWS-WHAT--
--AND YOU-- YOU CAN SEE THE FUTURE.
WHICH MEANS YOU'RE PROBABLY THE ONLY ONE WHO KNOWS WHETHER WE'RE GOING TO GET THROUGH ALL THIS.
RIGHT?
I DON'T KNOW-- NOT YET.
BUT MAYBE I CAN FIND OUT...
OHHH...

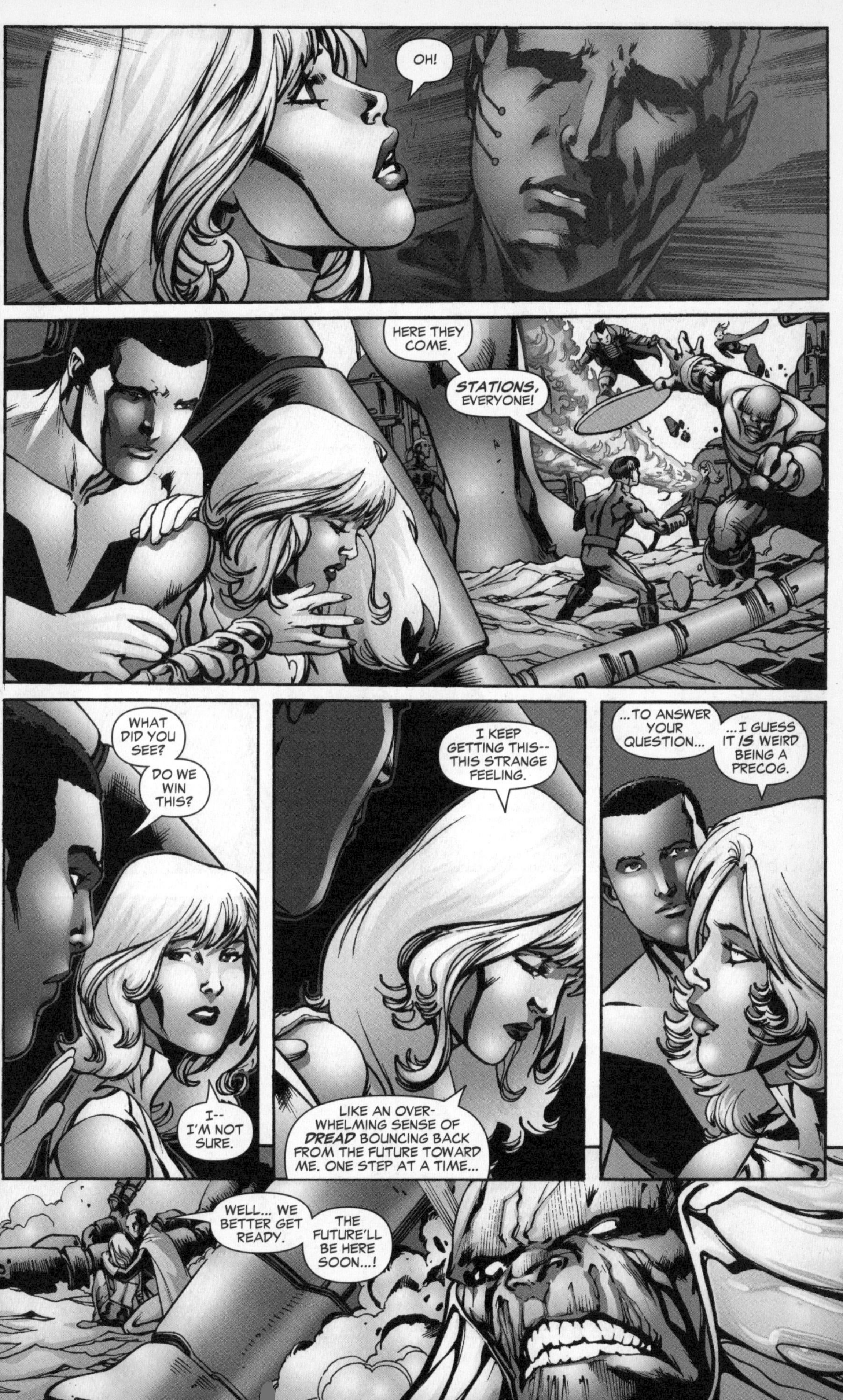
OH!
HERE THEY COME.
STATIONS, EVERYONE!
WHAT DID YOU SEE?
DO WE WIN THIS?
I-- I'M NOT SURE.
I KEEP GETTING THIS-- THIS STRANGE FEELING.
LIKE AN OVER-WHELMING SENSE OF DREAD BOUNCING BACK FROM THE FUTURE TOWARD ME. ONE STEP AT A TIME...
...TO ANSWER YOUR QUESTION...
...I GUESS IT IS WEIRD BEING A PRECOG.
WELL... WE BETTER GET READY.
THE FUTURE'LL BE HERE SOON...!

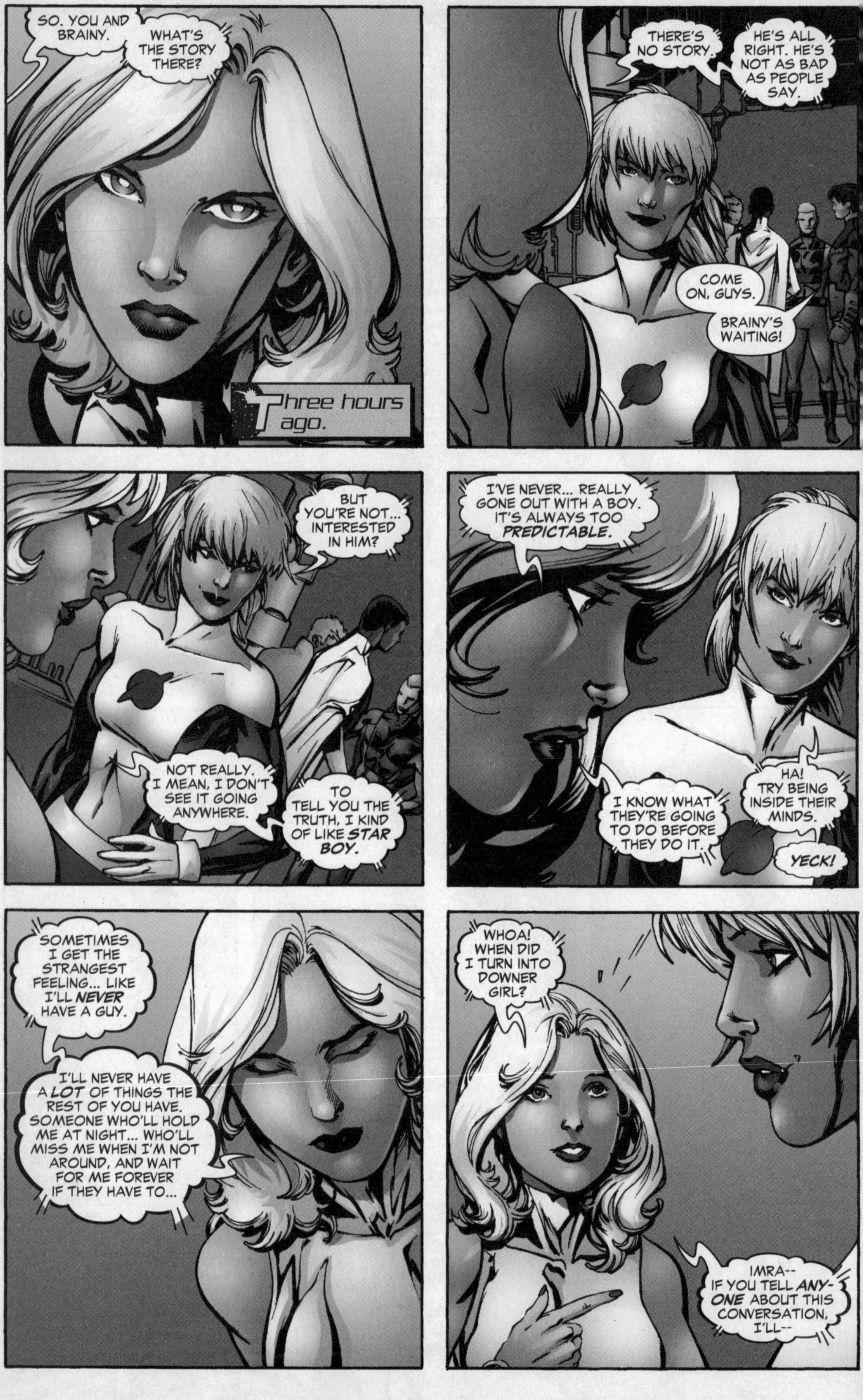
SO. YOU AND BRAINY.
WHAT'S THE STORY THERE?
Three hours ago.
THERE'S NO STORY.
HE'S ALL RIGHT. HE'S NOT AS BAD AS PEOPLE SAY.
COME ON, GUYS.
BRAINY'S WAITING!
BUT YOU'RE NOT... INTERESTED IN HIM?
NOT REALLY. I MEAN, I DON'T SEE IT GOING ANYWHERE.
TO TELL YOU THE TRUTH, I KIND OF LIKE STAR BOY.
I'VE NEVER... REALLY GONE OUT WITH A BOY. IT'S ALWAYS TOO PREDICTABLE.
I KNOW WHAT THEY'RE GOING TO DO BEFORE THEY DO IT.
HA! TRY BEING INSIDE THEIR MINDS.
YECK!
SOMETIMES I GET THE STRANGEST FEELING... LIKE I'LL NEVER HAVE A GUY.
I'LL NEVER HAVE A LOT OF THINGS THE REST OF YOU HAVE. SOMEONE WHO'LL HOLD ME AT NIGHT... WHO'LL MISS ME WHEN I'M NOT AROUND, AND WAIT FOR ME FOREVER IF THEY HAVE TO...
WHOA! WHEN DID I TURN INTO DOWNER GIRL?
IMRA-- IF YOU TELL ANY-ONE ABOUT THIS CONVERSATION, I'LL--

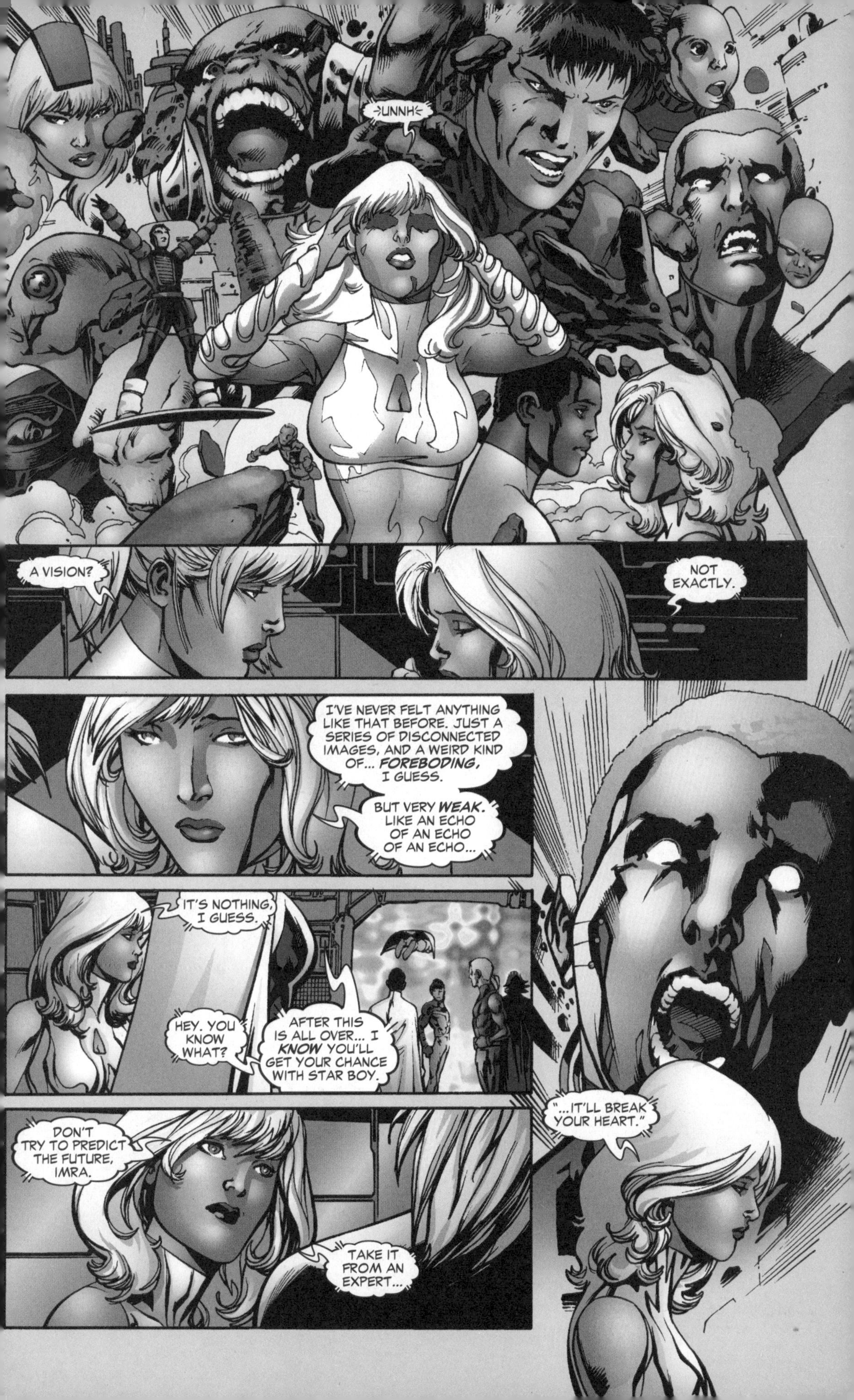
UNNH
A VISION?
NOT EXACTLY.
I'VE NEVER FELT ANYTHING LIKE THAT BEFORE. JUST A SERIES OF DISCONNECTED IMAGES, AND A WEIRD KIND OF... *FOREBODING,* I GUESS.
BUT VERY *WEAK.* LIKE AN ECHO OF AN ECHO OF AN ECHO...
IT'S NOTHING, I GUESS.
HEY. YOU KNOW WHAT?
AFTER THIS IS ALL OVER... I *KNOW* YOU'LL GET YOUR CHANCE WITH STAR BOY.
DON'T TRY TO PREDICT THE FUTURE, IMRA.
TAKE IT FROM AN EXPERT...
"...IT'LL BREAK YOUR HEART."

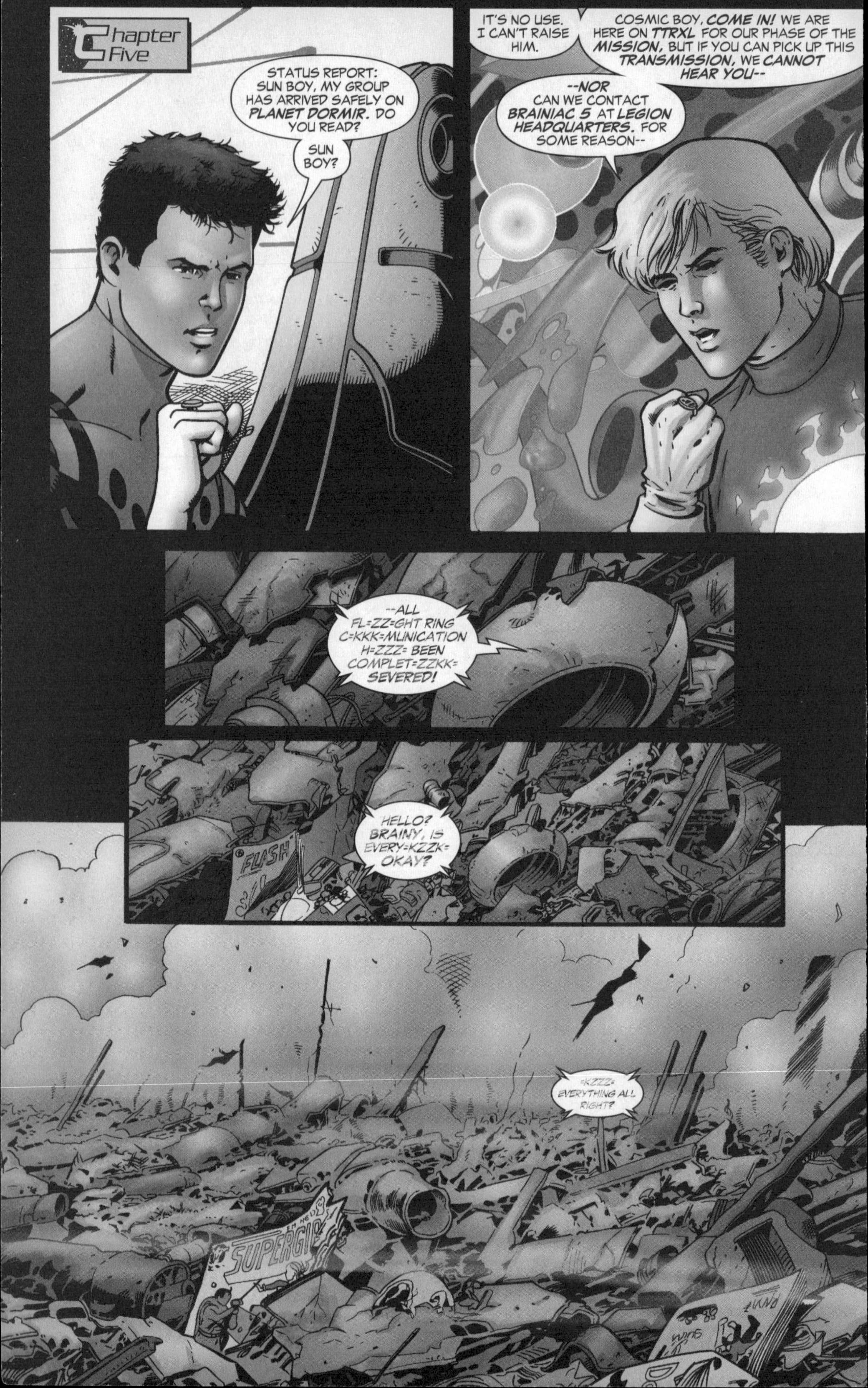

Chapter Five
STATUS REPORT: SUN BOY, MY GROUP HAS ARRIVED SAFELY ON PLANET DORMIR. DO YOU READ?
SUN BOY?
IT'S NO USE. I CAN'T RAISE HIM.
COSMIC BOY, COME IN! WE ARE HERE ON TTRXL FOR OUR PHASE OF THE MISSION, BUT IF YOU CAN PICK UP THIS TRANSMISSION, WE CANNOT HEAR YOU--
--NOR CAN WE CONTACT BRAINIAC 5 AT LEGION HEADQUARTERS. FOR SOME REASON--
--ALL FL=ZZ=GHT RING C=KKK=MUNICATION H=ZZZ= BEEN COMPLET=ZZKK= SEVERED!
HELLO? BRAINY, IS EVERY=KZZK= OKAY?
FLASH
=KZZZ= EVERYTHING ALL RIGHT?
SUPERGI

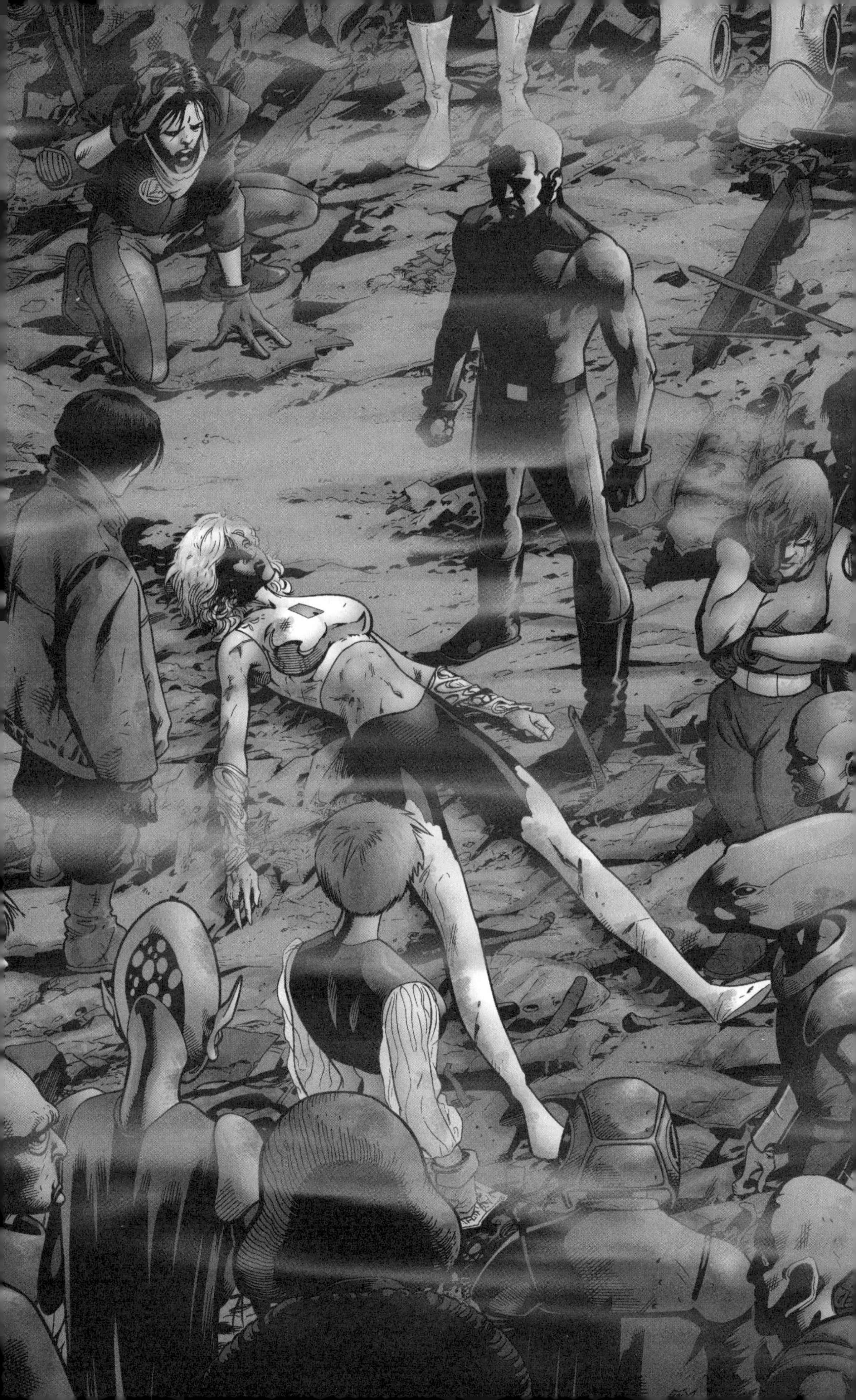

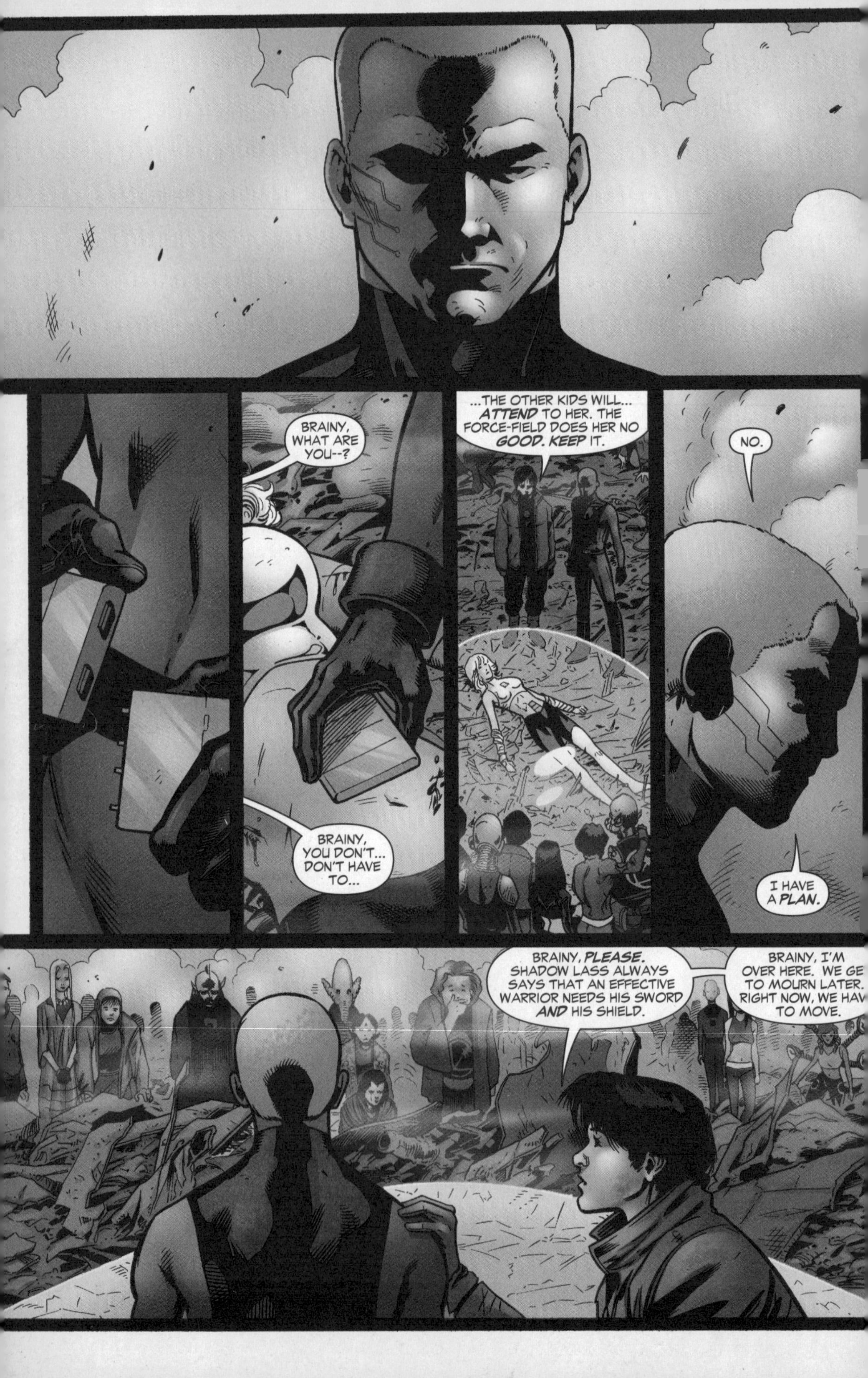
BRAINY, WHAT ARE YOU--?
BRAINY, YOU DON'T... DON'T HAVE TO...
...THE OTHER KIDS WILL... ATTEND TO HER. THE FORCE-FIELD DOES HER NO GOOD. KEEP IT.
NO.
I HAVE A PLAN.
BRAINY, PLEASE. SHADOW LASS ALWAYS SAYS THAT AN EFFECTIVE WARRIOR NEEDS HIS SWORD AND HIS SHIELD.
BRAINY, I'M OVER HERE. WE GE TO MOURN LATER. RIGHT NOW, WE HAV TO MOVE.

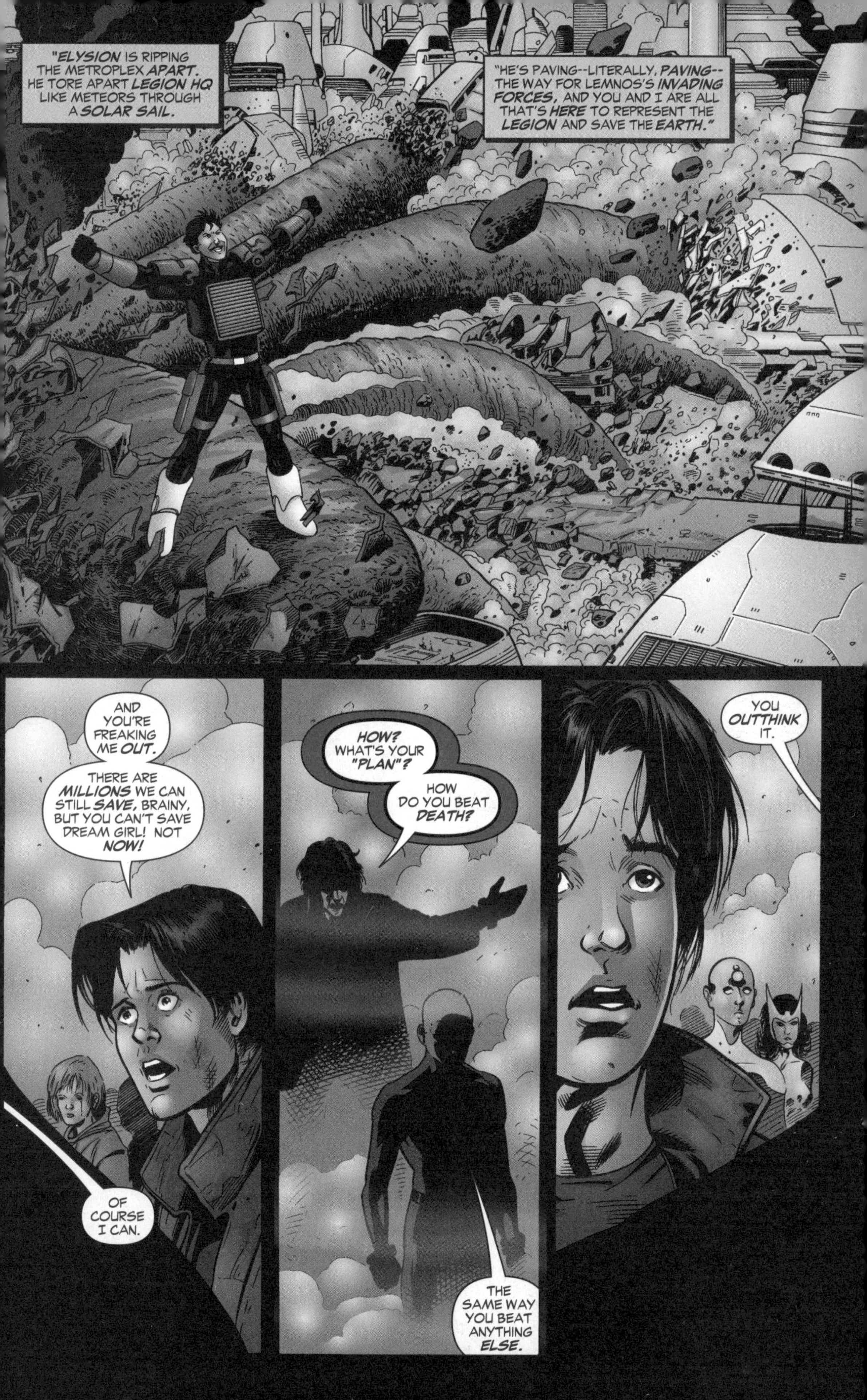
"ELYSION IS RIPPING THE METROPLEX APART. HE TORE APART LEGION HQ LIKE METEORS THROUGH A SOLAR SAIL.
"HE'S PAVING--LITERALLY, PAVING-- THE WAY FOR LEMNOS'S INVADING FORCES, AND YOU AND I ARE ALL THAT'S HERE TO REPRESENT THE LEGION AND SAVE THE EARTH."
AND YOU'RE FREAKING ME OUT.
THERE ARE MILLIONS WE CAN STILL SAVE, BRAINY, BUT YOU CAN'T SAVE DREAM GIRL! NOT NOW!
OF COURSE I CAN.
HOW? WHAT'S YOUR "PLAN"?
HOW DO YOU BEAT DEATH?
THE SAME WAY YOU BEAT ANYTHING ELSE.
YOU OUTTHINK IT.

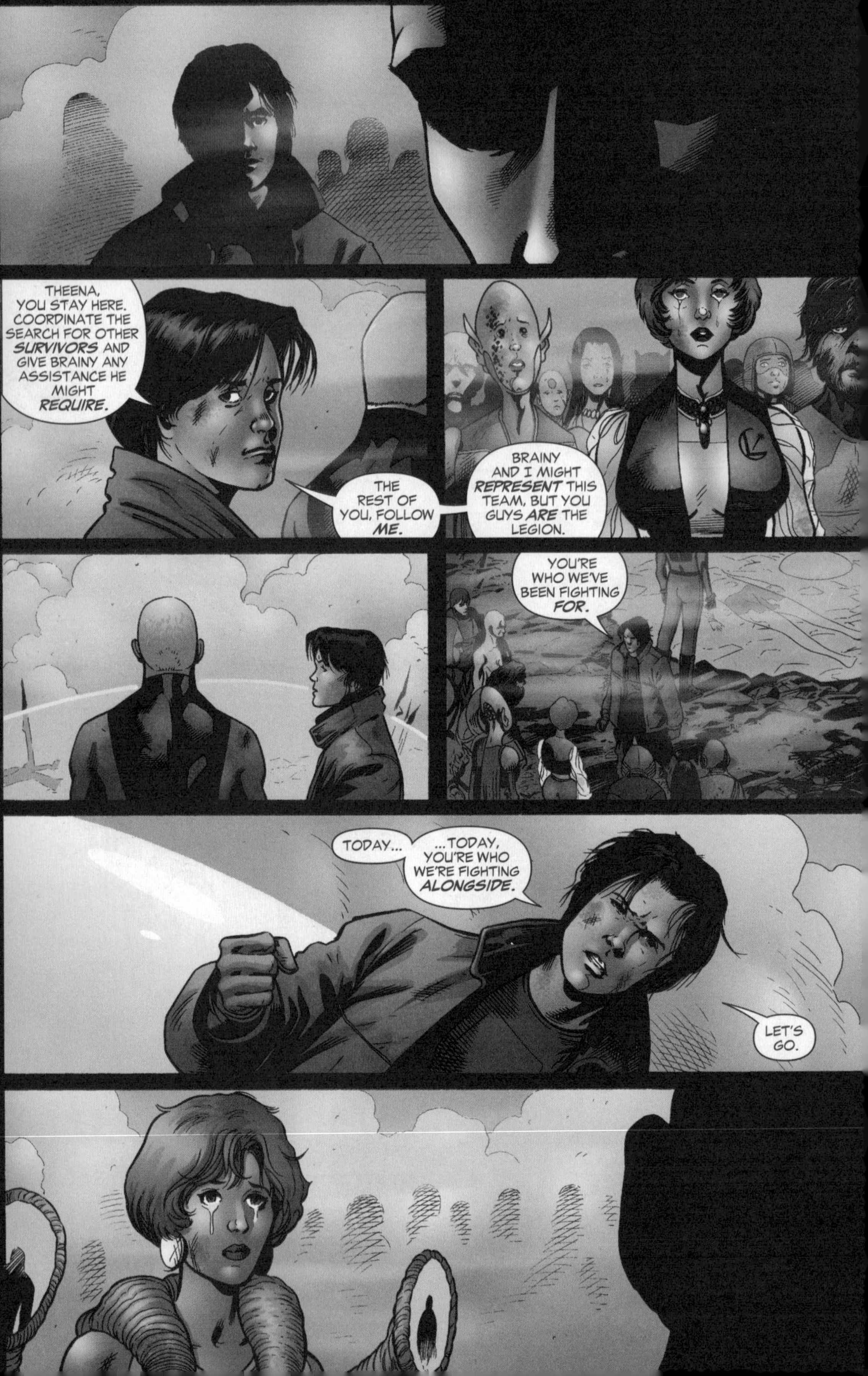
THEENA, YOU STAY HERE. COORDINATE THE SEARCH FOR OTHER SURVIVORS AND GIVE BRAINY ANY ASSISTANCE HE MIGHT REQUIRE.
THE REST OF YOU, FOLLOW ME.
BRAINY AND I MIGHT REPRESENT THIS TEAM, BUT YOU GUYS ARE THE LEGION.
YOU'RE WHO WE'VE BEEN FIGHTING FOR.
TODAY...
...TODAY, YOU'RE WHO WE'RE FIGHTING ALONGSIDE.
LET'S GO.

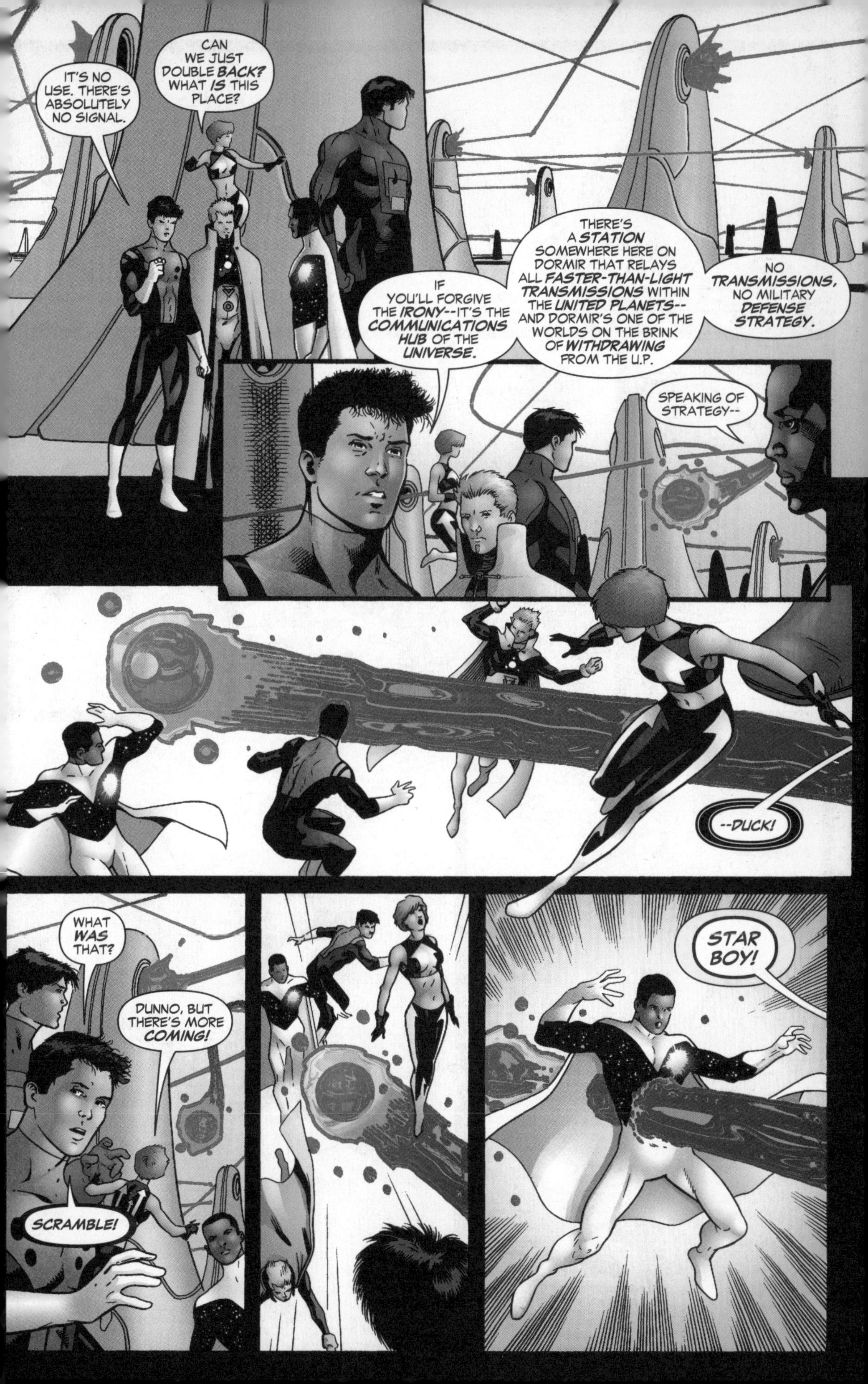
IT'S NO USE. THERE'S ABSOLUTELY NO SIGNAL.
CAN WE JUST DOUBLE BACK? WHAT IS THIS PLACE?
IF YOU'LL FORGIVE THE IRONY--IT'S THE COMMUNICATIONS HUB OF THE UNIVERSE.
THERE'S A STATION SOMEWHERE HERE ON DORMIR THAT RELAYS ALL FASTER-THAN-LIGHT TRANSMISSIONS WITHIN THE UNITED PLANETS--AND DORMIR'S ONE OF THE WORLDS ON THE BRINK OF WITHDRAWING FROM THE U.P.
NO TRANSMISSIONS, NO MILITARY DEFENSE STRATEGY.
SPEAKING OF STRATEGY--
--DUCK!
WHAT WAS THAT?
DUNNO, BUT THERE'S MORE COMING!
SCRAMBLE!
STAR BOY!

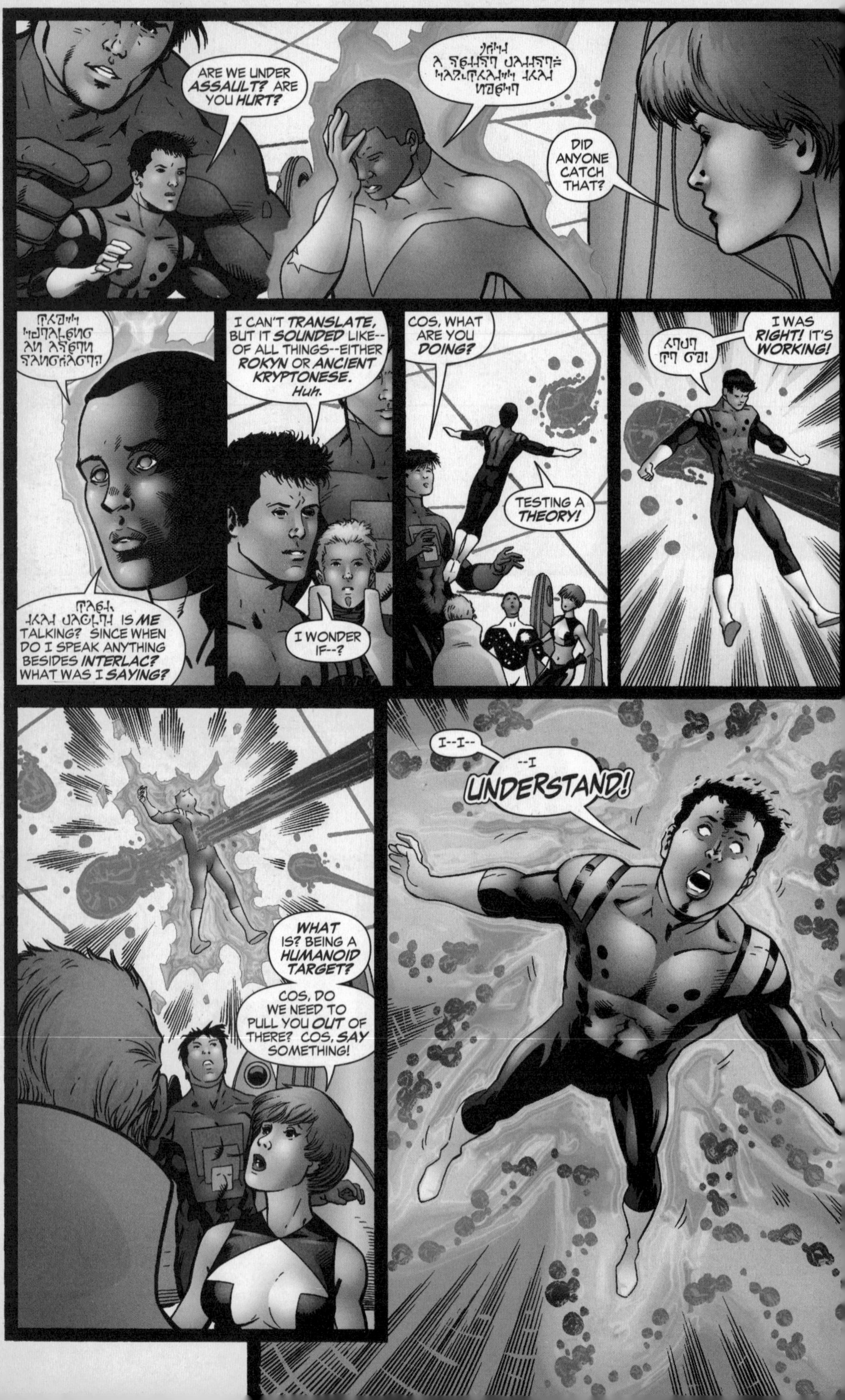
ARE WE UNDER ASSAULT? ARE YOU HURT?
DID ANYONE CATCH THAT?
I CAN'T TRANSLATE, BUT IT SOUNDED LIKE--OF ALL THINGS--EITHER ROKYN OR ANCIENT KRYPTONESE. Huh.
IS ME TALKING? SINCE WHEN DO I SPEAK ANYTHING BESIDES INTERLAC? WHAT WAS I SAYING?
I WONDER IF--?
COS, WHAT ARE YOU DOING?
TESTING A THEORY!
I WAS RIGHT! IT'S WORKING!
WHAT IS? BEING A HUMANOID TARGET?
COS, DO WE NEED TO PULL YOU OUT OF THERE? COS, SAY SOMETHING!
I--I--
--I UNDERSTAND!

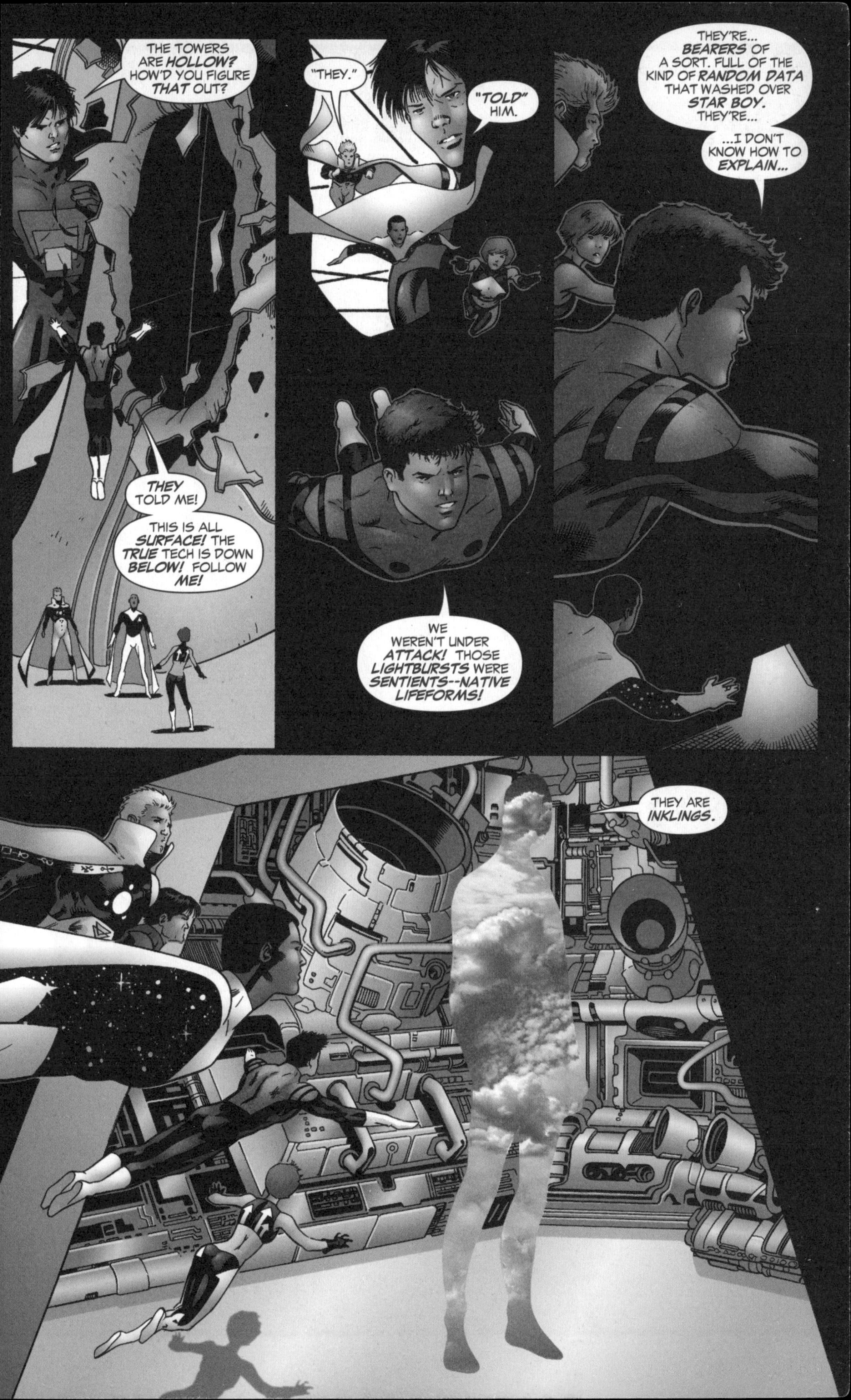
THE TOWERS ARE HOLLOW? HOW'D YOU FIGURE THAT OUT?
THEY TOLD ME!
THIS IS ALL SURFACE! THE TRUE TECH IS DOWN BELOW! FOLLOW ME!
"THEY."
"TOLD" HIM.
WE WEREN'T UNDER ATTACK! THOSE LIGHTBURSTS WERE SENTIENTS--NATIVE LIFEFORMS!
THEY'RE... BEARERS OF A SORT. FULL OF THE KIND OF RANDOM DATA THAT WASHED OVER STAR BOY. THEY'RE...
...I DON'T KNOW HOW TO EXPLAIN...
THEY ARE INKLINGS.

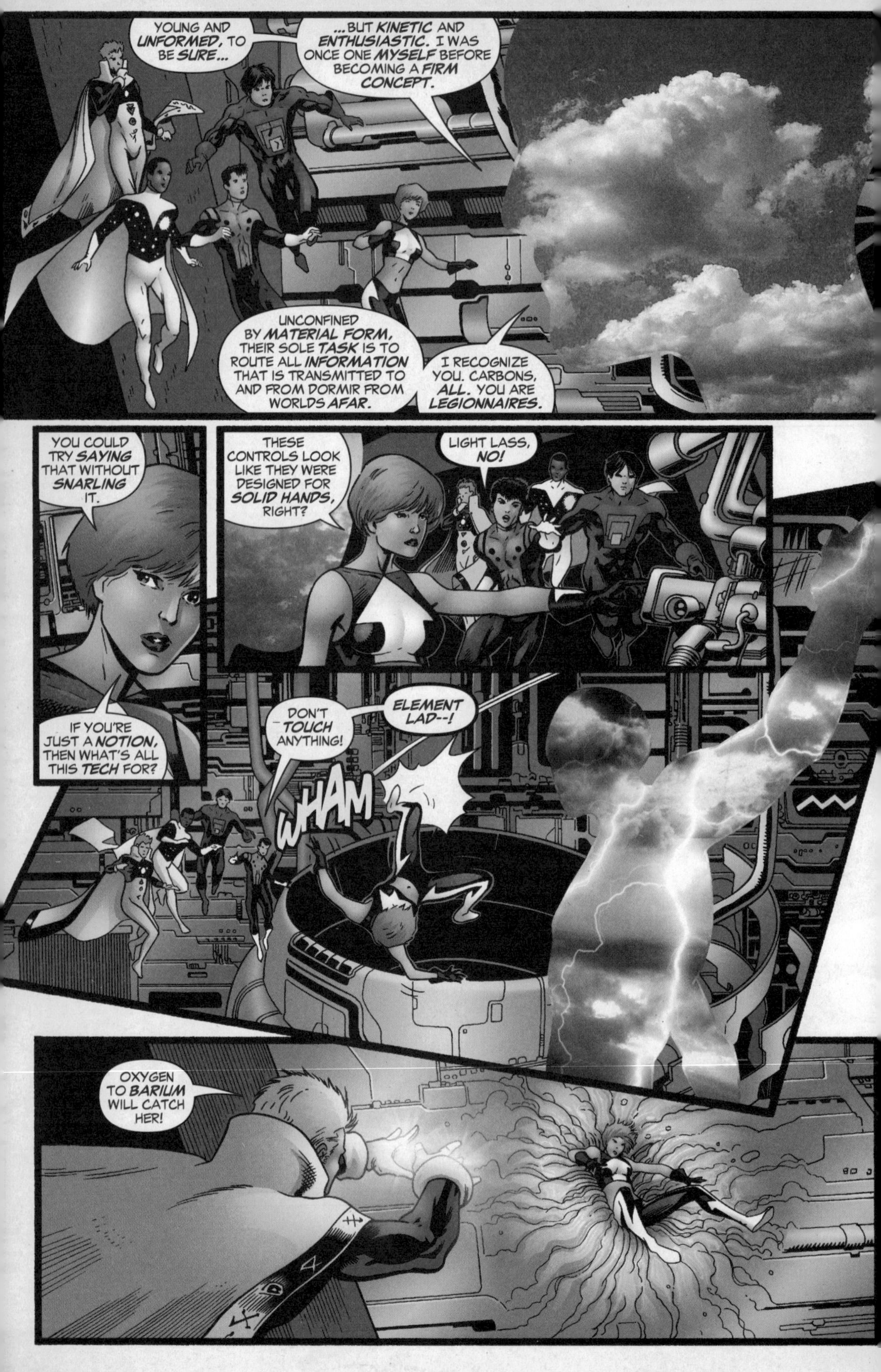
YOUNG AND UNFORMED, TO BE SURE...
...BUT KINETIC AND ENTHUSIASTIC. I WAS ONCE ONE MYSELF BEFORE BECOMING A FIRM CONCEPT.
UNCONFINED BY MATERIAL FORM, THEIR SOLE TASK IS TO ROUTE ALL INFORMATION THAT IS TRANSMITTED TO AND FROM DORMIR FROM WORLDS AFAR.
I RECOGNIZE YOU. CARBONS, ALL. YOU ARE LEGIONNAIRES.
YOU COULD TRY SAYING THAT WITHOUT SNARLING IT.
IF YOU'RE JUST A NOTION, THEN WHAT'S ALL THIS TECH FOR?
THESE CONTROLS LOOK LIKE THEY WERE DESIGNED FOR SOLID HANDS, RIGHT?
LIGHT LASS, NO!
DON'T TOUCH ANYTHING!
ELEMENT LAD--!
WHAM
OXYGEN TO BARIUM WILL CATCH HER!

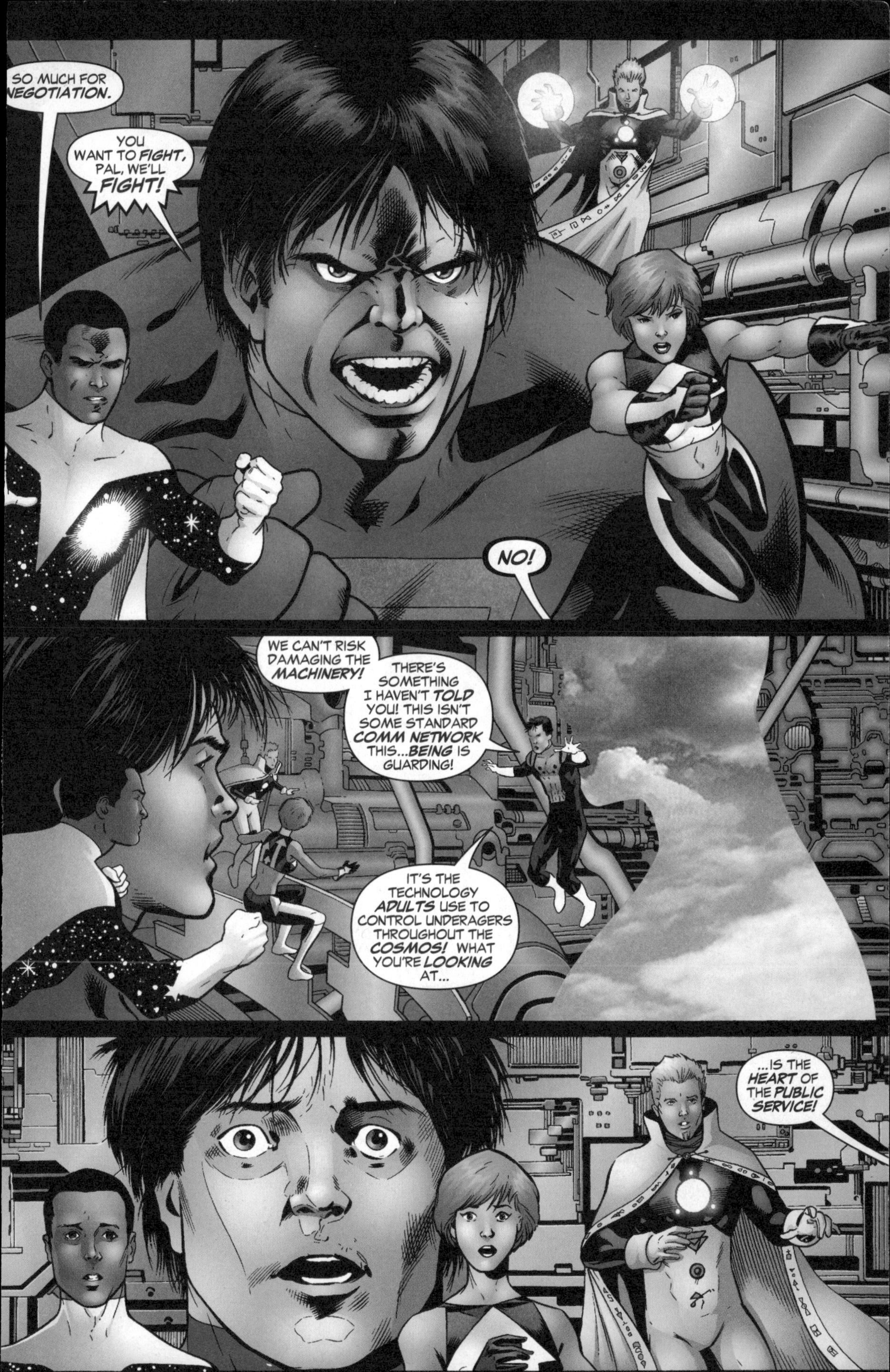
SO MUCH FOR NEGOTIATION.
YOU WANT TO FIGHT, PAL, WE'LL FIGHT!
NO!
WE CAN'T RISK DAMAGING THE MACHINERY!
THERE'S SOMETHING I HAVEN'T TOLD YOU! THIS ISN'T SOME STANDARD COMM NETWORK THIS...BEING IS GUARDING!
IT'S THE TECHNOLOGY ADULTS USE TO CONTROL UNDERAGERS THROUGHOUT THE COSMOS! WHAT YOU'RE LOOKING AT...
...IS THE HEART OF THE PUBLIC SERVICE!

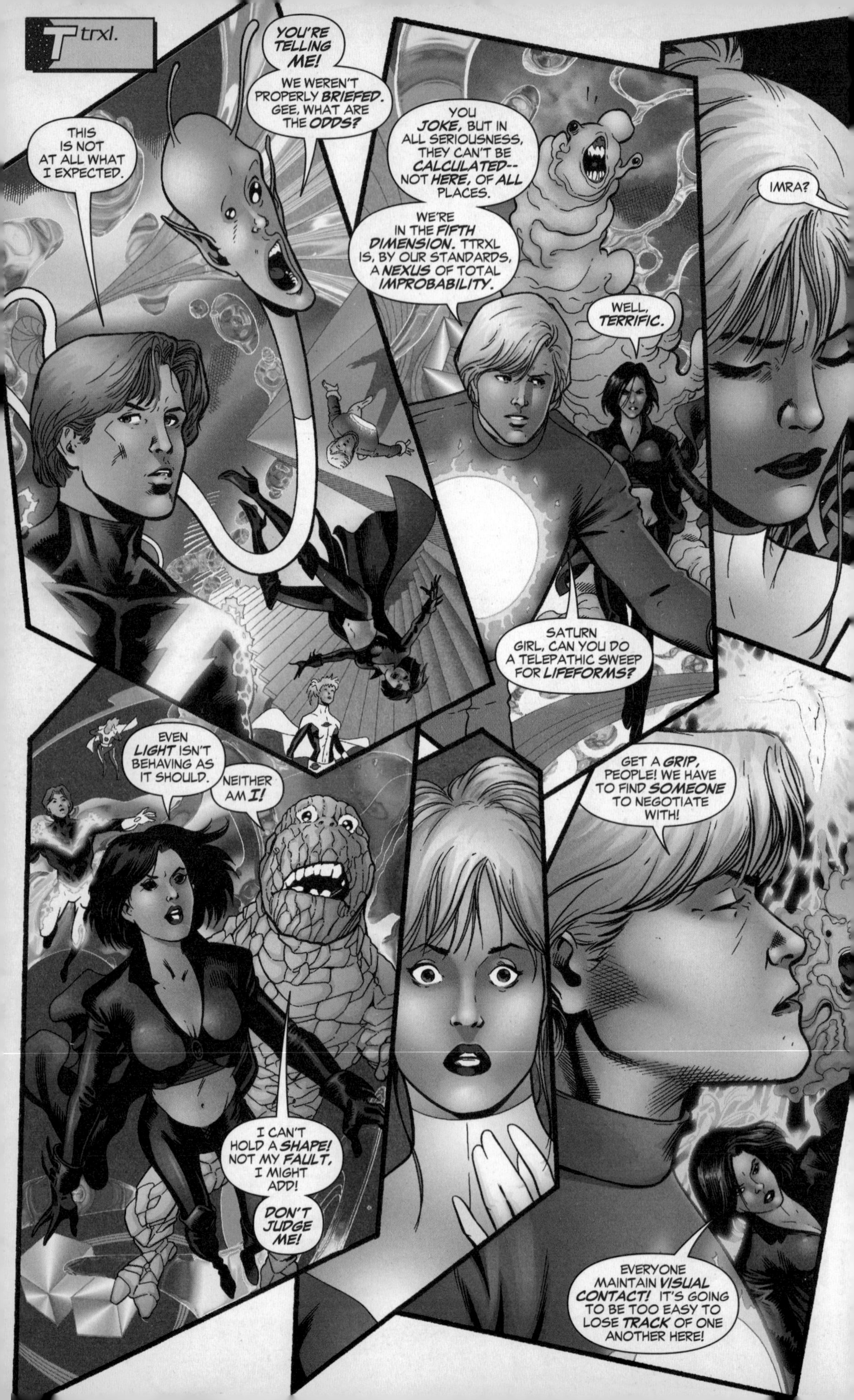
Ttrxl.
THIS IS NOT AT ALL WHAT I EXPECTED.
YOU'RE TELLING ME!
WE WEREN'T PROPERLY BRIEFED. GEE, WHAT ARE THE ODDS?
YOU JOKE, BUT IN ALL SERIOUSNESS, THEY CAN'T BE CALCULATED-- NOT HERE, OF ALL PLACES.
WE'RE IN THE FIFTH DIMENSION. TTRXL IS, BY OUR STANDARDS, A NEXUS OF TOTAL IMPROBABILITY.
WELL, TERRIFIC.
IMRA?
SATURN GIRL, CAN YOU DO A TELEPATHIC SWEEP FOR LIFEFORMS?
EVEN LIGHT ISN'T BEHAVING AS IT SHOULD.
NEITHER AM I!
I CAN'T HOLD A SHAPE! NOT MY FAULT, I MIGHT ADD!
DON'T JUDGE ME!
GET A GRIP, PEOPLE! WE HAVE TO FIND SOMEONE TO NEGOTIATE WITH!
EVERYONE MAINTAIN VISUAL CONTACT! IT'S GOING TO BE TOO EASY TO LOSE TRACK OF ONE ANOTHER HERE!

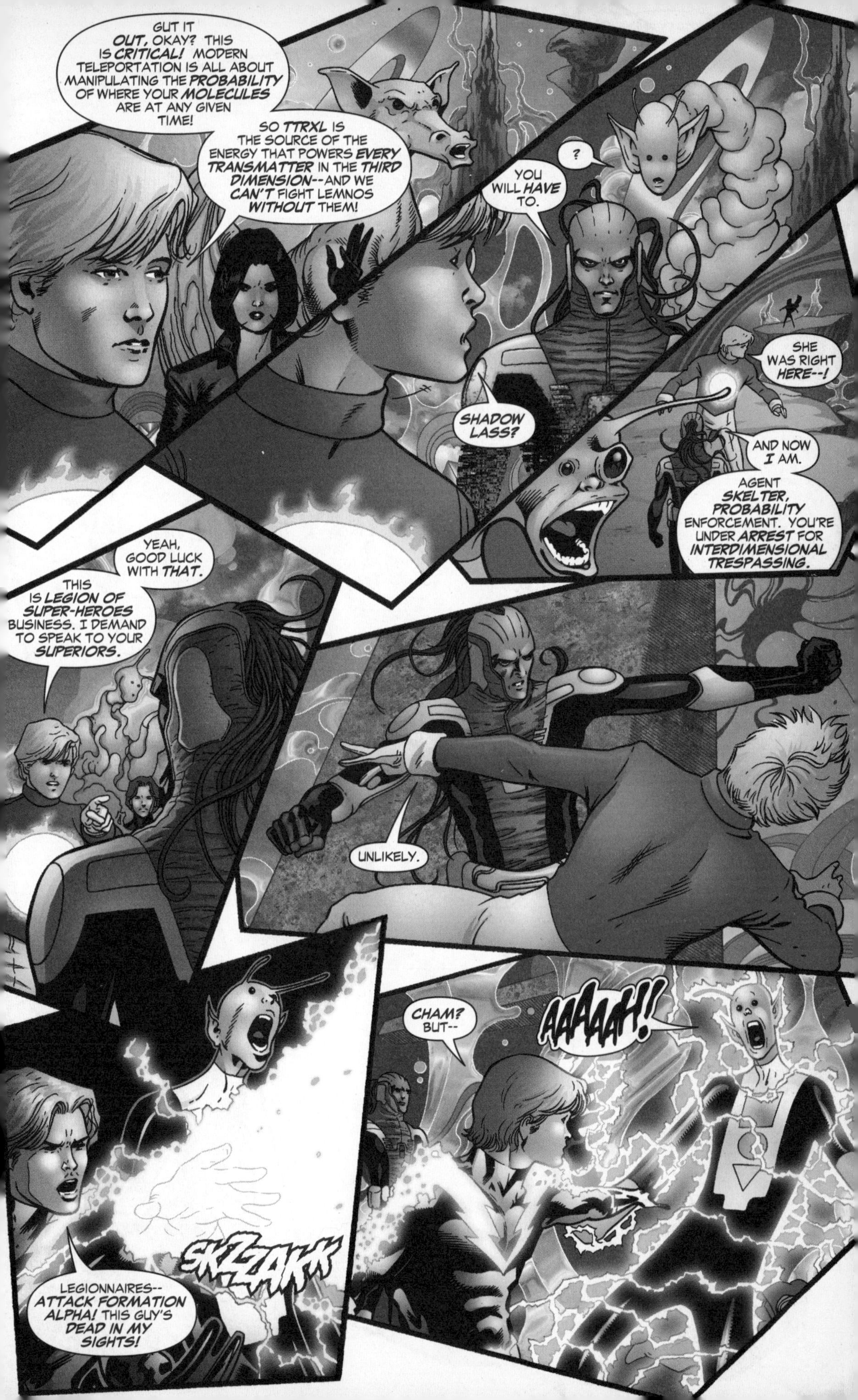
GUT IT OUT, OKAY? THIS IS CRITICAL! MODERN TELEPORTATION IS ALL ABOUT MANIPULATING THE PROBABILITY OF WHERE YOUR MOLECULES ARE AT ANY GIVEN TIME!
SO TTRXL IS THE SOURCE OF THE ENERGY THAT POWERS EVERY TRANSMATTER IN THE THIRD DIMENSION--AND WE CAN'T FIGHT LEMNOS WITHOUT THEM!
?
YOU WILL HAVE TO.
SHADOW LASS?
SHE WAS RIGHT HERE--!
AND NOW I AM.
AGENT SKELTER, PROBABILITY ENFORCEMENT. YOU'RE UNDER ARREST FOR INTERDIMENSIONAL TRESPASSING.
YEAH, GOOD LUCK WITH THAT.
THIS IS LEGION OF SUPER-HEROES BUSINESS. I DEMAND TO SPEAK TO YOUR SUPERIORS.
UNLIKELY.
SKZZAKK
LEGIONNAIRES--ATTACK FORMATION ALPHA! THIS GUY'S DEAD IN MY SIGHTS!
CHAM? BUT--
AAAAAH!!

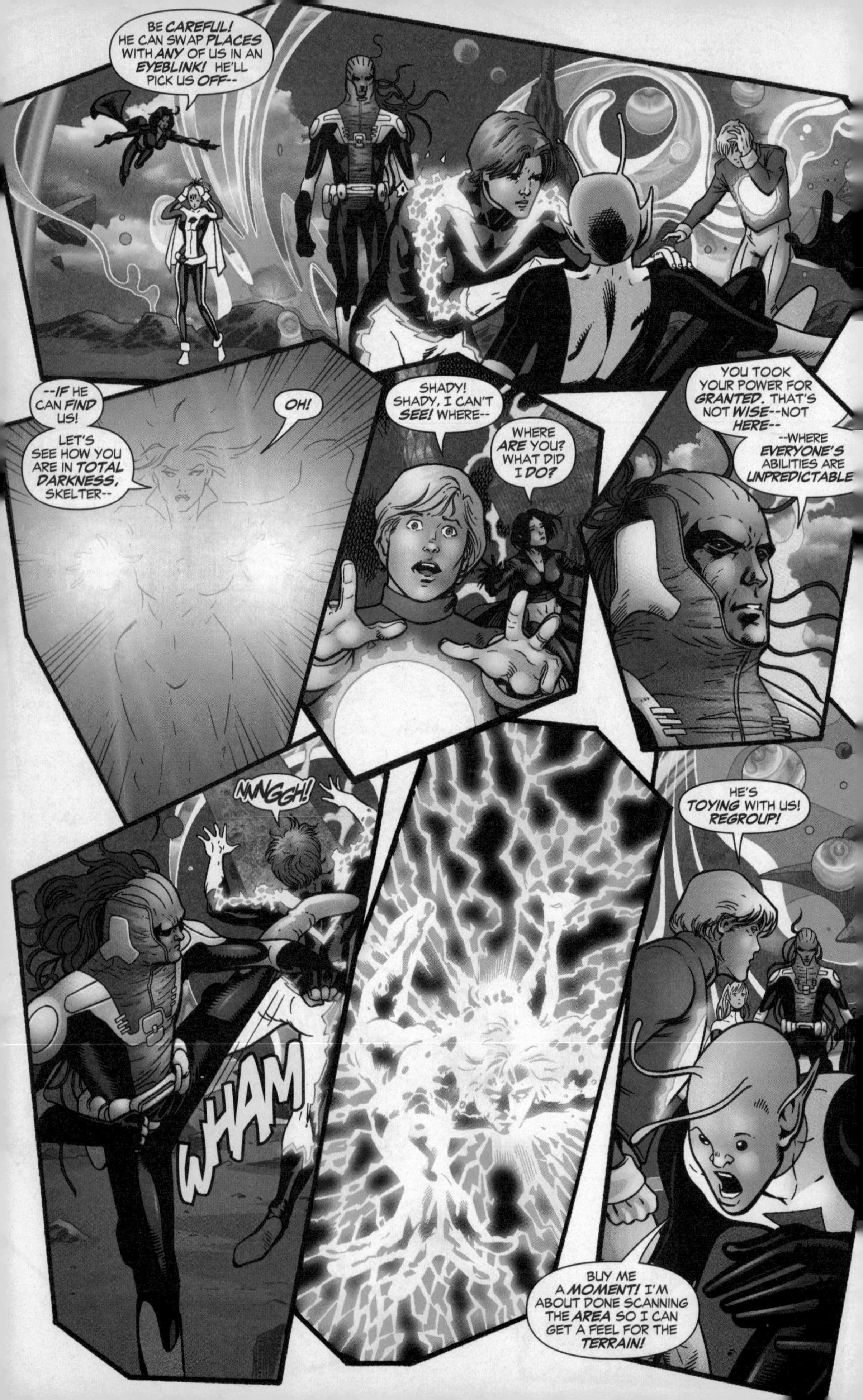

BE CAREFUL! HE CAN SWAP PLACES WITH ANY OF US IN AN EYEBLINK! HE'LL PICK US OFF--
--IF HE CAN FIND US!
LET'S SEE HOW YOU ARE IN TOTAL DARKNESS, SKELTER--
OH!
SHADY! SHADY, I CAN'T SEE! WHERE--
WHERE ARE YOU? WHAT DID I DO?
YOU TOOK YOUR POWER FOR GRANTED. THAT'S NOT WISE--NOT HERE--
--WHERE EVERYONE'S ABILITIES ARE UNPREDICTABLE
NNNGGH!
WHAM
HE'S TOYING WITH US! REGROUP!
BUY ME A MOMENT! I'M ABOUT DONE SCANNING THE AREA SO I CAN GET A FEEL FOR THE TERRAIN!

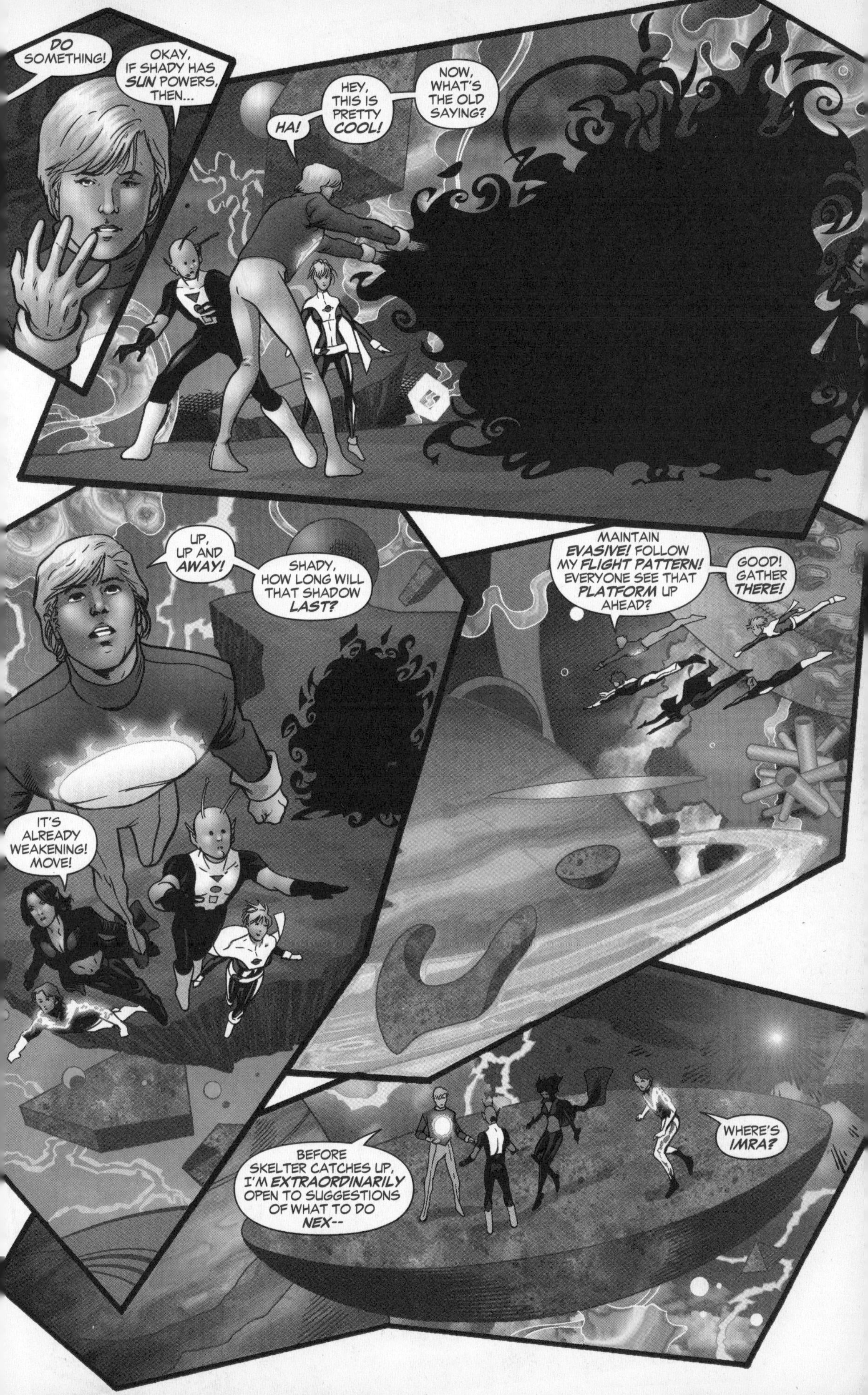
DO SOMETHING!
OKAY, IF SHADY HAS SUN POWERS, THEN...
HA!
HEY, THIS IS PRETTY COOL!
NOW, WHAT'S THE OLD SAYING?
UP, UP AND AWAY!
SHADY, HOW LONG WILL THAT SHADOW LAST?
IT'S ALREADY WEAKENING! MOVE!
MAINTAIN EVASIVE! FOLLOW MY FLIGHT PATTERN! EVERYONE SEE THAT PLATFORM UP AHEAD?
GOOD! GATHER THERE!
BEFORE SKELTER CATCHES UP, I'M EXTRAORDINARILY OPEN TO SUGGESTIONS OF WHAT TO DO NEX--
WHERE'S IMRA?

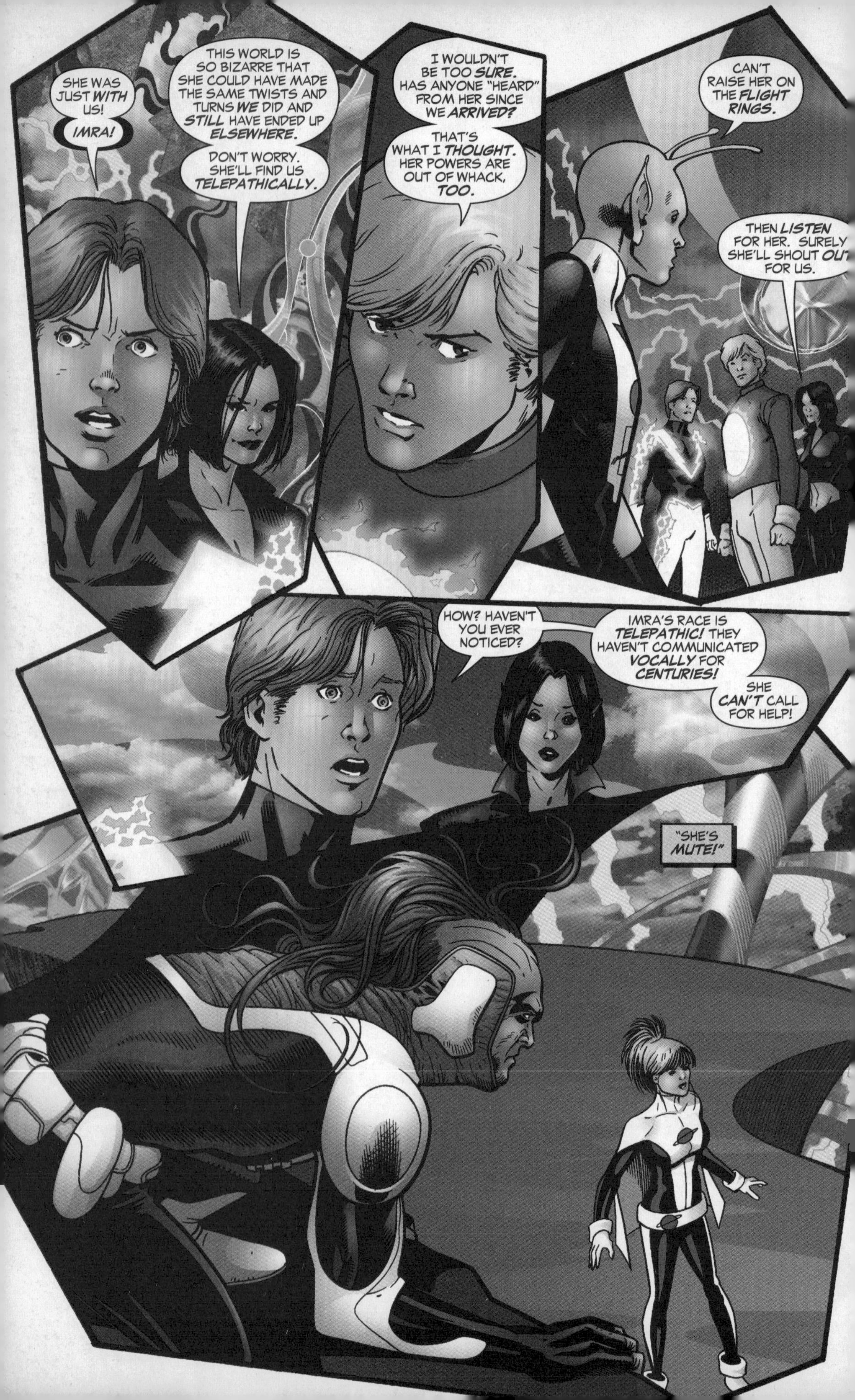
SHE WAS JUST WITH US!
IMRA!
THIS WORLD IS SO BIZARRE THAT SHE COULD HAVE MADE THE SAME TWISTS AND TURNS WE DID AND STILL HAVE ENDED UP ELSEWHERE.
DON'T WORRY. SHE'LL FIND US TELEPATHICALLY.
I WOULDN'T BE TOO SURE. HAS ANYONE "HEARD" FROM HER SINCE WE ARRIVED?
THAT'S WHAT I THOUGHT. HER POWERS ARE OUT OF WHACK, TOO.
CAN'T RAISE HER ON THE FLIGHT RINGS.
THEN LISTEN FOR HER. SURELY SHE'LL SHOUT OUT FOR US.
HOW? HAVEN'T YOU EVER NOTICED?
IMRA'S RACE IS TELEPATHIC! THEY HAVEN'T COMMUNICATED VOCALLY FOR CENTURIES!
SHE CAN'T CALL FOR HELP!
"SHE'S MUTE!"

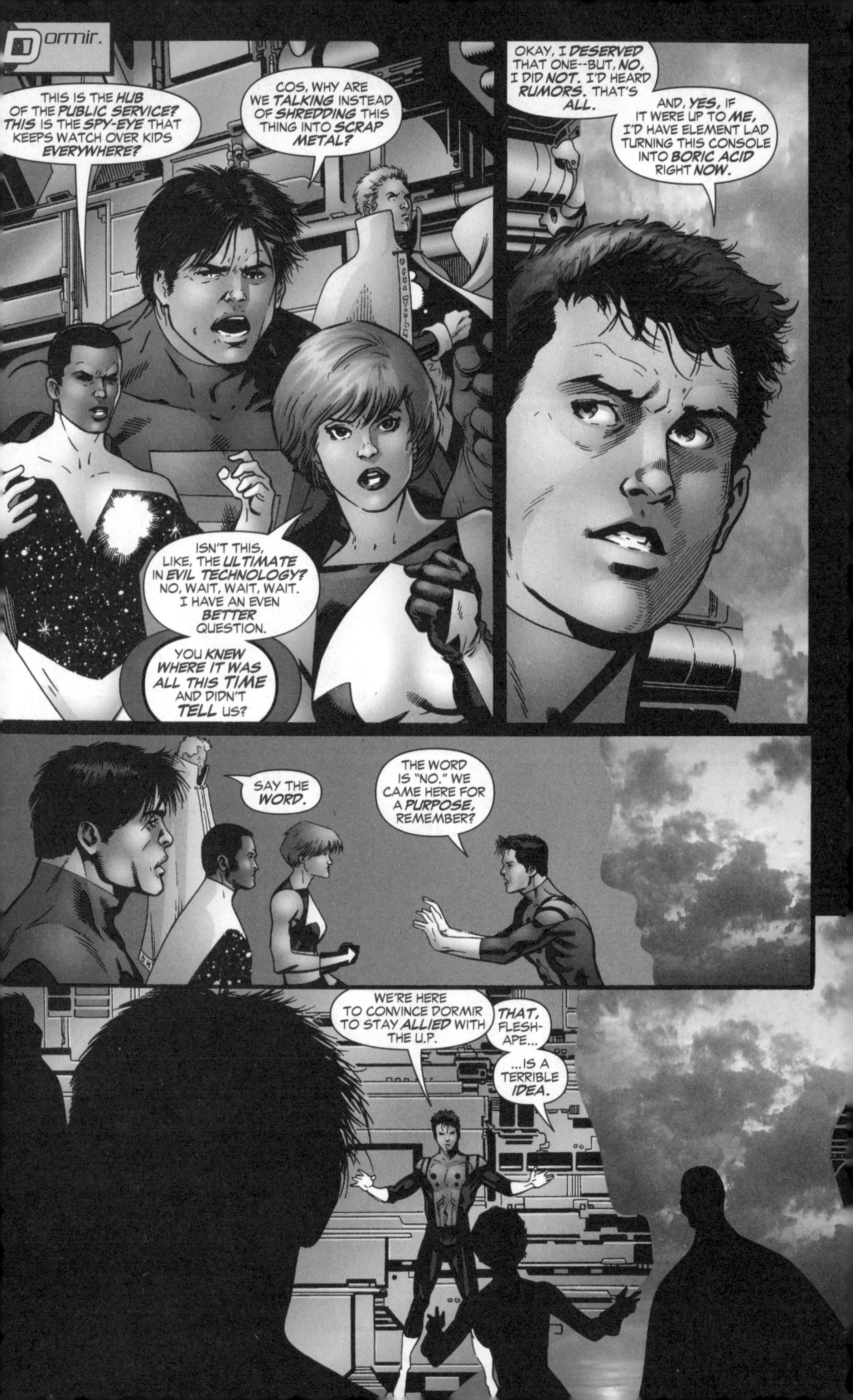

Dormir.
THIS IS THE HUB OF THE PUBLIC SERVICE? THIS IS THE SPY-EYE THAT KEEPS WATCH OVER KIDS EVERYWHERE?
COS, WHY ARE WE TALKING INSTEAD OF SHREDDING THIS THING INTO SCRAP METAL?
ISN'T THIS, LIKE, THE ULTIMATE IN EVIL TECHNOLOGY? NO, WAIT, WAIT, WAIT. I HAVE AN EVEN BETTER QUESTION.
YOU KNEW WHERE IT WAS ALL THIS TIME AND DIDN'T TELL US?
OKAY, I DESERVED THAT ONE--BUT, NO, I DID NOT. I'D HEARD RUMORS. THAT'S ALL.
AND, YES, IF IT WERE UP TO ME, I'D HAVE ELEMENT LAD TURNING THIS CONSOLE INTO BORIC ACID RIGHT NOW.
SAY THE WORD.
THE WORD IS "NO." WE CAME HERE FOR A PURPOSE, REMEMBER?
WE'RE HERE TO CONVINCE DORMIR TO STAY ALLIED WITH THE U.P.
THAT, FLESH-APE...
...IS A TERRIBLE IDEA.

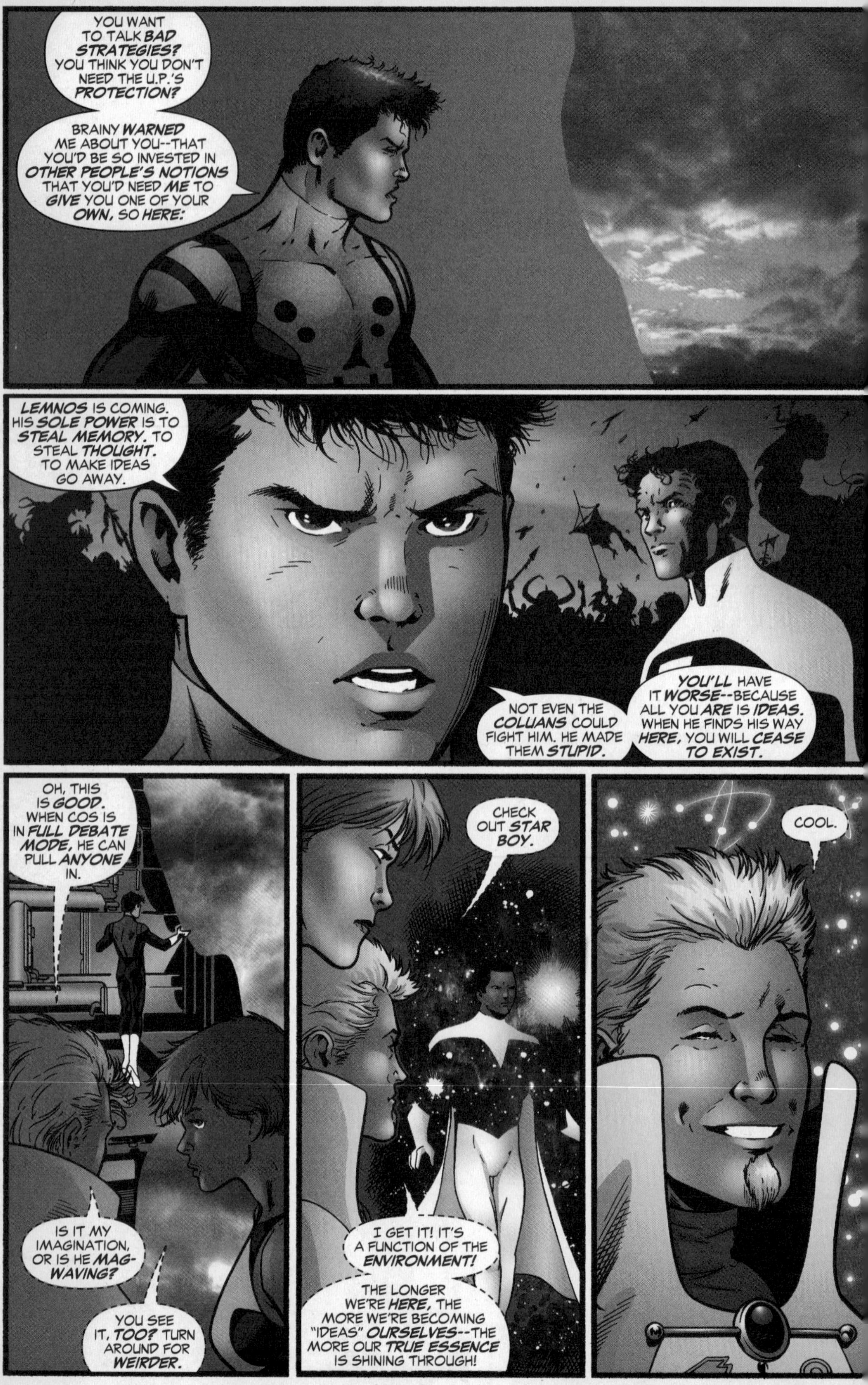
YOU WANT TO TALK BAD STRATEGIES? YOU THINK YOU DON'T NEED THE U.P.'S PROTECTION?
BRAINY WARNED ME ABOUT YOU--THAT YOU'D BE SO INVESTED IN OTHER PEOPLE'S NOTIONS THAT YOU'D NEED ME TO GIVE YOU ONE OF YOUR OWN, SO HERE:
LEMNOS IS COMING. HIS SOLE POWER IS TO STEAL MEMORY. TO STEAL THOUGHT. TO MAKE IDEAS GO AWAY.
NOT EVEN THE COLUANS COULD FIGHT HIM. HE MADE THEM STUPID.
YOU'LL HAVE IT WORSE--BECAUSE ALL YOU ARE IS IDEAS. WHEN HE FINDS HIS WAY HERE, YOU WILL CEASE TO EXIST.
OH, THIS IS GOOD. WHEN COS IS IN FULL DEBATE MODE, HE CAN PULL ANYONE IN.
IS IT MY IMAGINATION, OR IS HE MAG-WAVING?
YOU SEE IT, TOO? TURN AROUND FOR WEIRDER.
CHECK OUT STAR BOY.
I GET IT! IT'S A FUNCTION OF THE ENVIRONMENT!
THE LONGER WE'RE HERE, THE MORE WE'RE BECOMING "IDEAS" OURSELVES--THE MORE OUR TRUE ESSENCE IS SHINING THROUGH!
COOL.

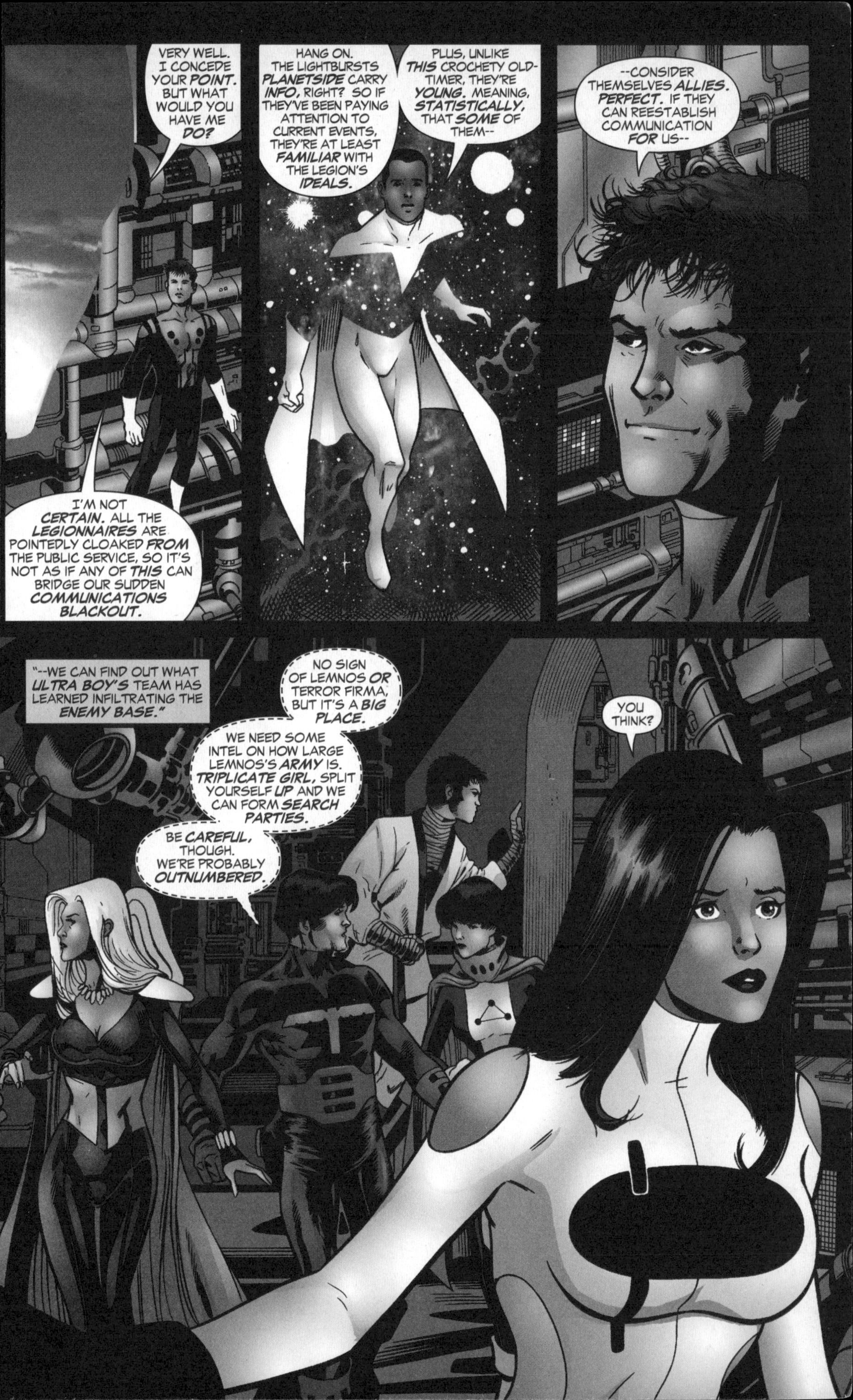
VERY WELL. I CONCEDE YOUR POINT. BUT WHAT WOULD YOU HAVE ME DO?
I'M NOT CERTAIN. ALL THE LEGIONNAIRES ARE POINTEDLY CLOAKED FROM THE PUBLIC SERVICE, SO IT'S NOT AS IF ANY OF THIS CAN BRIDGE OUR SUDDEN COMMUNICATIONS BLACKOUT.
HANG ON. THE LIGHTBURSTS PLANETSIDE CARRY INFO, RIGHT? SO IF THEY'VE BEEN PAYING ATTENTION TO CURRENT EVENTS, THEY'RE AT LEAST FAMILIAR WITH THE LEGION'S IDEALS.
PLUS, UNLIKE THIS CROCHETY OLD-TIMER, THEY'RE YOUNG. MEANING, STATISTICALLY, THAT SOME OF THEM--
--CONSIDER THEMSELVES ALLIES. PERFECT. IF THEY CAN REESTABLISH COMMUNICATION FOR US--
"--WE CAN FIND OUT WHAT ULTRA BOY'S TEAM HAS LEARNED INFILTRATING THE ENEMY BASE."
NO SIGN OF LEMNOS OR TERROR FIRMA, BUT IT'S A BIG PLACE.
WE NEED SOME INTEL ON HOW LARGE LEMNOS'S ARMY IS. TRIPLICATE GIRL, SPLIT YOURSELF UP AND WE CAN FORM SEARCH PARTIES.
BE CAREFUL, THOUGH. WE'RE PROBABLY OUTNUMBERED.
YOU THINK?

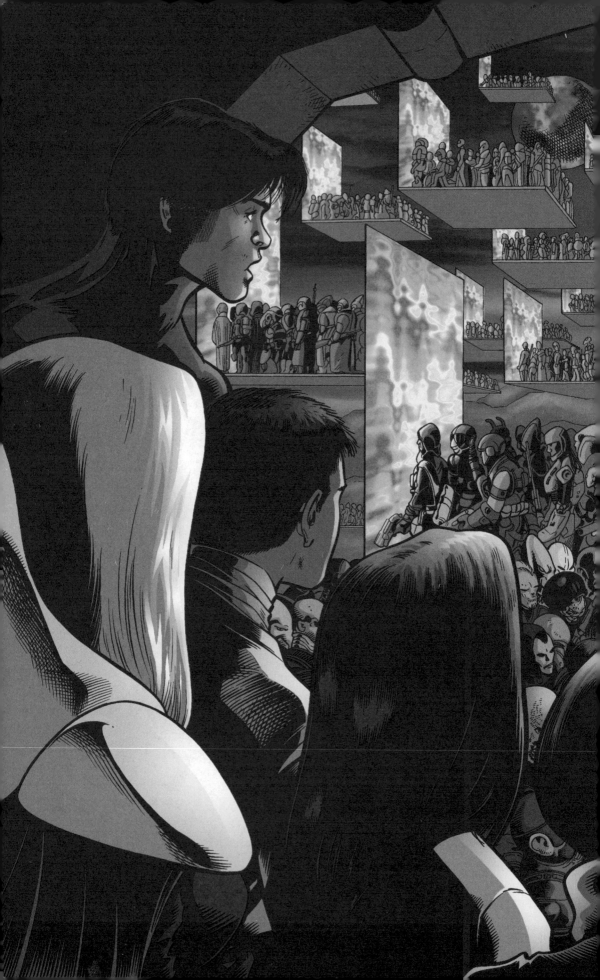

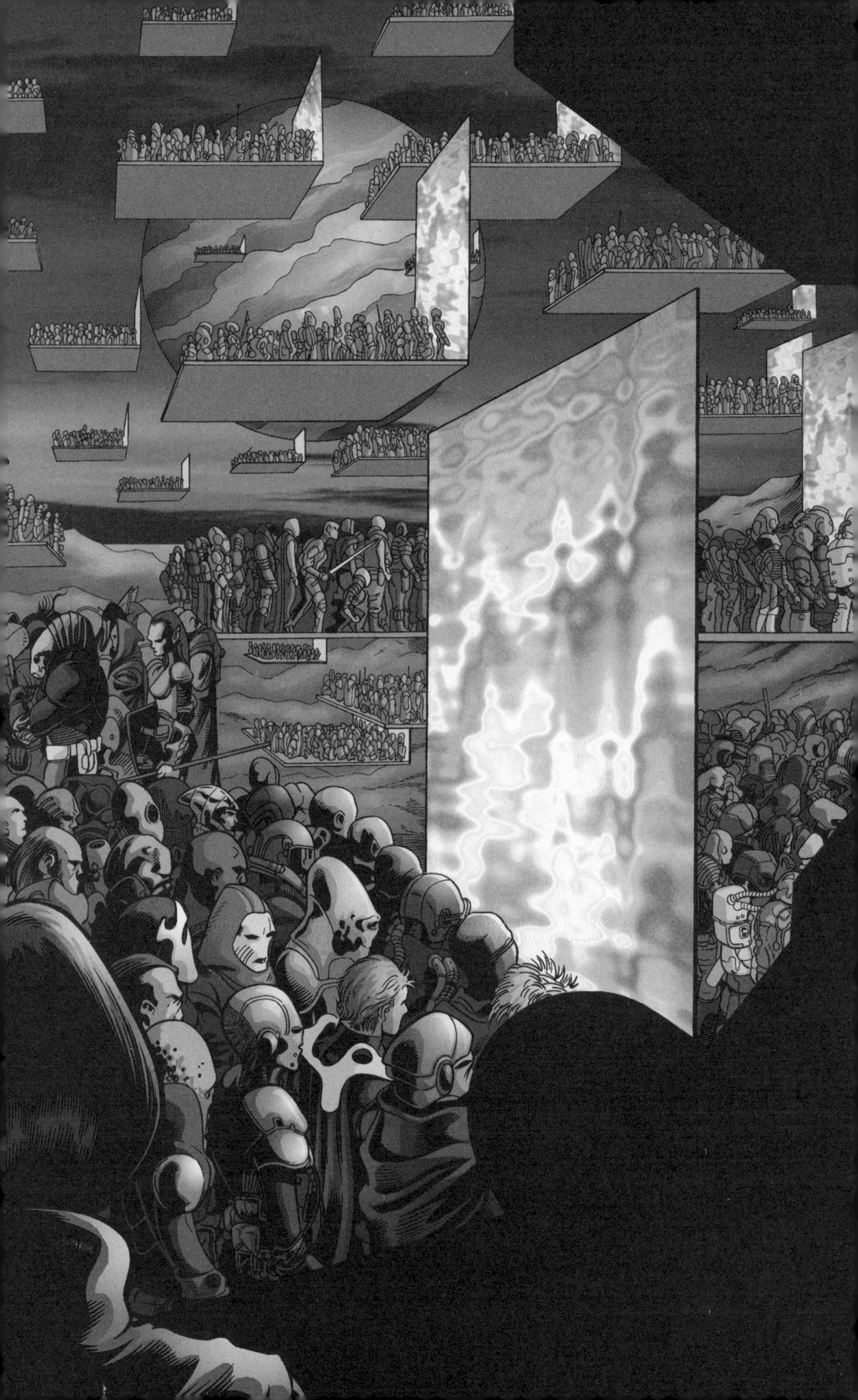

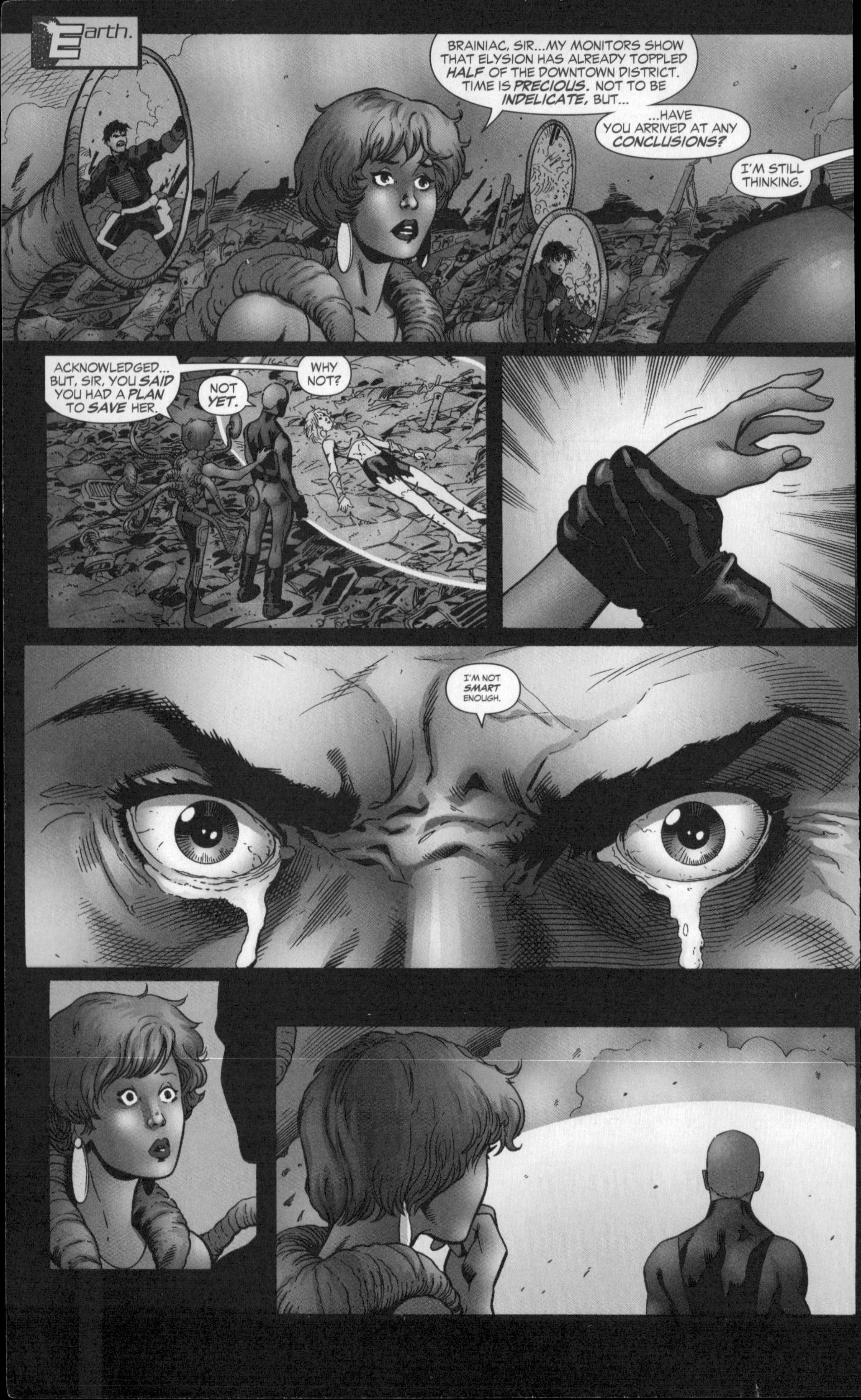
Earth.
BRAINIAC, SIR...MY MONITORS SHOW THAT ELYSION HAS ALREADY TOPPLED HALF OF THE DOWNTOWN DISTRICT. TIME IS PRECIOUS. NOT TO BE INDELICATE, BUT...
...HAVE YOU ARRIVED AT ANY CONCLUSIONS?
I'M STILL THINKING.
ACKNOWLEDGED... BUT, SIR, YOU SAID YOU HAD A PLAN TO SAVE HER.
NOT YET.
WHY NOT?
I'M NOT SMART ENOUGH.

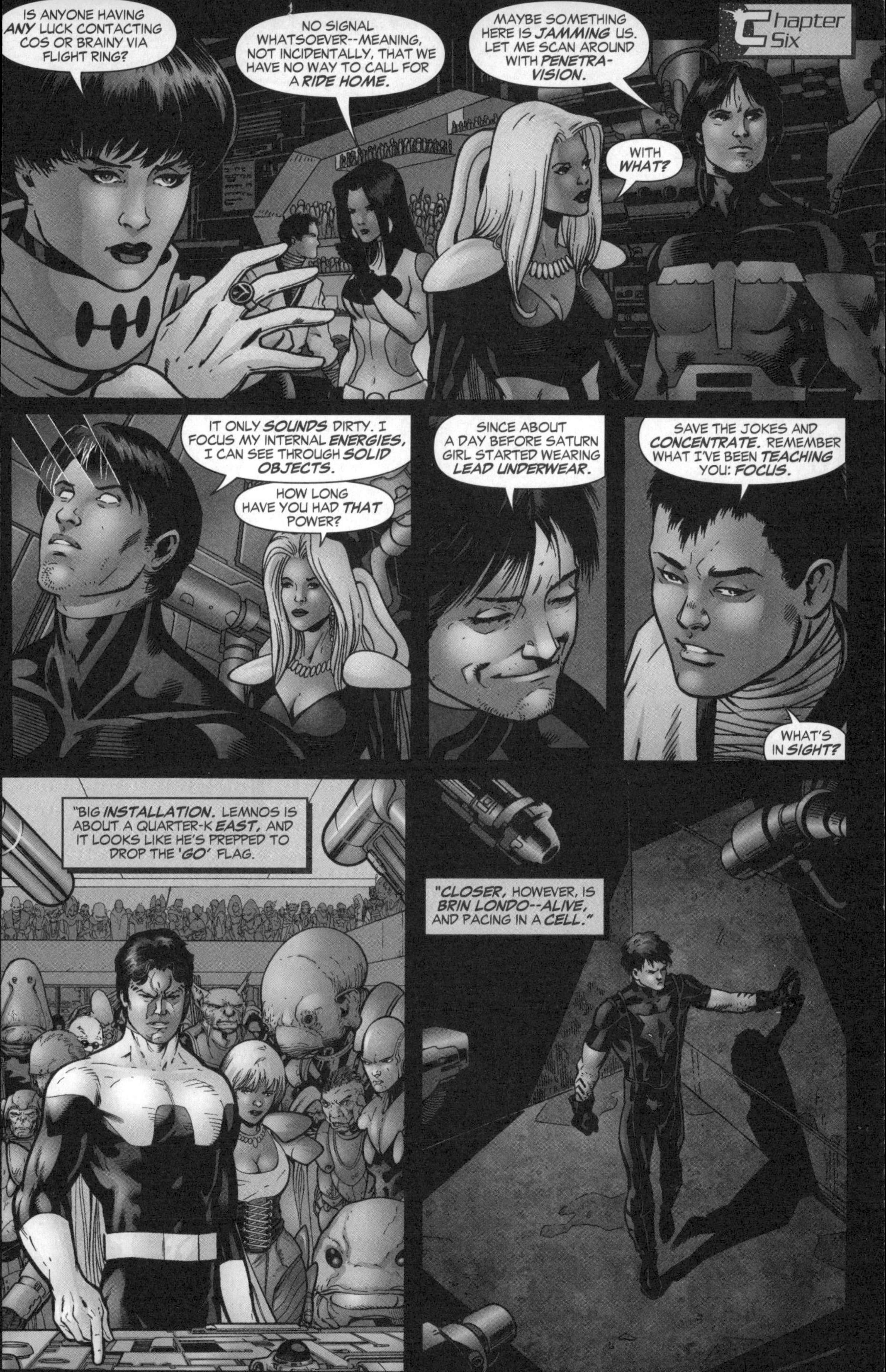
Chapter Six
IS ANYONE HAVING ANY LUCK CONTACTING COS OR BRAINY VIA FLIGHT RING?
NO SIGNAL WHATSOEVER--MEANING, NOT INCIDENTALLY, THAT WE HAVE NO WAY TO CALL FOR A RIDE HOME.
MAYBE SOMETHING HERE IS JAMMING US. LET ME SCAN AROUND WITH PENETRA-VISION.
WITH WHAT?
IT ONLY SOUNDS DIRTY. I FOCUS MY INTERNAL ENERGIES, I CAN SEE THROUGH SOLID OBJECTS.
HOW LONG HAVE YOU HAD THAT POWER?
SINCE ABOUT A DAY BEFORE SATURN GIRL STARTED WEARING LEAD UNDERWEAR.
SAVE THE JOKES AND CONCENTRATE. REMEMBER WHAT I'VE BEEN TEACHING YOU: FOCUS.
WHAT'S IN SIGHT?
"BIG INSTALLATION. LEMNOS IS ABOUT A QUARTER-K EAST, AND IT LOOKS LIKE HE'S PREPPED TO DROP THE 'GO' FLAG.
"CLOSER, HOWEVER, IS BRIN LONDO--ALIVE, AND PACING IN A CELL."

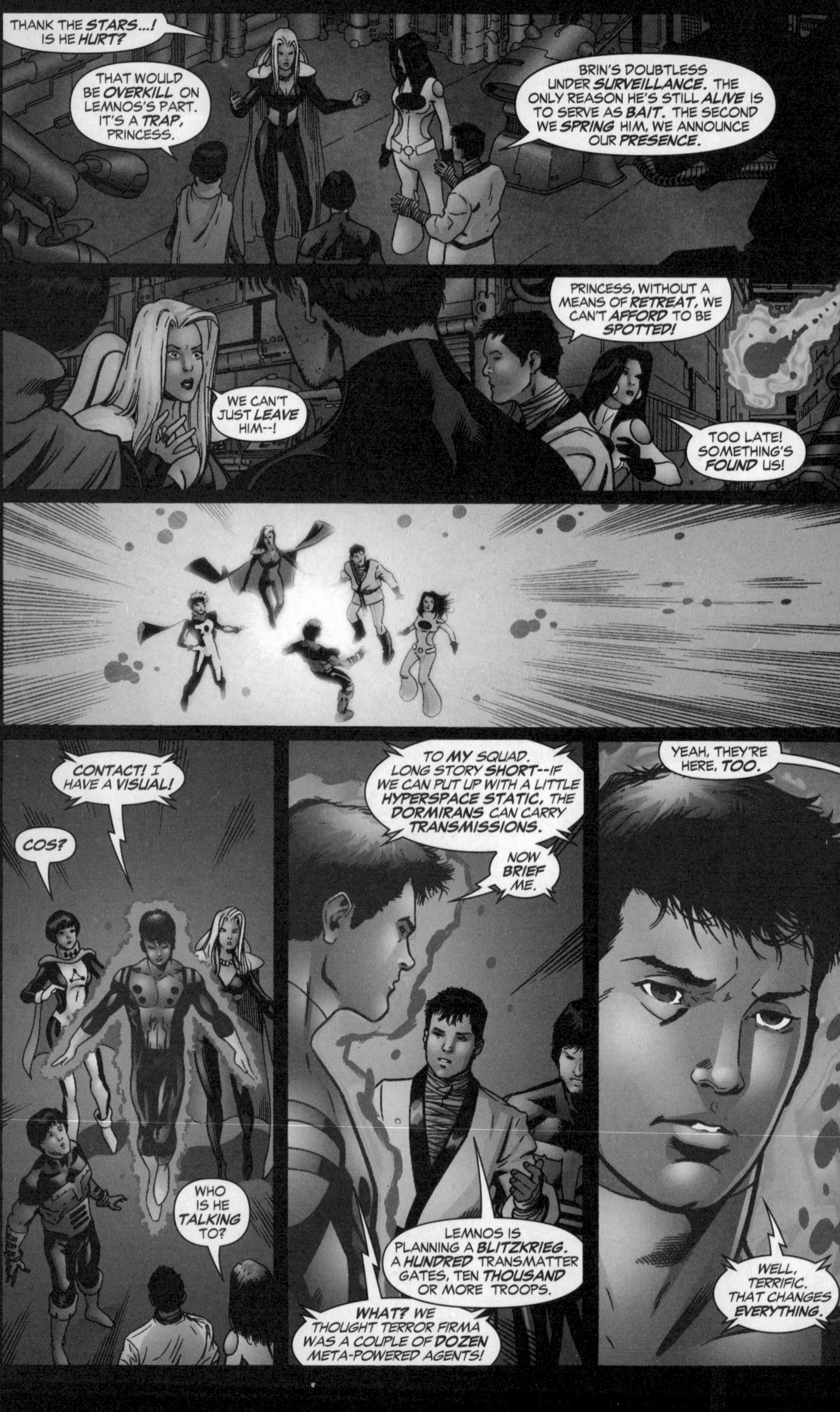

THANK THE STARS...! IS HE HURT?
THAT WOULD BE OVERKILL ON LEMNOS'S PART. IT'S A TRAP, PRINCESS.
BRIN'S DOUBTLESS UNDER SURVEILLANCE. THE ONLY REASON HE'S STILL ALIVE IS TO SERVE AS BAIT. THE SECOND WE SPRING HIM, WE ANNOUNCE OUR PRESENCE.
PRINCESS, WITHOUT A MEANS OF RETREAT, WE CAN'T AFFORD TO BE SPOTTED!
WE CAN'T JUST LEAVE HIM--!
TOO LATE! SOMETHING'S FOUND US!
CONTACT! I HAVE A VISUAL!
COS?
WHO IS HE TALKING TO?
TO MY SQUAD. LONG STORY SHORT--IF WE CAN PUT UP WITH A LITTLE HYPERSPACE STATIC, THE DORMIRANS CAN CARRY TRANSMISSIONS.
NOW BRIEF ME.
LEMNOS IS PLANNING A BLITZKRIEG. A HUNDRED TRANSMATTER GATES, TEN THOUSAND OR MORE TROOPS.
WHAT? WE THOUGHT TERROR FIRMA WAS A COUPLE OF DOZEN META-POWERED AGENTS!
YEAH, THEY'RE HERE, TOO.
WELL, TERRIFIC. THAT CHANGES EVERYTHING.

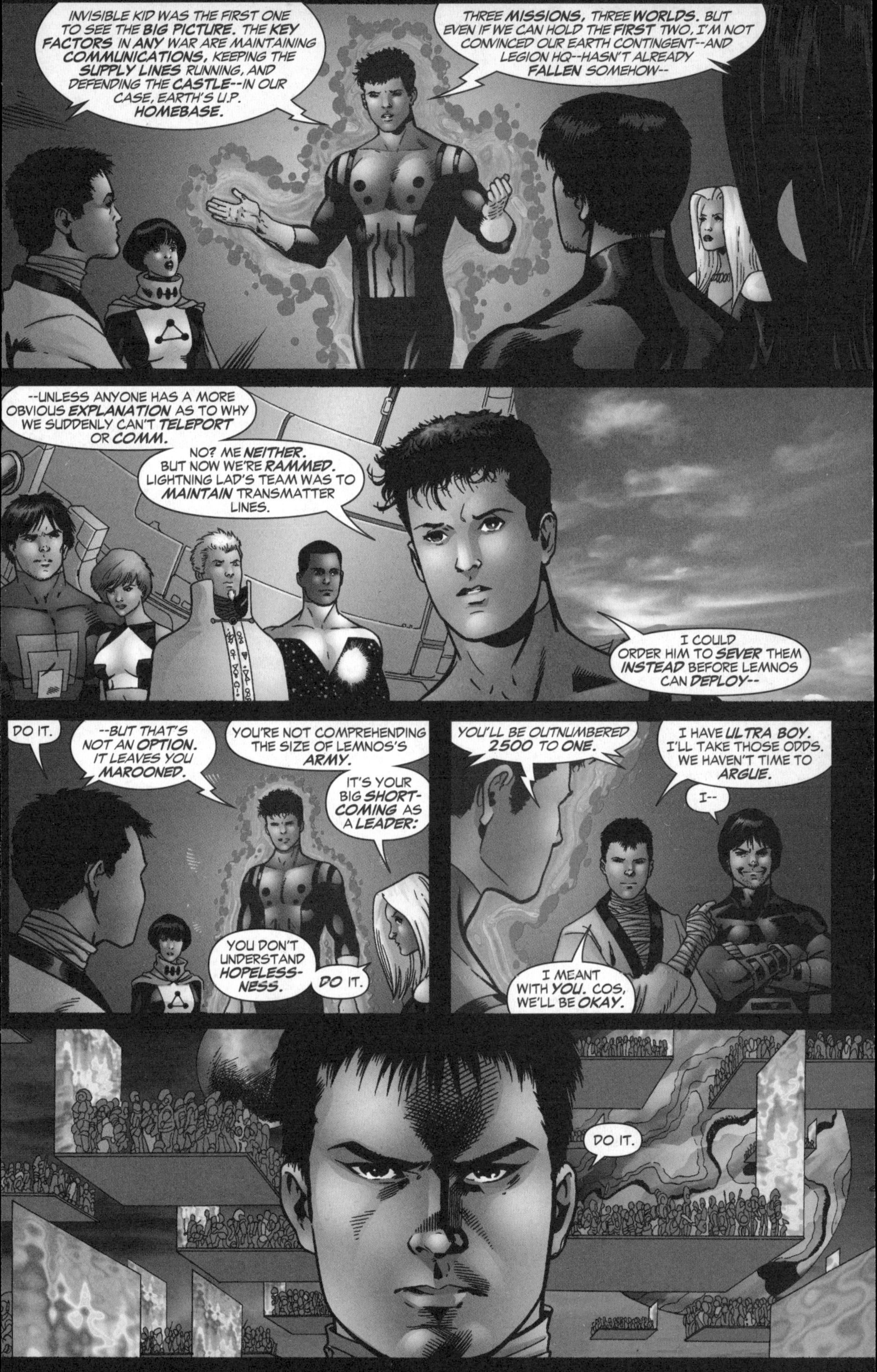

INVISIBLE KID WAS THE FIRST ONE TO SEE THE BIG PICTURE. THE KEY FACTORS IN ANY WAR ARE MAINTAINING COMMUNICATIONS, KEEPING THE SUPPLY LINES RUNNING, AND DEFENDING THE CASTLE--IN OUR CASE, EARTH'S U.P. HOMEBASE.
THREE MISSIONS, THREE WORLDS. BUT EVEN IF WE CAN HOLD THE FIRST TWO, I'M NOT CONVINCED OUR EARTH CONTINGENT--AND LEGION HQ--HASN'T ALREADY FALLEN SOMEHOW--
--UNLESS ANYONE HAS A MORE OBVIOUS EXPLANATION AS TO WHY WE SUDDENLY CAN'T TELEPORT OR COMM.
NO? ME NEITHER. BUT NOW WE'RE RAMMED. LIGHTNING LAD'S TEAM WAS TO MAINTAIN TRANSMATTER LINES.
I COULD ORDER HIM TO SEVER THEM INSTEAD BEFORE LEMNOS CAN DEPLOY--
DO IT.
--BUT THAT'S NOT AN OPTION. IT LEAVES YOU MAROONED.
YOU'RE NOT COMPREHENDING THE SIZE OF LEMNOS'S ARMY.
IT'S YOUR BIG SHORT-COMING AS A LEADER:
YOU DON'T UNDERSTAND HOPELESS-NESS.
DO IT.
YOU'LL BE OUTNUMBERED 2500 TO ONE.
I HAVE ULTRA BOY. I'LL TAKE THOSE ODDS. WE HAVEN'T TIME TO ARGUE.
I--
I MEANT WITH YOU. COS, WE'LL BE OKAY.
DO IT.

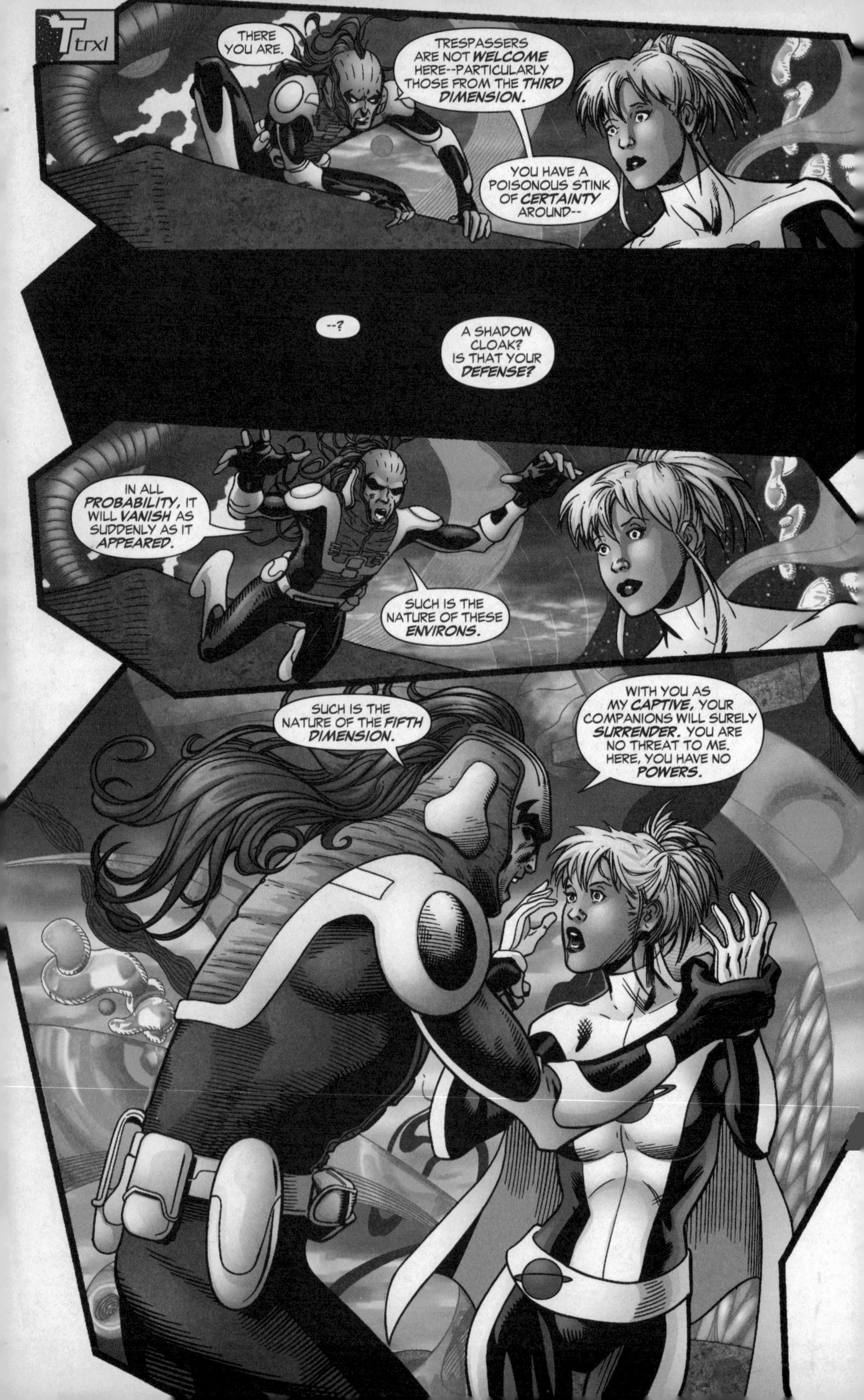
THERE YOU ARE.
TRESPASSERS ARE NOT WELCOME HERE--PARTICULARLY THOSE FROM THE THIRD DIMENSION.
YOU HAVE A POISONOUS STINK OF CERTAINTY AROUND--
--?
A SHADOW CLOAK? IS THAT YOUR DEFENSE?
IN ALL PROBABILITY, IT WILL VANISH AS SUDDENLY AS IT APPEARED.
SUCH IS THE NATURE OF THESE ENVIRONS.
SUCH IS THE NATURE OF THE FIFTH DIMENSION.
WITH YOU AS MY CAPTIVE, YOUR COMPANIONS WILL SURELY SURRENDER. YOU ARE NO THREAT TO ME. HERE, YOU HAVE NO POWERS.

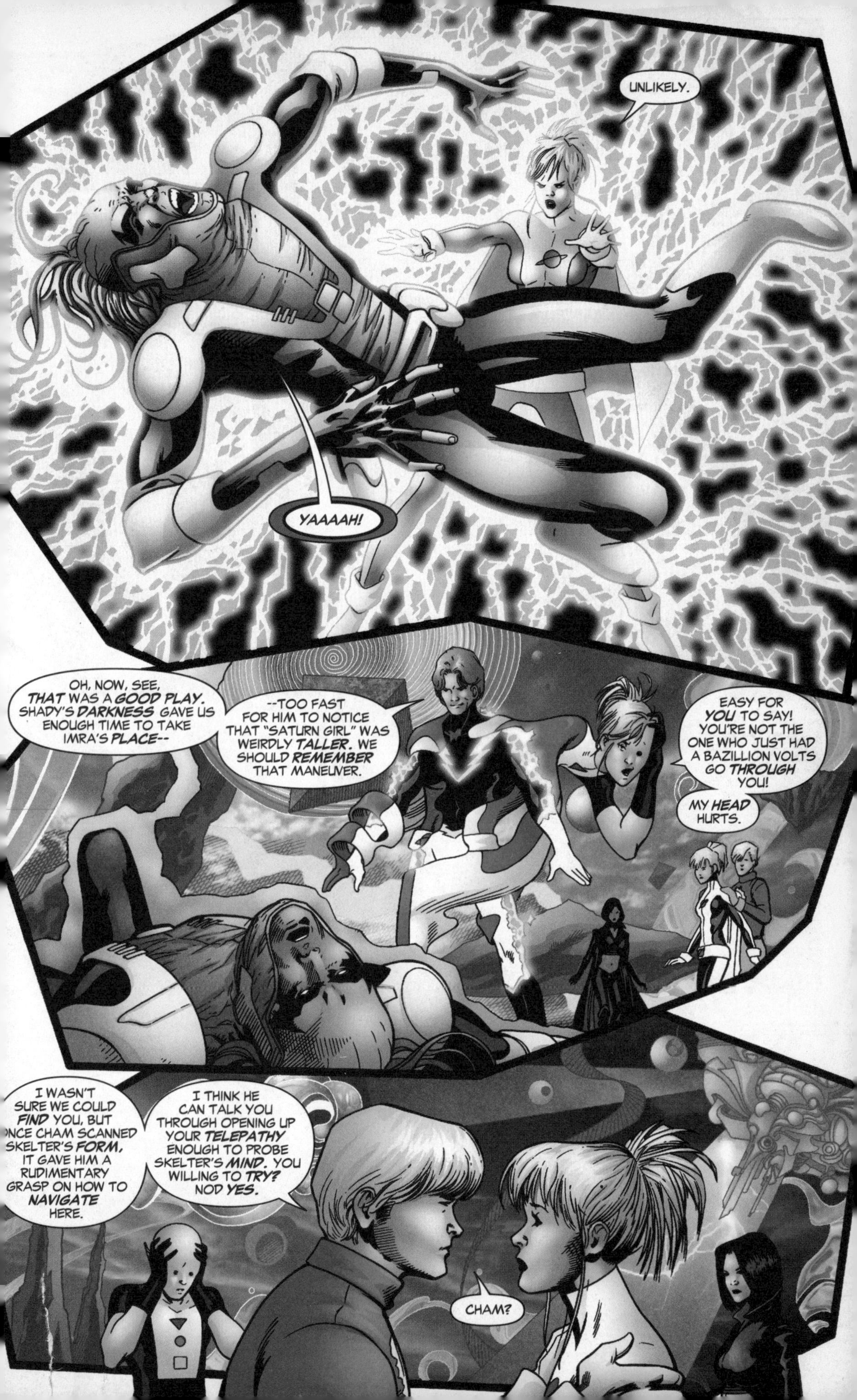
UNLIKELY.
YAAAAH!
OH, NOW, SEE, THAT WAS A GOOD PLAY. SHADY'S DARKNESS GAVE US ENOUGH TIME TO TAKE IMRA'S PLACE--
--TOO FAST FOR HIM TO NOTICE THAT "SATURN GIRL" WAS WEIRDLY TALLER. WE SHOULD REMEMBER THAT MANEUVER.
EASY FOR YOU TO SAY! YOU'RE NOT THE ONE WHO JUST HAD A BAZILLION VOLTS GO THROUGH YOU!
MY HEAD HURTS.
I WASN'T SURE WE COULD FIND YOU, BUT ONCE CHAM SCANNED SKELTER'S FORM, IT GAVE HIM A RUDIMENTARY GRASP ON HOW TO NAVIGATE HERE.
I THINK HE CAN TALK YOU THROUGH OPENING UP YOUR TELEPATHY ENOUGH TO PROBE SKELTER'S MIND. YOU WILLING TO TRY? NOD YES.
CHAM?

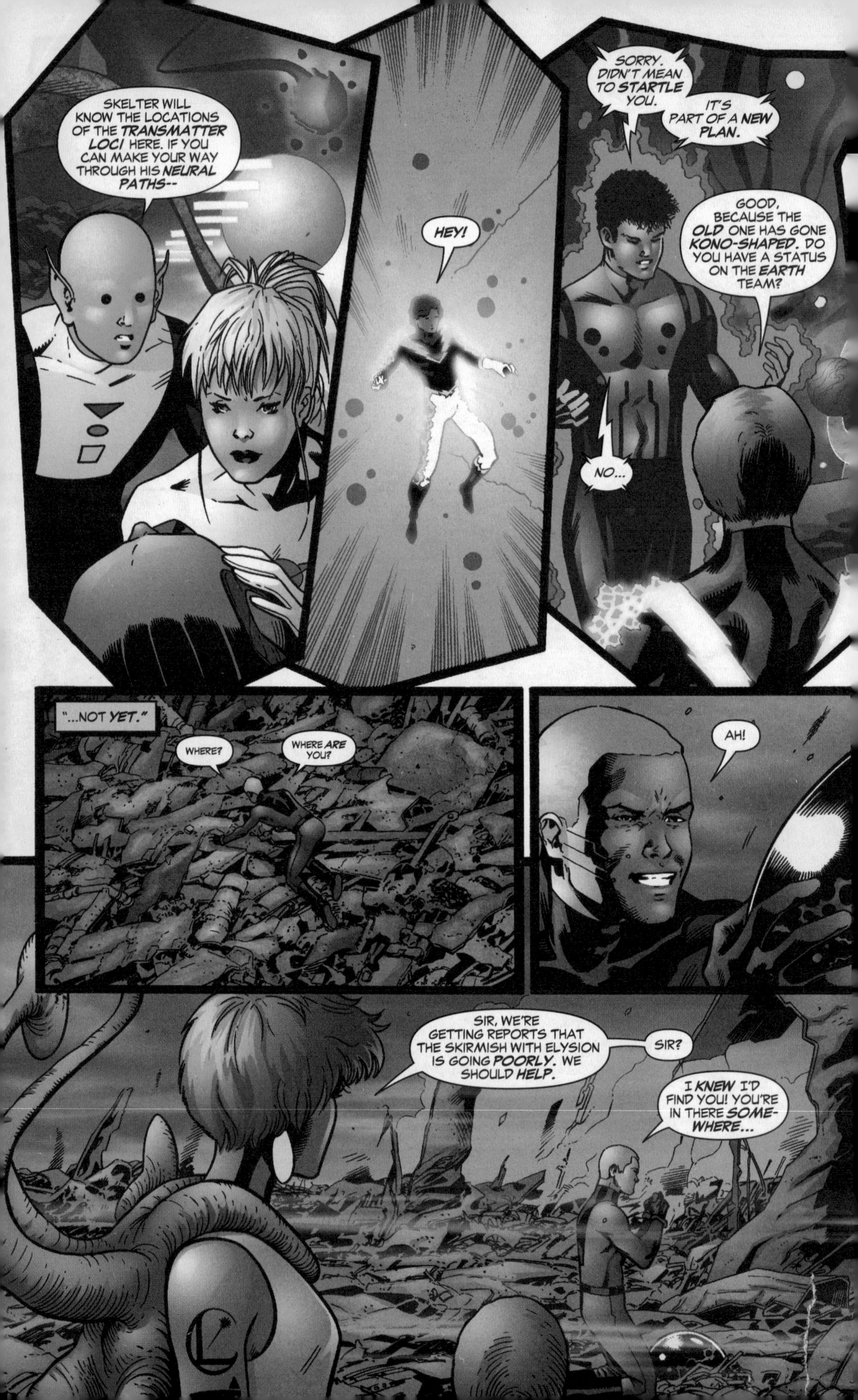
SKELTER WILL KNOW THE LOCATIONS OF THE TRANSMATTER LOCI HERE. IF YOU CAN MAKE YOUR WAY THROUGH HIS NEURAL PATHS--
HEY!
SORRY. DIDN'T MEAN TO STARTLE YOU.
IT'S PART OF A NEW PLAN.
GOOD, BECAUSE THE OLD ONE HAS GONE KONO-SHAPED. DO YOU HAVE A STATUS ON THE EARTH TEAM?
NO...
"...NOT YET."
WHERE?
WHERE ARE YOU?
AH!
SIR, WE'RE GETTING REPORTS THAT THE SKIRMISH WITH ELYSION IS GOING POORLY. WE SHOULD HELP.
SIR?
I KNEW I'D FIND YOU! YOU'RE IN THERE SOME-WHERE...

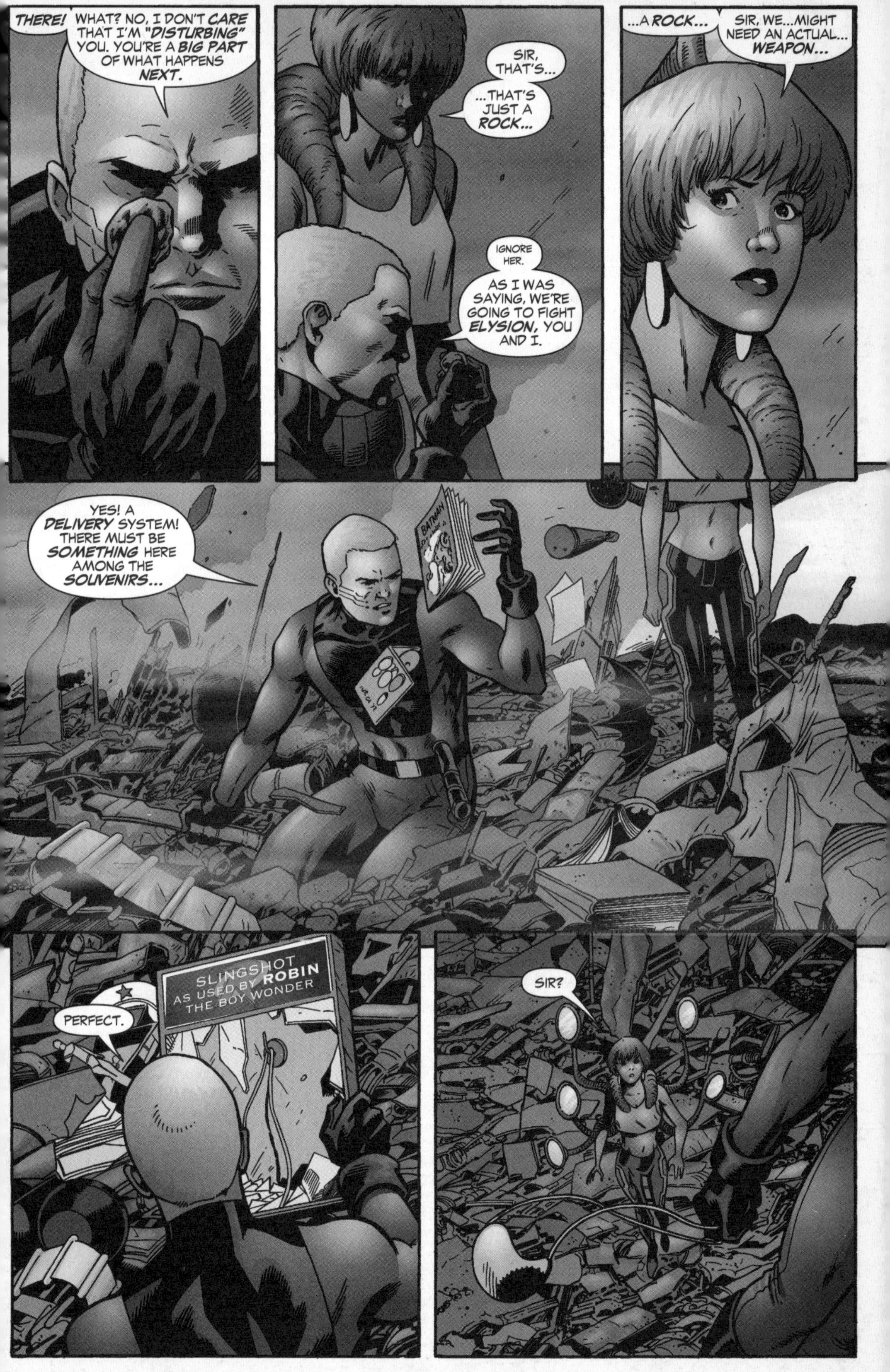
THERE!
WHAT? NO, I DON'T CARE THAT I'M "DISTURBING" YOU. YOU'RE A BIG PART OF WHAT HAPPENS NEXT.
SIR, THAT'S...
...THAT'S JUST A ROCK...
IGNORE HER.
AS I WAS SAYING, WE'RE GOING TO FIGHT ELYSION, YOU AND I.
...A ROCK...
SIR, WE...MIGHT NEED AN ACTUAL... WEAPON...
YES! A DELIVERY SYSTEM! THERE MUST BE SOMETHING HERE AMONG THE SOUVENIRS...
BATMAN
SLINGSHOT AS USED BY ROBIN THE BOY WONDER
PERFECT.
SIR?

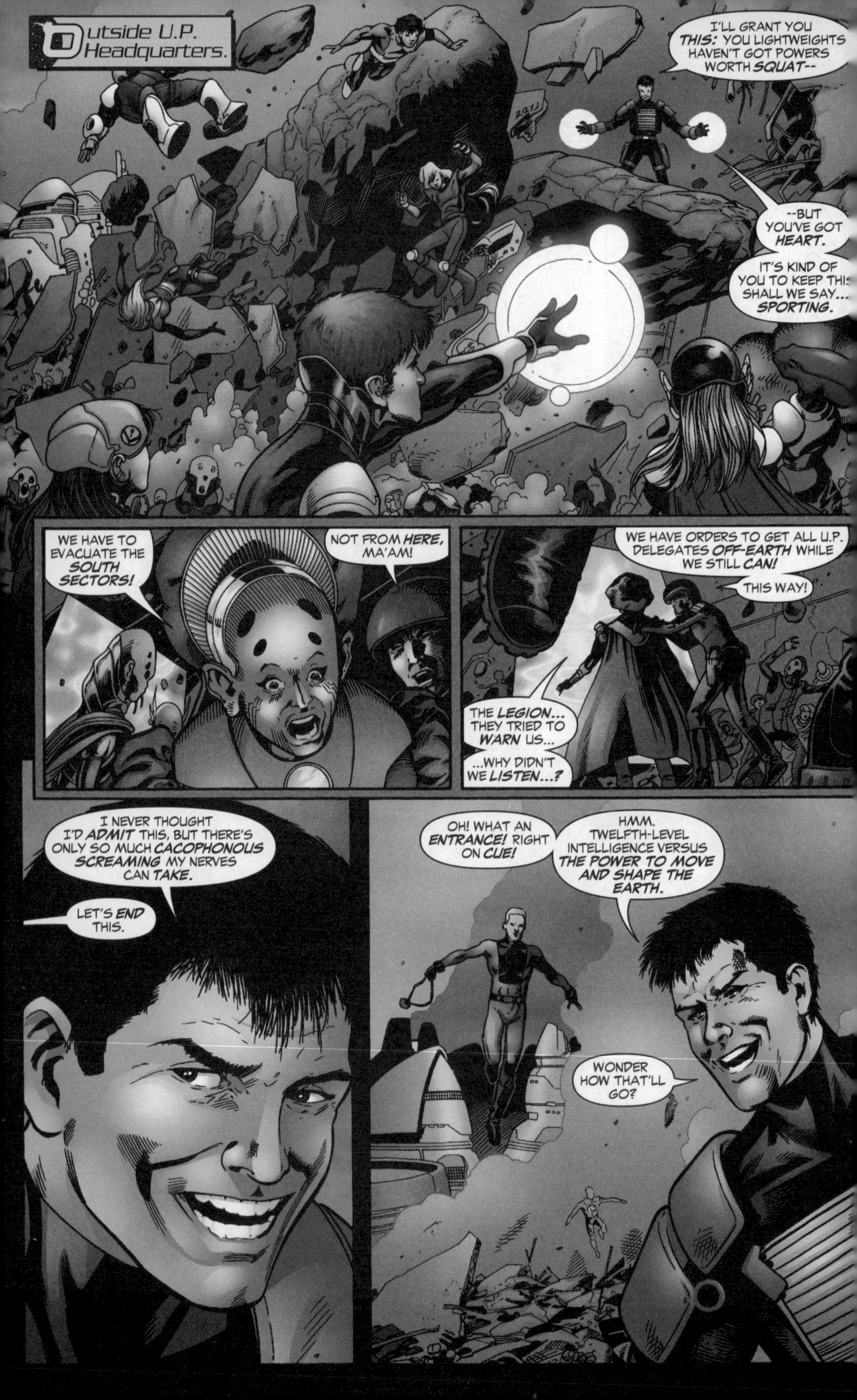
Outside U.P. Headquarters.
I'LL GRANT YOU THIS: YOU LIGHTWEIGHTS HAVEN'T GOT POWERS WORTH SQUAT--
--BUT YOU'VE GOT HEART.
IT'S KIND OF YOU TO KEEP THIS SHALL WE SAY... SPORTING.
WE HAVE TO EVACUATE THE SOUTH SECTORS!
NOT FROM HERE, MA'AM!
WE HAVE ORDERS TO GET ALL U.P. DELEGATES OFF-EARTH WHILE WE STILL CAN!
THIS WAY!
THE LEGION... THEY TRIED TO WARN US...
...WHY DIDN'T WE LISTEN...?
I NEVER THOUGHT I'D ADMIT THIS, BUT THERE'S ONLY SO MUCH CACOPHONOUS SCREAMING MY NERVES CAN TAKE.
LET'S END THIS.
OH! WHAT AN ENTRANCE! RIGHT ON CUE!
HMM. TWELFTH-LEVEL INTELLIGENCE VERSUS THE POWER TO MOVE AND SHAPE THE EARTH.
WONDER HOW THAT'LL GO?

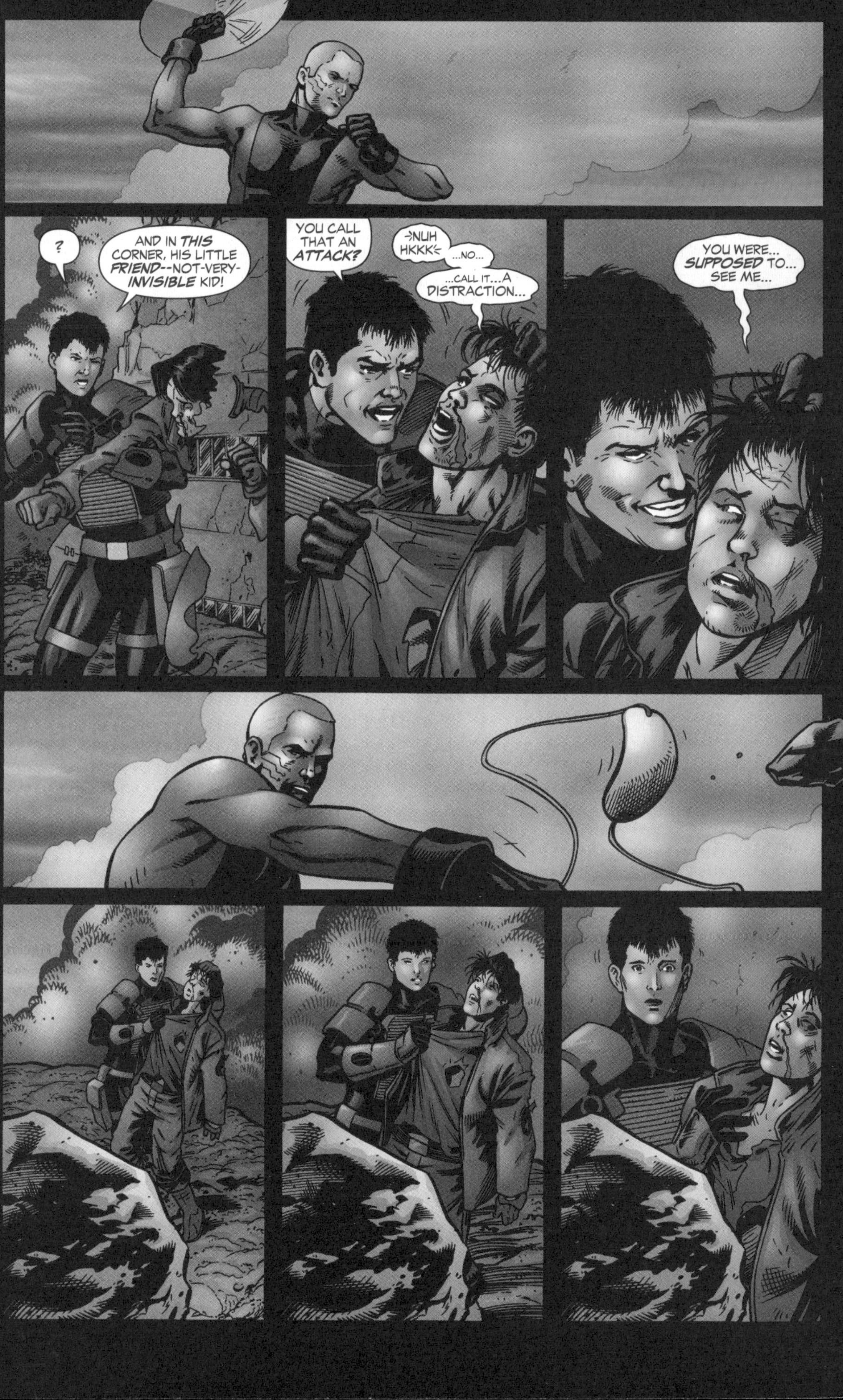
?
AND IN *THIS* CORNER, HIS LITTLE *FRIEND*--NOT-VERY-*INVISIBLE* KID!
YOU CALL THAT AN *ATTACK?*
NUH HKKK
...NO...
...CALL IT...A DISTRACTION...
YOU WERE... *SUPPOSED* TO... SEE ME...

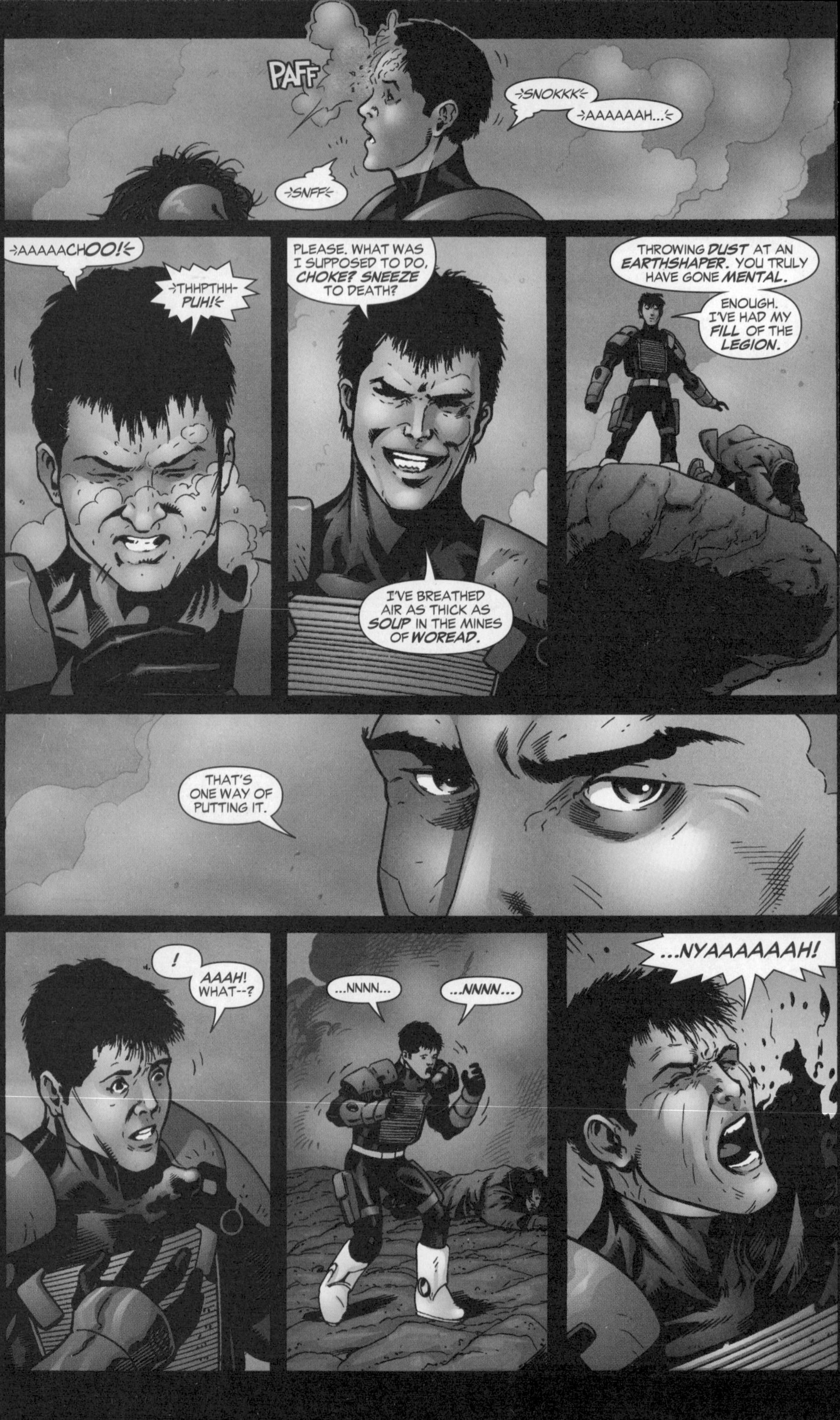
PAFF
SNOKKK
AAAAAAH...
SNFF
AAAAACHOO!
THHPTHH-PUH!
PLEASE. WHAT WAS I SUPPOSED TO DO, CHOKE? SNEEZE TO DEATH?
I'VE BREATHED AIR AS THICK AS SOUP IN THE MINES OF WOREAD.
THROWING DUST AT AN EARTHSHAPER. YOU TRULY HAVE GONE MENTAL.
ENOUGH. I'VE HAD MY FILL OF THE LEGION.
THAT'S ONE WAY OF PUTTING IT.
!
AAAH! WHAT--?
...NNNN...
...NNNN...
...NYAAAAAAH!

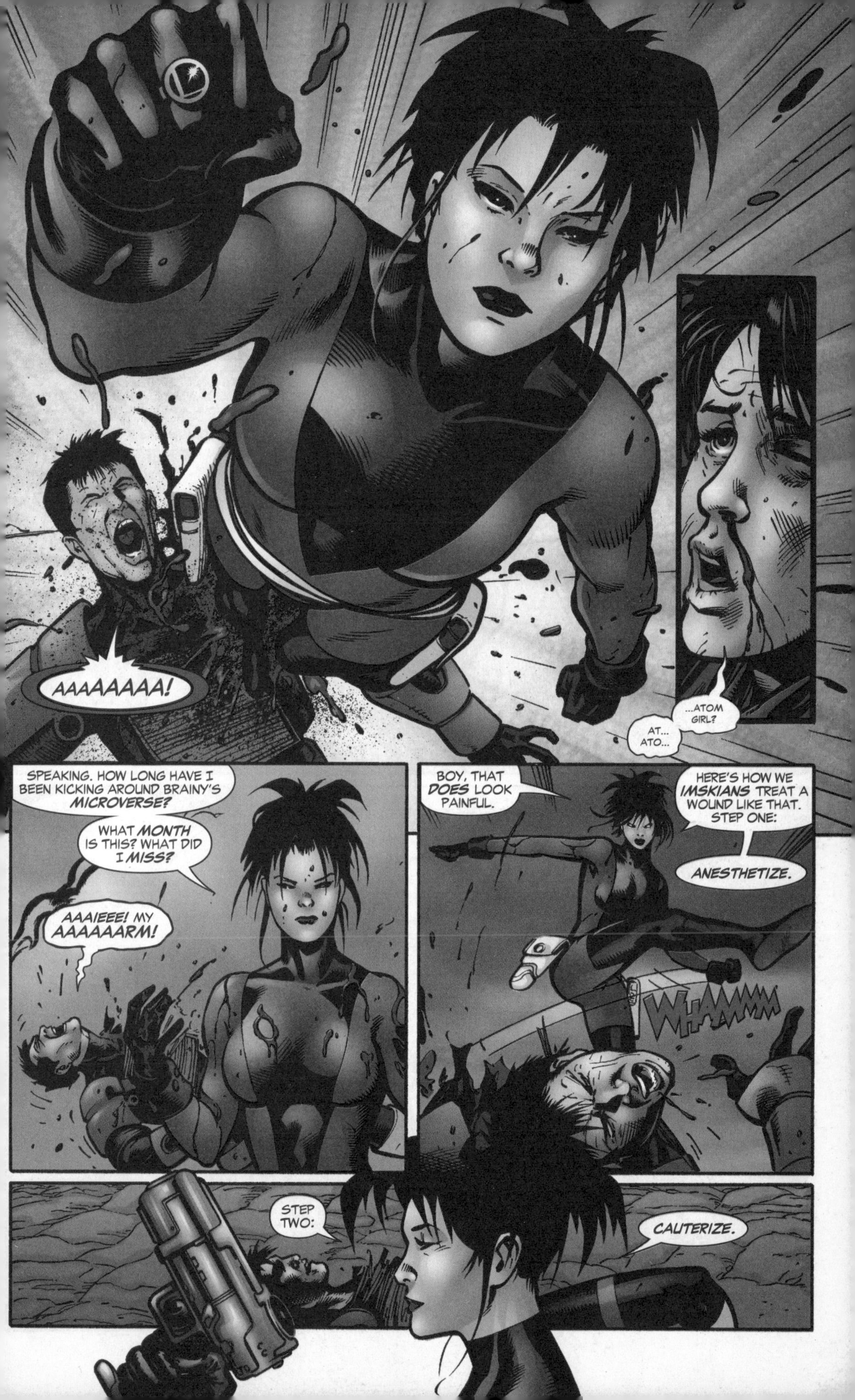
AAAAAAAA!
AT... ATO...
...ATOM GIRL?
SPEAKING. HOW LONG HAVE I BEEN KICKING AROUND BRAINY'S MICROVERSE?
WHAT MONTH IS THIS? WHAT DID I MISS?
AAAIEEE! MY AAAAAARM!
BOY, THAT DOES LOOK PAINFUL.
HERE'S HOW WE IMSKIANS TREAT A WOUND LIKE THAT. STEP ONE:
ANESTHETIZE.
WHAMMM
STEP TWO:
CAUTERIZE.

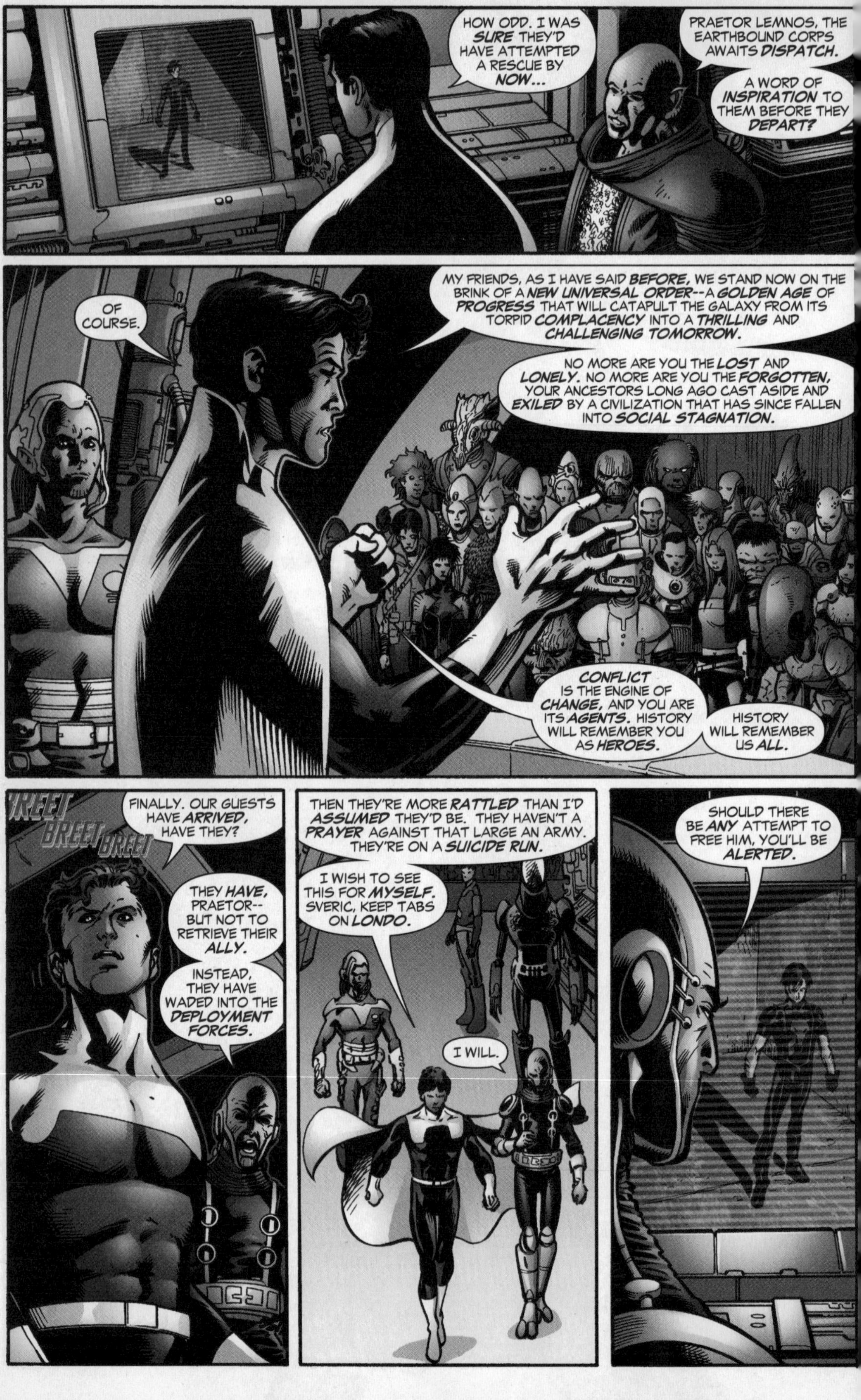
HOW ODD. I WAS SURE THEY'D HAVE ATTEMPTED A RESCUE BY NOW...
PRAETOR LEMNOS, THE EARTHBOUND CORPS AWAITS DISPATCH.
A WORD OF INSPIRATION TO THEM BEFORE THEY DEPART?
OF COURSE.
MY FRIENDS, AS I HAVE SAID BEFORE, WE STAND NOW ON THE BRINK OF A NEW UNIVERSAL ORDER--A GOLDEN AGE OF PROGRESS THAT WILL CATAPULT THE GALAXY FROM ITS TORPID COMPLACENCY INTO A THRILLING AND CHALLENGING TOMORROW.
NO MORE ARE YOU THE LOST AND LONELY. NO MORE ARE YOU THE FORGOTTEN, YOUR ANCESTORS LONG AGO CAST ASIDE AND EXILED BY A CIVILIZATION THAT HAS SINCE FALLEN INTO SOCIAL STAGNATION.
CONFLICT IS THE ENGINE OF CHANGE, AND YOU ARE ITS AGENTS. HISTORY WILL REMEMBER YOU AS HEROES.
HISTORY WILL REMEMBER US ALL.
BREET BREET
FINALLY. OUR GUESTS HAVE ARRIVED, HAVE THEY?
THEY HAVE, PRAETOR-- BUT NOT TO RETRIEVE THEIR ALLY.
INSTEAD, THEY HAVE WADED INTO THE DEPLOYMENT FORCES.
THEN THEY'RE MORE RATTLED THAN I'D ASSUMED THEY'D BE. THEY HAVEN'T A PRAYER AGAINST THAT LARGE AN ARMY. THEY'RE ON A SUICIDE RUN.
I WISH TO SEE THIS FOR MYSELF. SVERIC, KEEP TABS ON LONDO.
I WILL.
SHOULD THERE BE ANY ATTEMPT TO FREE HIM, YOU'LL BE ALERTED.

BRIN'S CELL. NO GUARDS, EVEN. I FEEL POSITIVELY *TAUNTED*. WHAT NOW?

LEAVE IT TO *ME*.

˙ᒋᑕᗐᕕᑎᕼ ᒋᗐᐳᑎ ᔕᑎᑕᗐᕼᗐᕕ ᐳᑎ ᑎᗐᐳ: ᕼᑎᕕᗐᑌ ᐱᔕᔕ ᑕᗐᐳᑎ ᑎᑎ ᑎᑕᑎᕼ ᕷᑎ ᗐᔕᑎᑎᕼᔕ ᗐᗐ ᑌᑕᑎᕼ ᑎᗐᑌ ᑎᑌ ᑎᗐ ᕕᗐᐳᑌ ᕷᑌ ᔕᑌᕼᑎᑌᑎᕼᔕᗐ

WELL, DON'T JUST *STAND* THERE!

GO *GET* HIM!

OH, NO... NO...

PHANTOM GIRL? GET *AWAY*! IT'S A *TRAP*!

WELL--*dur*!

WE'LL FIGHT OUR WAY *OUT*.

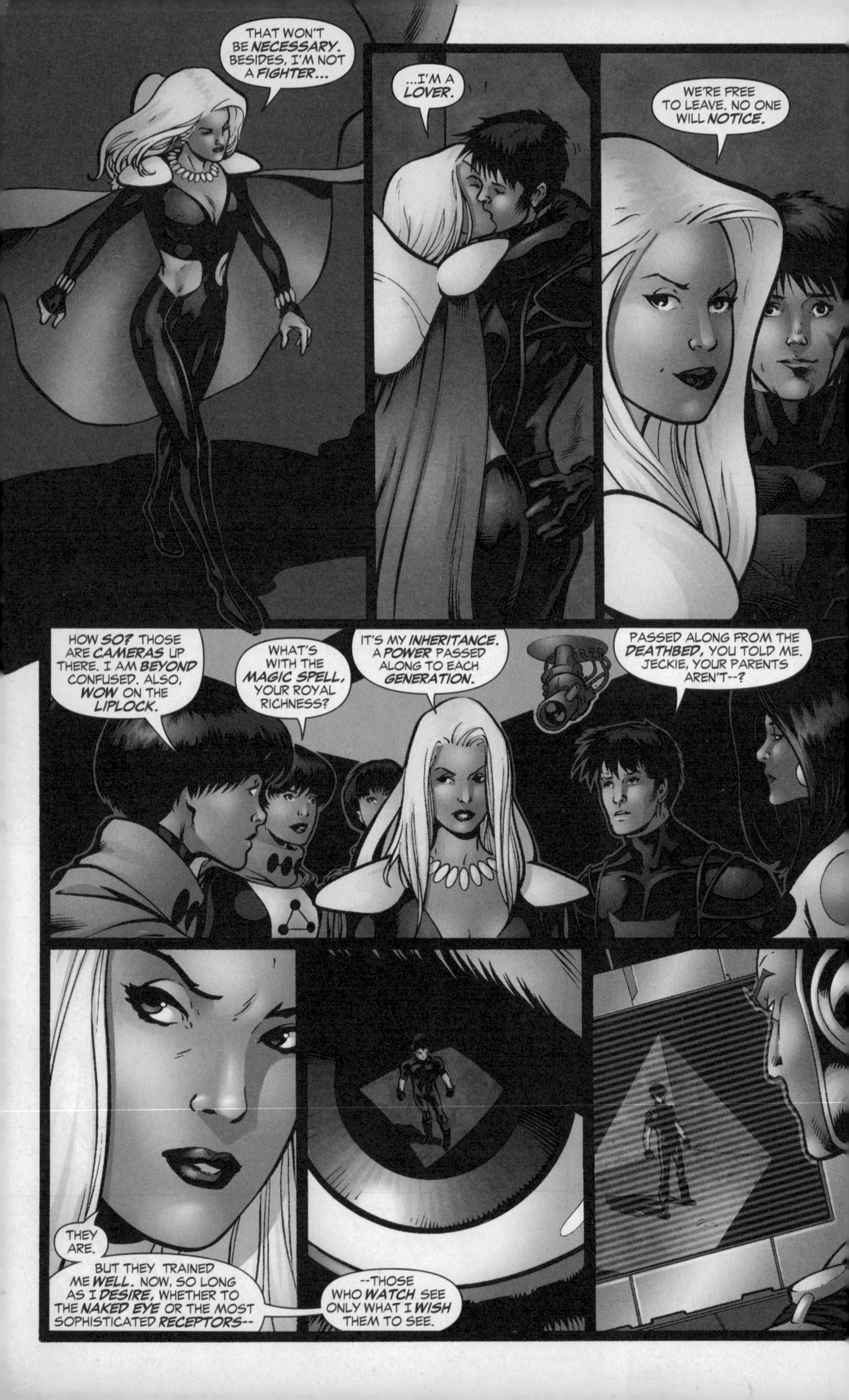
THAT WON'T BE NECESSARY. BESIDES, I'M NOT A FIGHTER...
...I'M A LOVER.
WE'RE FREE TO LEAVE. NO ONE WILL NOTICE.
HOW SO? THOSE ARE CAMERAS UP THERE. I AM BEYOND CONFUSED. ALSO, WOW ON THE LIPLOCK.
WHAT'S WITH THE MAGIC SPELL, YOUR ROYAL RICHNESS?
IT'S MY INHERITANCE. A POWER PASSED ALONG TO EACH GENERATION.
PASSED ALONG FROM THE DEATHBED, YOU TOLD ME. JECKIE, YOUR PARENTS AREN'T--?
THEY ARE.
BUT THEY TRAINED ME WELL. NOW, SO LONG AS I DESIRE, WHETHER TO THE NAKED EYE OR THE MOST SOPHISTICATED RECEPTORS--
--THOSE WHO WATCH SEE ONLY WHAT I WISH THEM TO SEE.

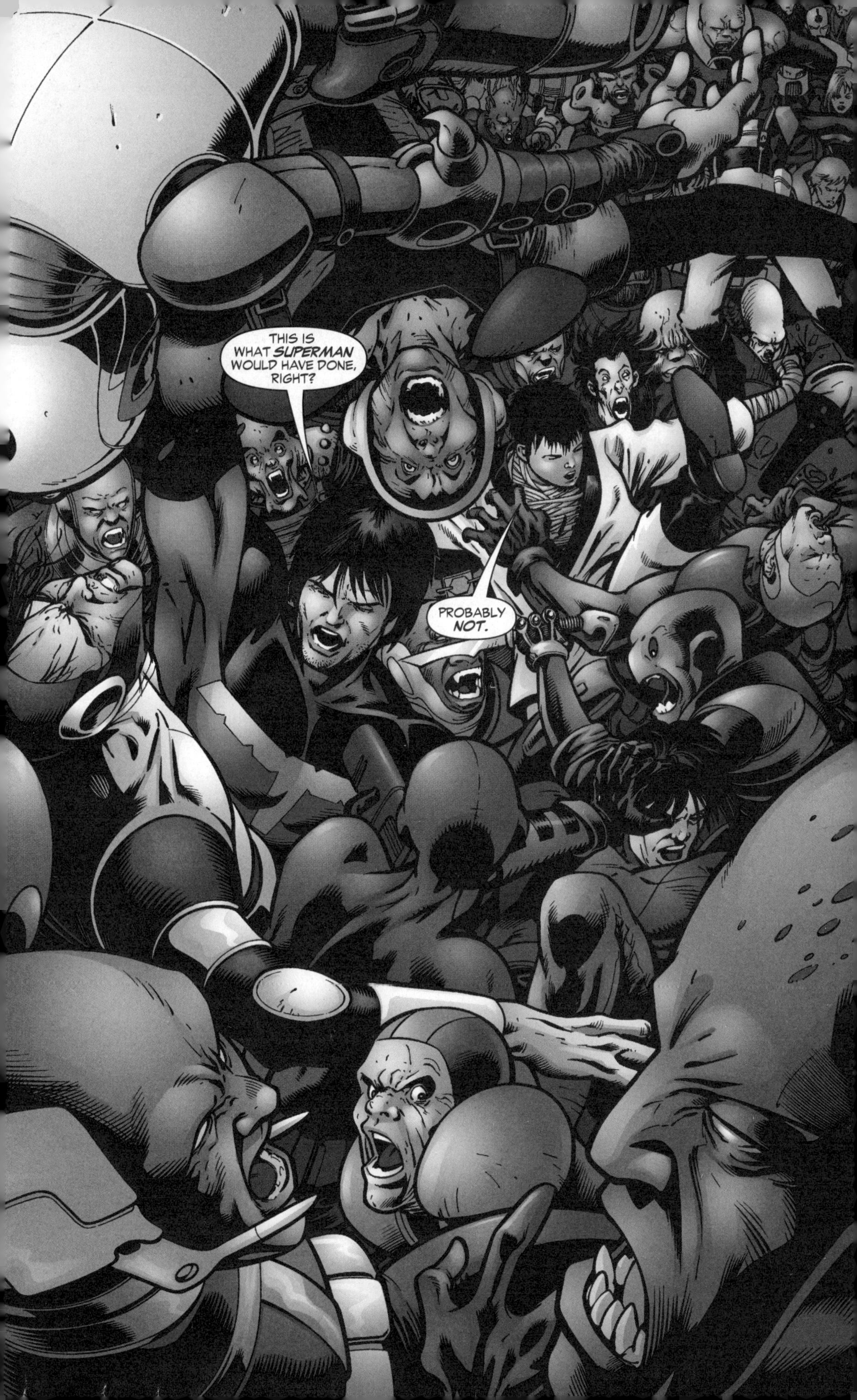
THIS IS WHAT SUPERMAN WOULD HAVE DONE, RIGHT?
PROBABLY NOT.

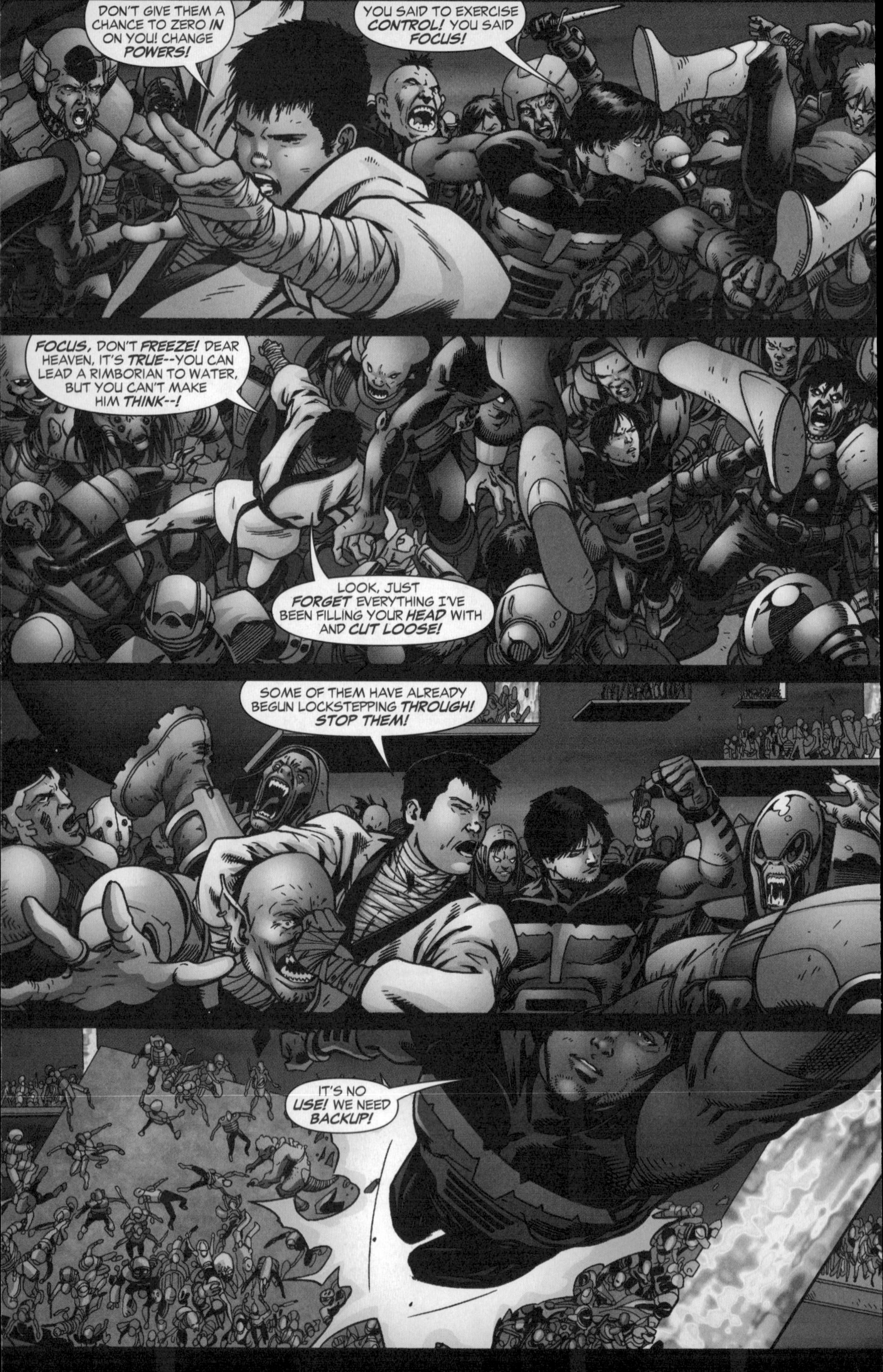
DON'T GIVE THEM A CHANCE TO ZERO IN ON YOU! CHANGE POWERS!
YOU SAID TO EXERCISE CONTROL! YOU SAID FOCUS!
FOCUS, DON'T FREEZE! DEAR HEAVEN, IT'S TRUE--YOU CAN LEAD A RIMBORIAN TO WATER, BUT YOU CAN'T MAKE HIM THINK--!
LOOK, JUST FORGET EVERYTHING I'VE BEEN FILLING YOUR HEAD WITH AND CUT LOOSE!
SOME OF THEM HAVE ALREADY BEGUN LOCKSTEPPING THROUGH! STOP THEM!
IT'S NO USE! WE NEED BACKUP!

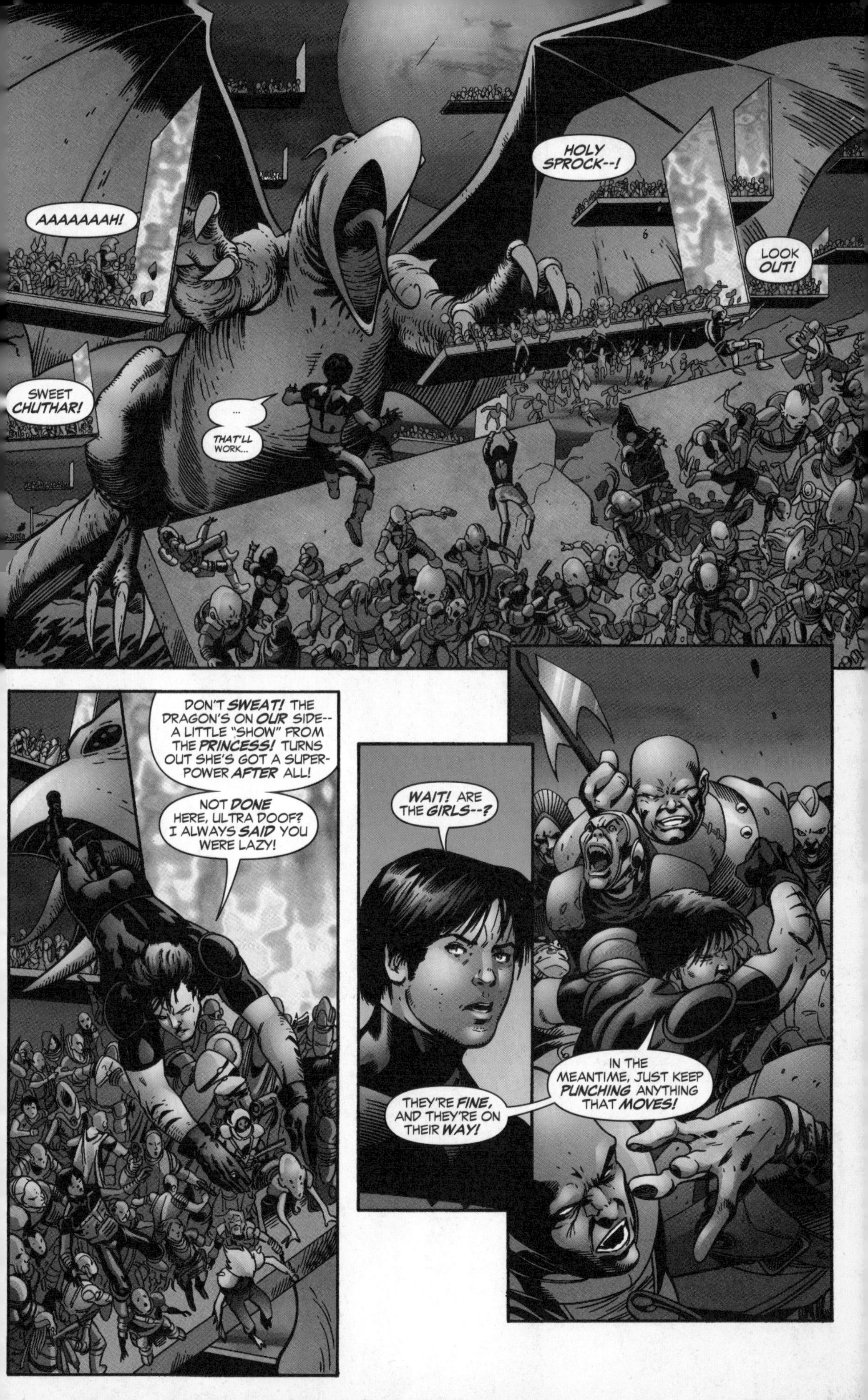
AAAAAAAH!
HOLY SPROCK--!
LOOK OUT!
SWEET CHUTHAR!
... THAT'LL WORK...
DON'T SWEAT! THE DRAGON'S ON OUR SIDE-- A LITTLE "SHOW" FROM THE PRINCESS! TURNS OUT SHE'S GOT A SUPER-POWER AFTER ALL!
NOT DONE HERE, ULTRA DOOF? I ALWAYS SAID YOU WERE LAZY!
WAIT! ARE THE GIRLS--?
THEY'RE FINE, AND THEY'RE ON THEIR WAY!
IN THE MEANTIME, JUST KEEP PUNCHING ANYTHING THAT MOVES!

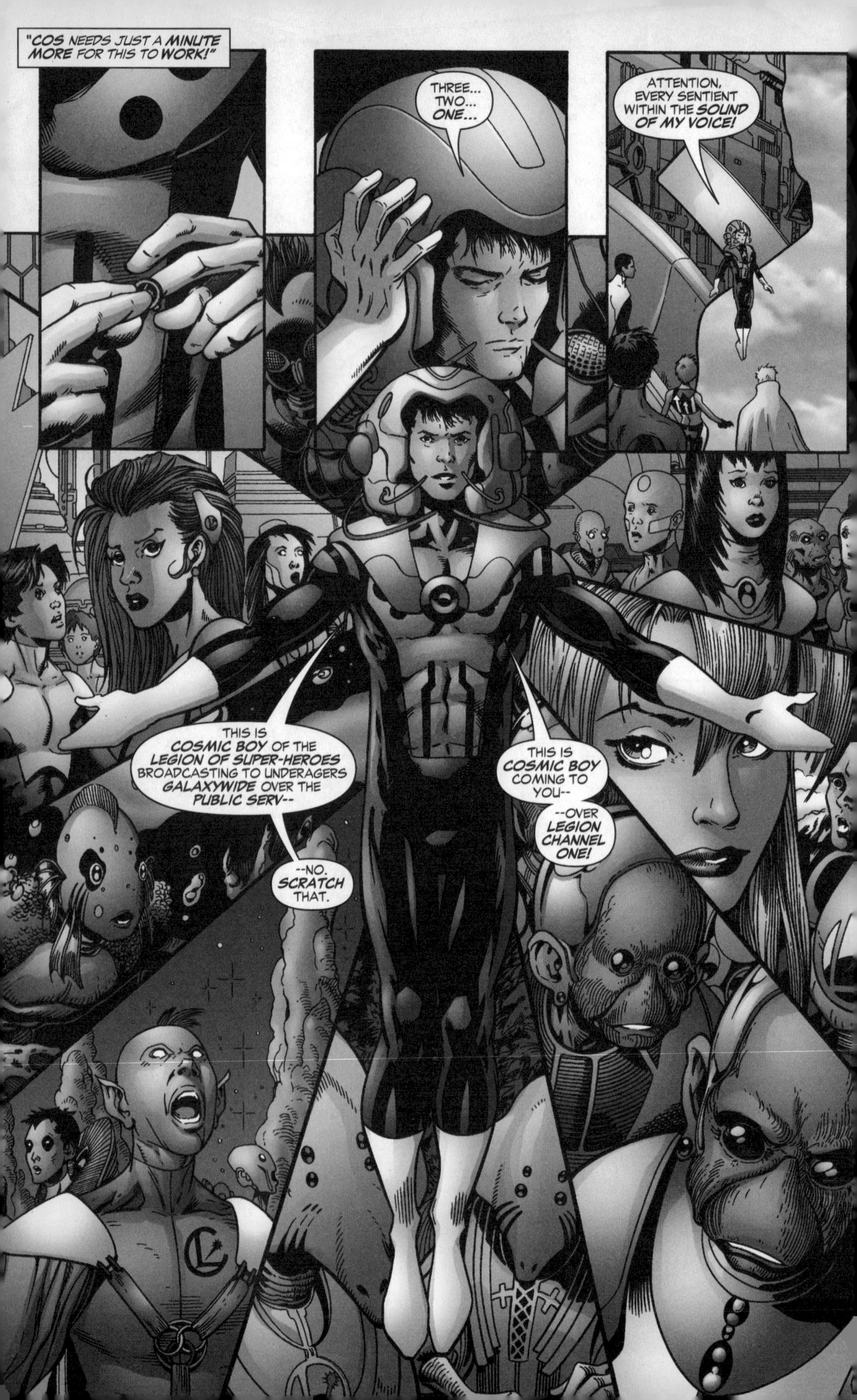
"COS NEEDS JUST A MINUTE MORE FOR THIS TO WORK!"
THREE... TWO... ONE...
ATTENTION, EVERY SENTIENT WITHIN THE SOUND OF MY VOICE!
THIS IS COSMIC BOY OF THE LEGION OF SUPER-HEROES BROADCASTING TO UNDERAGERS GALAXYWIDE OVER THE PUBLIC SERV--
--NO. SCRATCH THAT.
THIS IS COSMIC BOY COMING TO YOU--
--OVER LEGION CHANNEL ONE!

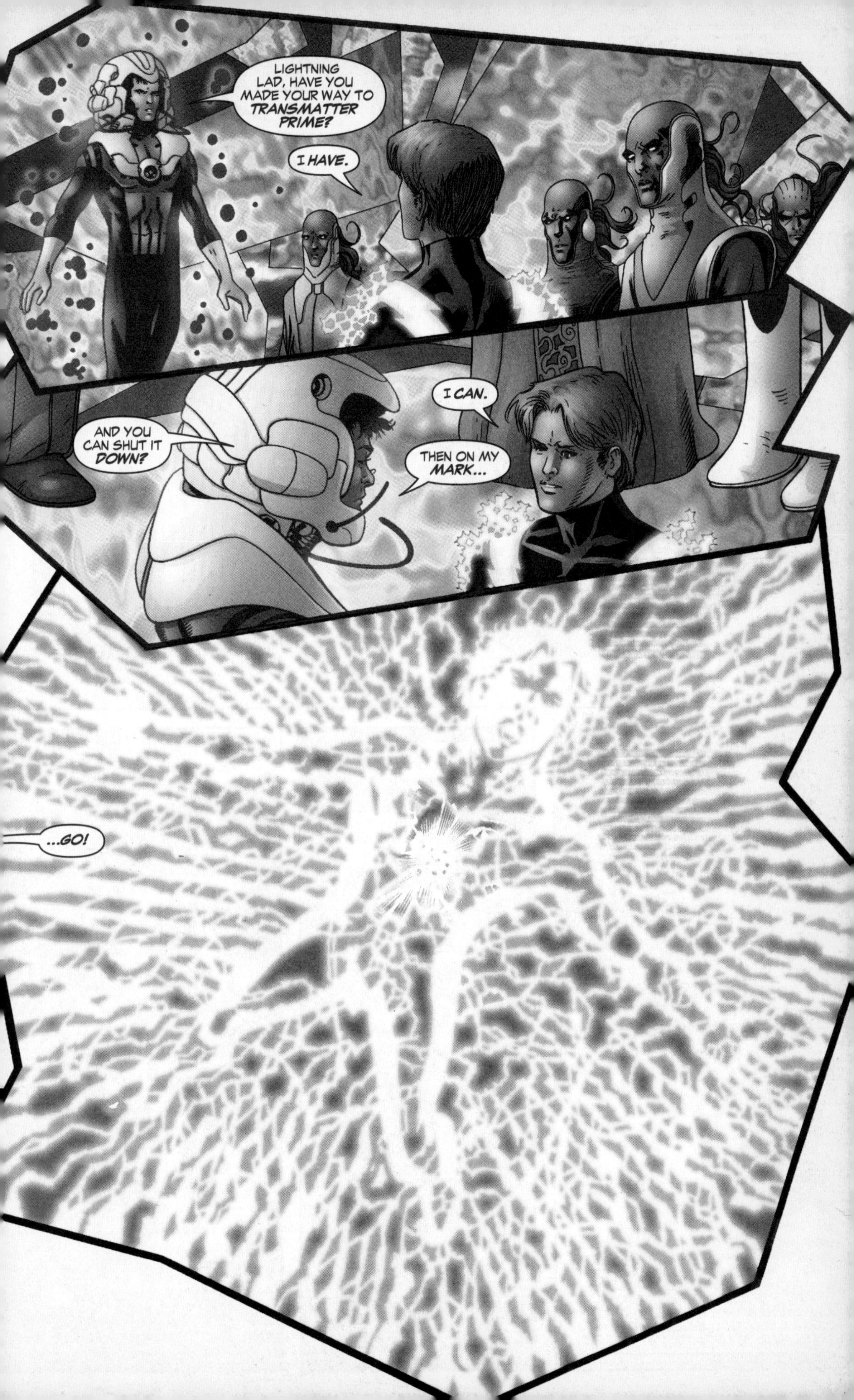
LIGHTNING LAD, HAVE YOU MADE YOUR WAY TO TRANSMATTER PRIME?
I HAVE.
AND YOU CAN SHUT IT DOWN?
I CAN.
THEN ON MY MARK...
...GO!

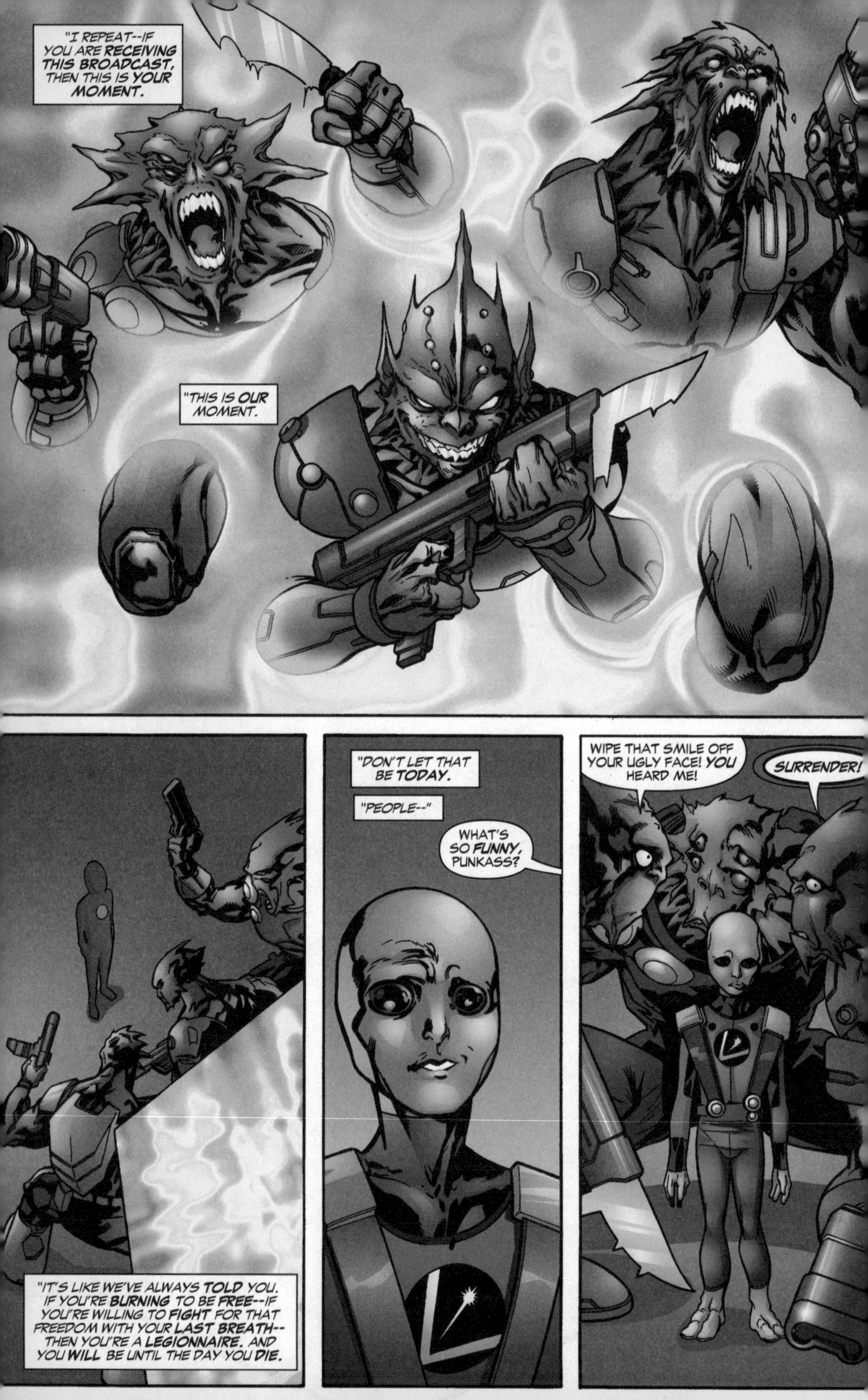
"I REPEAT--IF YOU ARE RECEIVING THIS BROADCAST, THEN THIS IS YOUR MOMENT.
"THIS IS OUR MOMENT.
"IT'S LIKE WE'VE ALWAYS TOLD YOU. IF YOU'RE BURNING TO BE FREE--IF YOU'RE WILLING TO FIGHT FOR THAT FREEDOM WITH YOUR LAST BREATH--THEN YOU'RE A LEGIONNAIRE. AND YOU WILL BE UNTIL THE DAY YOU DIE.
"DON'T LET THAT BE TODAY.
"PEOPLE--"
WHAT'S SO FUNNY, PUNKASS?
WIPE THAT SMILE OFF YOUR UGLY FACE! YOU HEARD ME!
SURRENDER!

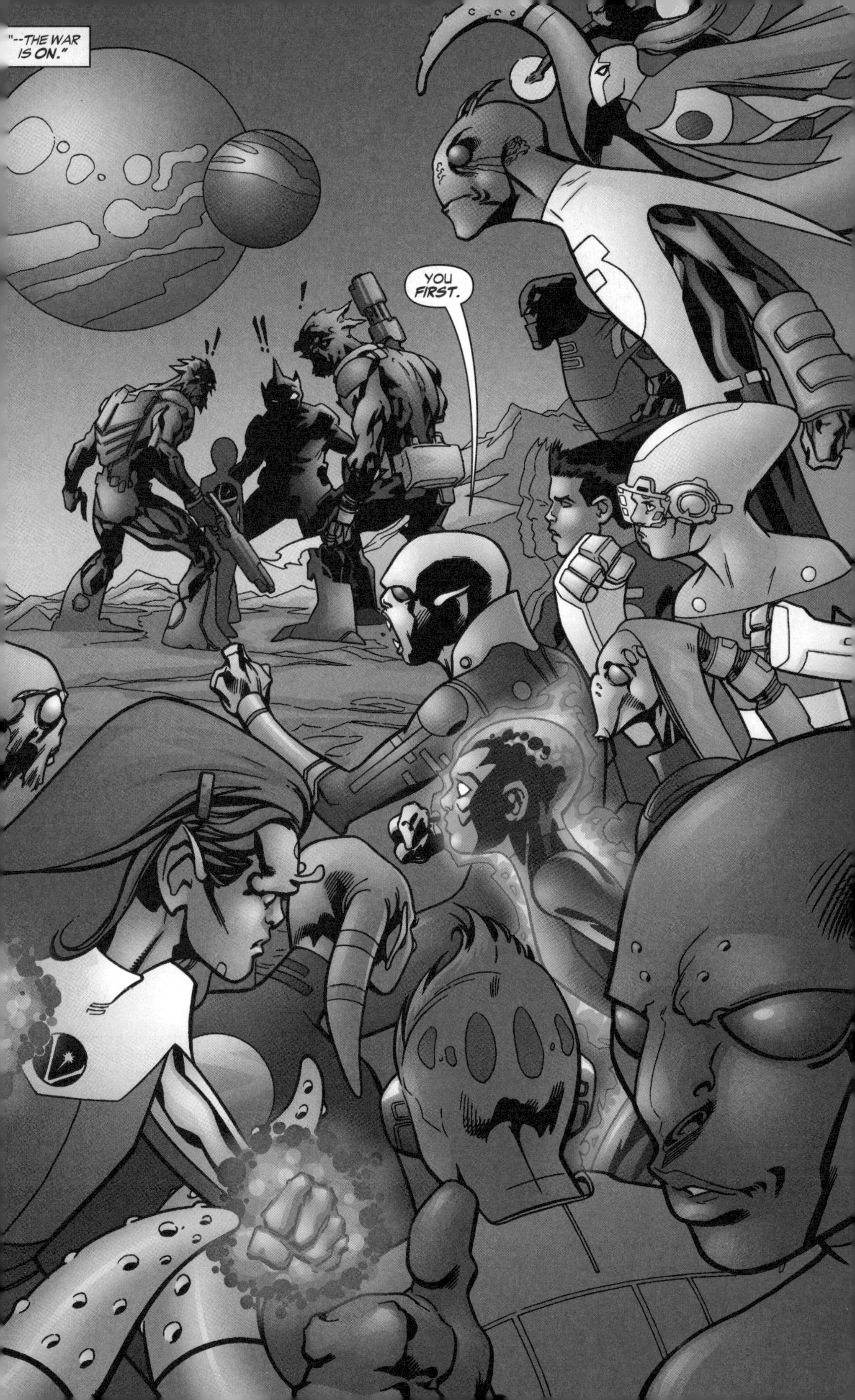
"--THE WAR IS ON."
!!
!!
!
YOU FIRST.

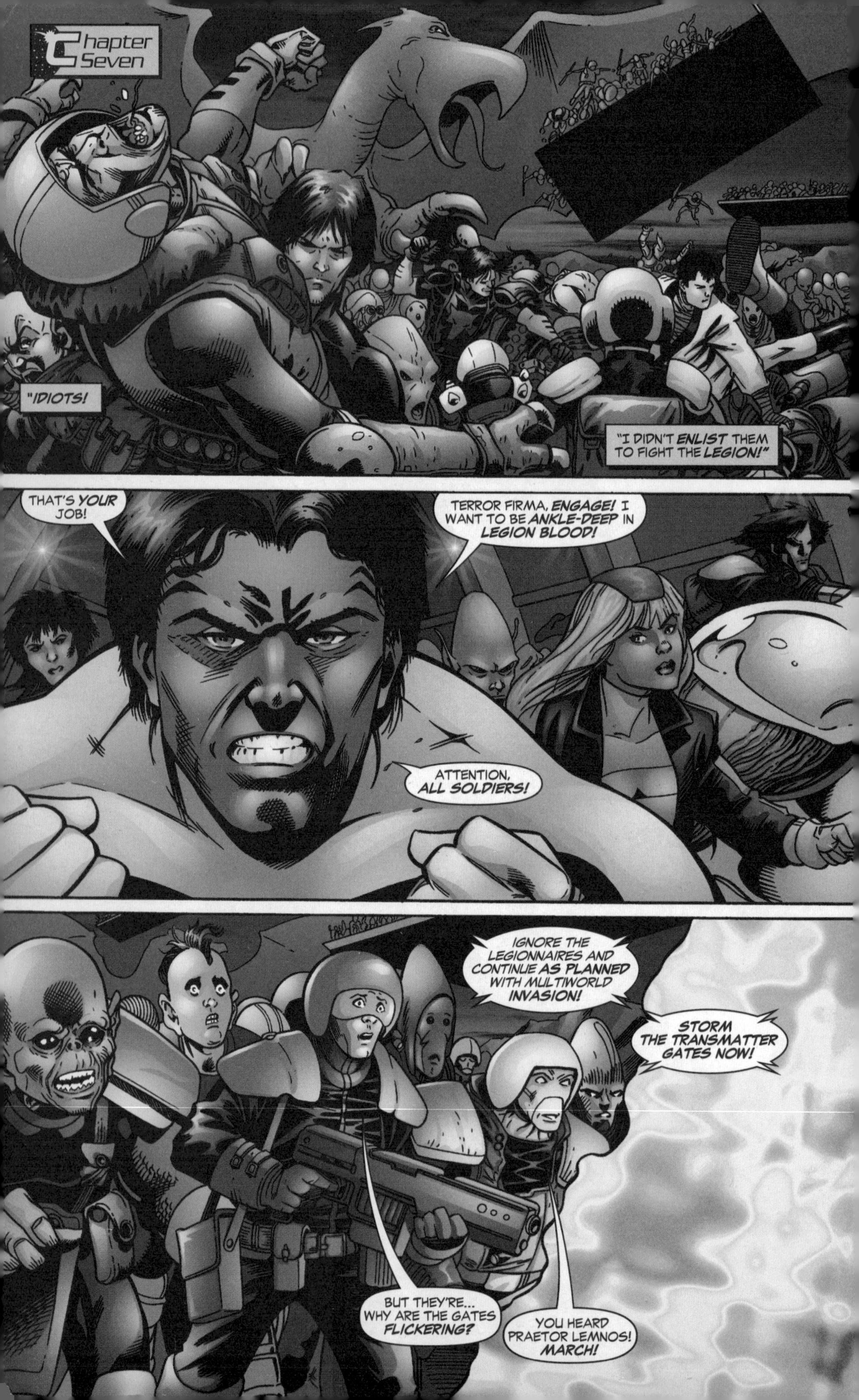
Chapter Seven
"IDIOTS!
"I DIDN'T ENLIST THEM TO FIGHT THE LEGION!"
THAT'S YOUR JOB!
TERROR FIRMA, ENGAGE! I WANT TO BE ANKLE-DEEP IN LEGION BLOOD!
ATTENTION, ALL SOLDIERS!
IGNORE THE LEGIONNAIRES AND CONTINUE AS PLANNED WITH MULTIWORLD INVASION!
STORM THE TRANSMATTER GATES NOW!
BUT THEY'RE... WHY ARE THE GATES FLICKERING?
YOU HEARD PRAETOR LEMNOS! MARCH!

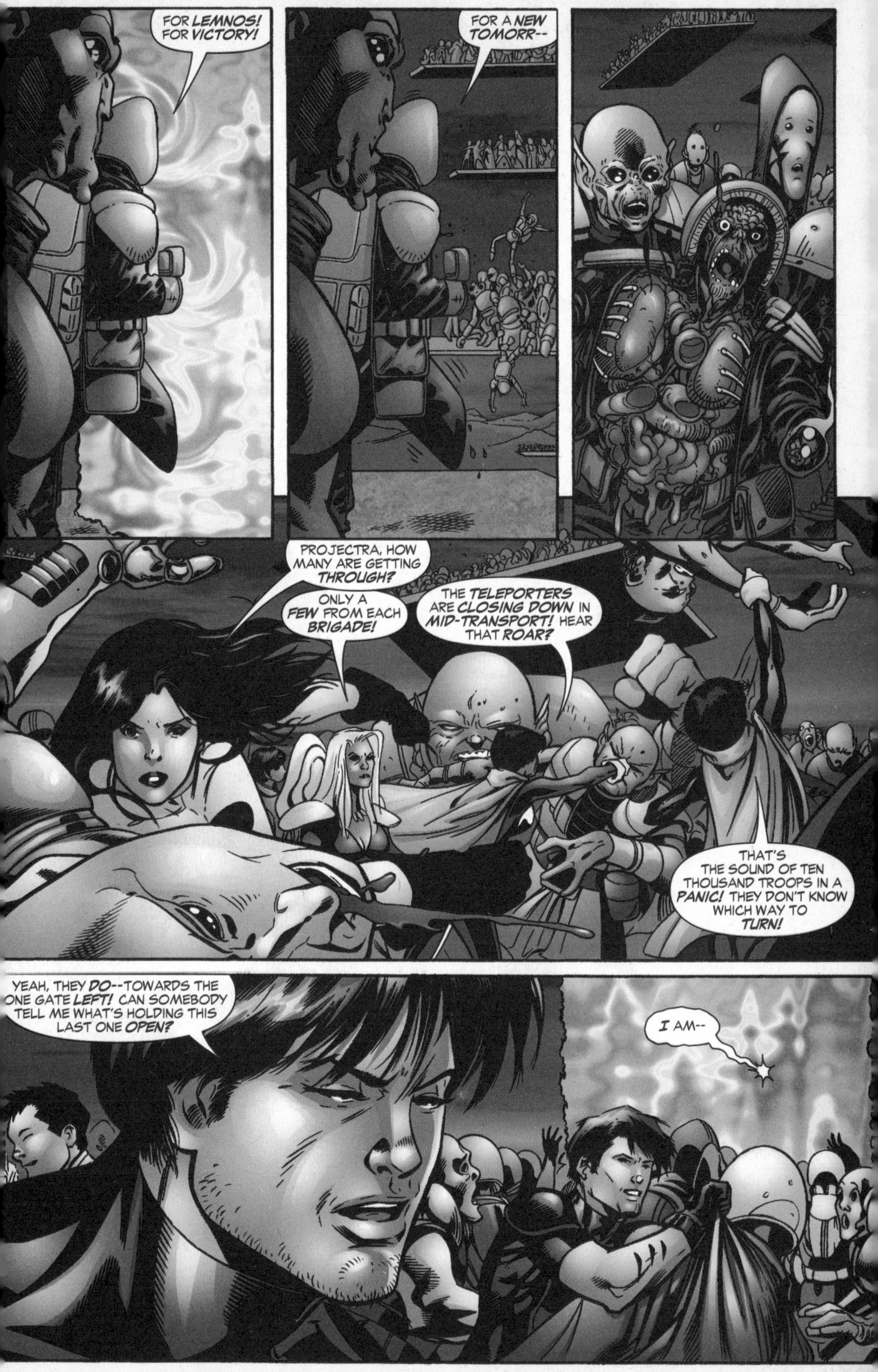
FOR LEMNOS! FOR VICTORY!
FOR A NEW TOMORR--
PROJECTRA, HOW MANY ARE GETTING THROUGH?
ONLY A FEW FROM EACH BRIGADE!
THE TELEPORTERS ARE CLOSING DOWN IN MID-TRANSPORT! HEAR THAT ROAR?
THAT'S THE SOUND OF TEN THOUSAND TROOPS IN A PANIC! THEY DON'T KNOW WHICH WAY TO TURN!
YEAH, THEY DO--TOWARDS THE ONE GATE LEFT! CAN SOMEBODY TELL ME WHAT'S HOLDING THIS LAST ONE OPEN?
I AM--

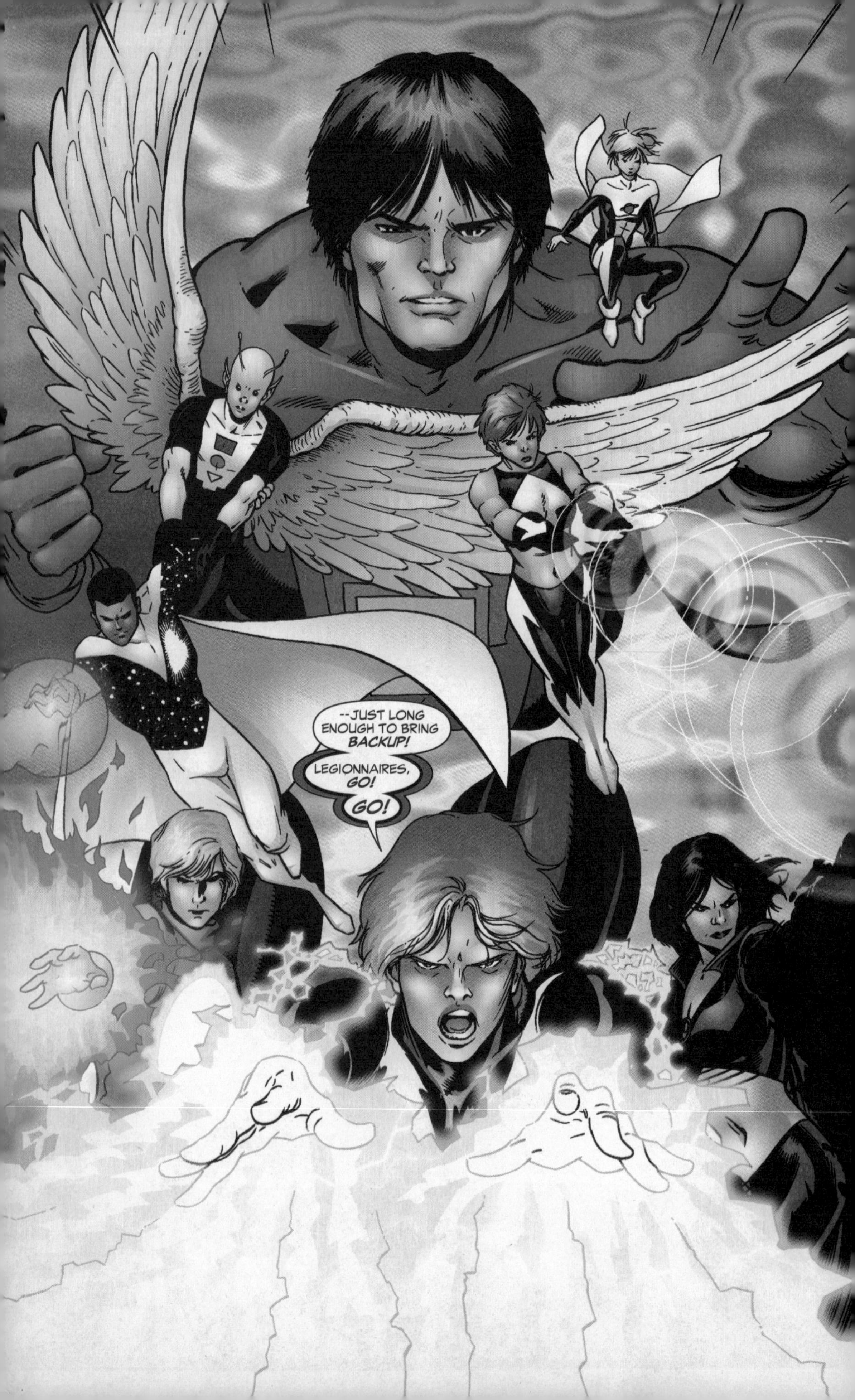
--JUST LONG ENOUGH TO BRING BACKUP!
LEGIONNAIRES, GO!
GO!

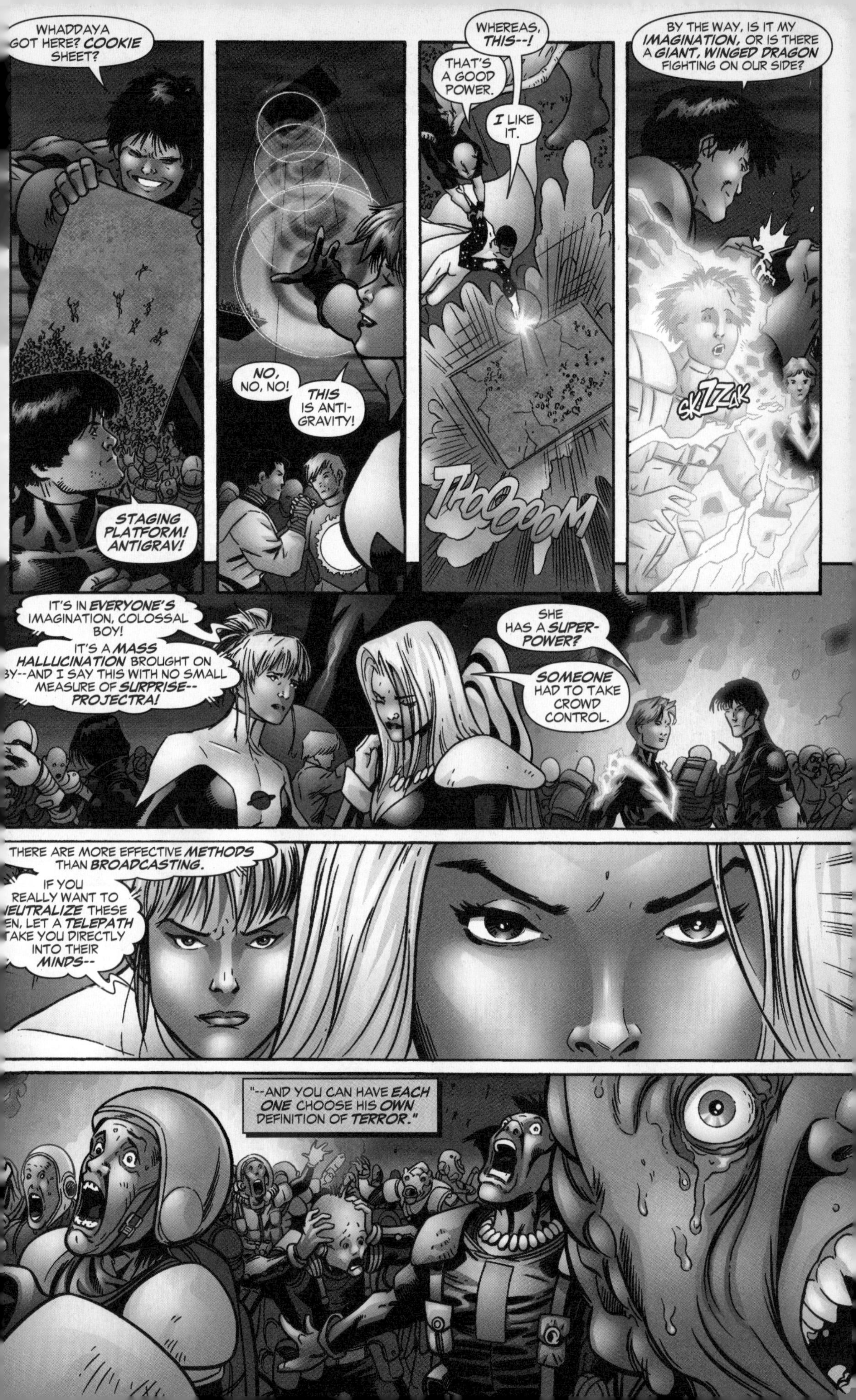
WHADDAYA GOT HERE? COOKIE SHEET?
STAGING PLATFORM! ANTIGRAV!
NO, NO, NO!
THIS IS ANTI-GRAVITY!
WHEREAS, THIS--!
THAT'S A GOOD POWER.
I LIKE IT.
THOOOOOM
BY THE WAY, IS IT MY IMAGINATION, OR IS THERE A GIANT, WINGED DRAGON FIGHTING ON OUR SIDE?
SKZZZAK
IT'S IN EVERYONE'S IMAGINATION, COLOSSAL BOY!
IT'S A MASS HALLUCINATION BROUGHT ON BY--AND I SAY THIS WITH NO SMALL MEASURE OF SURPRISE--PROJECTRA!
SHE HAS A SUPER-POWER?
SOMEONE HAD TO TAKE CROWD CONTROL.
THERE ARE MORE EFFECTIVE METHODS THAN BROADCASTING.
IF YOU REALLY WANT TO NEUTRALIZE THESE MEN, LET A TELEPATH TAKE YOU DIRECTLY INTO THEIR MINDS--
"--AND YOU CAN HAVE EACH ONE CHOOSE HIS OWN DEFINITION OF TERROR."

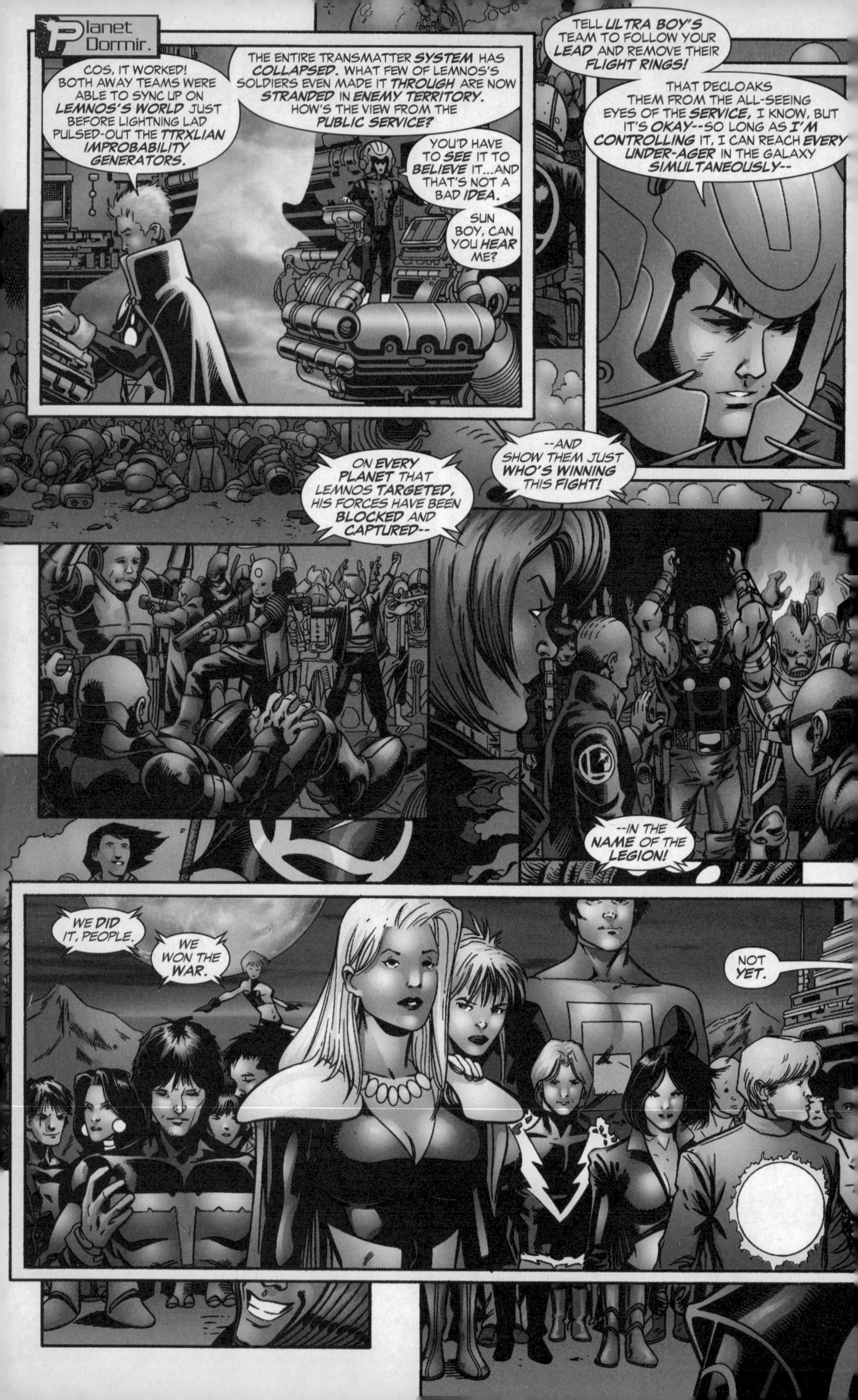
Planet Dormir.
COS, IT WORKED! BOTH AWAY TEAMS WERE ABLE TO SYNC UP ON LEMNOS'S WORLD JUST BEFORE LIGHTNING LAD PULSED-OUT THE TTRXLIAN IMPROBABILITY GENERATORS.
THE ENTIRE TRANSMATTER SYSTEM HAS COLLAPSED. WHAT FEW OF LEMNOS'S SOLDIERS EVEN MADE IT THROUGH ARE NOW STRANDED IN ENEMY TERRITORY. HOW'S THE VIEW FROM THE PUBLIC SERVICE?
YOU'D HAVE TO SEE IT TO BELIEVE IT...AND THAT'S NOT A BAD IDEA.
SUN BOY, CAN YOU HEAR ME?
TELL ULTRA BOY'S TEAM TO FOLLOW YOUR LEAD AND REMOVE THEIR FLIGHT RINGS!
THAT DECLOAKS THEM FROM THE ALL-SEEING EYES OF THE SERVICE, I KNOW, BUT IT'S OKAY--SO LONG AS I'M CONTROLLING IT, I CAN REACH EVERY UNDER-AGER IN THE GALAXY SIMULTANEOUSLY--
--AND SHOW THEM JUST WHO'S WINNING THIS FIGHT!
ON EVERY PLANET THAT LEMNOS TARGETED, HIS FORCES HAVE BEEN BLOCKED AND CAPTURED--
--IN THE NAME OF THE LEGION!
WE DID IT, PEOPLE.
WE WON THE WAR.
NOT YET.

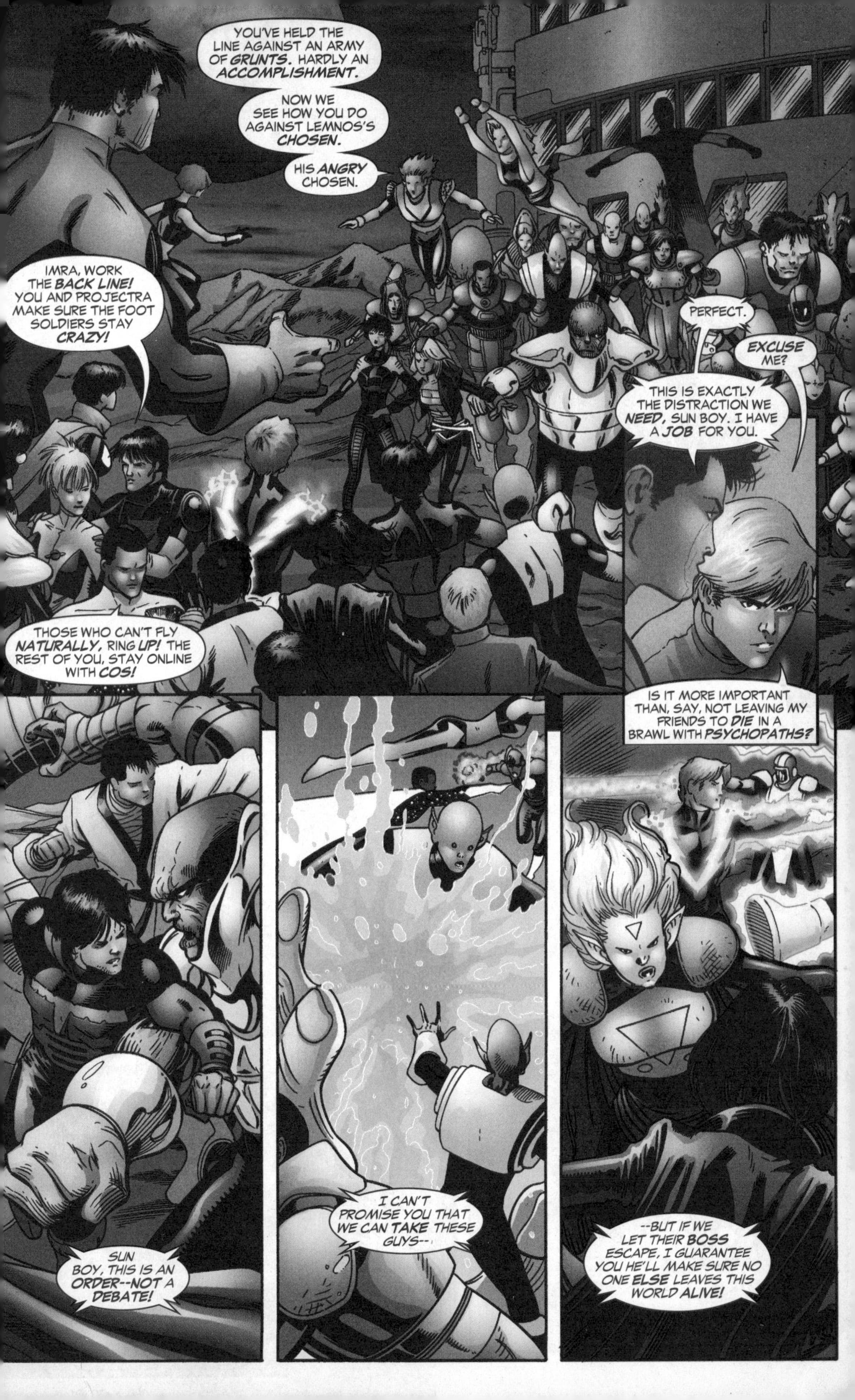
YOU'VE HELD THE LINE AGAINST AN ARMY OF GRUNTS. HARDLY AN ACCOMPLISHMENT.
NOW WE SEE HOW YOU DO AGAINST LEMNOS'S CHOSEN.
HIS ANGRY CHOSEN.
IMRA, WORK THE BACK LINE! YOU AND PROJECTRA MAKE SURE THE FOOT SOLDIERS STAY CRAZY!
THOSE WHO CAN'T FLY NATURALLY, RING UP! THE REST OF YOU, STAY ONLINE WITH COS!
PERFECT.
EXCUSE ME?
THIS IS EXACTLY THE DISTRACTION WE NEED, SUN BOY. I HAVE A JOB FOR YOU.
IS IT MORE IMPORTANT THAN, SAY, NOT LEAVING MY FRIENDS TO DIE IN A BRAWL WITH PSYCHOPATHS?
SUN BOY, THIS IS AN ORDER--NOT A DEBATE!
I CAN'T PROMISE YOU THAT WE CAN TAKE THESE GUYS--
--BUT IF WE LET THEIR BOSS ESCAPE, I GUARANTEE YOU HE'LL MAKE SURE NO ONE ELSE LEAVES THIS WORLD ALIVE!

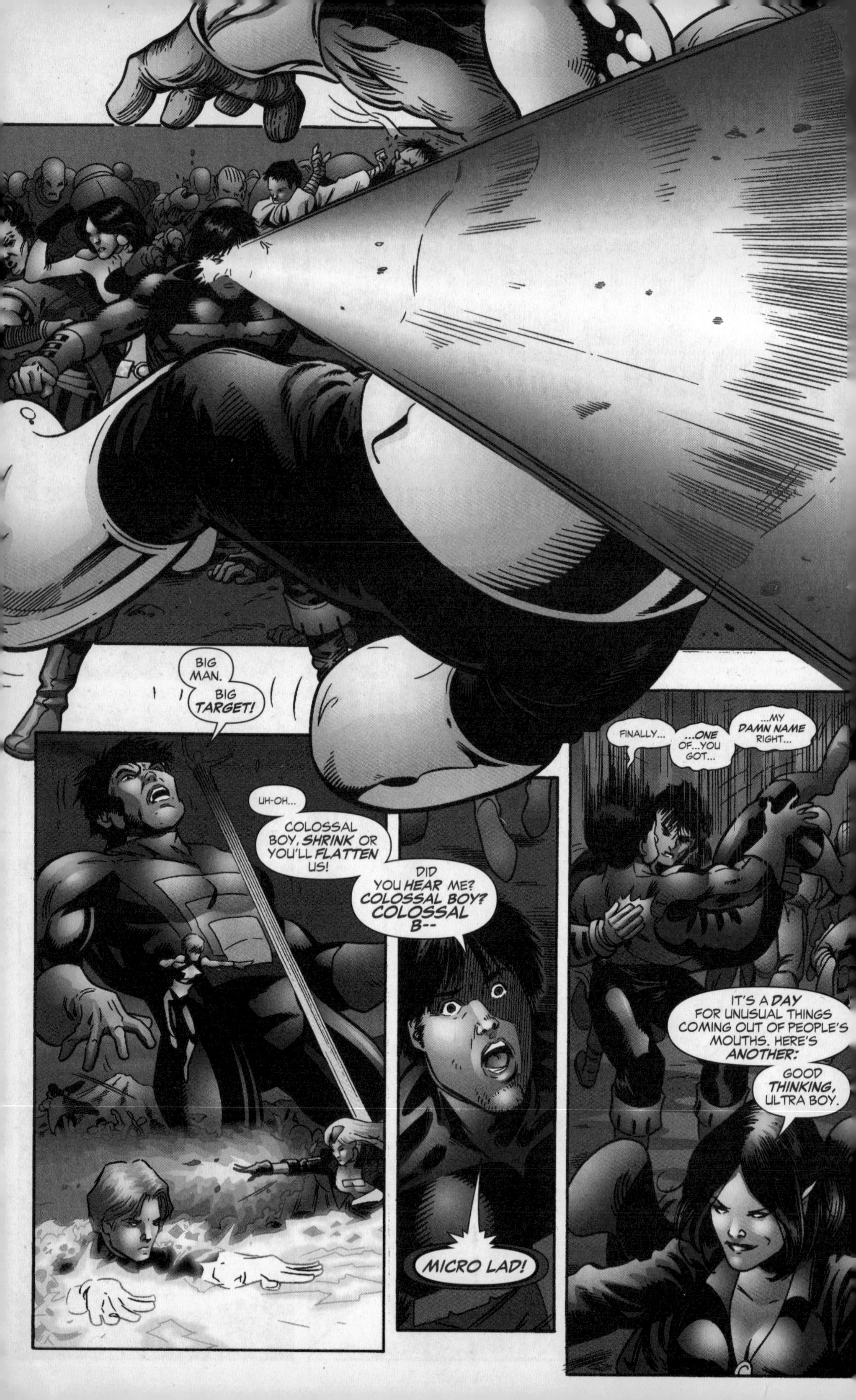
BIG MAN. BIG TARGET!
UH-OH...
COLOSSAL BOY, SHRINK OR YOU'LL FLATTEN US!
DID YOU HEAR ME? COLOSSAL BOY? COLOSSAL B--
MICRO LAD!
FINALLY...
...ONE OF...YOU GOT...
...MY DAMN NAME RIGHT...
IT'S A DAY FOR UNUSUAL THINGS COMING OUT OF PEOPLE'S MOUTHS. HERE'S ANOTHER:
GOOD THINKING, ULTRA BOY.

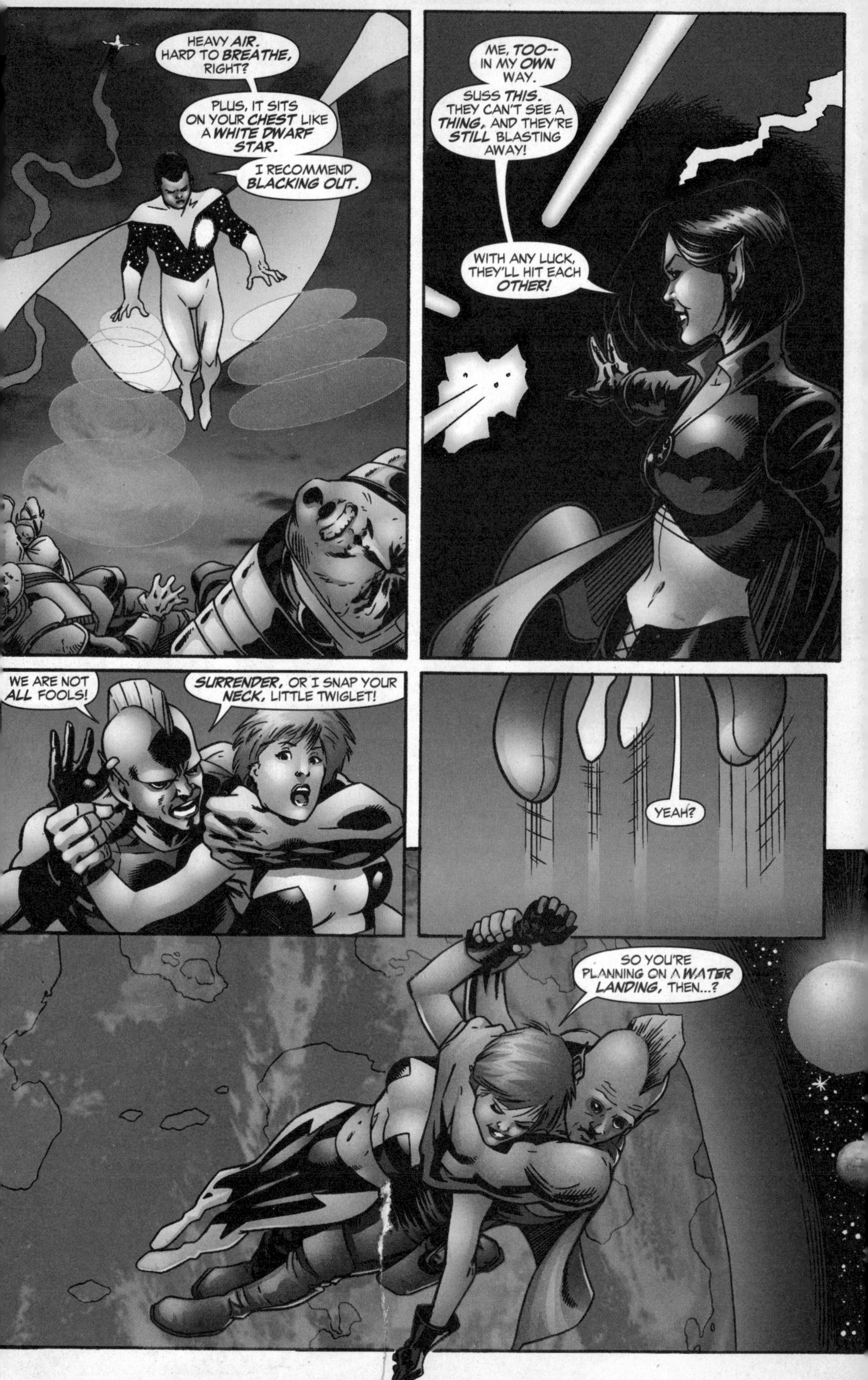
HEAVY AIR. HARD TO BREATHE, RIGHT?
PLUS, IT SITS ON YOUR CHEST LIKE A WHITE DWARF STAR.
I RECOMMEND BLACKING OUT.
ME, TOO-- IN MY OWN WAY.
SUSS THIS. THEY CAN'T SEE A THING, AND THEY'RE STILL BLASTING AWAY!
WITH ANY LUCK, THEY'LL HIT EACH OTHER!
WE ARE NOT ALL FOOLS!
SURRENDER, OR I SNAP YOUR NECK, LITTLE TWIGLET!
YEAH?
SO YOU'RE PLANNING ON A WATER LANDING, THEN...?

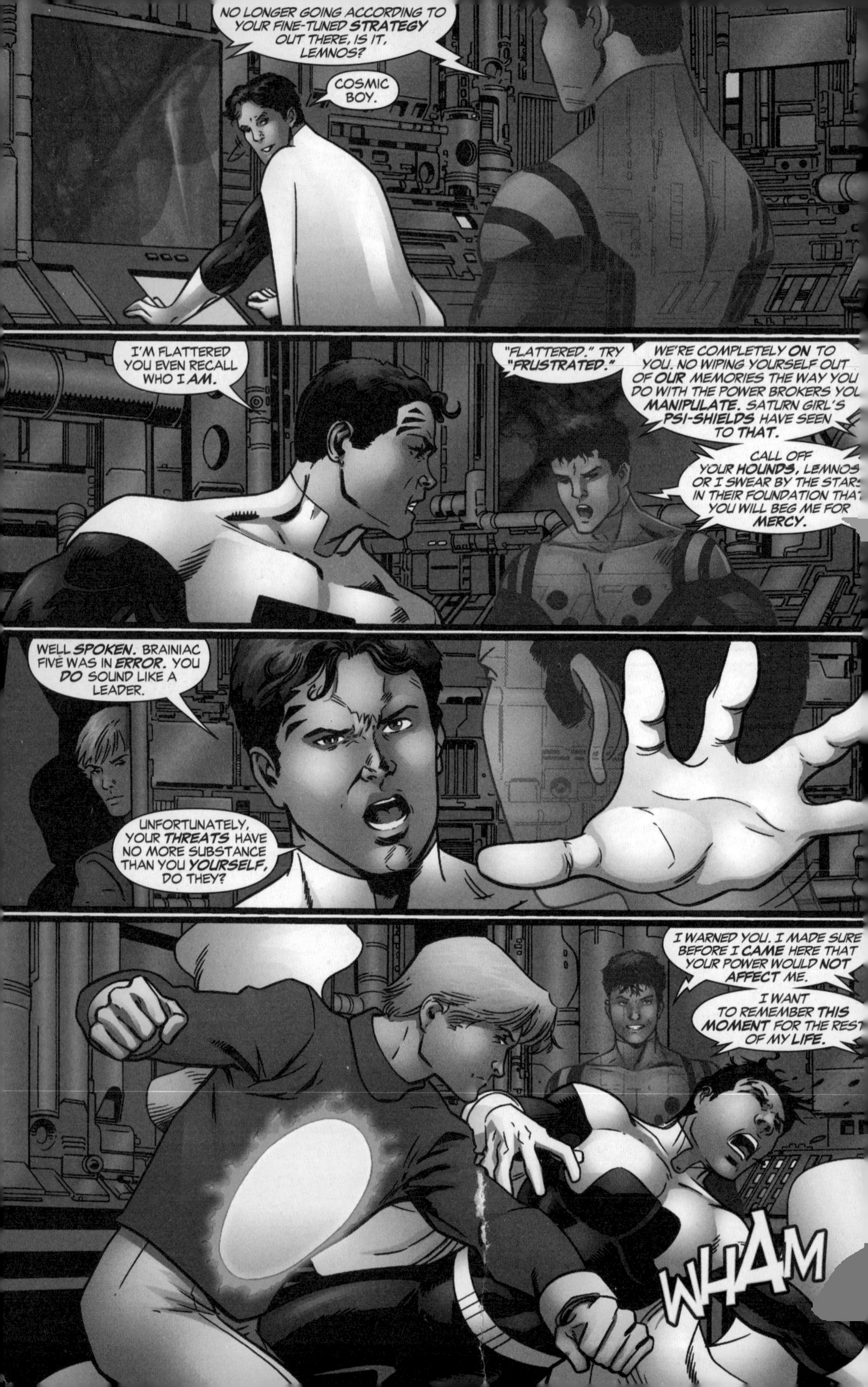
NO LONGER GOING ACCORDING TO YOUR FINE-TUNED STRATEGY OUT THERE, IS IT, LEMNOS?
COSMIC BOY.
I'M FLATTERED YOU EVEN RECALL WHO I AM.
"FLATTERED." TRY "FRUSTRATED."
WE'RE COMPLETELY ON TO YOU. NO WIPING YOURSELF OUT OF OUR MEMORIES THE WAY YOU DO WITH THE POWER BROKERS YOU MANIPULATE. SATURN GIRL'S PSI-SHIELDS HAVE SEEN TO THAT.
CALL OFF YOUR HOUNDS, LEMNOS OR I SWEAR BY THE STARS IN THEIR FOUNDATION THAT YOU WILL BEG ME FOR MERCY.
WELL SPOKEN. BRAINIAC FIVE WAS IN ERROR. YOU DO SOUND LIKE A LEADER.
UNFORTUNATELY, YOUR THREATS HAVE NO MORE SUBSTANCE THAN YOU YOURSELF, DO THEY?
I WARNED YOU. I MADE SURE BEFORE I CAME HERE THAT YOUR POWER WOULD NOT AFFECT ME.
I WANT TO REMEMBER THIS MOMENT FOR THE REST OF MY LIFE.
WHAM

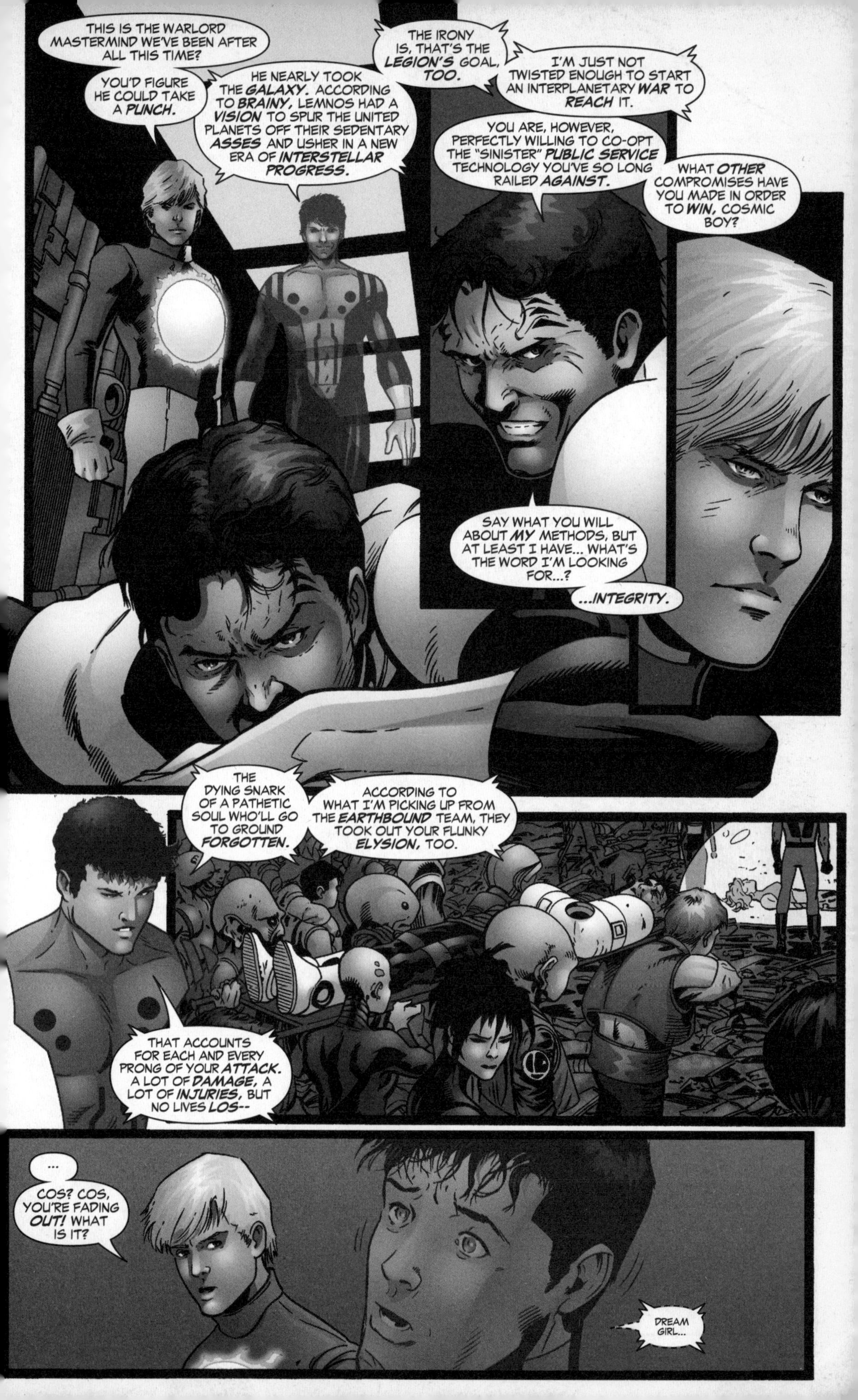

THIS IS THE WARLORD MASTERMIND WE'VE BEEN AFTER ALL THIS TIME?
YOU'D FIGURE HE COULD TAKE A PUNCH.
HE NEARLY TOOK THE GALAXY. ACCORDING TO BRAINY, LEMNOS HAD A VISION TO SPUR THE UNITED PLANETS OFF THEIR SEDENTARY ASSES AND USHER IN A NEW ERA OF INTERSTELLAR PROGRESS.
THE IRONY IS, THAT'S THE LEGION'S GOAL, TOO.
I'M JUST NOT TWISTED ENOUGH TO START AN INTERPLANETARY WAR TO REACH IT.
YOU ARE, HOWEVER, PERFECTLY WILLING TO CO-OPT THE "SINISTER" PUBLIC SERVICE TECHNOLOGY YOU'VE SO LONG RAILED AGAINST.
WHAT OTHER COMPROMISES HAVE YOU MADE IN ORDER TO WIN, COSMIC BOY?
SAY WHAT YOU WILL ABOUT MY METHODS, BUT AT LEAST I HAVE... WHAT'S THE WORD I'M LOOKING FOR...?
...INTEGRITY.
THE DYING SNARK OF A PATHETIC SOUL WHO'LL GO TO GROUND FORGOTTEN.
ACCORDING TO WHAT I'M PICKING UP FROM THE EARTHBOUND TEAM, THEY TOOK OUT YOUR FLUNKY ELYSION, TOO.
THAT ACCOUNTS FOR EACH AND EVERY PRONG OF YOUR ATTACK. A LOT OF DAMAGE, A LOT OF INJURIES, BUT NO LIVES LOS--
...
COS? COS, YOU'RE FADING OUT! WHAT IS IT?
DREAM GIRL...

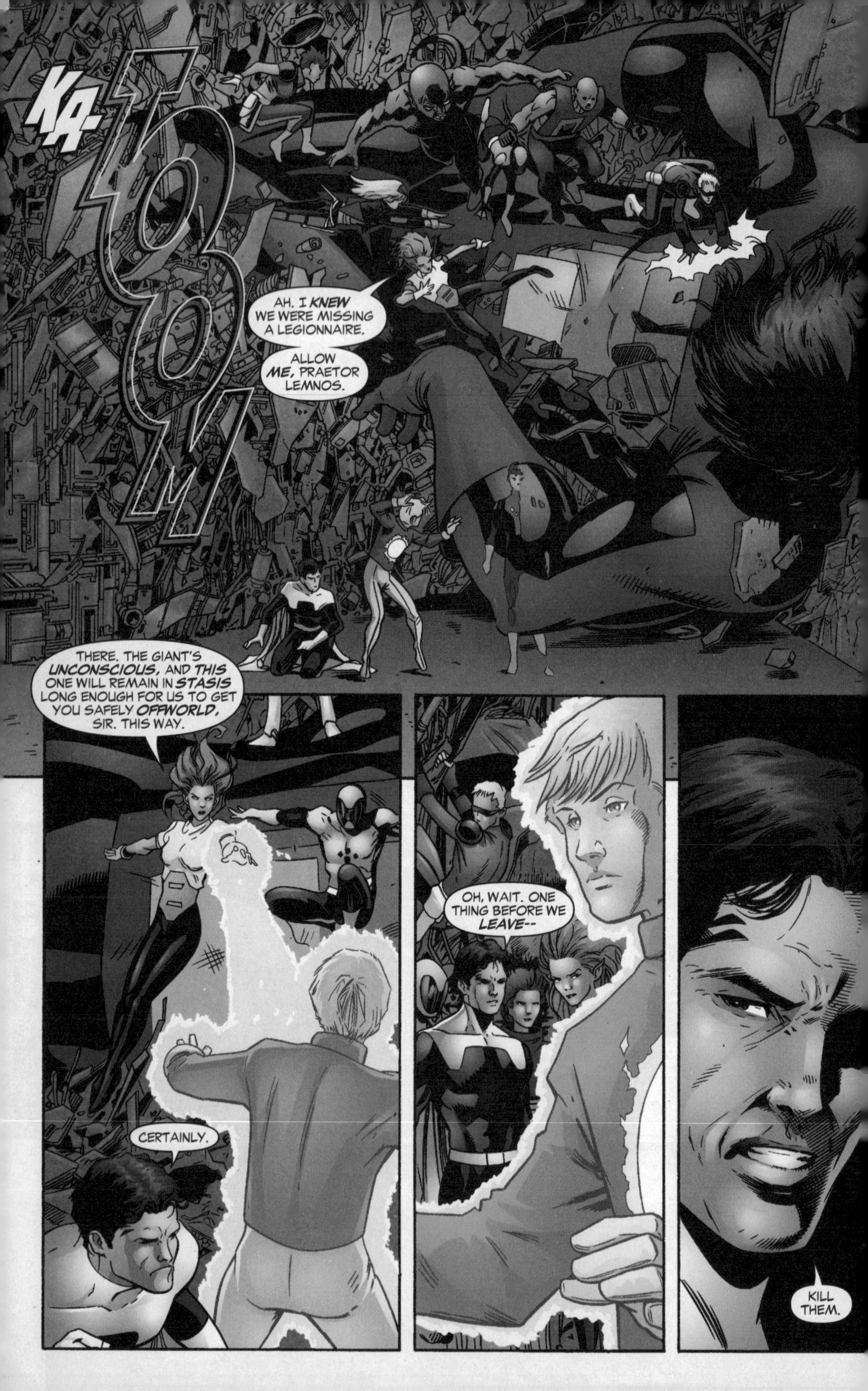
KA-THOOM
AH. I KNEW WE WERE MISSING A LEGIONNAIRE.
ALLOW ME, PRAETOR LEMNOS.
THERE. THE GIANT'S UNCONSCIOUS, AND THIS ONE WILL REMAIN IN STASIS LONG ENOUGH FOR US TO GET YOU SAFELY OFFWORLD, SIR. THIS WAY.
CERTAINLY.
OH, WAIT. ONE THING BEFORE WE LEAVE--
KILL THEM.

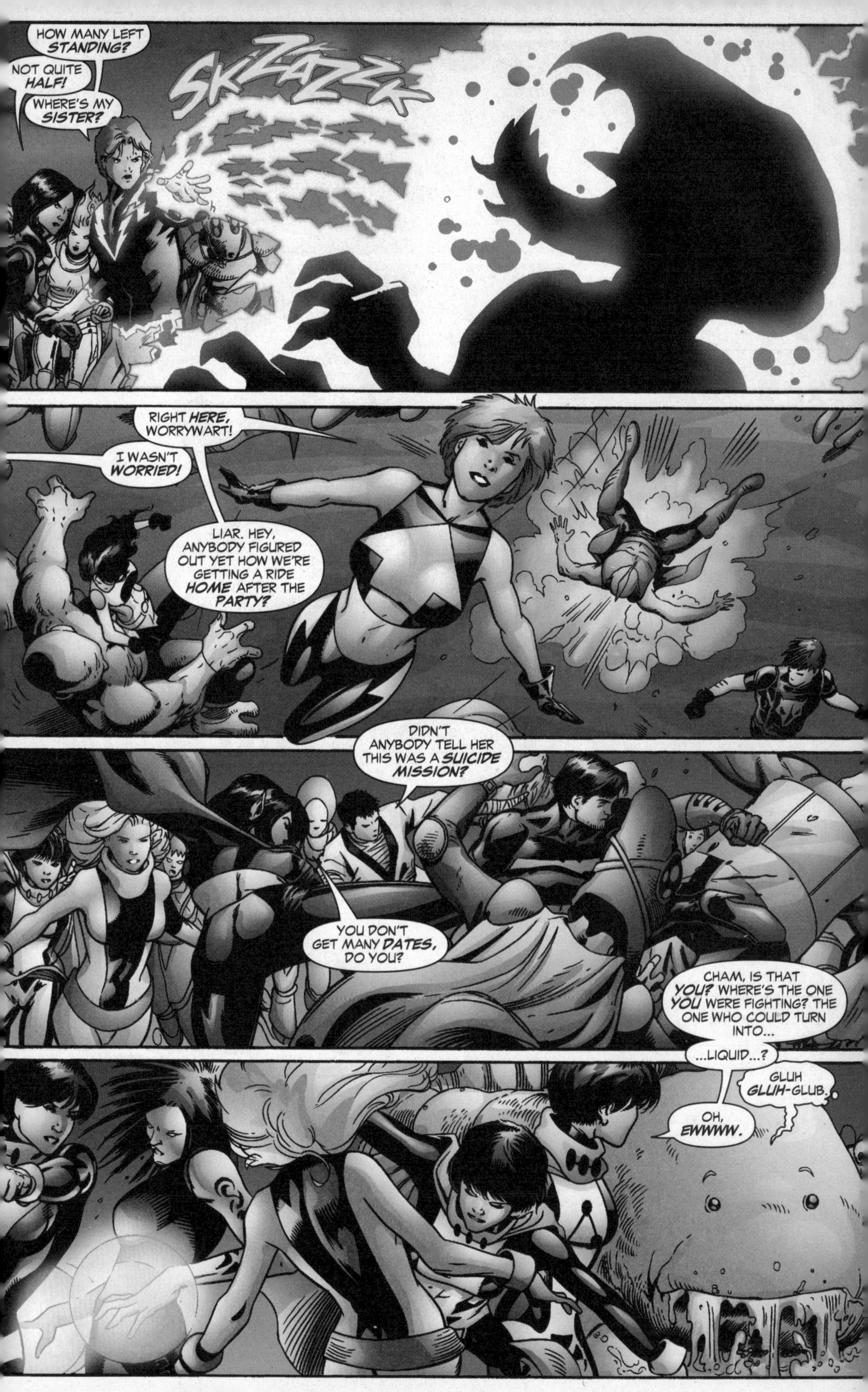
HOW MANY LEFT STANDING?
NOT QUITE HALF!
WHERE'S MY SISTER?
SKZAZZK
RIGHT HERE, WORRYWART!
I WASN'T WORRIED!
LIAR. HEY, ANYBODY FIGURED OUT YET HOW WE'RE GETTING A RIDE HOME AFTER THE PARTY?
DIDN'T ANYBODY TELL HER THIS WAS A SUICIDE MISSION?
YOU DON'T GET MANY DATES, DO YOU?
CHAM, IS THAT YOU? WHERE'S THE ONE YOU WERE FIGHTING? THE ONE WHO COULD TURN INTO...
...LIQUID...?
GLUH GLUH-GLUB.
OH, EWWWW.

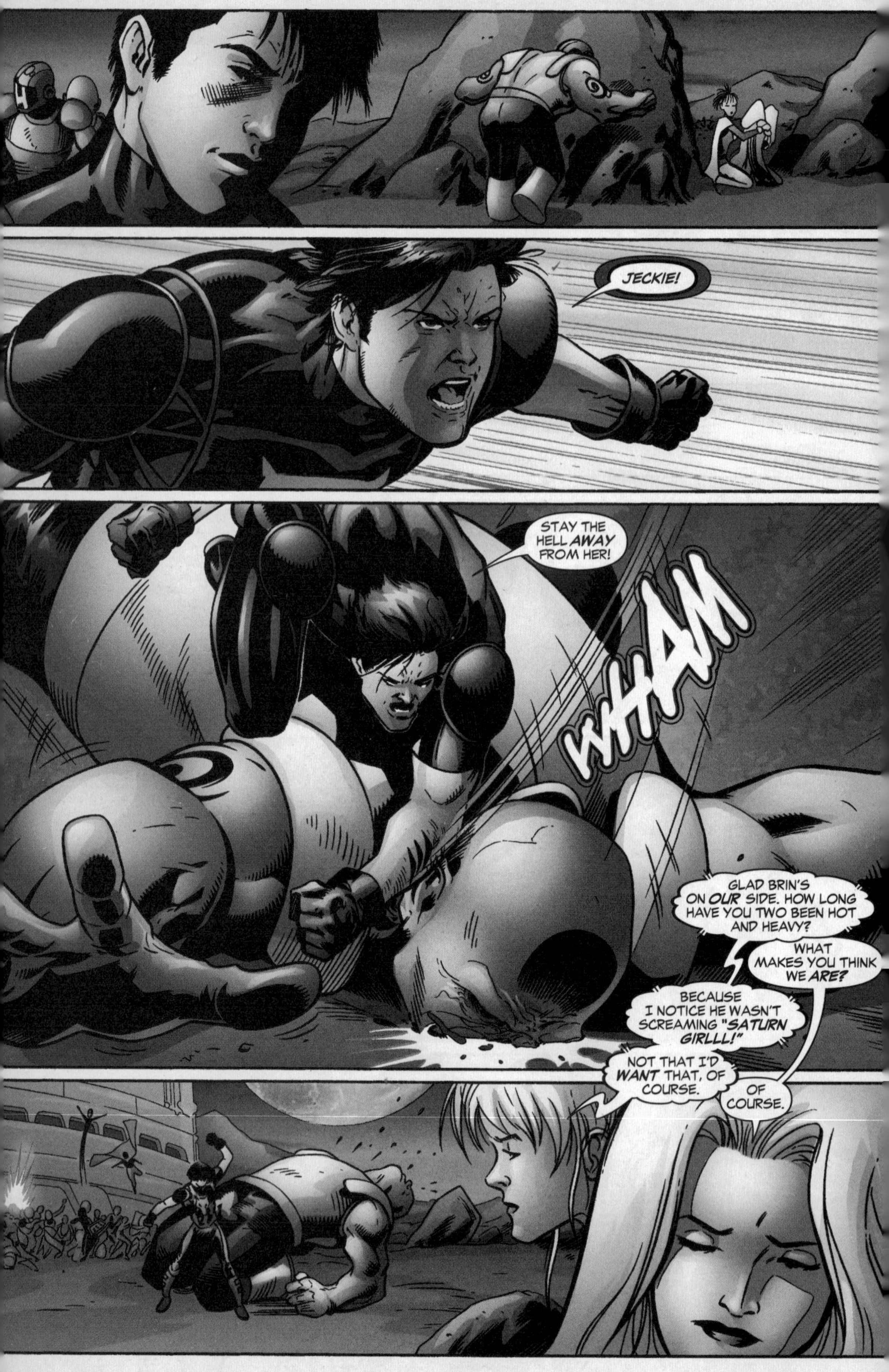
JECKIE!
STAY THE HELL AWAY FROM HER!
WHAM
GLAD BRIN'S ON OUR SIDE. HOW LONG HAVE YOU TWO BEEN HOT AND HEAVY?
WHAT MAKES YOU THINK WE ARE?
BECAUSE I NOTICE HE WASN'T SCREAMING "SATURN GIRLLL!"
NOT THAT I'D WANT THAT, OF COURSE.
OF COURSE.

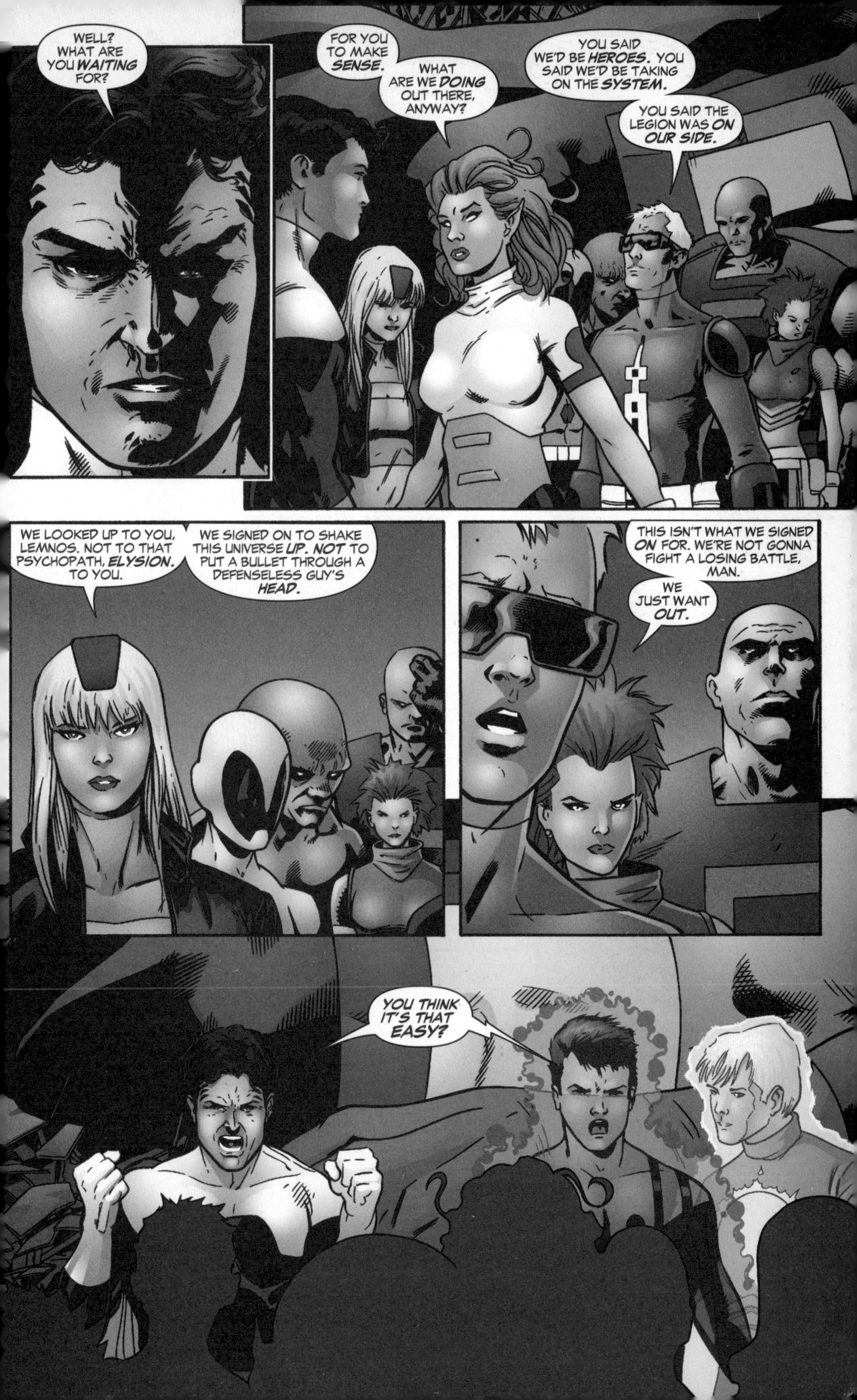

WELL? WHAT ARE YOU WAITING FOR?
FOR YOU TO MAKE SENSE.
WHAT ARE WE DOING OUT THERE, ANYWAY?
YOU SAID WE'D BE HEROES. YOU SAID WE'D BE TAKING ON THE SYSTEM.
YOU SAID THE LEGION WAS ON OUR SIDE.
WE LOOKED UP TO YOU, LEMNOS. NOT TO THAT PSYCHOPATH, ELYSION. TO YOU.
WE SIGNED ON TO SHAKE THIS UNIVERSE UP. NOT TO PUT A BULLET THROUGH A DEFENSELESS GUY'S HEAD.
THIS ISN'T WHAT WE SIGNED ON FOR. WE'RE NOT GONNA FIGHT A LOSING BATTLE, MAN.
WE JUST WANT OUT.
YOU THINK IT'S THAT EASY?

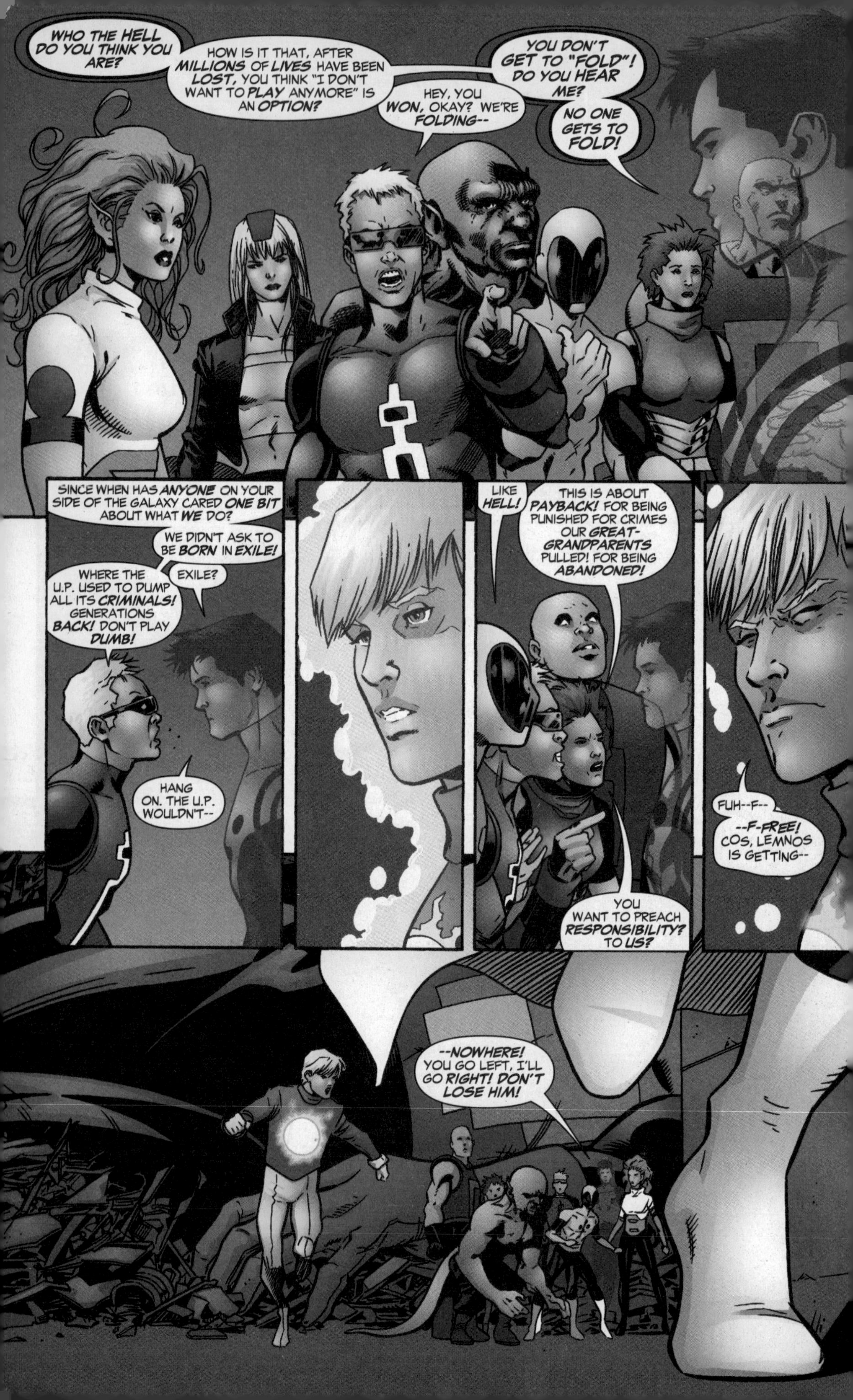
WHO THE HELL DO YOU THINK YOU ARE?
HOW IS IT THAT, AFTER MILLIONS OF LIVES HAVE BEEN LOST, YOU THINK "I DON'T WANT TO PLAY ANYMORE" IS AN OPTION?
HEY, YOU WON, OKAY? WE'RE FOLDING--
YOU DON'T GET TO "FOLD"! DO YOU HEAR ME?
NO ONE GETS TO FOLD!
SINCE WHEN HAS ANYONE ON YOUR SIDE OF THE GALAXY CARED ONE BIT ABOUT WHAT WE DO?
WE DIDN'T ASK TO BE BORN IN EXILE!
EXILE?
WHERE THE U.P. USED TO DUMP ALL ITS CRIMINALS! GENERATIONS BACK! DON'T PLAY DUMB!
HANG ON. THE U.P. WOULDN'T--
LIKE HELL!
THIS IS ABOUT PAYBACK! FOR BEING PUNISHED FOR CRIMES OUR GREAT-GRANDPARENTS PULLED! FOR BEING ABANDONED!
YOU WANT TO PREACH RESPONSIBILITY? TO US?
FUH--F--
--F-FREE! COS, LEMNOS IS GETTING--
--NOWHERE! YOU GO LEFT, I'LL GO RIGHT! DON'T LOSE HIM!

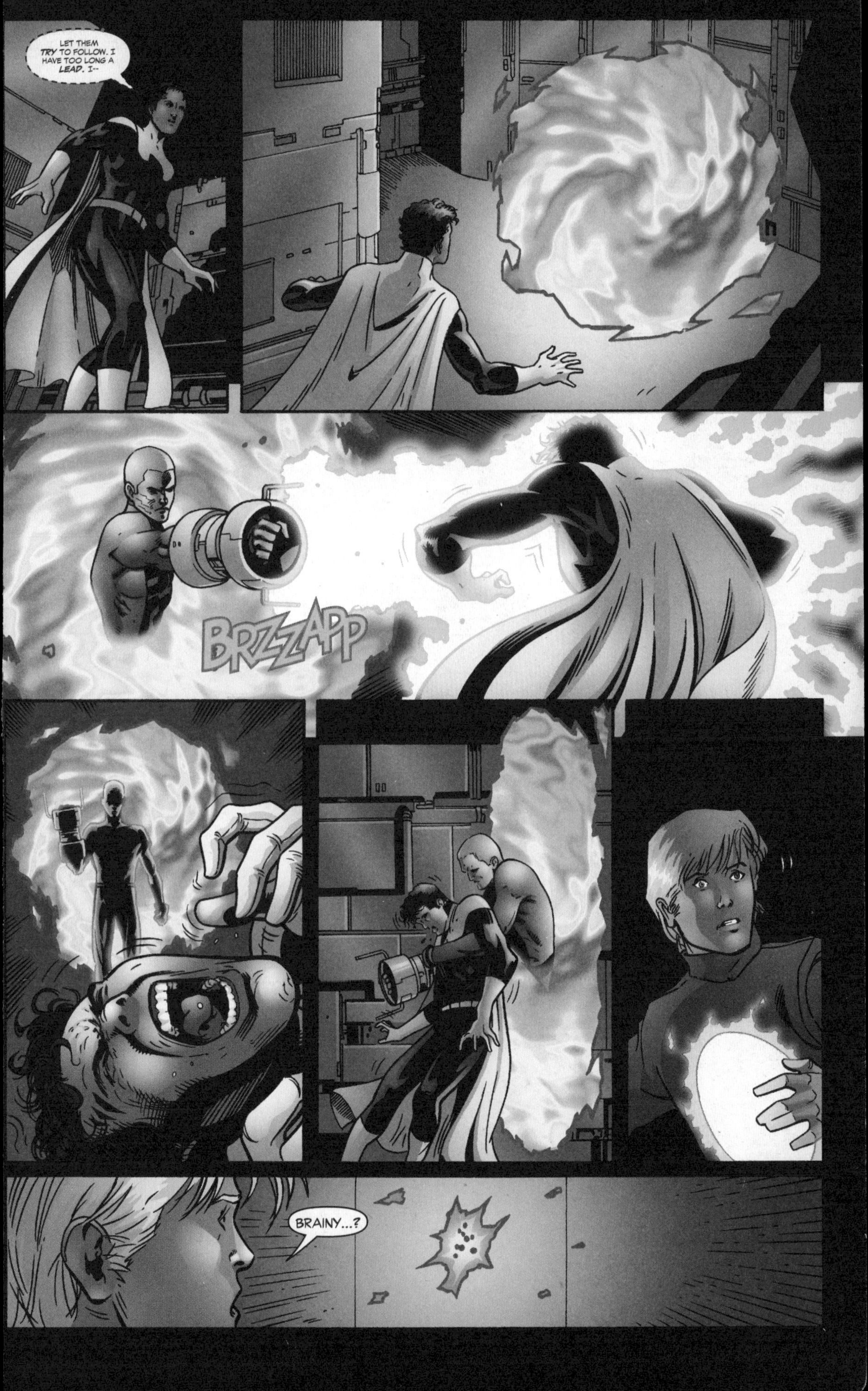
LET THEM TRY TO FOLLOW. I HAVE TOO LONG A LEAD. I--
BRZZAPP
BRAINY...?

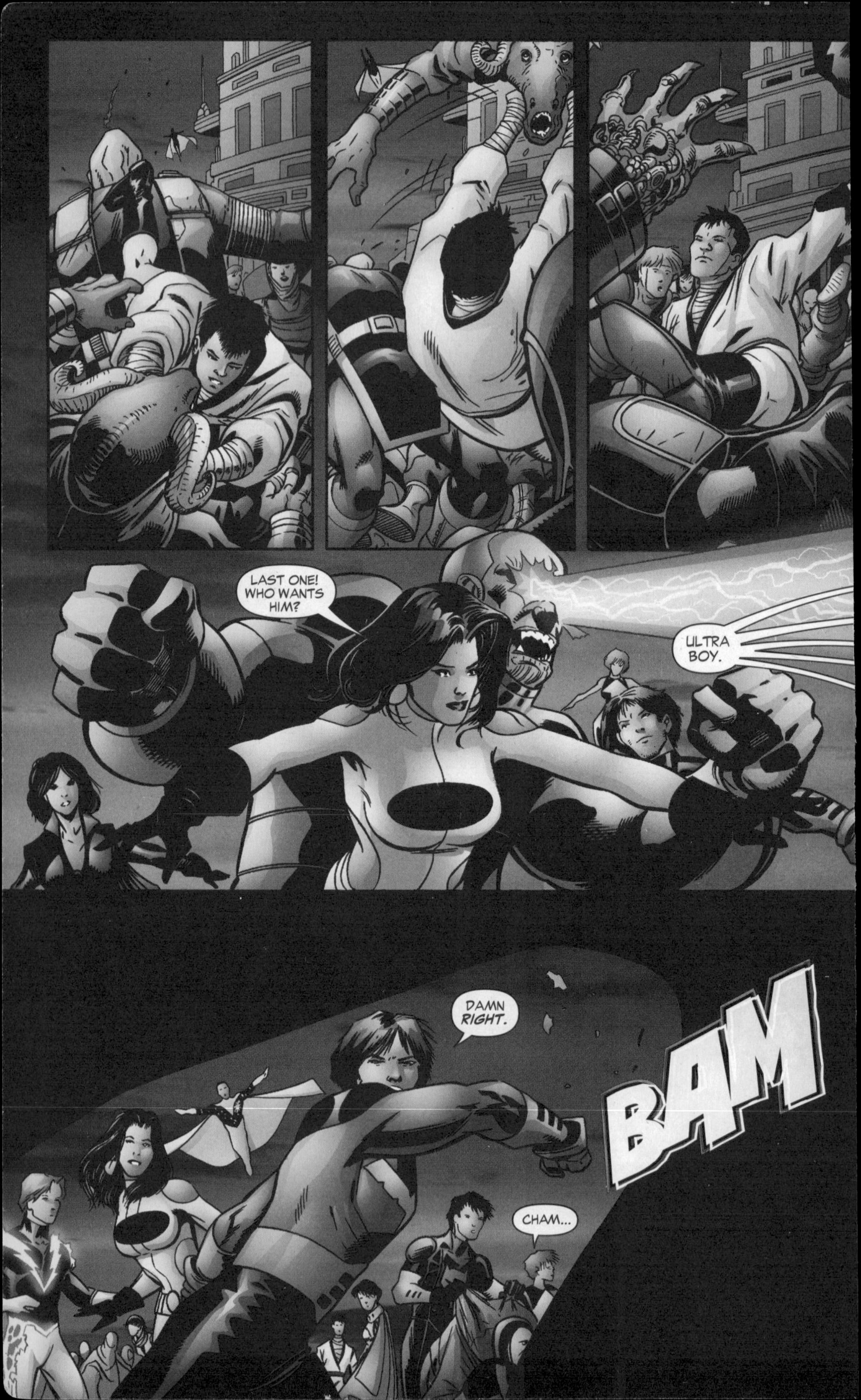
LAST ONE! WHO WANTS HIM?
ULTRA BOY.
DAMN RIGHT.
BAM
CHAM...

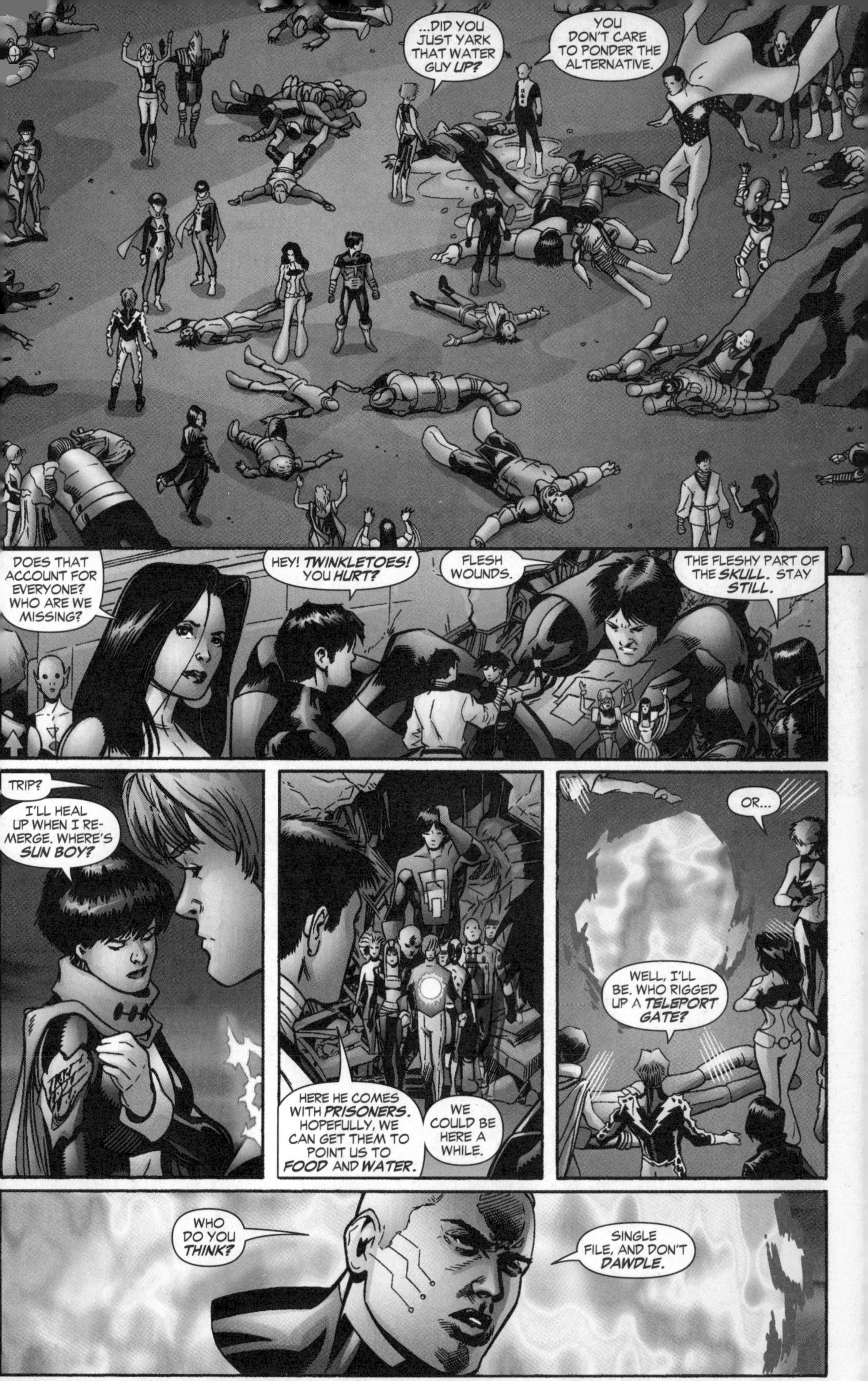
...DID YOU JUST YARK THAT WATER GUY UP?
YOU DON'T CARE TO PONDER THE ALTERNATIVE.
DOES THAT ACCOUNT FOR EVERYONE? WHO ARE WE MISSING?
HEY! TWINKLETOES! YOU HURT?
FLESH WOUNDS.
THE FLESHY PART OF THE SKULL. STAY STILL.
TRIP?
I'LL HEAL UP WHEN I RE-MERGE. WHERE'S SUN BOY?
HERE HE COMES WITH PRISONERS. HOPEFULLY, WE CAN GET THEM TO POINT US TO FOOD AND WATER.
WE COULD BE HERE A WHILE.
OR...
WELL, I'LL BE. WHO RIGGED UP A TELEPORT GATE?
WHO DO YOU THINK?
SINGLE FILE, AND DON'T DAWDLE.

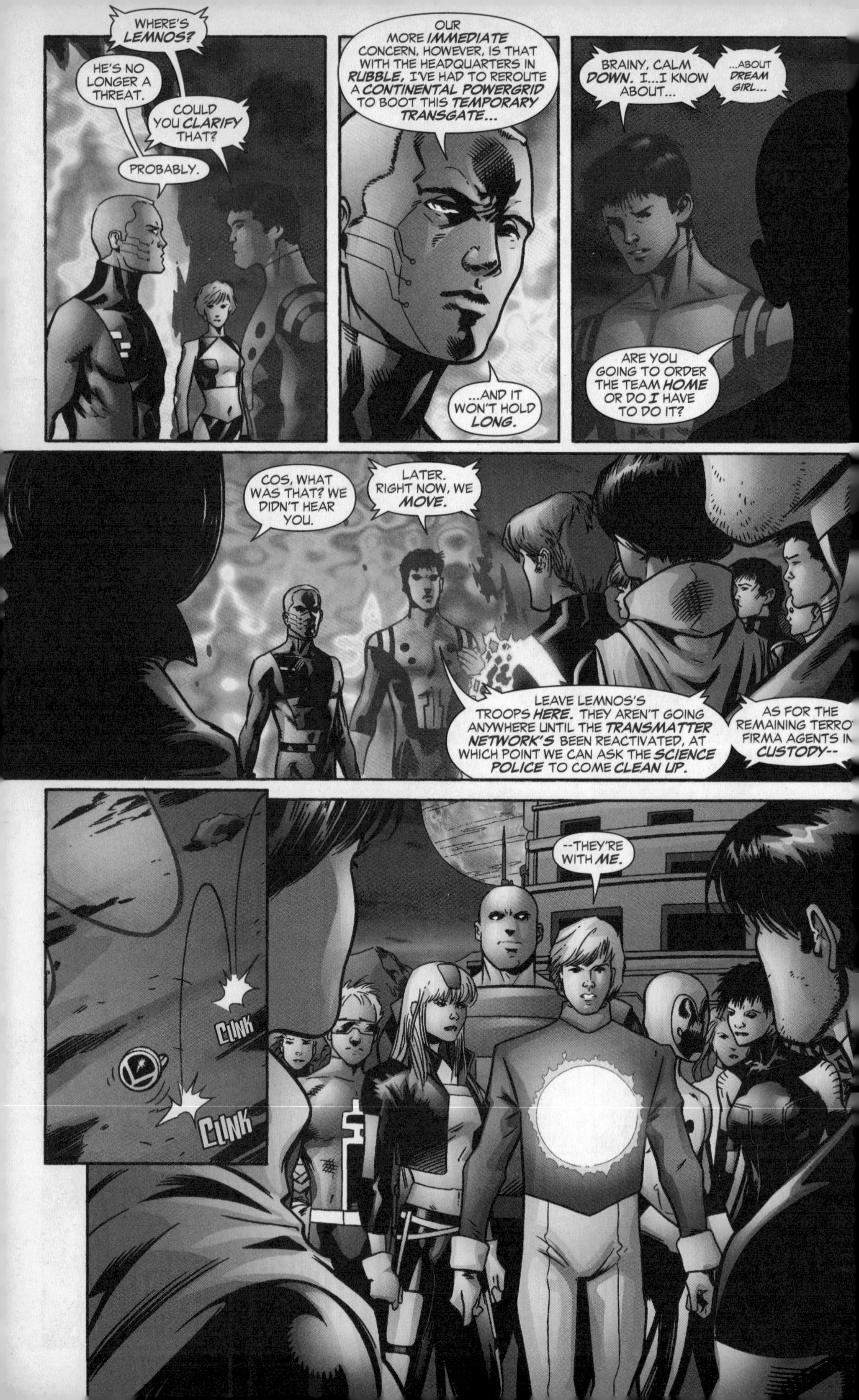
WHERE'S LEMNOS?
HE'S NO LONGER A THREAT.
COULD YOU CLARIFY THAT?
PROBABLY.
OUR MORE IMMEDIATE CONCERN, HOWEVER, IS THAT WITH THE HEADQUARTERS IN RUBBLE, I'VE HAD TO REROUTE A CONTINENTAL POWERGRID TO BOOT THIS TEMPORARY TRANSGATE...
...AND IT WON'T HOLD LONG.
BRAINY, CALM DOWN. I...I KNOW ABOUT...
...ABOUT DREAM GIRL...
ARE YOU GOING TO ORDER THE TEAM HOME OR DO I HAVE TO DO IT?
COS, WHAT WAS THAT? WE DIDN'T HEAR YOU.
LATER. RIGHT NOW, WE MOVE.
LEAVE LEMNOS'S TROOPS HERE. THEY AREN'T GOING ANYWHERE UNTIL THE TRANSMATTER NETWORK'S BEEN REACTIVATED, AT WHICH POINT WE CAN ASK THE SCIENCE POLICE TO COME CLEAN UP.
AS FOR THE REMAINING TERRO FIRMA AGENTS IN CUSTODY--
--THEY'RE WITH ME.
CLINK
CLINK

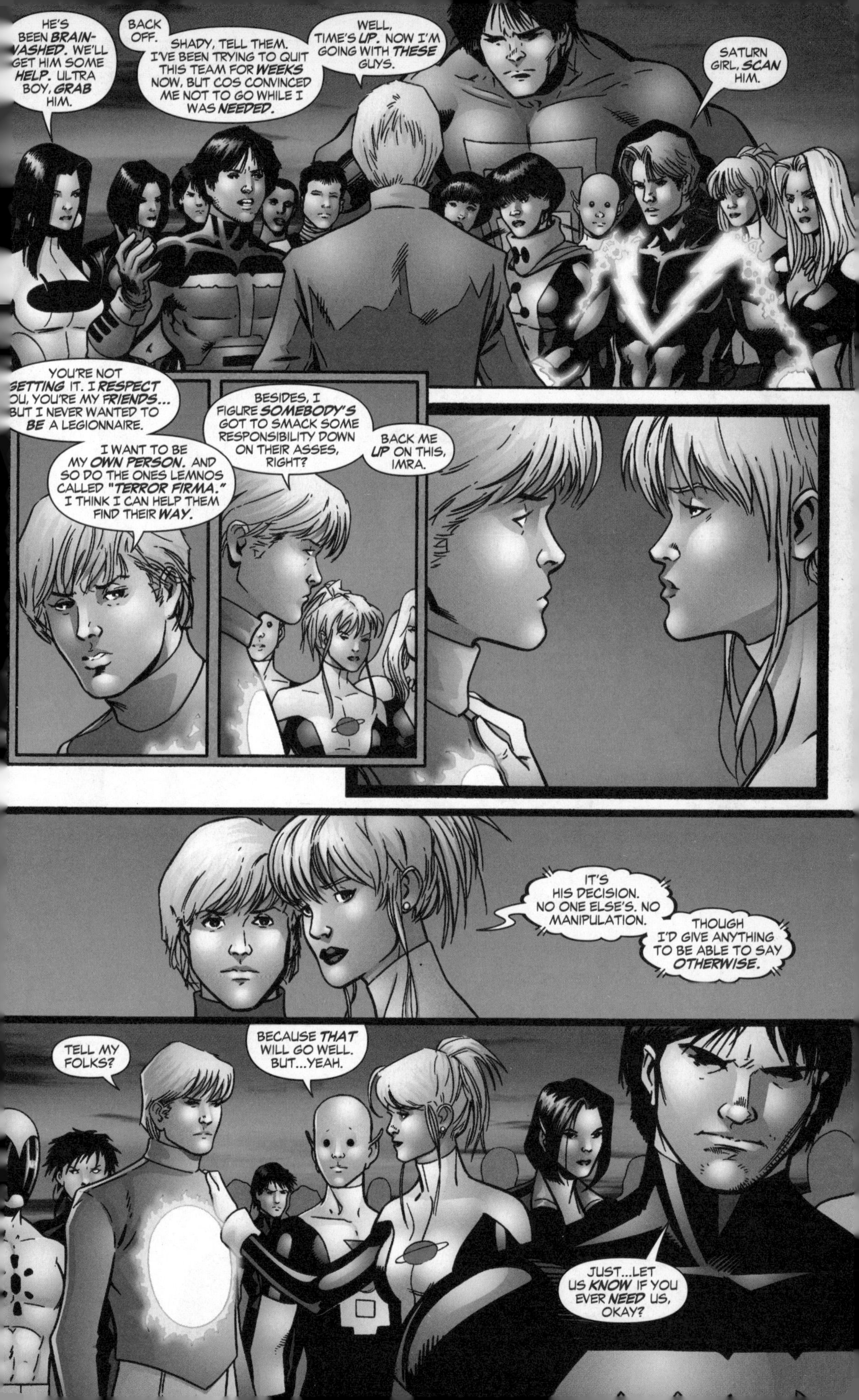
HE'S BEEN BRAIN-WASHED. WE'LL GET HIM SOME HELP. ULTRA BOY, GRAB HIM.
BACK OFF.
SHADY, TELL THEM. I'VE BEEN TRYING TO QUIT THIS TEAM FOR WEEKS NOW, BUT COS CONVINCED ME NOT TO GO WHILE I WAS NEEDED.
WELL, TIME'S UP. NOW I'M GOING WITH THESE GUYS.
SATURN GIRL, SCAN HIM.
YOU'RE NOT GETTING IT. I RESPECT YOU, YOU'RE MY FRIENDS... BUT I NEVER WANTED TO BE A LEGIONNAIRE.
I WANT TO BE MY OWN PERSON. AND SO DO THE ONES LEMNOS CALLED "TERROR FIRMA." I THINK I CAN HELP THEM FIND THEIR WAY.
BESIDES, I FIGURE SOMEBODY'S GOT TO SMACK SOME RESPONSIBILITY DOWN ON THEIR ASSES, RIGHT?
BACK ME UP ON THIS, IMRA.
IT'S HIS DECISION. NO ONE ELSE'S. NO MANIPULATION.
THOUGH I'D GIVE ANYTHING TO BE ABLE TO SAY OTHERWISE.
TELL MY FOLKS?
BECAUSE THAT WILL GO WELL. BUT...YEAH.
JUST...LET US KNOW IF YOU EVER NEED US, OKAY?

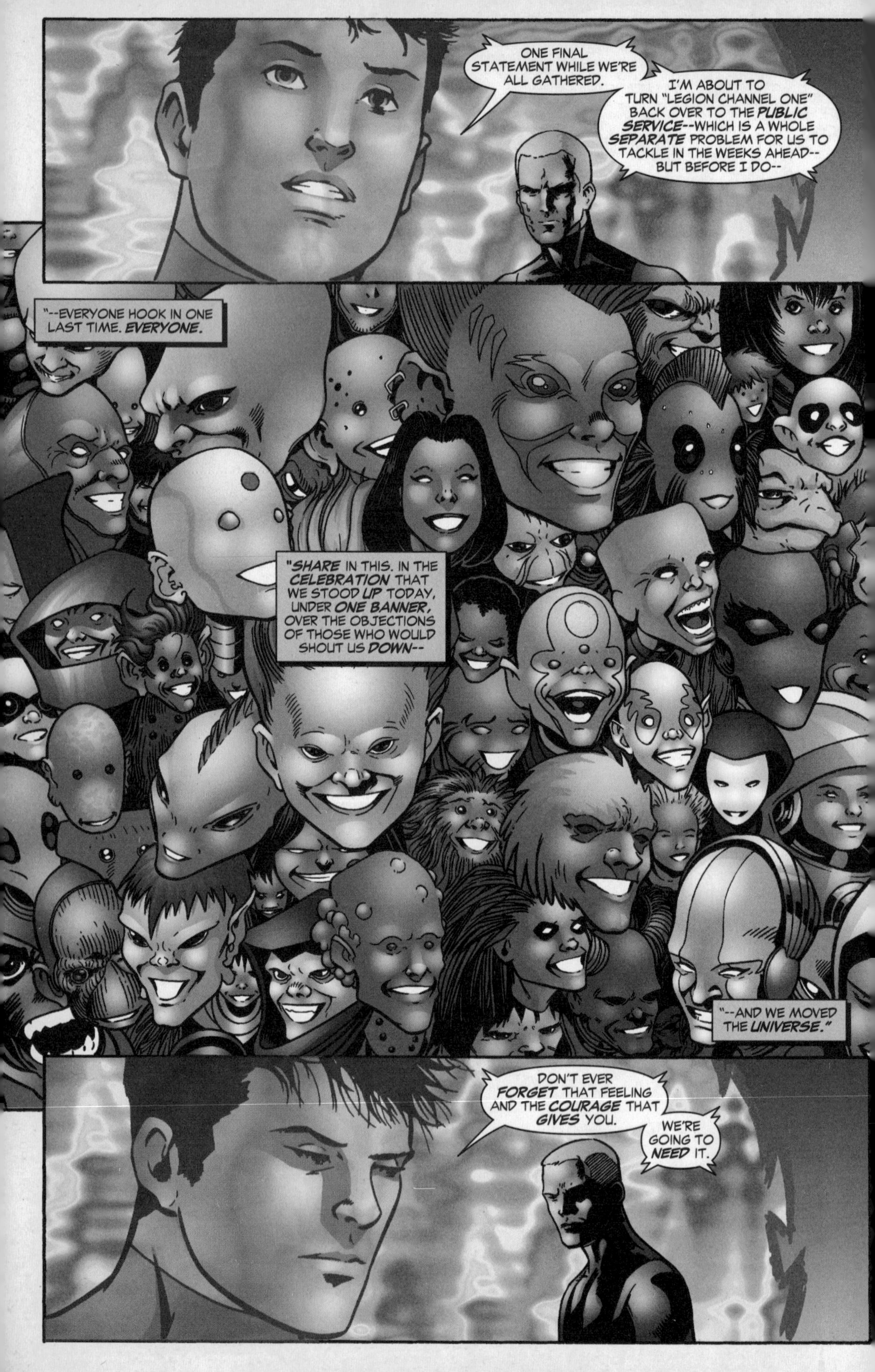
ONE FINAL STATEMENT WHILE WE'RE ALL GATHERED.
I'M ABOUT TO TURN "LEGION CHANNEL ONE" BACK OVER TO THE PUBLIC SERVICE--WHICH IS A WHOLE SEPARATE PROBLEM FOR US TO TACKLE IN THE WEEKS AHEAD--BUT BEFORE I DO--
"--EVERYONE HOOK IN ONE LAST TIME. EVERYONE.
"SHARE IN THIS. IN THE CELEBRATION THAT WE STOOD UP TODAY, UNDER ONE BANNER, OVER THE OBJECTIONS OF THOSE WHO WOULD SHOUT US DOWN--
"--AND WE MOVED THE UNIVERSE."
DON'T EVER FORGET THAT FEELING AND THE COURAGE THAT GIVES YOU.
WE'RE GOING TO NEED IT.

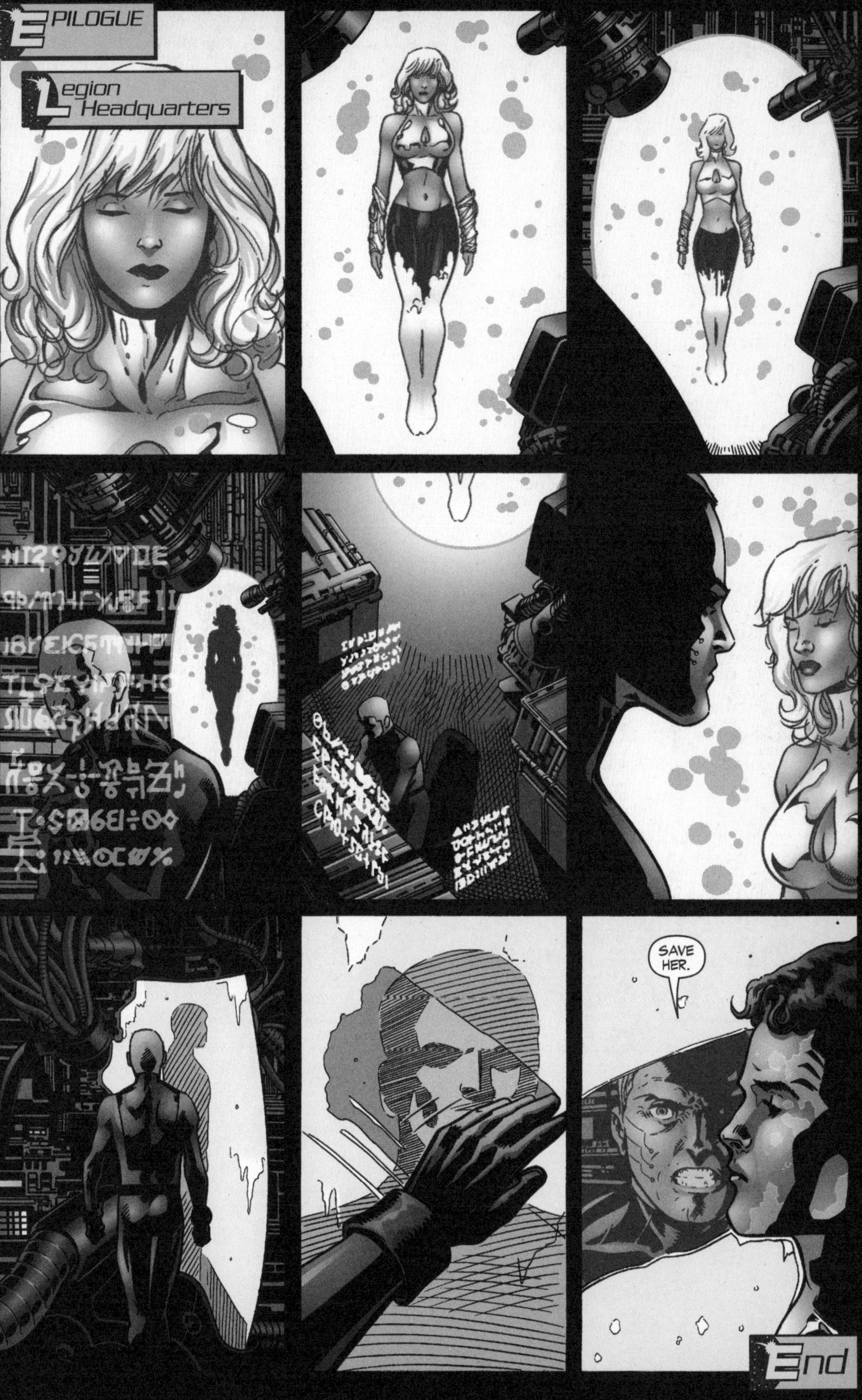
EPILOGUE
Legion Headquarters
SAVE HER.
End

LEGION OF SUPER-HEROES #7

Art by **Barry Kitson** with **Chris Blythe**

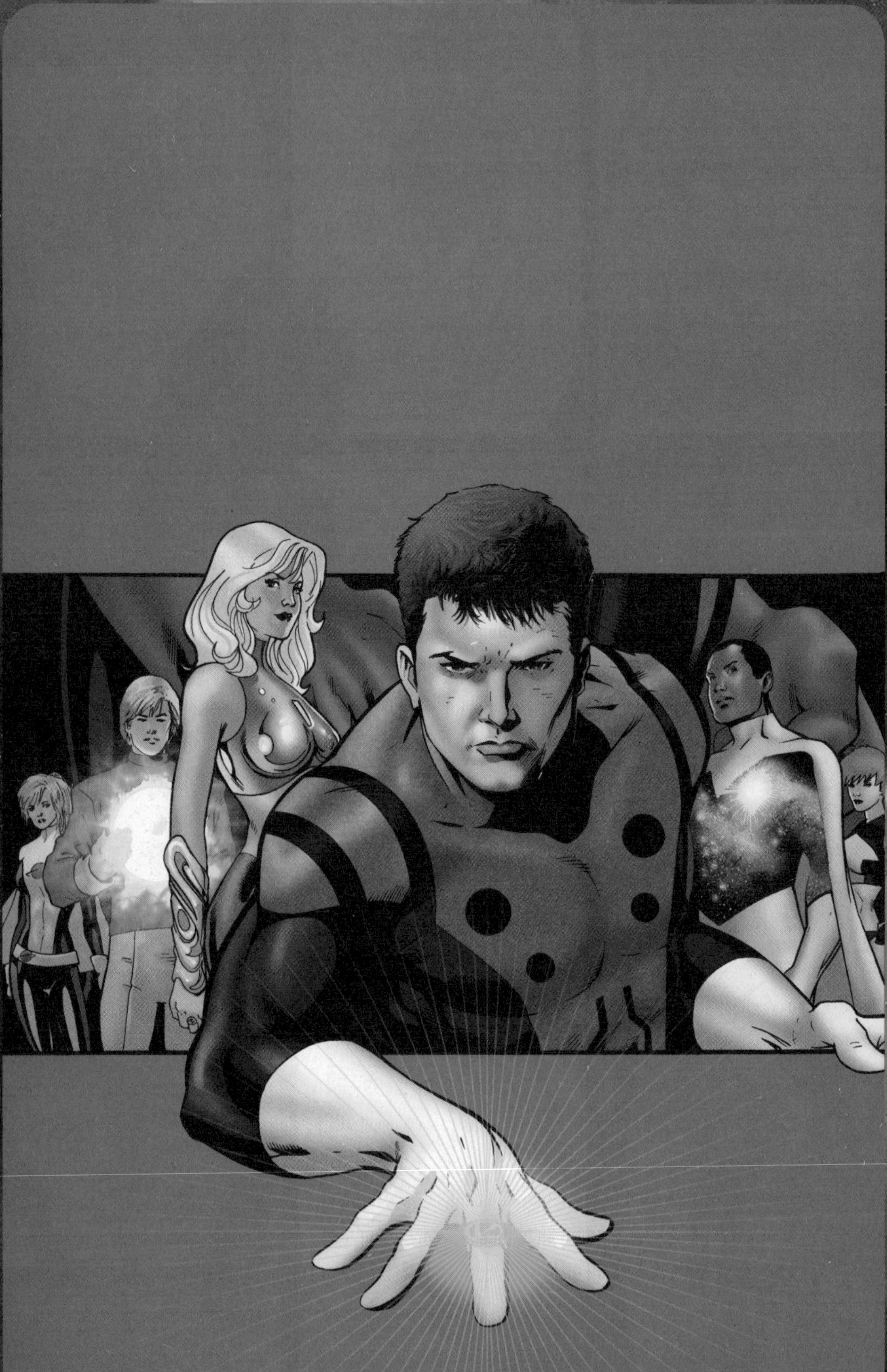

LEGION OF SUPER-HEROES #8

Art by **Barry Kitson** with **Chris Blythe**

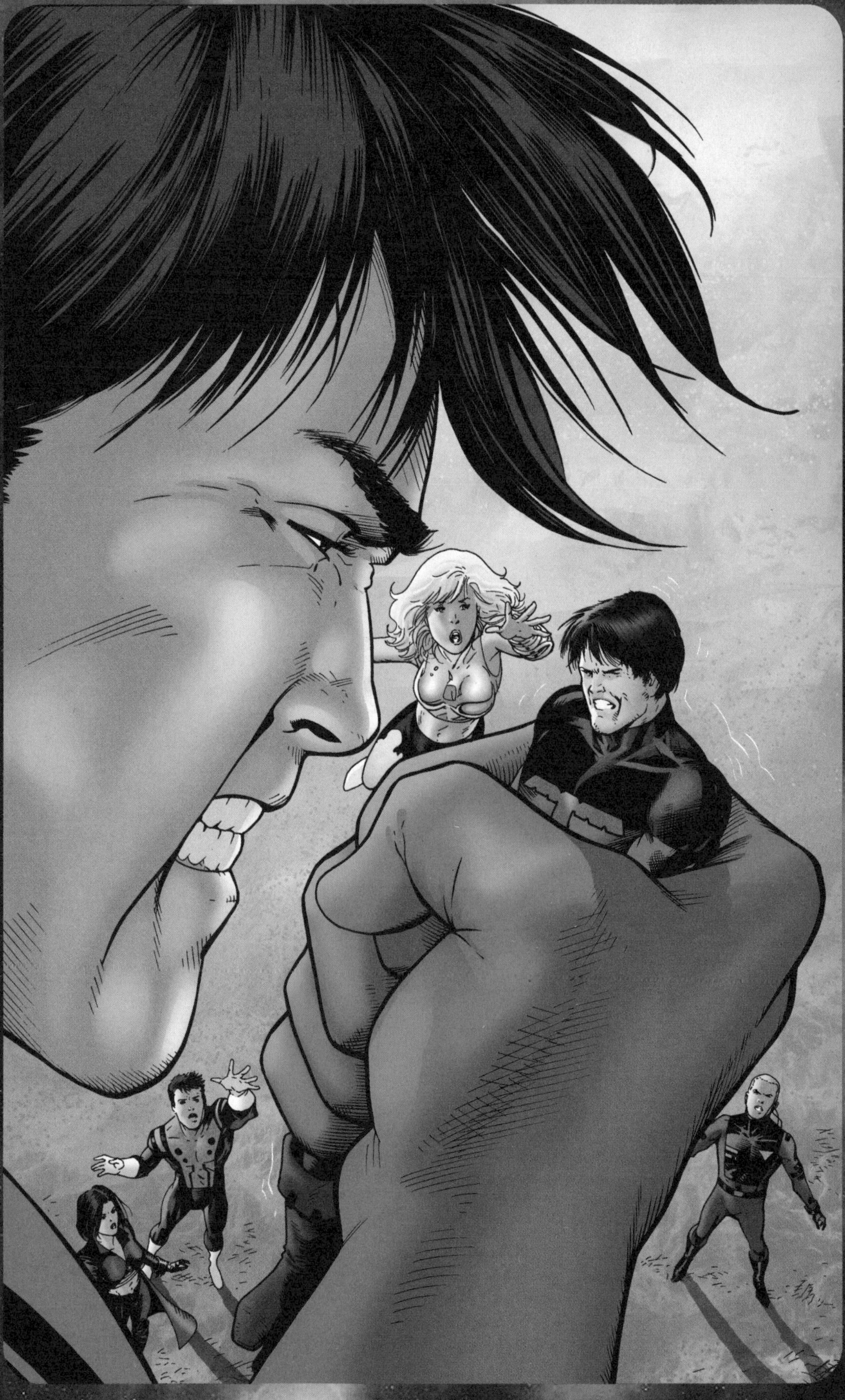

LEGION OF SUPER-HEROES #9

Art by **Barry Kitson & Mick Gray** with **Chris Blythe**

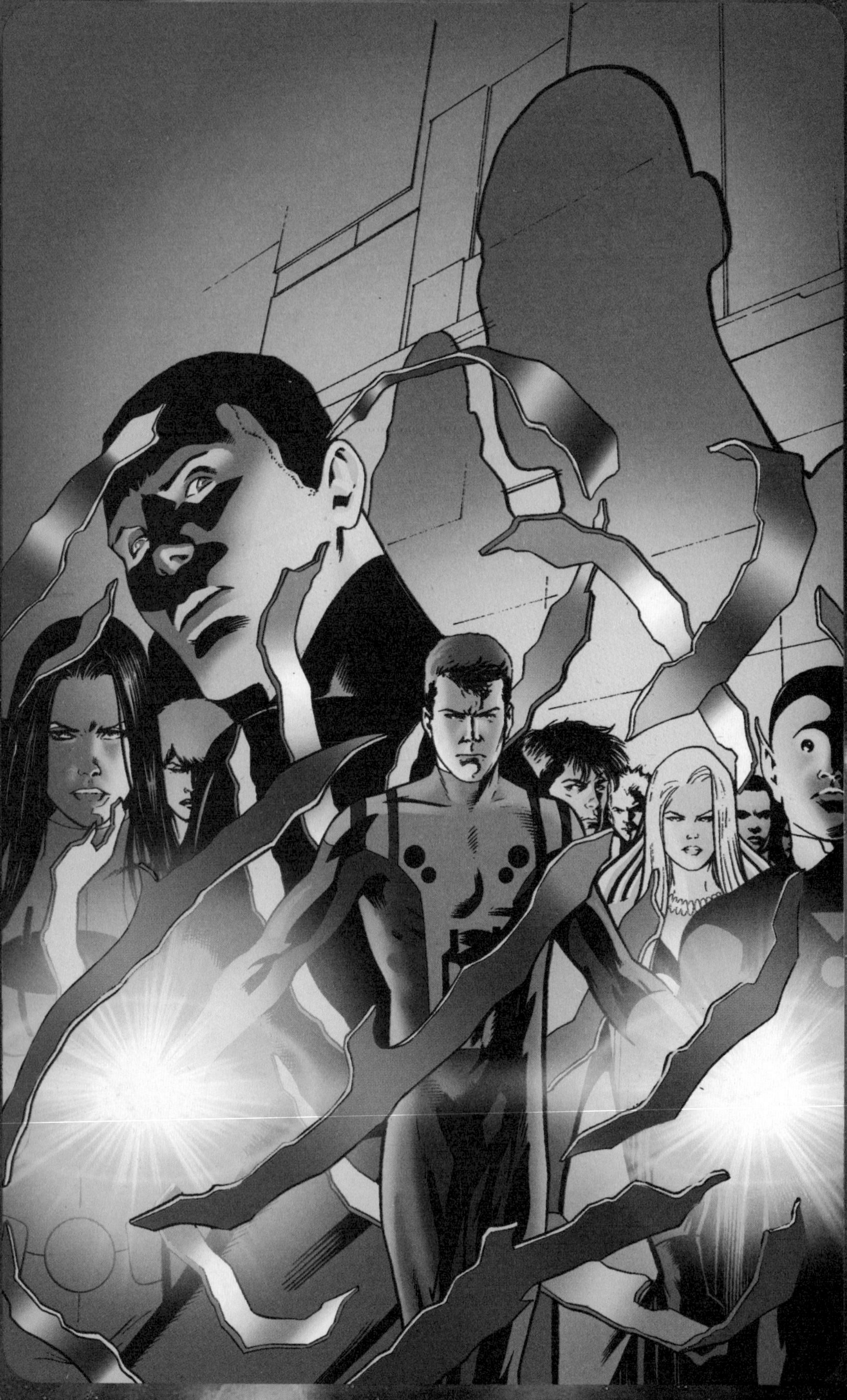

LEGION OF SUPER-HEROES #10

Art by **Barry Kitson & Mick Gray** with **Richard** & **Tanya Horie**

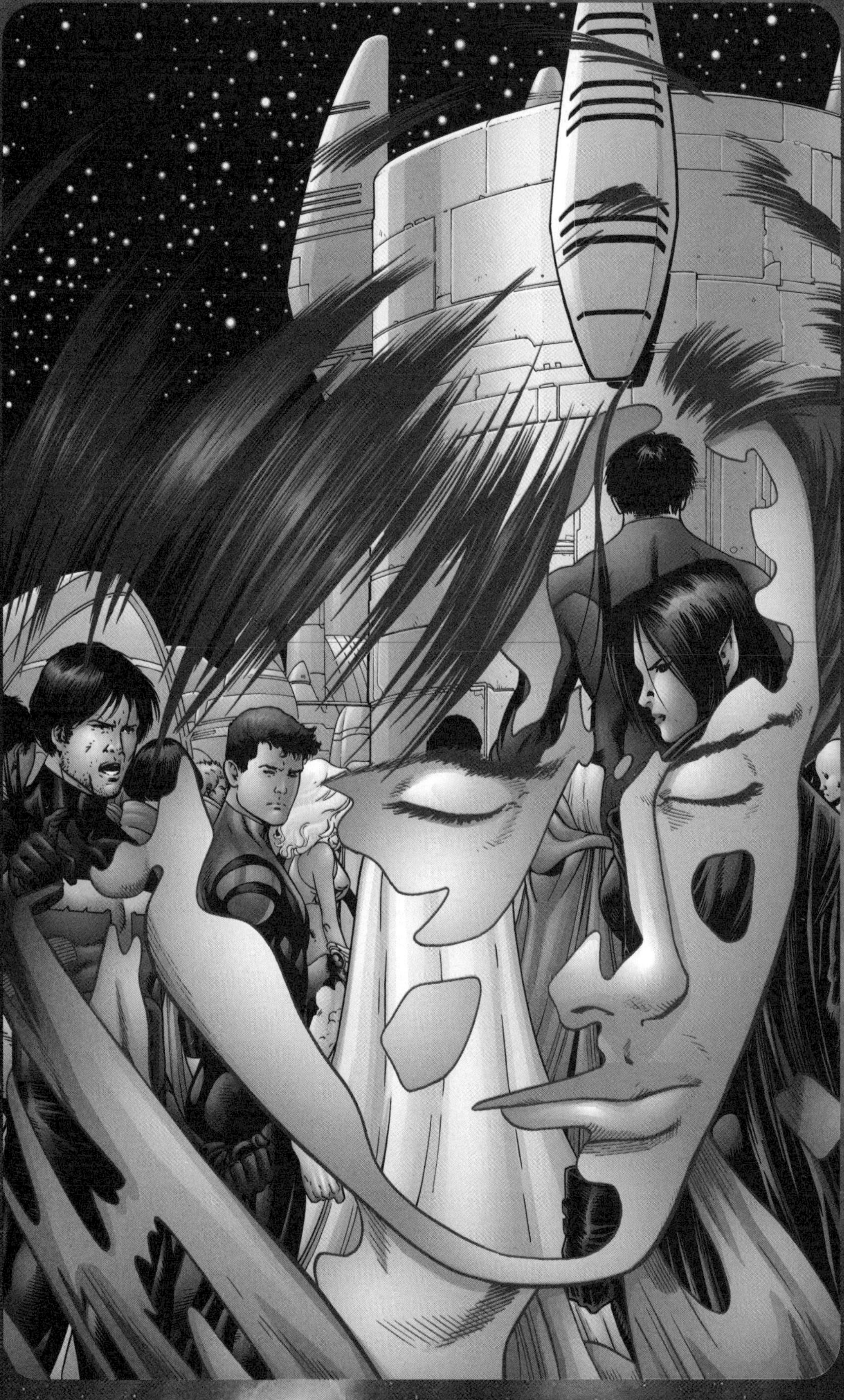

LEGION OF SUPER-HEROES #11

Art by **Barry Kitson** with **Sno-Cone**

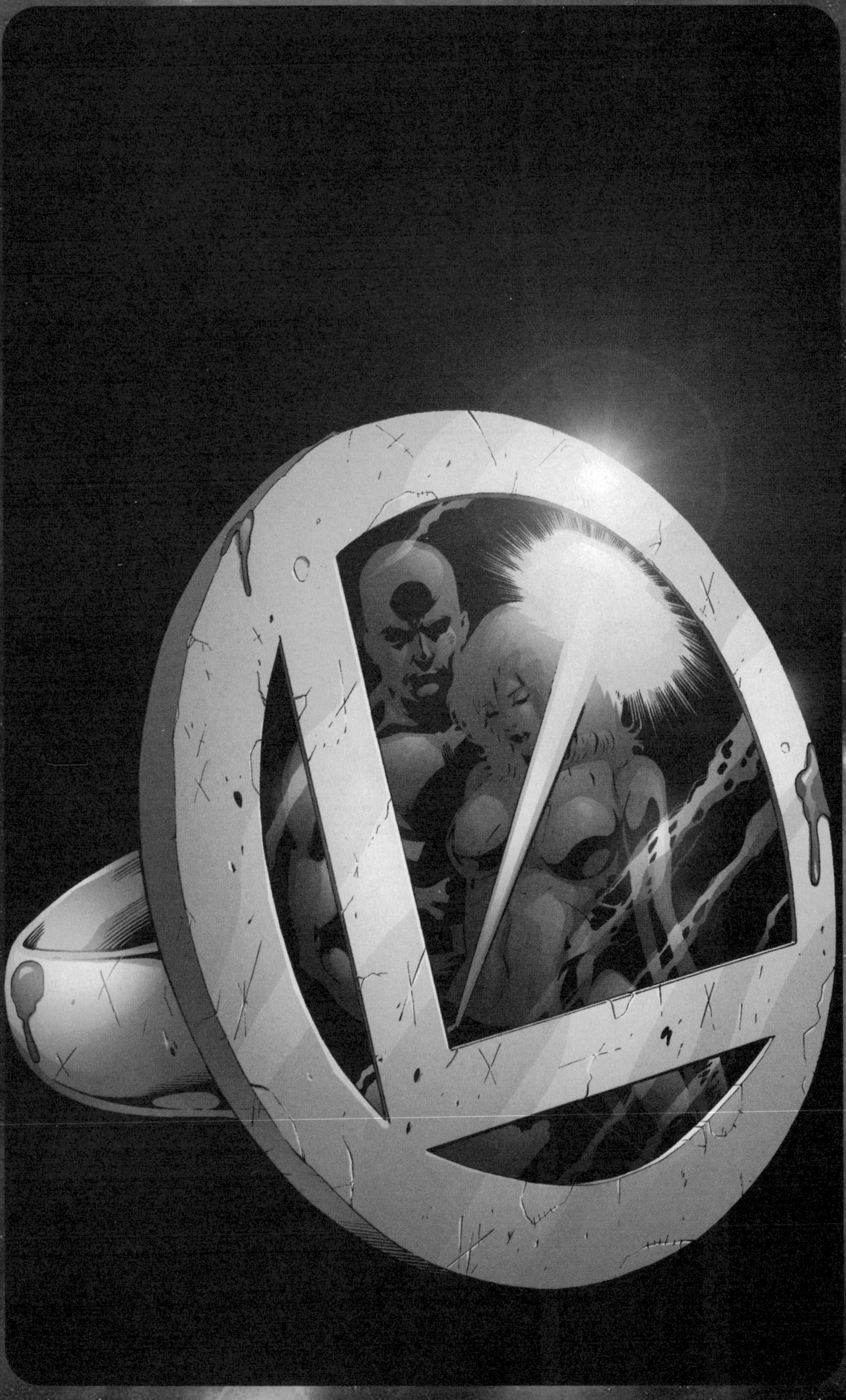

LEGION OF SUPER-HEROES #12

Art by **Barry Kitson** with **Sno-Cone**

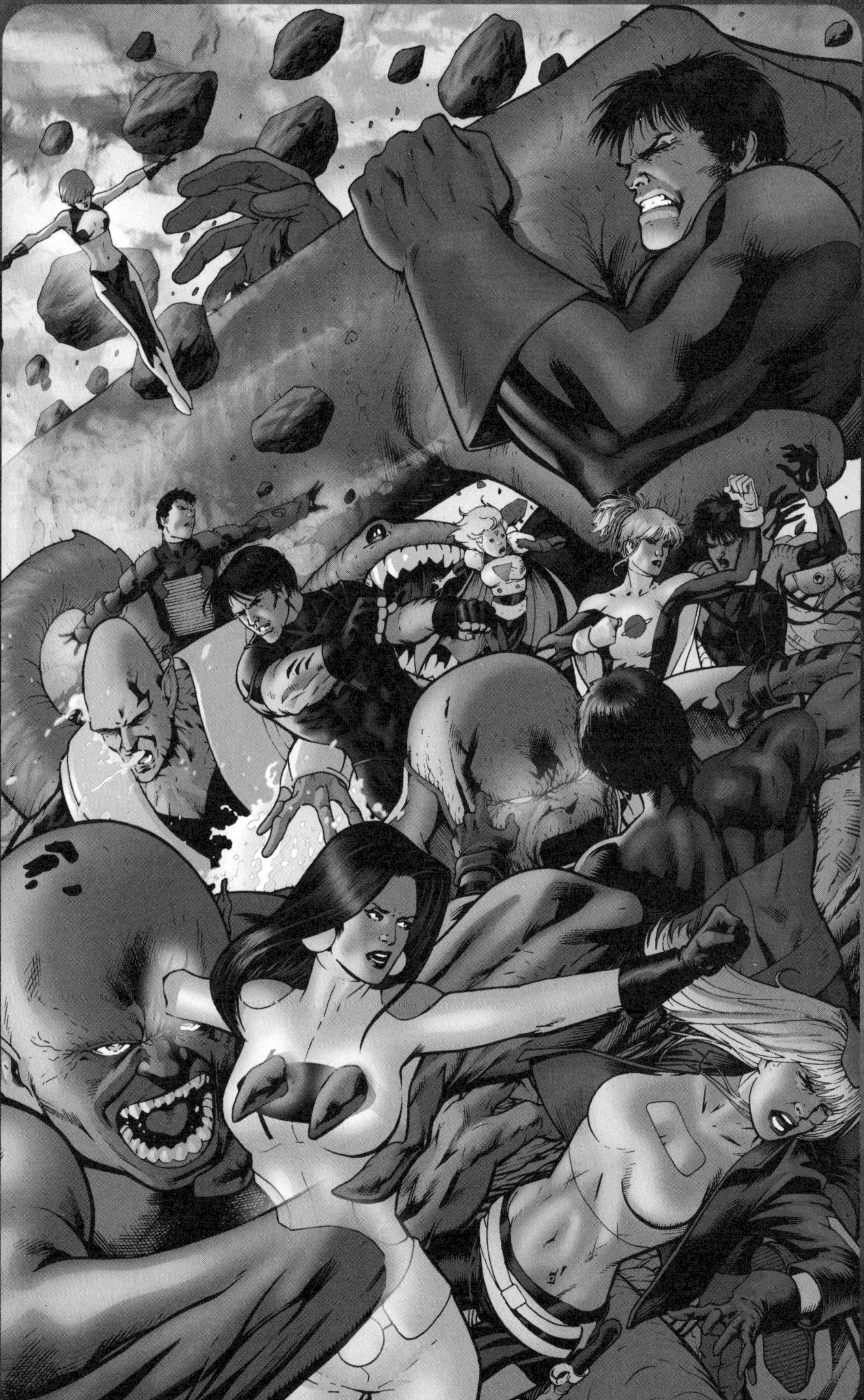

LEGION OF SUPER-HEROES #13

Art by **Barry Kitson** with **Sno-Cone**

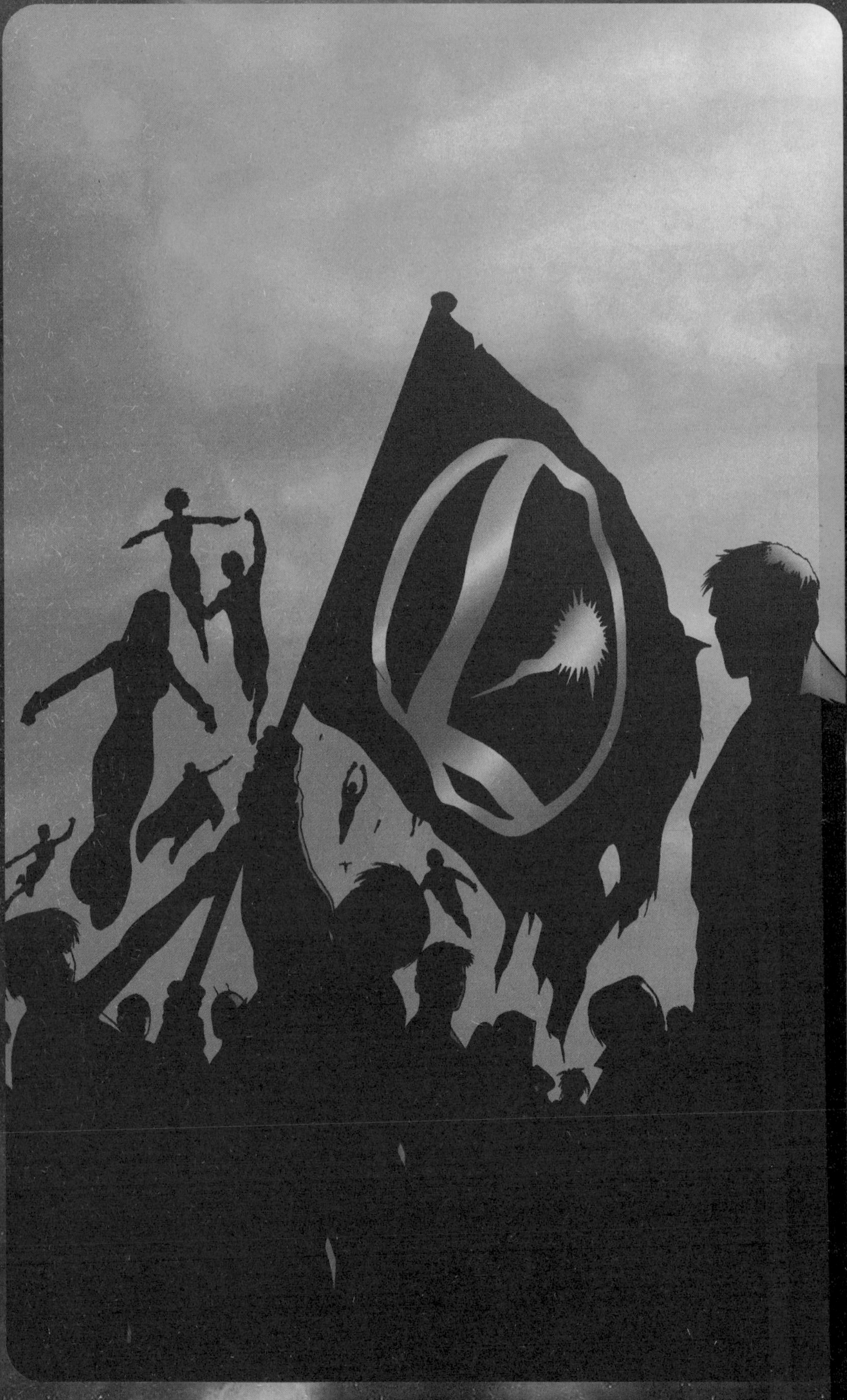

READ MORE ADVENTURES OF YOUR FAVORITE HEROES IN THESE COLLECTIONS FROM DC COMICS:

KINGDOM COME

THE GREATEST SUPER HERO EPIC OF TOMORROW!
ELSEWORLDS
KINGDOM COME
Mark WAID
Alex ROSS

Mark Waid and **Alex Ross** deliver a grim tale of youth versus experience, tradition versus change and what defines a hero. KINGDOM COME is a riveting story pitting the old guard — Superman, Batman, Wonder Woman and their peers — against a new uncompromising generation.

WINNER OF FIVE EISNER AND HARVEY AWARDS, INCLUDING BEST LIMITED SERIES AND BEST ARTIST

IDENTITY CRISIS

NEW YORK TIMES BEST-SELLING AUTHOR OF THE ZERO GAME
BRAD MELTZER
RAGS MORALES MICHAEL BAIR
IDENTITY CRISIS
Introduction by JOSS WHEDON, creator of BUFFY THE VAMPIRE SLAYER and FIREFLY

BRAD MELTZER
RAGS MORALES
MICHAEL BAIR

CRISIS ON INFINITE EARTHS

CRISIS
ON INFINITE EARTHS
MARV WOLFMAN
& GEORGE PÉREZ

MARV WOLFMAN
GEORGE PÉREZ

DC: THE NEW FRONTIER VOLUME 1

DC: The New Frontier
VOLUME ONE
BY DARWYN COOKE WITH DAVE STEWART

DARWYN COOKE
DAVE STEWART

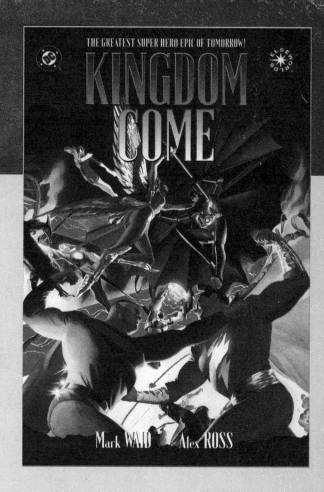

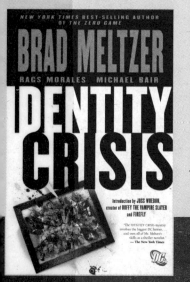

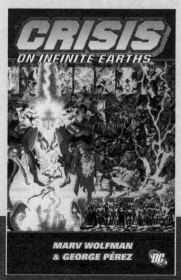

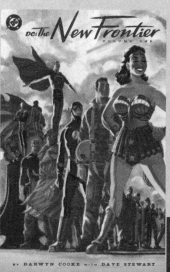